The Victoria History of the Counties of England

EDITED BY WILLIAM PAGE, F.S.A.

A HISTORY OF THE COUNTY OF BEDFORD

INDEX

INDEX TO THE VICTORIA HISTORY OF THE COUNTY OF BEDFORD

PUBLISHED FOR
THE UNIVERSITY OF LONDON
INSTITUTE OF HISTORICAL RESEARCH
REPRINTED FROM THE ORIGINAL EDITION OF 1914
BY
DAWSONS OF PALL MALL
FOLKESTONE & LONDON
1972

Issued by
Archibald Constable and Company Limited
in 1914

Reprinted for the University of London
Institute of Historical Research
by
Dawsons of Pall Mall
Cannon House
Folkestone, Kent, England
1972

ISBN: 0 7129 0535 9

Originally printed in Great Britain by
W. H. Smith & Son, London
Reprinted in Belgium by Jos Adam, Brussels

CONTENTS OF INDEX VOLUME

THE VICTORIA HISTORY OF THE COUNTIES OF ENGLAND

The publication of the volumes of this series which form the history of the county of Bedford is due to the financial support afforded by the Right Hon. the Viscount Hambleden, the Right Hon. the Viscount Alverstone, G.C.M.G., the Right Hon. the Lord Ashcombe, Mr. O. E. D'Avigdor Goldsmid, D.L., Mr. Somerset A. Beaumont, D.L., and the late Mr. Frank McClean, F.R.A.S., of whose public spirit and generosity it is here desired to make special recognition.

GENERAL INDEX

NOTE.—The Domesday Introduction and Translation of the Domesday Text are indexed separately in Vol. I. The articles on Geology, Palaeontology, Botany and Zoology being usually in the form of lists are not indexed, The following less obvious abbreviations are used:—adv., advowson; b., brother; cast., castle; chant., chantry; chap., chapel; coll., college; ct., court; ctss., countess; d., daughter; dchss., duchess; dk., duke; D. and C., Dean and Chapter; f., father; hund., hundred; ind., industries; man., manor; mchnss., marchioness; m., mother; mon., monastery; par., parish; pop., population; sch., school; sis., sister; sts., streets; vsct., viscount; vsctss., viscountess; w., wife.

Aaron, iii, 2, 363
Abbas, iii, 23
Abbesse, Will., iii, 251
Abbey Close (Bedford), iii, 6
Abbey Farm (Renhold), iii, 215
Abbot, Chas., ii, 173; Rev. Chas., i, 37, 41-50, 52, 54-6, 58-63, 79; Maurice, iii, 325; Sir Rich., ii, 59; Rob., iii, 325
Abbots Lands, ii, 383
Abbots Langley (Herts.), ch., ii, 317
Abbotsley (Hunts.), ii, 71
Abergavenny, Geo., Lord, iii, 229; Jno. de Hastings, Lord, iii, 229, 233
Abernon, *see* D'Abernon
Abingdon (Berks), ii, 48
Abingdon Abbey, ii, 211; iii, 345
Abraham the Jew, iii, 291, 383
Accleia, *see* Oakley
Achelai, *see* Oakley
Achi, ii, 339
Ackroyd, Rawson, iii, 132
Ackworth, *see* Acworth
Aclai, *see* Oakley
Acton Burnell, iii, 71
Acworth, Frances, iii, 388; Geo., ii, 39, 360, 362, 363; iii, 126, 203, 386; John, ii, 362, 373, 374, 380; Rich., iii, 203, 204; Will., ii, 362
Adam (vicar of Oakley), iii, 333; the clerk, iii, 23
Adams, Agnes, iii, 50; J. Reynal, iii, 384; Mrs. J. W., ii, 222; Rob., ii, 335; Theo., ii, 335; iii, 432; Thos., iii, 50, 104; Will., ii, 40
Addington, Gt. (Northants), i, 189
Addington, Rev. Hen., ii, 282; Joseph, iii, 206, 209; J., i, 123; Luke, ii, 255; P., i, 100, 101, 110, 116, 119, 120, 122, 125, 126, 128, 130, 139; Thos. A., ii, 282; W., i, 132; W. J., ii, 190
Adelitha, iii, 426
Adeliza, iii, 240
Adelmare, Cesar, ii, 159
Adelold, iii, 101
Adey, Dan. Goodson, ii, 317, 319
Adingrave, Alice de, iii, 384; Eleanor, iii, 292; Ellen de, iii, 384; Hen. de, iii, 384; Jno. de, iii, 384; Thos., iii, 217 *n*, 384
Adingrave's Close (Renhold), iii, 217
Ad Pontes, ii, 4
Adrian IV., pope, i, 359 *n*
Adser the Black, iii, 401
Adye, Rev. Fran. W., ii, 317, 319
Adyngraves, *see* Adingrave
Ædgiva, ii, 207
Ælfgifu, iii, 345
Ælfhelm, ii, 237; iii, 150
Ælfleda, iii, 124
Ælfric, iii, 128
Æthelwine, ii, 19, 20, 21
Affa, w. of Alfhelm, ii, 237
Agricultural Machinery Works, ii, 125, 137
Agricultural Organization Soc., ii, 142
Agriculture, ii, 108-9, 129-42
Agylon, Agnes, ii, 234 *n*; Rob., ii, 234 *n*
Aickin, Eleanor, iii, 133; Fran., iii, 133
Aieworde, *see* Eyworth
Aiken, Pet., iii, 72 *n*
Ailesbury, earl of, ii, 57, 58, 60, 61, 63, 267; iii, 19, 296, 361, 362; Rob., earl of, iii, 272, 290 *n*, 292, 317, 324, 325; Thos., earl of, ii, 59; iii, 271, 314, 315
Ailey, Chas., ii, 190
Ailey Green, i, 29
Ailwin, ii, 294
Aisseworde, *see* Eyworth
Akeman Street, ii, 5
Akle, *see* Oakley
Alava, archd. of, iii, 327
Alban, St., arms, ii, 368
Albemarle, ctss. of, iii, 130, 395, 398; Hawis, ctss. of, iii, 284, 285, 286; Isabel, ctss. of, iii, 285; earls of, ii, 28; iii, 29, 395; Bald., ii, 350; iii, 285; Will., iii, 284, 285, 286
Alberd, Amieia, ii, 287; Amy (Anne), iii, 429; Lucy, ii, 287; iii, 429; Reginald, ii, 81; Rich., ii, 81; Will., ii, 287; iii, 429
Alberic, cnt., *see* Vere, Aubrey de
Albingi, *see* Daubeney
Albini, *see* Daubeney
Albone, Dan, ii, 127
Albreda, iii, 175
Albyn, Rob., iii, 60
Aldeburgh, Rich. de, iii, 17
Alderman, Robt., iii, 57
Aldermanbury Manor, iii, 23
Aldgate, Friars Minor, ii, 239; Nuns Minoresses, i, 326 *n*
Aldridge, Amb., iii, 449
Alee, Agnes, iii, 366; Eliz., iii, 366; Rob., iii, 366
Alevold, iii, 78
Alexander III, pope, i, 314 *n*, 353 *n*, 378, 388; ii, 154, 209, 309, 312, 332, 380; iii, 127, 143, 179, 276, 278
Alexander, E., iii, 426, 428; Jos. T. B., iii, 60, 76, 80; *see* Lincoln, bps. of
Alexandra, Queen, i, 100
Aley Green, ii, 314
Aleyn, Hen., iii, 230; Jno., iii, 230, 231; Kath., iii, 230; *see also* Allen
Alfelinus, *see* Ælfhelm
Alfhelm, *see* Ælfhelm
Alford, Lady, ii, 185 *n*; Jno., vsct., ii, 66 *n*; Sir Edw., ii, 212
Alfred, King, i, 269, 276, 297, 310; ii, 18, 73; iii, 345
Alfwold, iii, 338
Algae, i, 59-60
Algar, iii, 89, 418
Aliams Fee (Totternhoe), iii, 448, 449
Alington, C., ii, 197; Jno., ii, 207, 301; Julius, ii, 206, 207, 301; iii, 310; Sara, ii, 207, 301; Will., ii, 207; Rev. Will., ii, 207, 301
Allanson, Jno., ii, 165
Allcroft, John d', iii, 304
Allen, Eliz., ii, 337; Rev. Hunter B., iii, 189; Jno., iii, 319; J., i, 127; P., ii, 199; Will., ii, 337; —, i, 135; iii, 317; *see also* Aleyn
Allen, W. H., Son & Co., ii, 126
Alley, Fran, ii, 362; Jno., ii, 362
Alli, iii, 52, 77
Allic, iii, 138
Allington Hill, i, 116
All Souls Coll. (Oxf.), iii, 424
Almar, i, 300; ii, 215; iii, 38, 92
Alneto, Alice de, iii, 110; Hen. de, iii, 114 *n*; Hugh de, iii, 110, 200; Sarah de, iii, 110, 111; Will. de, iii, 110, 116; fam., iii, 113
Alnthorpe, Alice, ii, 322; Walt., ii, 322
Alnutt, Alf., iii, 338
Alric, ii, 282; iii, 258, 260, 459
Alsey, Will. de, iii, 91 *n*
Alsi, iii, 37, 44, 77; *see also* Ulsi
Alston, Alex. R., iii, 90; Andr., ii, 299; Anne, iii, 66; A. R., iii, 88; Sir Crewe, iii, 73; Sir Edw., iii, 119; Eliz., iii, 73; Frances, iii, 76; Jno., iii, 78, 83; Sir Justinian, iii, 73; Justinian, iii, 77; Sir Rowland, ii, 62, 66 *n*; iii, 50; Rowland C., iii, 50, 73, 77, 102; Temperance, iii, 73 *n*; Sir Thos., ii, 44, 63 *n*; iii, 51, 72 *n*, 73; Thos., ii, 66 *n*; iii, 73, 77, 83; Vere J., iii, 76; Sir Will., iii, 74; Will., iii, 73, 75, 76, 77, 78, 83, 102; Capt., ii, 70; fam., ii, 44, 66; iii, 72
Altham, Alicia Annesley, Lady, iii, 411
Althorpe, iii, 102
Alton (Hants), ii, 31
Alvric, ii, 278, 321, 322, 329; the priest, iii, 159
Alwey, Anne, ii, 354; Dorothy, ii, 354; Mary, ii, 354; Ralph, ii, 354
Alwin, ii, 224, 248, 267 *n*, 277, 753; iii, 114, 137, 211, 276, 314, 344

Aiwold, iii, 74, 84
Alwyn, *see* Alwin
Amaury, Edm. de, iii, 384; Sir John, iii, 384; Jno. de, iii, 384
Ambrose, iii, 433
Amersham, Jno. of, i, 381
Ames, Levi, ii, 374; Lionel, ii, 357, 374
Amesbury Priory (Wilts), i, 404; iii, 403
Amethella, *see* Ampthill
Amphibal, St., arms of, ii, 368
Ampthill, i, 145, 324, 336 *n*, 337, 346, 367; ii, 36, 38, 39, 40, 44, 46, 55, 56, 66, 67, 102, 115, 133, 195, 266, 293, 320, 323, 376, 381; iii, 197, 267, 268, 289, 313, 320, 455; adv., iii, 273; 'Alameda,' iii, 269; almshouses, iii, 268, 269, 270; castle of, ii, 147; iii, 270; char., iii, 274, 275; Chas. I at, ii, 41; ch., i, 315 *n*, 333, 334, 335 *n*, 344, 352; iii, 268, 273; clock-tower, iii, 268; cross, iii, 270; deanery of, i, 347; 'Duke's Cottages,' iii, 269; hosp., iii, 275; ind., iii, 268; inns in, iii, 268; man., ii, 95, 96, 147, 308, 327; iii, 270, 271, 272, 285, 361; mkts. and fairs, ii, 88; iii, 268, 269, 271, 272; moot-hall, iii, 268; pks., iii, 270, 272, 292; Queen Kath. at, ii, 122, 123; iii, 353; rectory, iii, 273, 333; Rom. rem., ii, 4; schs., ii, 181; vicarage, i, 316 *n*
Ampthill, hon., i, 357; ii, 39, 145, 147, 267, 295, 321, 322, 376; iii, 82, 205, 251, 252, 271, 272, 276, 281, 285, 287, 290, 292, 294, 301, 306, 314, 317, 318, 321, 324, 325, 326, 331, 339, 347, 361, 376, 396, 418, 419, 442, 443, 452, 459
Ampthill, Emily, Lady, iii, 270; Ld., iii, 144, 149; Arth., Ld., ii, 66
Ampthill, Jno., i, 384
Ampthill Fields (Maulden), iii, 316
Ampthill House, i, 122; ii, 61; iii, 270
Ampthill Moor, i, 50
Ampthill Park, i, 7, 65, 108, 126 ii, 61, 147, 197
Ampthill Woods, i, 63
Anabaptists, i, 344; iii, 432
Anable, Will., iii, 145, 366
Ancaster, duke of, ii, 191
Anderson, Awdry, Lady, ii, 233; Cath., ii, 233; Sir Edm., ii, 211, 231, 232, 233; iii, 106, 452; Edm., ii, 231, 233; Eliz., iii, 452; Sir Fran., ii, 233; Fran., ii, 231; Judith, ii, 231, 233; J. O., ii, 199; Magdalen, Lady, ii, 231, 233; Marg., ii, 233; Mary, ii, 233; R. E. H., ii, 200; Simpson, ii, 277; Sir Steph., ii, 231, 233; Steph., ii, 231
Andrew, Ann, iii, 222; Benj., ii, 320; Bern., i, 399
Andrews, Benj., ii, 317; Joan, ii, 317; Jno., ii, 262; Jonas, iii, 33; Rich., ii, 347; Will., ii, 262
Angell, Helen, ii, 382 *n*; Thos., ii, 301
Anglo-Danish remains, i, 282
Anglo-Saxon burials, i, 175, 177, 184, 185; cemetery, i, 176, 186, 187; iii, 297, 402; remains, i, 175; ii, 8, 11, 17, 242; iii, 57, 297, 439; weapons, i, 177, 182, 183, 190, 285 *n*
Anne (of Cleves), Queen, iii, 271; (of Denmark), Queen, ii, 210, 295, 297, 339; iii, 219, 276; (w. Rich. II), Queen, iii, 16
Annesley, Alicia, *see* Altham, Lady; Joan, iii, 170; Jno., iii, 170; Will., iii, 82
Annestey, Jno., iii, 385
Anscell, *see* Ansell
Anschetil, *see* Aschil
Ansell, Edw., ii, 281; Eliz., iii, 184; Thos., ii, 323; iii, 184, 195
Anselm, i, 371
Ansfrid, iii, 37
Anstey, Eliz., iii, 150; Sir Hen., ii, 41; —, ii, 363
Anthony, fam., *see* Antonie
Anti, iii, 418
Antonie, Jno., iii, 92; Lee, ii, 65, 132, 187; Mark, iii, 88, 92; Rich., iii, 92
Apothecaries' Soc., Gideon de Lanie (Delaune), master of, iii, 219
Appelond, Jno., i, 397
Applewood, ii, 341, 342
Appley Corner (Haynes), ii, 338, 342
Apprentices, iii, 18
Aprice, Edm., ii, 346; Isaac, ii, 346; Jane, ii, 346; Jno., ii, 346; Rob., ii, 346; Will., ii, 346; —, i, 363; iii, 48
Ap Rys, *see* Aprice
Apsley Green, iii, 296
Apthorp (Apthorpe), E. E., ii, 199; Steph., ii, 280
Archdale, G., ii, 190
Archer, Alice, iii, 50; Gilb., iii, 376; Nich., i, 384 *n*; Rich., iii, 50; Rev. Thos., i. 336 *n*; ii, 325; iii, 289 *n*, 290, 295, 296; Tim., ii, 292; Dr., iii, 233
Archiaco, Aymer de, ii, 351, 352 *n*; Mabel de, ii, 351
Ardens, fam., *see* Ardern
Ardens, man., *see* Arderns
Ardern, Eustacia de, iii, 220; Nichola, iii, 84; Rob. de, iii, 84; Thos. de, iii, 220, 221; Will., ii, 271, 342 *n*, 343, 344
Arderns, man. (Roxton), iii, 220
Ardren, *see* Ardern
Ardres, man. (Turvey), iii, 110, 112
Ardres, Baldwin des, *see* Guînes, count of; Ernulf de, iii, 46, 74, 78, 101, 111; Hugh de, iii, 112; Isolda de, iii, 112; Jno. de, iii, 112; Rich. de, iii, 112; Rob. de, iii, 110, 111, 112; Sarah, *see* Alneto; Thos. de, iii, 112
Ardys, Dorothy, iii, 216; Jno., iii, 216; Thos., iii, 216
Argentein, *see* Argentine
Argentine, Dav., iii, 159; Joan, ii, 215, 216; John, ii, 215, 216; Margery, iii, 283; Matilda de, iii, 310; Rich. de, iii, 310
Aris, Eliz., iii, 157; Jos., iii, 157
Arkwright, A., iii, 88; Esmé, ii, 189; Rob., ii, 189
Arlesey, i, 173-4, 278, 312; ii, 234, 260, 262, 263, 270, 300, 324; adv., ii, 265; char., ii, 265; ch., i, 313, 324 *n*, 348 *n*; ii, 261, 263, 264, 265; coins, ii, 261; earthworks, ii, 261; ind., ii, 261; man., ii, 207, 223; mkts. and fairs, ii, 88, 262; mills, ii, 263; Nonconf., ii, 265; pottery (Samian), ii, 4; rectory, ii, 265; sch., ii, 181; vicar, i, 342; vicarage, ii, 206, 316; wkhouse., ii, 104
Arlesey Bury, ii, 261, 263, 342; man., ii, 262, 263, 265; mills, ii, 262
Arlesey Siding, sch., ii, 181
Armada, ii, 40
Armington, Will., iii, 112
Armstrong, A. A., iii, 297
Arnald, *see* Arnold
Arnesby (Leics.), i, 382, 384
Arnold, Edw., ii, 236; Grey, ii, 295; Hen., ii, 91; Jno., iii, 185; Kath., iii, 382; Marg., ii, 295; iii, 380; Mich., iii, 310
Arrouasians, i, 349, 387 *n*, 388, 388 *n*
Arschil, *see* Aschil
Arthorw, Jno., iii, 154; Marg., iii, 154
Artificial stone ind., ii, 127
Arundel, earl of, iii, 199
Aschil, ii, 300, 381; iii, 181, 184, 186, 262, 344, 381, 383
Asgar, ii, 361
Ashbrookfield (Wootton), iii, 331 *n*
Ashburnham, Sophia, ctss. of, iii, 132; earls of, iii, 22; Bert., iii, 130; Geo., iii, 130, 132 *n*; Jno., iii, 130; Eliz., Lady, iii, 126; Kath., Lady, iii, 130; Lds., iii, 270, 311; Jno., iii, 322; Will., iii, 126, 130
Ashburnham, Jno., ii, 51, 52, 61; iii, 270, 272, 322, 323; fam., iii, 132
Ashby, prior of, iii, 148 *n*
Ashby, Dav. de, ii, 357, 366; Isabel of, i, 360; Jno. of, i, 370; Rob. de, iii, 30
Ashcroft, —, ii, 168
Asheldon Close (Marston Moretaine), iii, 311
Ashfield, Florence, ii, 289; Geo., ii, 296; Margery, ii, 296; Patience iii, 361; Rich., iii, 361; Rob., ii, 296; Thos., iii, 302; —, iii, 305
Ashley, Alice, iii, 191; Eliz., iii, 207; Gilb., iii, 207; Hen., iii, 191
Ashridge, iii, 362
Ashridge Coll. (Bucks), iii, 448
Ashton, Sir Edw., ii, 43; Frances, ii, 179; iii, 351, 367, 368; Mary, iii, 436; Matth., ii, 298, 299; Nich., iii, 272, 437; Pet., ii, 299; Rob., iii, 436; Will., iii, 436, 438
Ashwell, Jno., i, 380, 381; Rich., ii, 385
Ashwell Street, i, 176
Askyllus (Anskyldus), ii, 315
Aspedon (Kent), ii. 256 *n*
Aspin, Anne, iii, 91; Jno., iii, 91
Aspinall, Jas., iii, 304; Nich., ii, 167, 168, 169
Aspley, Alice de, ii, 337; Nich. de, ii, 337; Rog. de, ii, 337
Aspley Bury, man., ii, 294, 295, 296
Aspley End, ii, 295 *n*
Aspley Guise, i, 372 *n*; ii, 91, 96, 114, 199, 329; iii, 276, 336, 338, 342, 394, 398; adv., iii, 339, 342; chants., iii, 342; char., iii, 343; ch., i, 315, 371 *n*, 378, 379, 380; iii, 338, 340, 342; Glebe Farm, iii, 338; ind., iii, 338; man., iii, 338; mkt. and fairs, ii, 88; iii, 340; mills, iii, 340; Nonconf., iii, 338; Old House, The, iii, 338; rectory, iii, 342; sch., ii, 181; iii, 338
Aspley Heath, ii, 181
Aspley House (Aspley Guise), iii, 338
Aspley Woods, , 42, 52, 56, 58, 79, 108; iii, 338
Asplion, Kath., ii, 257
Assandun, battle of, ii, 20
Asscheton, *see* Ashton
Assheton, *see* Ashton
Astell, Edm., ii, 356 *n* Eliz., iii, 231; Jno., ii, 228; Rich., ii, 228; iii, 231; Will. ii, 66 *n*,

INDEX

Astell (*cont.*)
228; Will. H., ii, 228; Will. T., ii, 228; fam., ii, 66
Astewood, *see* Astwood
Aston Bury, man., ii, 315
Aston Flamville, iii, 216 *n*
Astrey, Alice, ii, 295 *n*; iii, 293, 300; Dorothy, iii, 382, 438, 446; Fran., iii, 187, 442; Geo., iii., 193; Sir Hen., iii, 442; Hen., iii, 376, 380, 442; Jas., iii, 442; Lora, iii, 193; Mary, ii, 338; iii, 193, 380; Ralph, ii, 40 *n*, 295 *n*; iii, 146, 293, 300, 380, 442, 454; Rich., iii, 442; Susanna, iii, 382; Will., iii, 442; fam., iii, 379
Astwick, ii, 96, 201, 203, 205, 248, 281, 291; iii, 69, 96 *n*; adv., ii, 203, 206; chap., i, 314 *n*, 315 *n*, 318, 392; char., ii, 206; ch., ii, 203, 205, 206; Ch. Farm, ii, 203; man., ii, 203, 204, 205, 262; iii, 44, 77; mills, ii, 203, 204; Samian pottery, ii, 4; Rom. Brit. weapons, ii, 41; rectory, ii, 206
Astwick, Elias of (de), i, 314 *n*; ii, 203; Jno. of (de), i, 379, 381; ii, 203, 204, 289; Walt. de, ii, 203; Will. (de), ii, 203, 204, 205; Rich. de, ii, 203; Sim. de, ii, 203
Astwick Bury, ii, 203
Astwick Mills, i, 142
Astwood, ii, 187; iii, 116
Astwood, Jno., iii, 428; Nich. iii, 30
Asty Wood (Stagsden), iii, 96
Athall, Will., i, 398
Athelgyth, iii, 431
Athelney, i, 276
Athelstan, King, ii, 314 *n*, 350 *n*; iii, 345
Athol, Dav., earl of, iii, 3, 281
Atkins, Annabella, iii, 133; Edw., iii, 193, 296; Sir Hen., iii, 133; Thos., iii, 133; Will., iii, 246; Lady, ii, 42
Atkinson, Alex., ii, 241; C. B., ii, 199; Thos., iii, 201
Atoun, Jno., i, 393
Attelburgh, Sibyl, i, 360
Atterton, Jno., iii, 251
Atwood, Agnes, ii, 363 *n*; Thos., ii, 363 *n*, 373, 375
Aubervill, hon. of, iii, 377, 419
Aubervill, Will. de, iii, 377, 419
Auckland, canon of, i, 327
Audele, *see* Audley
Audley, Alice, iii, 192; Anna, iii, 295; Hen., ii, 342, 344, 353; iii, 132, 147, 408; Jas. de, iii, 299; Rob., ii, 43; Sir Thos., iii, 13; Thos., iii, 295; Will, ii, 40; —, ii, 44, 54
Audley End, iii, 131
Auferney Wood, ii, 342
Augustinian Canons, *see* Austin Canons
Auncells (Milton Bryant), iii, 419
Aungeyn, Rog., iii, 346
Aunsell, *see* Ansell
Austin, Fran. M., iii, 332; Rob., ii, 232; Thos. G., ii, 119; W., ii, 198
Austin Canons, i, 349, 350, 363 *n*, 371-87, 388 *n*, 395 *n*; ii, 154; iii, 21 *n*, 173
Austin Nuns, i, 387, 388
Austria, Jno., archdk. of, iii, 458; Lewis, archdk. of, iii, 458
Avalon, Hugh of, *see* Lincoln, Hugh, bp. of
Aveline, iii, 285
Avenay, Rob., iii, 310
Avenel, Eliz., ii, 296 *n*; Jno., ii, 296, 297; Juliana, ii, 296; Kath.,
Avenel (*cont.*)
ii, 219; Mary, ii, 219; Rob., ii, 296
Avery, Hen. of, ii, 289 *n*; Jno., iii, 91 *n*; Will., iii, 368
Aves, Eliz., iii, 361; Rich., iii, 361
Avrenches, Matilda d', iii, 452; Will. d', iii, 452
Awdley, *see* Audley
Axholme, Isle of, ii, 31
Aydrop, Thos., iii, 106, 195
Aylesbury (Bucks), ii, 46; iii, 383, 393, 401, 402; ch., i, 311; gaol, ii, 26; iii, 7
Aylesbury, earls of, *see* Ailesbury
Aylesbury, Jno., ii, 364; Kath., iii, 77, 191; Sir Thos., iii, 191; Thos., iii, 77
Aylesford (Kent), i, 170
Aylyff, Jno., iii, 39
Aynel, Ad., ii, 360; Jno., ii, 360; iii, 453; Rog., ii, 360; Will., ii, 360; iii, 453
Aynsworth, Eliz., ii, 179; Sim., iii, 285, 454; Thos., ii, 179
Azelin, iii, 236

Baa, *see* Bathonia
Babs, man., iii, 146
Babyngton (Babington), Sir Will., ii, 276, 277, 280, 323; Will., ii, 276, 145
Bach, Maria G., iii, 53, Thos., iii, 53
Backenho, man. (Thurleigh), i, 297; iii, 106
Backnoe End Farm (Thurleigh), iii, 104
Bacon, Sir Fran., iii, 253, 285; Rob., iii, 95, 106; Will., iii, 95; fam., ii, 233
Baddyngho, Joan, iii, 217 *n*
Badelesdone, *see* Battlesden
Badlesmere, Barth. de, ii, 384, 385; Giles de, ii, 384; Marg. de, ii, 284, 385
Bagley, Hen., iii, 94, 116; Matth., iii, 94, 175
Bagley's Spinney (Stagsden), iii, 96
Bagot, Chas., iii, 434; Frances, iii, 434
Bagshaw (Bagshawe), Edm., iii, 193, 326; Edw., iii, 193; Mary, iii, 193; Rev. R. S., ii, 285
Bailey, W., i, 100
Bailiff's, man. (Luton), ii, 350, 361
Baird, Sir Dav., ii, 67
Baker, Ann, iii, 278; Jas., iii, 327; Joan, ii, 329, 330; Jno., ii, 39; Rev. R. S., i, 291; Rev. Thos., ii, 181 *n*; iii, 128; Thos., iii, 327; Will., ii, 329, 330; fam., iii, 277
Baker's Wood (Leighton Buzzard), iii, 400, 405
Bakeworthe Field (Barton), ii, 309
Baldock (Herts), ii, 207, 214
Baldock (Baldok), Agnes de, ii, 254 *n*; Nich., i, 381; — de, ii, 254 *n*
Baldric, iii, 426
Baldry, Hen., iii, 400
Baldwin, the Miller, iii, 216
Baldwin, Fran., iii, 167; Thos., iii, 167
Baleok, Beatrice de, iii, 281
Baliol, *see* Balliol
Ball, Jno., ii, 35; Lucy, iii, 356 *n*; Rich., iii, 356; Rog., iii, 211
Ballard, Sam., iii, 280
Ballidon in the Peak, chap., i, 372 *n*; man., i, 376
Ballington Bottom (Herts), iii, 337, 455
Balliol (Baliol), Clemence de, i, 354; Devorguilla de, ii, 30, 238; iii, 297; Jno. de, ii, 30, 238; iii, 297; fam., ii, 30
Balliol Coll. (Oxf.), ii, 30; iii, 29
Balls, man., *see* Babs, man.
Ball's Pasture Field (Turvey), iii, 117
Bamford, Rev. Rob., ii, 209, 222; iii, 33
Bamforth, Rob., iii, 18
Bamforth & Co., ii, 127
Banbury, iii, 80
Banks, Sir Jos., ii, 135
Bankworth, Judith, iii, 434
Baptist, Jane, iii, 183; Jno., iii, 183
Baptists, i, 344; ii, 214, 222, 241, 242, 245, 255, 270, 271, 280, 299, 303, 312, 344, 374, 375, 381, 384, 387; iii, 6, 31, 32, 49, 89, 94, 100, 104, 109, 136, 157, 165, 209, 214, 234, 238, 275, 279, 284, 308, 314, 320, 338, 367, 389, 414, 415, 451
Barantyn, Drew, iii, 299; Eliz., iii, 299; Joan, iii, 299; Jno., iii, 299
Barber (Barbar, Barbor, Barbour), Agnes, ii, 316, 373; Alice, iii, 430, 449; Anne, ii, 259, 380; Bridg., iii, 28; Christian, ii, 380; Eliz., ii, 281 *n*; Geo., ii, 383; iii, 449; Hugh, ii, 162; Jno., ii, 89 *n*, 281 *n*, 373; iii, 21, 28, 293; Rich., i, 334; ii, 383; Rob., ii, 316; iii, 259, 425, 430; Rog., ii, 342; iii, 432; Thos., ii, 380; iii, 311, 425; Will., ii, 380; —, iii, 261
Bardolf (Bardolphe), Agnes, iii, 372; Will., ii, 30; iii, 372; fam., iii, 390 *n*
Barescote, Sim., i, 382
Baret, Hen., iii, 356 *n*; Jno., iii, 257; Rich., iii, 356 *n*
Barewood (Little Staughton), iii, 165
Barford, Gt., i, 303, 312, 335 *n*; ii, 133, 190, 280, 315; iii, 12; 181–5; adv., iii, 185; bridge, iii, 3, 181, 228; char., iii, 33, 185; ch., i, 315 *n*, 380; iii, 181, 184, 185, 222; hall, iii, 181; man., ii, 207; iii, 181, 184; mills, iii, 181, 184; Nonconf., iii, 181; rectory, i, 317; iii, 184 *n*; sch., ii, 182; ship money, iii, 180; vicarage, i, 316 *n*; iii, 181
Barford, Gt., hund., ii, 113; iii, 34, 180, 195, 199, 205
Barford, Little, ii, 25, 44, 71, 72, 197, 201, 206–9; iii, 310; adv., ii, 209; Barford House, ii, 206; char., ii, 209; chs., ii, 206, 207, 208, 209; man., ii, 206-8; mill, ii, 208; rectory, ii, 206; Rowe's Cottage, ii, 206
Barford, Geoff. of, iii, 184; Hugh of, iii, 184; Will., i, 399
Barkedich (Bed.), iii, 1 *n*, 21
Barker (Barkere), Agatha, ii, 334; Hen., ii, 334; Hugh, ii, 162; Jno. le, iii, 143; Rob., ii, 162, 169; Thos., ii, 335; iii, 177
Barking Abbey, i, 322 *n*; iii, 307; abbess, i, 312; iii, 306
Barle, Alianor, iii, 145; Jno., iii, 145
Barleigh, Dorothy, iii, 306
Barlow, Will., bp., *see* Lincoln, bps. of; —, i, 119; ii, 133
Barnacke, Edm., ii, 243; Joan, ii, 243; Jno., ii, 243; Mary, ii, 243; iii, 191; Will., ii, 243; iii, 191

Barnard, Ellen, iii, 273; Jno., iii, 273; J. H., i, 127; ii, 195, 196, 197; Rich., ii, 368, 369, 373; Sir Rob., ii, 64; iii, 20; Talbot, iii, 301; Thos., ii, 66 *n*; iii, 238; Thos. H., iii, 297; fam., ii, 66; *see also* Bernard and Burnard
Barnardiston, Geo., iii, 245, 246; Hen., iii, 245; Joan, iii, 245; Jno., iii, 245, 246, 255; Marg., iii, 245; Sir Nath., iii, 146; Rob., iii, 245; Sam., iii, 146; Sir Thos., ii, 356, 359; Thos., ii, 359
Barnes, Geo., iii, 403, 429; Jno., i, 336, 337; iii, 429; Ralph, i, 369 *n*; Sam. E., ii, 242
Barnett, Curtis, ii, 211; —, ii, 190, 211
Barnham, Fran., iii, 403, 429
Barnhard, *see* Barnard
Barons' War, ii, 17, 27, 30, 31, 33, 350
Barre, Agnes de la, ii, 359; Eliz., ii, 256; Jno., ii, 256; Thos., ii, 256
Barringer, Will., iii, 104
Barrington, Joan, ii, 204 *n*
Barrows, *see* Burials and Burial Urns
Barr's Place (Eaton Bray), iii, 375
Barrymore, Ld., ii, 192
Bartholomew, iii, 90; Ellen, w. of, iii, 90
Bartholomew, C., iii, 90
Barthon, *see* Barton-in-the-Clay
Bartlow (Essex), Rom. rem., ii, 12
Barton, *see* Barton-in-the-Clay
Barton, Geoff. of, i, 377; Jas., iii, 117; Louisa, iii, 117; Mary, iii, 117; Dr., ii, 167; —, ii, 169
Barton Hills, ii, 71, 308, 344, 381
Barton-in-the-Clay, ii, 25, 50, 77, 82, 87, 129, 306, 308–13, 384; iii, 59; adv., ii, 312; char., ii, 313; ch., i, 313; ii, 308, 311, 312; ind., ii, 117; man, i, 312; ii, 80, 308-10, 313; mills, ii, 310; Nonconf., ii, 312; iii, 32; petrifying spring at, i, 31; ii, 308; prehist. rem., i, 162, 174; ii, 308; rectory, ii, 308, 312; sch., ii, 181
Barton-on-Humber, iii, 131
Barwick, Pet., ii, 295
Barworth, *see* Barwythe
Barwythe (Studham), iii, 429; chant., i, 325 *n*, 326 *n*; iii, 428, 432; chap., i, 318; ch., iii, 431; Grove, the, iii, 430; man., iii, 426
Barwythe House, iii, 428
Basingham (Basingeham), Agnes (de), ii, 234 *n*; iii, 70; Beatrice de, iii, 71 *n*; Jno. de. iii, 71; Rob. (de), ii, 234 *n*; iii, 70; Walt. de, iii, 426
Baskerfield, Mary, iii, 415
Baskerville, Thos., iii, 351, 363
Basmead, man., iii, 190, 192, 193; man. house, i, 306
Basmey, *see* Basmead
Basset (Bassett), Agnes, i, 398; Alianor, iii, 145; Fran., ii, 66 *n*; Fulk, iii, 84; Sir Jno., iii, 145, 146; Jno., ii, 289; iii, 145; Juliane, i, 357; Kath., iii, 145; Nich., i, 353; Norman, iii, 145; Ralph, iii, 57, 58; Rich., i, 353; ii, 23; iii, 107; Rob., iii, 125 *n*, 145; Sim., i, 398 *n*; Sybil, iii, 145; Thurstan, iii, 107; Will., iii, 145, 146; fam., ii, 66; iii, 22
Bassets, man. (Milton Ernest), iii, 145, 146
Basseville, Alice de, i, 360
Bassingbourn(e), Kath., ii, 346; Mary, ii, 219; Thos., ii, 346; iii, 22; Warin de, ii, 219
Bates, Geo., iii, 404; Rev. Thos., ii, 316 *n*, 318 *n*
Bateson, Will., ii, 385
Bates's Close (Cardington), iii, 238
Bath, Jno., earl of, ii, 336, 339; Thos., mqs. of, ii, 341
Bath, Agnes de, iii, 192; Eliz. de, iii, 192; Fulk of, ii, 238; Joan of, ii, 238; Osbert de, iii, 192; Reg. de, iii, 192; *see* Bathonia
Bath and Wells, bp. of, ii, 38, 310; iii, 192
Bathonia, Anne de, iii, 221; Walt. de, iii, 221; *see* Bath
Bathurst, Allen, Ld., ii, 60 *n*; iii, 344, 384
Batrachians, i, 102-3
Batsford, Sampson de, iii, 74; Wm. de, iii, 74
Battams, Geo., iii, 52; Thos., ii, 138; iii, 52
Batten, Eliz., iii, 335; Jas., iii, 335; Rich., iii, 335
Batthyany, count, ii, 194
Battison, Thos., ii, 172; iii, 17
Battlesden, ii, 96, 356; iii, 336, 343–5; adv., iii, 345; char., iii, 345, 368; ch., iii, 343, 344, 345; Hill Farm, iii, 343; lake, i, 136; man., iii, 343, 344; pk., i, 125; iii, 343, 400, 421; rectory, iii, 343; sch., ii, 181; vicar of, iii, 345
Battlesden, Thos., i, 401
Battlesden Abbey, iii, 65
Battye, Will., iii, 437
Bawde, Jane, iii, 391; Thos., iii, 391
Bawdery, Will., iii, 407
Baxter, Jno. de, ii, 309; —, i, 343
Bay, Sim. de, iii, 85
Bayeux, man., *see* Ocle-cum-Clapham
Bayeux, bp. of, i, 313; iii, 96, 114, 126, 223, 370, 376, 419, 449 *n*
Bayeux, Eliz. de, iii, 154: Joan de, iii, 155; Marg. de, iii, 155; Rich. de, iii, 130, 154; Rob. de, iii, 154; Sim. de, iii, 130; Will. de, iii, 130
Bayford, ii, 317
Bayley, Ellen, iii, 428; Jas., iii, 310; Will., iii, 428
Bayliffe, Chas., ii, 280
Bayncroft, *see* Beancroft
Baynes, Mary, iii, 31, 32
Bayonne, bp. of, ii, 38
Bayons, Will., iii, 162
Beacher, *see* Beecher
Beadlow Farm (Clophill), ii, 321
Beamont, *see* Beaumont
Beancroft (Marston Moretaine), iii, 308; man., iii, 311
Beancroft Farm (Marston Moretaine), iii, 311
Beauchamp, bar., i, 300 *n*, 393; iii, 61, 92, 97, 386
Beauchamp, Lord de, iii, 162
Beauchamp, Alice de, iii, 191; Ant., ii, 337; Beatrice de, iii, 44, 46, 97, 114, 215, 235, 329, 330, 383; Cicely de, ii, 351, 352; Edith, Lady, iii, 136; Edith de, ii, 203; iii, 137; Ela de, ii, 30 *n*; iii, 14, 44, 45, 46, 136 *n*, 186, 215, 234, 235, 295, 329, 330; Eliz., Lady, ii, 324; iii, 140, 230, 317, 380; Eliz. de, i, 357, 383 *n*; ii, 248, 296, 324; iii, 295, 326, 330; Ellen de, i, 377; Emma, iii, 41; Geoff. de, ii, 211, 324; Hen., ii, 339; iii, 41, 403; Hugh de, i, 297, 361, 377, 381 *n*, 382 *n*, 383, 384, 385, 386, 394; ii, 143, 203, 204, 207, 208, 211, 215, 243, 271, 281, 300, 302, 336, 339, 344, 381; iii, 9, 36, 37, 40, 42, 44, 61, 91, 96, 107, 113, 114, 136, 138, 145, 159, 171, 181, 186, 190, 193, 197, 199, 203, 204, 205, 206, 207, 210, 216, 234, 238, 240, 248, 257, 258, 259, 260, 262, 266, 291, 292, 315, 375, 418, 424; Ida de, i, 379; iii, 213, 235, 334; Isabel de, iii, 329; Joan de, ii, 324; iii, 12, 234, 330, 331; Sir Jno., iii, 136, 137; Jno. de, ii, 29, 31, 203, 307, 339; iii, 12, 41, 44, 45, 190, 196, 215, 234, 235, 295, 329, 351; Marg., iii, 41, 137; Maud de, ii, 243, 300, 339; iii, 44, 77, 97, 262, 329; Miles de, ii, 24, 25; iii, 9, 24; Oliver de, i, 385 *n*; iii, 190, 193; Payn (Pain) de, i, 377, 392; ii, 206, 267, 271, 276, 339, 341, 343; iii, 9, 24, 166, 240; Philippa, ii, 248; iii, 190, 210; Ralph, ii, 208, 243, 251; iii, 191, 199, 200-1, 221 *n*; Reg. de, ii, 34 *n*; Rich. de, ii, 296; iii, 219, 403; *see also* St. Amand, Lord; Roais de, *see* Rohesia; Rob. de, iii, 9; Rog. de, i, 325 *n*, 386; ii, 34, 243, 245, 321; iii, 41, 42, 52, 136, 190, 191, 196, 199, 200, 201, 272; Rohesia (Rohese, Rose) de, i, 390, 392; ii, 154, 267, 271, 274, 276, 341, 343; iii, 9, 210; Sibyl de, *see* Patishull; Sim. de, i, 303, 314 *n*, 361, 371 *n*, 377, 378, 379, 385 *n*, 390 *n*, 391, 392; ii, 23, 24, 26, 29, 154, 155, 203, 206, 218, 267, 271, 276, 302, 338, 339; iii, 8, 9, 10, 12, 37, 98, 100, 137, 139, 159, 185, 203, 208, 210, 214, 235, 236, 237, 242, 261, 266, 329, 334, 342, 348, 378, 402; Thos. de, i, 373; ii, 321; Sir Walt., iii, 317; Sir Will. de, ii, 324; iii, 140, 187, 230, 380; Will. de, i, 361, 362, 379, 380, 390 *n*, 391, 392 *n*; ii, 27, 28, 29, 71, 203, 206, 243, 244, 245, 248, 267, 271, 276, 296, 300, 339, 341, 343; iii, 10, 11, 12, 14, 44, 52, 98 *n*, 137, 162, 166, 192, 199, 203, 208, 210, 213, 215, 216 *n*, 235, 237, 242, 292, 293, 295, 317, 331, 334, 375, 383; fam., i, 382, 385, 390 *n*; ii, 23, 25 *n*, 31; iii, 43, 52, 61, 212, 236, 237, 342
Beaudesert (Leighton Buzzard), iii, 414
Beaufort, Hen., bp., *see* Lincoln, bps. of; Jno., *see* Somerset, dk. of; Lady Marg., iii, 41
Beaulieu, man., i, 351 *n*, 352
Beaulieu Priory, i, 313, 315 *n*, 316 *n*, 318 *n*, 349, 350, 351, 352, 377 *n*, 385; ii, 87, 270, 321-5, 342, 344; iii, 148, 273, 316, 318, 319, 320; priors, i, 352
Beaumanor (Leics.), iii, 380
Beaumont, Edw., iii, 432; Hugh de, ii, 24, 39; Joan, iii, 437; Jno., iii, 28; Marg., iii, 301; Rob., ii, 379, *see also* Leicester, earl of; Thos., iii, 437; Will., ii, 379, iii, 432; capt., iii, 297; —, i, 99; fam., i, 382
Becheleswordc, *see* Biggleswade
Becher, Jno., iii, 215; Sir Will. iii, 215, 216 *n*; Will. ii, 224 *n*, 316; iii, 215; capt., ii, 194
Beck, A. C., iii, 64, 66
Beckering, John de, iii, 322
Beckerings Park (Ridgmont), ii, 145, 147; iii, 322

INDEX

Beckerings Pk. Farm (Ridgmont), iii, 320
Beckerings Pk. Lodge Farm, iii, 322
Becket, Rob., iii, 316; Thos., i, 378; ii, 26, 27, 154; —, ii, 168; iii, 194
Beckford, Will., iii, 372, 448, 455
Beckworth, Jos. F., iii, 335; Mary, iii, 335
Bedanforda, *see* Bedford
Bedcanforda, *see* Bedford
Bedcott, Rich., iii, 209; Sarah, iii, 209; Will., iii, 209
Beddington (Surr.), iii, 427
Bedeforda, *see* Bedford
Bedell, Gabriel, iii, 113; Matth., iii, 304; Thos., iii, 259; Will., iii, 326
Bedford, ii, 23, 34, 39, 42, 54 *n*, 55, 56, 57, 59, 60 *n*, 63, 64, 73, 105, 116, 340; iii, 1-33, 73, 117, 253; Adams Manufacturing Co., ii, 127; Agricultural Inst., iii, 320; Allen Inst., ii, 127; Angling Club, i, 99; A. S. rem, i, 176, 185, 190; archdry., ii, 214; archds., i, 313, 315 *n*, 319, 320, 323, 332, 334, 336 *n*, 341, 348, 378, 384 *n*, 396, 397; ii, 29, 152, 154, 155, 213, 265, 270, 356; iii, 334, 355, 359, 431; artificial stone works, ii, 127; assessment, ii, 153; iii, 1, 2; assizes, iii, 22, 71, 276; bailiff, ii, 155; iii, 19; bedell of beggars, iii, 3, 8; bp. of, i, 332; Black Death, i, 328; bridge, iii, 1, 4, 30, 44; bridewell, iii, 7; chamberlain, ii, 58; chant., i, 329 *n*; chaps., i, 324; iii, 6; char., ii, 153, 156, 157, 170, 172, 174, 181; iii, 31, 32, 33; Chas. I., ii, 52-53; chs., i, 107, 176, 281, 310, 311, 311 *n*, 312, 315 *n*, 324 *n*, 325 *n*, 326, 331 *n*, 339, 340, 343, 346 *n*, 347 *n*, 371 *n*, 380, 396, 397; ii, 92, 152, 153, 155; iii, 2, 4, 24, 52; coll. ch. (St. Paul's), ii, 25, 152, 153, 154, 155, 156, 161, 172, 176, 214, 311-13, 315 *n*, 345, 349, 379, 380; iii, 2, 4, 24, 25, 114, 236; Corn Exchange, ii, 176; Crown Building Soc., iii, 214; deanery, i, 347; Earl Cowper buildings, ii, 177; earthworks, i, 280, 281, 282, 284; engineering works, ii, 126; electric works, ii, 126; gaols, ii, 26, 55, 103; iii, 1, 7, 8, 306, 361, 379; gate-houses, iii, 1, 4, 7; gilds, i, 330; ii, 92, 155, 156; hosp., iii, 6; ind., ii, 109, 126, 127; iii, 5; inns, ii, 62, 99, 170, 209, 222; iii, 5, 6, 7, 11, 12, 30; ironworks, ii, 125, 126, 137; Jewry, i, 321; iii, 2; King's ditch, iii, 8; leper hosp., i, 349; library, iii, 4; Longholm Meadows, i, 110; man., iii, 23, 75, 114, 184; mkt. cross, iii, 2; mkts. and fairs, ii, 88, 105, 140, 268; iii, 1, 3, 21, 24, 35, 441; mayor and corp., i, 354, 395-398; ii, 41, 55, 57, 58, 59, 64, 153, 155, 156, 160, 161, 162, 165, 166, 167, 169, 173; iii, 3, 5, 16-23, 29, 30; mills, i, 397; iii, 9, 24; mint, iii, 2; Moot Hall, iii, 2; Nonconf., i, 344; iii, 30, 31; pars., iii, 1, 5, 6; pk., iii, 5; parl. repre., ii, 34, 64; iii, 20, 21; place-names, iii, 8; postal service, ii, 99; prehist. rem., i, 146, 147, 150, 161, 174; races, iii, 8; rebellion, iii, 3; recorder, ii, 58; iii, 19, 155; rectors, i, 337, 338, 341 *n*, 343;
Bedford (*cont.*)
ii, 164, 176; rectories, i, 331 *n*, 339 *n*; Rom. rem., ii, 1, 4, 5, 8; Rupert, pr., ii, 46; schs., i, 42; ii, 109, 141, 149-85; iii, 2, 3, 5, 6, 9, 25; sessions, i, 369; iii, 159; ship-money, ii, 41; siege, iii, 1; tournaments, iii, 2; vicarages, i, 316 *n*; ii, 168; Vulcan Works, ii, 127; Yeomanry, ii, 70
Bedford, bar., i, 364, 377, 379; ii, 22, 26 *n*, 215, 218, 300, 305, 339, 344, 381; iii, 9, 12-15, 40, 46, 52, 71 *n*, 77, 83, 89, 90, 96-8, 107, 114, 125, 134, 136-8, 145, 159, 162, 166, 181, 186, 199, 204-5, 210-12, 215-16, 236, 238, 240, 248, 258, 260, 264, 293, 295, 329-31, 338-9, 375, 383, 418, 423; hon., ii, 283; iii, 90, 166, 203, 206, 210, 216, 346
Bedford, barons of, iii, 12, 37; Jno., iii, 77; Payn, i, 385 *n*, 390; Isabella, ctss. of, ii, 39; Marg., ctss. of, ii, 277; Mary, ctss. of, ii, 39 *n*; dchss. of, i, 110, 136; Gertrude, iii, 318, 361; Jaquetta, ii, 225 *n*, 282; iii, 118; dks., i, 99, 102, 103, 186; ii, 7, 15, 63, 64, 65, 66, 70, 108, 130, 131, 132-36, 138, 139, 141, 146, 147, 171, 172, 173, 177, 181 *n*, 183 *n*, 184 *n*, 185 *n*, 188, 189, 192, 193, 194, 197, 267; iii, 11, 12, 19, 20, 23, 30, 94, 95, 100, 102, 107, 139, 140, 142, 149, 150, 159, 191, 195, 201, 203, 204, 205, 207, 210, 211, 224, 240, 242, 262, 264, 266, 270, 272, 273, 276, 286, 288, 291, 292, 296, 305, 306, 307, 308, 310, 311, 313, 315, 320, 321, 322, 323, 324, 325, 342, 343, 344, 345, 361, 362, 376, 391, 395, 396, 398, 417, 418, 419, 421, 422, 423, 458, 461, 462; Fran., ii, 130, 135, 137, 139, 140; iii, 104, 204, 214, 271, 286, 305, 458, 459; Geo., ii, 39, 39 *n*; Hastings, ii, 140; Herbrand A., ii, 140; iii, 104, 292, 396, 459, 461; Jasper, ii, 39; Jno., ii, 39, 62, 68, 135, 358; iii, 18, 207, 209, 286, 290, 314, 318, 324, 457, 461, 462; Will., ii, 61; Wriothesley, ii, 61; iii, 376; earls of, ii, 54, 56; iii, 142, 302; Edw., iii, 143, 203; Fran., ii, 40, 42, 185 *n*, 277; iii, 203, 376, 459, 462; Hugh, ii, 24, 39; iii, 9; Ingelram, ii, 39; Jno., ii, 39, 266; iii, 459; Will., ii, 43
Bedford, Cecilia of, iii, 215; Hen. of, i, 326; Hugh de, ii, 39; Isaac de, iii, 2 *n*; Jno. (of), i, 381, 384; Martha, iii, 236; Matth. of, i, 384; Rob. of, i, 388; Sam., ii, 54 *n*; Rev. Thos., iii, 236; Thos., iii, 236; Will. (of), i, 399; ii, 55
Bedford Abbey, i, 311, 377; iii, 1, 6
Bedford Castle, i, 186, 281, 285, 296, 320, 362, 364, 372, 378; ii, 5, 23, 27-9, 33; iii, 2, 12, 13, 204, 353; mill, iii, 23; siege, i, 382; ii, 24, 28, 144 *n*; iii, 7, 9, 10, 11, 24
Bedford Coll. (Lond.), ii, 177
Bedford-cum-Kyrkeby, *see* Bedford Major
Bedford Grammar Sch., ii, 149, 152-77, 199, 200
Bedford House (London), ii, 57 *n*, 63 *n*
Bedford Level, ii, 61 *n*
Bedford Major, preb., ii, 153
Bedford Minor, preb., ii, 153-4
Bedford St. Mary, *see* Bedford Major
Bedfordshire, agricultural societies, ii, 140, 142
Bedfordshire Chamber of Agriculture, ii, 140, 142
Bedfordshire Game Protection Society, ii, 198
Bedfordshire Regt., ii, 45, 67-70; iii, 149
Bedford Verd, *see* Bedford Minor
Bedingfield, Sir Edm., iii, 15; Sir Edw., iii, 296; Hen., iii, 296; Marg., iii, 15
Bedlow, man. (Clophill), ii, 322, 325; fair, ii, 323; mill, iii, 387
Beech, Mary, iii, 328; Thos., iii, 326
Beecher (Beacher), Eliz., iii, 218; Mary, iii, 304; Sir Will., iii, 203; Will., iii, 218, 304; —, ii, 262; fam. iii, 218
Beeches, man. (Pulloxhill), ii, 377
Beechwood Park (Hemel Hempstead), i, 116
Beedles, —, ii, 170
Bee-keeping, ii, 142
Beers, Geo., ii, 188
Beeston, i, 365; ii, 242; iii, 227, 242-4, 246-8, 250; chant., ii, 242; man., i, 364; iii, 247; mill, iii, 247; Nonconf., ii, 246
Beeston, Hen., ii, 166, 171
Beeston-Caldecote, man., *see* Perots
Beeston Leys (Northill), iii, 247, 251
Beetles, *see* Coleoptera
Beggary, hamlet, *see* Begwary
Beggary, Joan de, iii, 196; Rich. de, iii, 196; Rog. de, iii, 196
Begwary (Eaton Socon), iii 198; man., i, 305; iii, 196-7
Begwary Brook (Eaton Socon), iii, 189
Begwary Farm (Eaton Socon), iii, 190, 197
Beidforda, *see* Bedford
Bek, Thos., bp., i, 362 *n*, 401
Bekering, Jno. de, iii, 322
Bekeryng, *see* Beckerings Park
Bel, *see* Bell
Belcher, Miss, ii, 177
Bele, *see* Bell
Belers, Rog. de, ii, 336
Belfield, Ant., iii, 428; Hen., iii, 428; Jno., iii, 428; Will., iii, 382, 428-30, 432
Belgrave (Leics.), ii, 162
Belgrave, Marg., iii, 196; Rich., iii, 196
Belknappe (Belknap), Juliana, ii, 296; Rob., ii, 287, 296
Bell (Bel, Bele, Belle), Joan, iii, 403; John (le), iii, 184, 258, 403; Rob., iii, 105, 443; Sim. le, iii, 257, 258; Thos. iii, 184; Will., iii, 220
Bellamy, Rob., ii, 40
Bellasis, Jane, ii, 345; Jno., ii, 345
Belle, *see* Bell
Bell End (Kempston), iii, 297
Bello, Jno. de, iii, 353
Bells, man., iii, 155
Belrap, Alward, iii, 386
Belsham, Thos., iii, 9; Will., iii, 9
Belturbet, Will., Ld., iii, 140
Belvoir, hon., iii, 107, 112, 113, 149, 426
Belvoir, Rob. de Ros, ld. of, ii, 31 *n*
Belvoir Castle, iii, 112
Bendish, Hen., ii, 252; Will., iii, 163
Bendlowes, Will., iii, 300
Benedict, St., i, 350, 355, 363 *n*, 367, 392

Benedictine monks, i, 349, 351-3, 374, 376 *n*; iii, 403, 446
Benedictine nuns, i, 353-61
Benery (Oakley), iii, 149
Benett, *see* Bennett
Benham (Ravensden), iii, 210
Benington, Eliz., i, 360
Benison, Geo. T., ii, 382, 383
Bennell, Will., iii, 355
Bennets, man., ii, 350, 359, 361
Bennett (Benett, Bennet), Grace, iii, 282; Jno., iii, 8 *n*; J., i, 123, 136, 137; Sim., iii, 282; Thos., ii, 106, 136, 137; Will., ii, 107, 137; —, ii, 130; iii, 387
Benson, Jas., iii, 208
Bentham, Rev. Jos., iii, 122, 417; Sam., ii, 166
Bentley, Anne, iii, 429; Jno., iii, 429; Thos., iii, 364
Beodeford, i, 310 *n*
Beranforda, *see* Barford
Berdefeud, Jno. de, iii, 40
Bereford, par., *see* Barford
Bereford, Agnes de, ii, 362; Alice de, ii, 362; Bald. de, ii, 360, 362; Edm. de, ii, 362; Eliz., ii, 362; Hen. de, iii, 184; Humph. de, iii, 184; Joan de, ii, 362; Will. de, ii, 362; fam., iii, 181 *n*
Berell, Jno., iii, 247
Berells, man., *see* Buddenho
Beresford, Anne C., ii, 343
Berewode (Studham), iii, 428
Bergh, Rob. de, ii, 309
Berkeford, *see* Barford
Berkeley, Isabel, Lady de, ii, 340; Ld., iii, 346; Jas., Ld. de, ii, 340; Will., visct., ii, 301; iii, 13; Cath., iii, 205; G. C. G., ii, 187, 188, 194; Sir Jno., ii, 51, 52; Jno., iii, 205; Maurice, iii, 13 *n*; fam. iii, 342
Berkford, *see* Barford
Berkhampstead (Herts), ii, 47, 157, 317; iii, 358; cast., iii, 362
Berkley, *see* Berkeley
Bermondsey Priory, iii, 9, 24
Bernake, *see* Barnacke
Bernard, St., i, 361
Bernard, ii, 223; iii, 5
Bernard, Alice, iii, 116; Eleanor, ii, 286; Sir Jno., ii, 286; Marg., ii, 286; Nich., ii, 223; Odo, ii, 223; Rich., iii, 116; Rog., ii, 223 *n*; *see also* Barnard and Burnard
Berners, Mary, ii, 252
Berridge, Jno., i, 345, 346
Berrington, —, iii, 234
Berry, Dan., iii, 61
Berryfield (Lidlington), iii, 305
Berrystead (Goldington), iii, 205
Bertona, *see* Barton-in-the-Clay
Bertuna, *see* Barton-in-the-Clay
Besebrigg (Sharnbrook), iii, 91
Beseville, Marina de, ii, 275
Best, Ant., iii, 212; Hen., iii, 23; Mary, iii, 206
Bethune, Alice de, ii, 356; Bald. de, ii, 349-50, 357, 360
Beton, Cicely, iii, 249, 250
Betterton, Fran., ii, 162
Bettesworth, Charlotte G., iii, 443; Jno., ii, 357; Dr., ii, 357
Betts, Jno., ii, 171
Bevan (Bevin, Beywin, Beyum), Benj., iii, 322 *n*; Rich., iii, 322; Thos., iii, 322; Walt., iii, 321, 322; Will., iii, 320, 322; fam., iii, 322
Bevans, man., iii, 322
Bevell (Bevill), Fran., iii, 392; Hen., iii, 361; W., ii, 194
Beverley, Eliz., iii, 198; Jas., ii, 44, 323-4; iii, 201, 273; Rob., ii, 322, 374; Thos., iii, 198, 201; Will., iii, 198
Bevin, *see* Bevan
Beyum, Beywin, *see* Bevan
Bicheno, —, ii, 133
Bickenhill (Warws.), i, 360
Bickleswade, *see* Biggleswade
Bickley, Fran., iii, 261; Rich., iii, 261
Biddenham, iii, 31, 34, 36, 46, 66, 82, 175, 176, 210, 219; adv., iii, 36, 37, 39, 40; bridge, iii, 44; chants., i, 324, 325 *n*, 329, 334; ii, 92; iii, 40, 43, 47, 49; char., iii, 40; ch., i, 326, 329 *n*; iii, 36, 38, 39; ind., ii, 138; man., iii, 36, 37, 38, 78, 110; mills, iii, 38, 47; palaeolithic impl., iii, 36; place-names, iii, 40; pop., ii, 115; prebends, ii, 153; prehist. rem., i, 28, 33, 145, 174; rectory, iii, 40; Rom. rem., ii, 5, 6, 7; sch., ii, 181; vicarage, i, 329 *n*, 341; wells, ii, 2, 5, 7
Biddenham, Jno. of, i, 381; Will. of, i, 381
Biddlesden (Bucks), iii, 343 *n*
Bidwell (Houghton Regis), iii, 390
Biedcanforda, *see* Bedford
Bigg, Abigail, iii, 444; Abra., iii, 444; Agnes, iii, 444; Fran., iii, 443, 444; Jno., iii, 201; Mary, iii, 444; Sarah, iii, 444
Biggin Spinney (Roxton), i, 121
Biggin Wood (Everton), ii, 226
Biggin Wood (Tempsford), i, 307; earthwork, ii, 251
Biggin Wood, Little (Everton), ii, 226
Biggleswade, ii, 44, 45 *n*, 54, 95, 116, 201, 209, 214; iii, 7, 18, 70, 75 *n*, 202, 205, 227 *n*, 242, 260; adv., ii, 214; agric., ii, 133; bridge, ii, 209, 210; boro., ii, 212; chaps., ii, 214; char., ii, 179-81 *n*, 214-15; ch., i, 317; ii, 210, 213, 214, 217; coins (Brit.), i, 173; ii, 210; common, ii, 190, 209; dean of, i, 347; fishery, ii, 212; gilds, i, 330; ii, 179, 214; harriers, ii, 190; highway robbery, ii, 99; ind., i, 39; ii, 127, 138, 139, 212, 213; man., ii, 88, 210-12, 214, 253; mkts. and fairs, ii, 88, 209, 210, 212, 214; mills, ii, 212; moat, ii, 209; Nonconf., ii, 214; parl. div., ii, 66, 67; place-names, ii, 210; pop., ii, 113; prebend., i, 324, 334, 338, 343; prehist. rem., i, 173, 174; races, ii, 191; rectory, i, 329; ii, 214; Rom. rem., ii, 4, 6, 209, 212; schs., ii, 179-81, 214; sports, ii, 189, 199; vicar of, i, 329; vicarage, i, 317, 341; ii, 214; wells, i, 13, 26
Biggleswade, hund., ii, 18, 113, 116 *n*, 143, 201-55
Biggleswade, Jno., i, 385
Bigland, Cornelius, ii, 183 *n*, 374
Bigod (Bygod), Hugh, ii, 223; Maud, ii, 223; Rog. le, ii, 268; *see also* Norfolk, earl of
Bilenda, Hen. de, i, 372
Bilkemore, man., ii, 377, 378
Bilkemore, Anastasia de, ii, 378; Matilda de, ii, 378; Sir Rob. de, ii, 337, 338; Rob. de, ii, 378
Billenden, *see* Billington
Billesdon, *see* Billington
Billing, Walt. de, iii, 173
Billington (Gt. and Little), iii, 399, 400, 402, 404; chap., i, 341; ii, 114; iii, 414, 417; ch., iii, 411; Cock Inn, iii, 400; man., iii, 406, 407; man. house, iii, 400; Nonconf., iii, 415; prehist. rem., i, 162; rectory, iii, 414; sch., ii, 181
Billington, Joan, iii, 406; Jno., iii, 406, 407
Billyndon, *see* Billington
Birchall's Wood (Eversholt), iii, 375
Birchfield, man., iii, 181, 182
Birchmore, i, 370; ch., i, 370; iii, 462; man., iii, 461; man. house, iii, 462; rectory, i, 370; water-works, iii, 457
Bird, Jno., ii, 344; Thos., iii, 22, 311
Birds, i, 104-37
Birdshill, i, 50
Birrell, Eliz., ii, 289; Hen., ii, 289
Biscott (Biscot), i, 310; ii, 374; Bear's Moat, ii, 360 *n*; ch., i, 346; ii, 374; earthworks, i, 305; man., ii, 350, 360-3; mill, ii, 366; Nonconf., ii, 374; springs, i, 19; vicarage, ii, 374
Biscott (Biscot), Ad. of, i, 322 *n*, 395 *n*; Godfrey of, ii, 356
Biscott Grange, Rom. rem., ii, 8
Biscott Place, ii, 362 *n*
Bishop, Hen., iii, 120
Bissopescote, *see* Biscott
Bithray, Chas., iii, 52; Thos., iii, 52; Uriah, iii, 51
Bitlesden, *see* Battlesden
Blachesou, *see* Bletsoe
Black, Ad., ii, 357 *n*; Arth., iii, 331
Blackborne Hall, iii, 104, 183; man., iii, 105
Blackborne Hall Farm (Thurleigh), iii, 104
Black Death, ii, 88-90, 278; iii, 3, 78, 93, 100, 158, 299, 301, 318
Black Friars, *see* Friars, Black
Black Pond (Thurleigh), i, 289
Blackwell, iii, 456
Blaigny (Blegner), Ernald de, ii, 215 *n*; Thos. de, ii, 215 *n*
Blake (Blak), Jex, ii, 175; Steph., ii, 276 *n*
Blakelandes (Wootton), iii, 331 *n*
Blakesley (Northants), i, 394
Blankfront, man., *see* Potsgrove
Blankfront (Blancfront), Hen., iii, 422, 423; Rob., iii, 422; Will., iii, 422; W. de, i, 315 *n*
Blaydes, Fanny M., ii, 385; —, ii, 385
Bleadon (Somers.), iii, 54
Bleak Hall (Biggleswade), ii, 209
Blechesham, *see* Bletsoe
Blechesho, *see* Bletsoe
Blegner, *see* Blaigny
Bletchley (Bucks), ii, 30 *n*, 71
Bletnesho, *see* Bletsoe
Bletsoe, i, 297; ii, 30, 40, 96; iii, 34, 40-43, 59, 61, 234 *n*, 293, 461; adv., iii, 41, 43; cast., i, 301, 302; iii, 40, 42; chant., iii, 43; chap., i, 325 *n*; char., iii, 43; ch., i, 325 *n*; iii, 40, 42, 43; earth-works, i, 301, 302, 303; hermit, i, 350; man., i, 325 *n*; ii, 34 *n*; iii, 40, 41; mill, iii, 42; pk., i, 44; pop., ii, 115; rector, iii, 43; sch., ii, 181; vicar, ii, 327 *n*, 336
Bletsoe, Agnes, iii, 119; Anne, iii, 119; Eliz., iii, 119; Will., iii, 119, 120
Blikeslane (Caddington), ii, 315
Bliss, Math. F., iii, 310
Blisworth (Northants), i, 386
Blofield, Edw., iii, 286; Eliz., iii, 294; Giles, iii, 294; Mary, iii, 294

INDEX

Blomfield (Bloomfield), Sir Arth., ii, 214; Fran., ii, 349; Rob., ii, 266
Bloodworth, Chas., iii, 60; Nich., ii, 345 *n*
Bloody Battle Bridge, i, 285 *n*
Bloomfield, *see* Blomfield
Bloomsbury Square (London), ii, 57 *n*
Blosseville, Gilb. de, iii, 64, 65; Sim. de, iii, 65
Blott, Jno., iii, 67; Will., iii, 67
Blounham, *see* Blunham
Blount, Mountjoy, *see* Newport, earl of
Blow, T. B., i, 43, 50
Blows Downs (Dunstable), prehist. rem., i, 170, 172
Bluck Moor (Maulden), iii, 316
Bludeworth, *see* Bloodworth
Bluet, Will., ii, 224 *n*
Blundell, Alan, ii, 210; Eliz., Lady, iii, 235; Emma, ii, 210; Sir Fran., iii, 13; Sir Geo., ii, 59; iii, 13, 14, 15, 235; Geo., ii, 44; Jno., ii, 210, 253, 268 *n*, 271, 275, 286 *n*, 329; iii, 246; Rich., ii, 253; Rob., ii, 289 *n*; Rog., ii, 329; Sim., ii, 210; Will., ii, 210; Will. N., iii, 15, 235; fam., iii, 247
Blundells, farm (Harlington), iii, 381
Blundells, man. (Caldecote), *see* Caldecote, Upper
Blundells, man. (Harlington), iii, 380, 381
Blundells, man. (Silsoe), ii, 329, 330
Blunham, ii, 147, 201, ; iii, 31, 243; adv., iii, 233; char., iii, 233; ch., iii, 228, 231, 232, 233; fraternity, ii, 245, 325; iii, 233, 237, 255, 264; gild, i, 330; lands in, i, 380; ii, 92; iii, 231; man., iii, 228, 229, 236; man. house, iii, 228; mkt., ii, 88; iii, 229; pop., ii, 116; sch., ii, 181
Blunham, Dan. L., i, 368 *n*, 369
Blunham House (Blunham), ii, 197; iii, 228
Blunham Mill, i, 101
Blunham with Moggerhanger and Chalton, iii, 227, 228-33
Blunt, Eliz., iii, 366; Hugh le, iii, 98; Jno., iii, 225, 366; Mountjoy, *see* Newport, earl of; Rich., iii, 225; Will., iii, 225; —, ii, 165
Blyth-King, Mrs., iii, 453
Bobelin, Sim., iii, 391 *n*
Boderigan, Hen. de, ii, 354; Sibil de, ii, 354
Bodleian Library (Oxford), iii, 295
Boheme, Geo., ii, 69
Bohun, Eleanor de, iii, 171; Eliz. de, iii, 172; Frank de, ii, 351; Humph. de, *see* Hereford, earl of; Jno. de, ii, 306, 351, 354; iii, 171, 175; Marg. de, iii, 175; Maud de, ii, 223 *n*; Sybil de, ii, 351, 353, 354; Will. de, *see* Northampton, earl of; fam., iii, 283
Boileau, W. H., ii, 195
Bokland, man., ii, 230 *n*
Boklond, Kath. de, ii, 219; Ralph de, 219
Bold, Rev. Arth., iii, 61; Martha, iii, 61
Bole, Thos., i, 384; Will., iii, 240
Bolebec, Hugh de, i, 366; iii, 310, 314, 459; Isabel, iii, 314; Walt., iii, 314, 459 *n*
Boleyn, Anne (queen), iii, 111, 172
Boleyn, Anne, ii, 355; Geoff., ii, 355; Thos., ii, 363
Bolingbroke, earls of, ii, 44, 49, 63; iii, 19, 41, 60 *n*; Paulet, iii, 41, 137, 177; Oliver, ii, 56; iii, 35, 123, 125, 137, 163, 179, 180, 257
Bolle, Sir Chas., iii, 196
Bolnhurst (Bulehestre, Bolehestre), ii, 56, 115; iii, 123-8, 143, 149, 153, 223; adv., iii, 125, 127, 128; char., iii, 128; ch., i, 312, 314, 315 *n*; iii, 124-8; earthwork, i, 275; farms, iii, 124; man., iii, 124, 125, 396; moats, iii, 124; place-names, iii, 124; rector, ii, 181 *n*; iii, 128; sch., ii, 181
Bolstrode, Edm., iii, 286, 288
Boltere, Joan, iii, 220; Rich., iii, 220
Bolton, Rowland, ii, 299
Bond, Jno., ii, 180; iii, 408
Bondi, the Staller, ii, 383
Boner, Julian, iii, 154; Thos., iii, 154
Boniface, archbp., i, 322, 374; pope, i, 354, 359; iii, 170
Bonsey, H. D., iii, 19
Bonville, Eliz., iii, 89; Will., iii, 89
Boot, Will., ii, 304
Booth, Will., iii, 342
Borard, Rich. de, *see* Bossard
Borchard, Sim., iii, 112
Bord, Hen., ii, 295
Borgred, iii, 120
Borham, Hen. de, ii, 380
Borne, Eliz., iii, 22; Rich., iii, 7, 22; Will., iii, 22, 335
Borns, Nich., iii, 285, 437
Borough, Randall, iii, 246
Boroughbridge, battle, ii, 231, 300, 339; iii, 12
Borret (Borred), iii, 90, 133, 162, 176
Borrett, Jno., ii, 295
Borstall, Will., iii, 244
Bosanquet, Dav., iii, 185
Bosard, *see* Bossard
Boscombe, Alestan of, ii, 223, 261
Bosgrove, Frances, iii, 216; Jno., iii, 216
Bosom (Bosoun, Bosum, Bosun, Buzum), Alex., iii, 97, 219; Anne, iii, 97; Barth., iii, 97; Edm., iii, 97, 98; Eliz., iii, 97; Goditha, iii, 219; Ida, iii, 97; Joan, iii, 97; Jno., iii, 97; Marg., iii, 219, 329; Walt., iii, 97; Will., iii, 97, 219, 329; fam., iii, 97
Bosoms, man. (Stagsden), iii, 97
Bosoun, fam., *see* Bosom
Bossard, Giles, iii, 139; Hugh, iii, 139, 142; Joan, iii, 139, 150; Jno., iii, 139; Rich., ii, 31 *n*; iii, 107, 149, 150; Sim. de, iii, 149
Bossington, i, 145
Bostocke, Edm., iii, 261
Bosun, fam., *see* Bosom
Boswell, Jas., iii, 257; Thos., iii, 135
Bosworth (Leics.), iii, 231 *n*
Bosworth, Jno. of, i, 387
Botany, i, 37-67
Botecourt, *see* Botetourt
Boteler, Alex. le, iii, 372; Alice, iii, 39, 89; Anne, iii, 37, 438; Awdry, ii, 233; Eliz., iii, 40; Geo., iii, 89, 90, 92, 95; Grace, iii, 37; Helen, iii, 37, 66; Sir Jno., iii, 89; Jno., iii, 89; Mary, iii, 37, 66; Sir Oliver, iii, 89, 90; Oliver, iii, 68; Sir Phil., iii, 90, 95; Sir Thos., iii, 37; Thos., iii, 37, 46, 66, 372; Ursula, iii, 31, 39, 82; Sir Will., ii, 41, 45, 54 *n*; iii, 39, 40, 64, 66, 90, 94, 438; Will., ii, 58; iii, 37, 39, 40, 46,
Boteler (*cont.*)
68, 82, 89; fam. iii, 39, 266; *see also* Butler
Botelers (Bucks), man., iii, 372
Boteley, Sir Jno., iii, 314 *n*
Botelstan, *see* Battlesden
Botetourt (Boteturt), Andr., iii, 390; Eliz., ii, 203; iii, 13; Joan de, ii, 364; Jno., ii, 275; iii, 13, 96; iii, 46, 235, 330; Maud (Matilda), ii, 203, 256, 275; iii, 330; fam., iii, 181, 212, 283, 342
Botevilein, *see* Butvillein
Bothe, Maud, ii, 210, 211, 220; Rob., ii, 204, 211, 224 *n*, 226
Botlesford, Geoff. de, iii, 426; Jno. de, iii, 426; Rob. de, iii, 426; Walt. de, iii, 426, 428; Will. de, iii, 426
Botte, Ralph, iii, 376
Bott End (Wilshamstead), iii, 328
Bott End (Wootton), iii, 329
Bottler, *see* Boteler
Botvileyns (Hinwick or Brayes Farm), man., iii, 58, 84
Bouchier, *see* Bourchier
Boughton, Edw., iii, 301; Eliz., iii, 301; Rich., ii, 328; iii, 301; Thos., ii, 328; Will., ii, 328; iii, 301
Boughton End (Lidlington), i, 45, 47; iii, 305
Boulde, Phil., iii, 285, 288
Boulogne, hon., iii, 74, 90, 101, 111
Boulogne, Eustace, count of, iii, 46, 78, 101; Reg., count of, ii, 255
Boulogne, Faramus (Pharus) de, iii, 372, 461
Boulton, Harry, ii, 188
Bourchier, Eliz., ii, 316; Humph., ii, 316, 317; Thos., iii, 272
Bourne, i, 387 *n*, 388 *n*; iii, 302
Bourne, Edw., ii, 167; iii, 27; Jno., iii, 311; Susanna, iii, 27; Will., ii, 39; iii, 23, 311; —, ii, 166, 171
Bourne End (Cranfield), iii, 275, 278, 329
Boveden, Nich. de., iii, 449; Sarah de, iii, 449
Bover, Edw., iii, 456 *n*
Bovey, Sir Ralph, iii, 254
Bovil (Boweles, Bowell, Bowles, Boyvill, Bueles, Builli, Buly), Cecilia de, iii, 252; Diana, iii, 382; Eliz., i, 356, 358; Eustace de, ii, 336; Hen. de, iii, 219; Ingeramus de, iii, 173; Sir Jno. de, iii, 183; Jno., ii, 336; iii, 57, 219, 221, 248, 252, 254; Matilda, iii, 183; Nich. de, iii, 379; Pet. de, ii, 294, 336; iii, 252; Sim. de, iii, 211; Thos., ii, 254-5; Will., ii, 172; —, ii, 312, 332; iii, 131; fam., iii, 210
Bow Church (Lond.), iii, 368
Bowdler, Eliz., iii, 286; Thos., iii, 286
Boweles, fam., *see* Bovil
Bowell, fam., *see* Bovil
Bowels (Bowells), man., ii, 336, 337; iii, 45, 46, 252, 253
Bowels, fam., *see* Bovil
Bowels fields (Northill), iii, 245
Bowells Wood (Bromham), iii, 44
Bowen, Alb. E., iii, 88, 92, 95; Mrs., iii, 395
Bower, Dr., iii, 297
Bowes Close (Wootton), iii, 332
Bowles, fam., *see* Bovil
Bowskell, Thos., iii, 17
Bowyer, Sir Will., iii, 393
Box (Boxe), Anne, iii, 220; Hen., ii, 281 *n*; Sir Ralph, iii, 250; Will., iii, 220
Box End (Kempston), mills, iii, 302
Boxes, man., *see* Throckmortons

Boxhedge Farm (Cranfield), iii, 275
Box Hill (Surrey), i, 40
Boyden, Mrs., iii, 146
Boyvill, *see* Bovil
Bozeat (Northants), iii, 63
Brace, Fran., iii, 154, 240
Bracebridge, John de, iii, 332
Brache, man., ii, 350, 356, 357, 361, 363; mill, ii, 356, 366
Brache, Andr. de la, ii, 356, 359
Brache Farm (Luton), ii, 375
Brachull, Lescelina de, ii, 381 *n*; Will. de, ii, 381 *n*
Braci, Aldulf de, iii, 370, 372; Mascelin de, iii, 370
Brackley, Thos., Ld., iii, 393
Bradbeer, J., ii, 198
Bradbourne-in-the-Peak, i, 373, 376; chaps., i, 372; ch., i, 372; man, i, 372 *n*, 377
Bradenham (Bucks), iii, 415
Bradshaw (Bradshawe), Hen., ii, 361; Joan, ii, 361; Nich., iii, 221; —, ii, 216; fam., iii, 43
Bradwell (Bucks), i, 6
Brady, Dr., i, 97
Braham, Rich. de, iii, 213
Brahi, *see* Bray
Braibroc, *see* Braybrook
Braithwayte, Rich., ii, 245
Brakebergh, *see* Brogborough
Brakin, Eliz., iii, 200
Bramblehanger, ii, 374; man., ii, 350, 362, 363, 366
Bramblehanger, Alan de, ii, 360 *n*, 362
Brambles (Rubi), i, 54-5
Bramingham, Gt. (Luton), ii, 363
Bramingham, Little, ii, 363, 366
Brampton (near Huntingdon), ii, 24
Brampton, Ld., ii, 235
Bramston, Arth., iii, 145; Withers, iii, 145; Mrs., iii, 145
Brandreth, Alice, iii, 407; Anne, iii, 407; Hen., iii, 391-3, 407; H. C. G., iii, 367, 391, 393; Nehemiah, iii, 392; Mrs., iii, 391, 393; fam., ii, 243; iii, 389
Branson, G. H., ii, 200
Brantfield, Jno., Ld., ii, 347
Branting, ii, 224
Braose (Brewose), Aliva de, ii, 300, 339; iii, 12, 262; Payn de, ii, 143; Will. de, ii, 300, 339, 341; iii, 44, 219 *n*, 262, 329
Brasenose Coll. (Oxford), iii, 117
Brasier, *see* Brazier
Brasington, Edw., iii, 130 *n*
Brasses, i, 355 *n*; ii, 209, 213, 218, 229, 233, 236, 240, 250, 258, 265, 269, 279, 287, 292, 299, 312, 319, 328 *n*, 331, 338, 343, 347, 373, 379; iii, 25, 28, 39, 47, 53, 63, 87, 95, 100, 103, 108, 116, 120, 121, 127, 131, 135, 143, 167, 174, 177, 179, 185, 193, 200, 208, 218, 222, 233, 235 *n*, 237, 239, 240 *n*, 241, 250, 266, 273, 283, 295, 304, 307, 312, 315, 328, 334, 340, 366, 373, 378, 385, 387-8, 393, 411, 413, 423, 425, 434, 438, 446, 450
Brass foundries, ii, 350
Brassington, Edw., ii, 365
Bray, Ada de, ii, 253; Anselm de, ii, 330; Sir Edm., ii, 346; iii, 373; Edm., iii, 44, 85, 371, 397, 456; Sir Edw., ii, 340; iii, 13, 298, 391; Edw., ii, 340; iii, 371, 397; Eliz., ii, 340; iii, 371; Hugh de, ii, 253, 330; iii, 314; Isabella de, iii, 191; Jane, iii, 373; Joan, iii, 97; Sir Jno., ii, 340; Jno., ii, 301; iii, 371; Mary, ii, 340; Matilda de, iii, 314; May, Lady,
Bray (*cont.*)
iii, 298; Sir Reg., ii, 301, 340, 344, 346; iii, 13, 22, 44, 78, 85, 298, 344, 371, 396; Reg., i, 399; ii, 340; iii, 85; Rich., ii, 312; iii, 163; Rob. de, ii, 328, 339; iii, 40, 43, 91, 98; Rog. de, ii, 34, 221, 230; iii, 98, 191; Temperance, ii, 341 *n*; Thos. de, i, 325 *n*; ii, 34 *n*, 330, 332; Will. de, ii, 379; iii, 6, 427; —, ii, 194; fam., iii, 98, 211, 370, 375
Braybrook (Braibroc, Braybroke), Alianora, iii, 188; Christina (de), i, 361, 364; ii, 237, 247; iii, 194; Eleanor, iii, 317, 380; Eliz. (de), ii, 296, 324; iii, 187, 230, 317, 380; Sir Gerard (de), i, 385, 389, 403 *n*; ii, 276-7, 280; iii, 52, 130, 140, 162, 186, 230, 243-4, 380; Gerard de, ii, 35, 276-7, 287 *n*, 296, 323, 334; iii, 65, 140, 184, 186-9, 199, 229-30, 317, 333, 380; Hen. (de), i, 361, 364, 385 *n*; ii, 27, 28, 237, 239, 247-8; iii, 10, 11, 194, 353; Isabella, ii, 276, 280, 323; Joan (de), ii, 276 *n*; iii, 186, 199, 230 *n*; Sir Jno., iii, 186; Jno. de, ii, 72; iii, 229; Mabel de, iii, 186; Marg. de, iii, 187; Maud, iii, 380; Sir Reg., ii, 227; iii, 230 *n*; Reg., ii, 296; iii, 140 *n*, 194; Rich. de, iii, 196; Rob., i, 329; iii, 189, 193-4, 349; —, iii, 140; fam., iii, 236, 326
Braye (Bray), Anne, Lady, ii, 340; Jane, Lady, ii, 340; iii, 373; Joan, Lady, iii, 208; Ld., iii, 240, 372-3; Edm., Ld., ii, 301, 340, 341 *n*, 343; iii, 13, 23, 208, 344, 371, 392; Jno., Ld., ii, 340; iii, 204, 344
Brayes, man., *see* Bromham
Brayfield (Northants), ch., i, 387, 388, 389; rectory, i, 389
Brayne Corner (Ridgmont), iii, 321
Braynforth, Rob., ii, 214
Brays, man. (Husborne Crawley), iii, 396-7
Brazier (Brasier), John, iii, 458; Thos., ii, 310; Will., ii, 312 *n*
Breach (Maulden), iii, 314
Breadalbane, Amabel (Amabella), ctss. of, ii, 327
Breauté, Alice de, iii, 70 *n*; Falkes (Fawkes, Fulk) de, i, 320, 354, 362, 364, 378, 379; ii, 27, 28, 29, 350; iii, 10, 11, 23, 24, 282, 339, 342, 353; Marg. de, iii, 11; Will. de. iii, 10, 11, 70 *n*; Will. M. de, ii, 28
Brecknock, Alice, iii, 429; Dav., iii, 429; Jno., iii, 429; Lettice, iii, 429; Marg., iii, 429
Bredham, Jno., iii, 157
Bredyman, Edith, i, 335 *n*; iii, 419, 436; Edm., iii, 82, 419, 436; Geo., ii, 377; iii, 82, 376, 419, 436
Brent, Sir Nath., i, 337, 339; iii, 69
Brereton, Rev. C., ii, 174; Jane, Lady, ii, 340; Joan, iii, 23, 205, 208, 392; Jno., ii, 173, 174; Thos., ii, 173, 174; Sir Urian, ii, 340; iii, 23, 205, 208, 344, 392
Breton, Amabilla le, iii, 405; Gozelin le, iii, 405, 421, 422; Hugh le, iii, 405, 422; Juliana le, iii, 422; Rich. le, ii, 305; Walt. le, iii, 405; Will. le, i, 373, 374, 377, 396; *see also* Briton
Brett (Bretti, Britt), Alice, iii, 428, 431; Hugh, iii, 428, 431; Sir
Brett (*cont.*)
Jno., iii, 259, 260; Owen, ii, 44; iii, 259, 260; Rob., iii, 443; Will., iii, 443
Bretville, Geoff., ii, 253; Will. de, ii, 253
Brewer, Will., ii, 219; fam., iii, 194
Brewers' Brash (Wootton), iii, 311 *n*
Brewer's Hill Farm (Houghton Regis), iii, 368, 394
Brewose, *see* Braose
Breybrok, *see* Braybrook
Brian, *see* Bryan
Briant, *see* Bryant
Briars Stockings Copse (Eversholt), iii, 375
Bricheno, Will., iii, 154
Brick Farm (Ravensden), iii, 210
Brickground Plantation, iii, 394
Brickhill, Bow (Bucks), ii, 71
Brickhill, Gt. (Bucks), i, 376; ii, 40, 46, 53, 162; postal service, ii, 99
Brickhill, Little (Bucks), ii, 2, 3, 46; iii, 271
Brick industry, ii, 117, 261, 304, 314; iii, 128, 157, 175, 186, 210, 215, 280, 297, 307, 329, 451
Brickwood, Jno., iii, 194
Brickwork, ii, 364, 365
Brictric, iii, 129, 146
Bridge, Rich., iii, 55
Bridges, Bridg., iii, 255; Brook, iii, 21; Eliz., iii, 255; Giles, iii, 339; Haselfoote, iii, 255; Thos., iii, 255
Bridgman, Sir Orlando, ii, 52
Bridgewater (Bridgwater), ctsses. of, iii, 417, 432; Penelope, ii, 373; earls of, iii, 451; Jno., iii, 146 *n*, 391, 393; Jno. W., iii, 427, 428; Arabella, Lady, iii, 137
Bridle, Geo., ii, 172; —, ii, 173
Bridlington, Geoff., prior of, i, 353 *n*
Brienne, Rob. de, iii, 9
Briers, Anne, Lady, ii, 377-9; Anne, ii, 377; Arabella, Lady, ii, 377, 379; Sir Will., ii, 377-80; Will., ii, 379
Brigg (Brigge), Thos. atte, i, 325 *n*; iii, 284; fam., iii, 351
Briggs, Geo., iii, 367
Brightman, Thos., ii, 344
Brightwell (Herts), iii, 425
Brihtnoth, ii, 20
Brikulle, Thos. de, iii, 343
Brill (Bucks), i, 400
Brin, Mary, ii, 102
Brinklo, Jno., i, 398
Briscoe, Anne, ii, 295 *n*; Jno., ii, 295
Brisey, Mabel, iii, 458; Rog., iii, 458
Bristol, Jno., earl of, iii, 45, 49
Bristow, Herb., ii, 256
Britain, Baron, ii, 244; Will., ii, 244
Britens, man., i, 402; ii, 82; iii, 291, 292
British remains, ii, 1, 2, 8, 314; iii, 176, 350, 402
Briton (Britton), Hugh, i, 314 *n*; Jno., ii, 305; Marg., ii, 305; iii, 292; Rich., ii, 305; Rog., ii, 305; Will., ii, 305; iii, 292; *see also* Breton
Britt, *see* Brett
Brittany, Jno. de, earl of Richmond, *see* Richmond
Brittons, man., *see* Britens, man.
Briwere, Joan, iii, 119; Rob. (de la), iii, 119; Will. (de), iii, 119, 122, 162

Broad Green (Cranfield), iii, 275
Broad Green Farm (Cranfield), iii, 278
Broadmead (Wootton), iii, 335
Broc, le, fam., iii, 210
Brocas, Anne, iii, 407; Barn., ii, 379; iii, 406, 407; Edith, iii, 419, 436; Eliz., iii, 407; Jno., iii, 407; Rob., ii, 379; iii, 406, 407; Will., iii, 407
Brocborough, *see* Brogborough
Brockeborowe, *see* Brogborough
Brocket, Edw., ii, 357; Sir Jno., ii, 355, 357; Jno., ii, 357
Brockton, —, ii, 195
Brodo, ii, 232
Brogborough (Lidlington), i, 306
Brogborough (Ridgmont), Cromwell at, iii, 321; man., iii, 71 *n*, 321, 322; pk., ii, 55, 147; iii, 322, 323
Brogborough Hill (Ridgmont), iii, 320
Brogborough Pk. Farm (Ridgmont), iii, 320, 321
Brogborough Round House, *see* Brogborough Pk. Farm
Broi, *see* Broy
Broilg, *see* Broy
Broken Wharf (London), iii, 33
Bromeclose (Old Warden), iii, 255
Bromflete, Edw., ii, 277; Hen., *see* Vessy; Marg., iii, 91, 118, 121; Sir Thos., iii, 91, 118, 119; Thos, iii, 91, 121
Bromhall, Oliver, ii, 244
Bromham, ii, 60, 92, 96, 198, 252, 253; iii, 12, 14, 34, 37, 40, 44-9, 55, 96, 183, 302; adv., i, 316 *n*, 384; iii, 47, 48; chant., iii, 49; bridge, iii, 36; char., iii, 49; Chas. I. at, iii, 45; ch., i, 315 *n*, 382, 384; iii, 47, 48, 49, 153; hall, i, 141; ii, 44, 46 *n*, 60; iii, 44; man., iii, 13, 37, 44, 45, 46, 47, 78, 311; mills, iii, 44, 47; pk., i, 112, 120, 126; iii, 44; pop., ii, 115; rectory, iii, 47, 49; Rom. rem., ii, 5, 6, 15; sch., ii, 181
Bromham, Jno. de, iii, 47; Sim. de, iii, 47
Bromholme, *see* Bromham
Bromley, Ld. Chancellor, ii, 180
Bromsall, Eliz., iii, 231; Frances, iii, 243; Marg., iii, 233; Owen T., iii, 231, 244; Ralph, ii, 59; Thos., ii, 59, 246; iii, 231, 233, 243, 250
Bronze Age, i, 168-70, 270; iii, 117, 439, 448
Brooke (Brook), Anne, iii, 419; Arth., iii, 419; Duke, iii, 208, 209; Eliz., ii, 227; Sir Geo., iii, 140, 187, 208, 230, 236; Sir Hen., iii, 208; Joan, ii, 227; Marg., iii, 208; Sir Thos., ii, 227; Thos., ii, 296; iii, 140, 187, 198; Sir Will., iii, 187, 208; fam., ii, 262; iii, 205
Brookbanks, A. J., ii, 214
Brook End (Eversholt), iii, 375
Brook End (Keysoe), iii, 136; Nonconf., iii, 136
Brook End (Northill), iii, 242
Brook End (Stotfold), ii, 300
Brook Farm (Holcot), iii, 386
Brook Farm (Ravensden), iii, 209
Brook Farm (Wilden), iii, 223
Brooks, Ann, iii, 286; Cath., iii, 286, 288; F. G., ii, 199, 200; Geo., iii, 61, 238, 286; Jane, ii, 214, 304; Jno. H., iii, 286; Jno. T., iii, 286; Maj. J. H., i, 117, 127, 137, 140; ii, 146; iii, 284; Kath. M. F. B., iii, 284; —, ii, 146
Broom, iii, 227, 256, 260, 261, 267; hall, iii, 256; Man. Farm., iii, 256
Brotherhood Hall (Leighton Buzzard), iii, 415
Broughberrowe (Lidlington), iii, 305
Broughton (Bucks), iii, 131, 330, 402; adv., i, 383; barony of, ii, 294; ch., i, 382, 383, 384
Broughton, Anne, i, 402; iii, 436, 440; Cath., iii, 440; Eliz., ii, 243; Sir Jno., i, 402; ii, 243; Jno. (de), ii, 212, 289; iii, 158, 346, 380, 384, 436, 440, 444; Kath., i, 402; ii, 243, 289; Mary, iii, 346, 440; Sir Rob., iii, 436; Rob., ii, 243; iii, 158, 440; fam., iii, 312, 381, 446
Broughton End (Lidlington), iii, 305
Broun, *see* Brown
Brounder, Alice, iii, 140; Rich., iii, 140
Brounsford, Isabel de, iii, 247; Will. de., iii, 247
Brown (Broun), Andr., iii, 433; Eleanor, ii, 257; Hen., iii, 351; Humph., iii, 231, 443; Jno., ii, 257, 310, 342 *n*; Rev. J. E., ii, 92 *n*; Lancelot (Capability), ii, 325, 355; Rog., i, 326; —, ii, 44, 62, 90; *see also* Brun
Browne, Ant., iii, 193; Cath., ii, 347; iii, 443; Christiana, iii, 443; Geo., iii, 443; Lewis, iii, 443; Mabel, Lady, iii, 244; Mabel, ii, 323; Mary, Lady, ii, 207; Mary, ii, 262, 342 *n*; iii, 443; Matth., ii, 323; Maj.-Gen. Rich., ii, 47, 48; iii, 402; Rich., iii, 244, 250; Sir Sam., ii, 206, 207; Sam., ii, 44, 55, 204, 262, 265; iii, 366; Sir Thos., iii, 244; Thos., ii, 204, 234, 262, 323; iii, 133; Will., i, 394; ii, 158; iii, 321; *see also* Brun
Browning, Jno., iii, 182; Capt., ii, 189
Brownlow, earls of, ii, 66 *n*, 184 *n*, 185 *n*, 220, 222; iii, 368, 427, 428, 429, 432, 448; Adelbert W., iii, 451; Jno. W., iii, 451; Ld., ii, 216; iii, 145
Broy, Margery de, iii, 40; Osbert de, iii, 40, 42, 91; Phil. de, i, 378; ii, 26, 27; Walt. de, iii, 40; fam. iii, 43, 48
Bruce, Ld., ii, 58, 147, 310, 323; iii, 286; Ld. Chas., iii, 315; Edw. Ld., ii, 267, 322; iii, 267, 294, 337; Ld. Edw., iii, 331; Rob. Ld., ii, 55, 56, 325; iii, 290; *see also* Ailesbury, earl of; Thos., Ld., iii, 290, 317
Bruce (Bruse), Alice, iii, 445; Chas., iii, 294; Christiana, iii, 299; Gylis, iii, 445; Honora, iii, 325; Isabel, ii, 237, 278; iii, 299; Sir Jno., iii, 445; Rich., iii, 299; Rob., i, 382, 384 *n*, 388; ii, 30, 237, 267, 278; iii, 65, 195, 260, 299; Thos., iii, 318 *n*; *see also* Ailesbury, earl of
Brucebury, man. (Kempston), iii, 299
Brudenell, Alice, iii, 182; Cath., ii, 239; iii, 150; Edm., iii, 150, 182; Rob., ii, 239; iii, 150; Sir Thos., iii, 150 *n*
Bruert, Will., iii, 189
Brugge, *see* Brigge
Bruham, *see* Bromham
Brun (Brune), Jno. le, iii, 129, 130; Sarah le, iii, 129; Will. le, iii, 129; *see also* Brown, Browne
Bruneham, *see* Bromham
Brunstanethorp, ii, 21
Bruse, *see* Bruce
Bruton, Jno., i, 393
Bryan (Brian), Sir Fran., i, 330, 331, 367, 368 *n*, 370; ii, 316; iii, 197, 325, 459 *n*, 461; Geoff., ii, 336; Iolenta, ii, 336; Joan, ii, 215, 336; Jno., ii, 325, 345 *n*; iii, 274, 296, 316, 418; Mabel, ii, 336; Pet., ii, 336; iii, 418; Rob., ii, 336; iii, 418; Rog., ii, 215, 216; Sir Will., iii, 382
Bryant (Briant), Jno., iii, 261, 393, 414; J., ii, 292; iii, 374
Bryteville, Hugh de, iii, 182; Jno. de, iii, 182; Will. de, iii, 182
Brytvilles, man., *see* Birchfield
Buchanan, Arch., ii, 385; Jane, ii, 385
Buck, Sir Chas., iii, 436, 438; Frances, iii, 436; Sir John, iii, 436; Mary, Lady, iii, 436; Sir Will., iii, 436
Buckby (Northants), i, 360
Buckby, Anne, ii, 281 *n*; Mary, ii, 281; Rich., ii, 281, 285; Will., ii, 265, 281
Buckden (Hunts), ii, 38, 39
Buckhurst, Ld., ii, 253
Buckingham, ii, 47, 67; iii, 1 ch., i, 311
Buckingham, Anne, duchess of, iii, 173; dks. of, ii, 53; iii, 110, 154, 298; Edw., iii, 106, 126, 156, 172; Hen., iii, 171, 283; Humph., iii, 78, 85, 171-2, 422; Hen., earl of, iii, 36; Humph., earl of, iii, 36; Walt., earl of, ii, 385; iii, 315
Buckingham, Jno., *see* Lincoln, bps. of; Rich. of, i, 397; Will. of, i, 397
Buckinghamshire, archd. of, i, 354 *n*; iii, 28; bishopric, i, 332; ind., ii, 121, 123, 124; parl. repre., ii, 34; sheriffs of, ii, 29 *n*, 30 *n*, 32, 40
Buckland, Joan de, iii, 452; Matilda de, iii, 452; Will. de., iii, 452
Bucklow, iii, 34-5, 36 *n*
Buckmaster, C., iii, 417; Jno., iii, 415, 449; Rich., iii, 415
Buckstead (Studham), iii, 368
Buckwood Stubbs, iii, 337, 390
Buckworth, Jos. F., iii, 330; Mary, iii, 330
Buddenho (Berells and Frenches), man., iii, 247-8
Buddenho (Bodenho), Jno. de, iii, 30; Nicolaa de, iii, 247; Rich. de, iii, 247
Budewell (Turvey), iii, 114
Budna, iii, 242, 248, 250
Bueles (Buels), fam., *see* Bovil
Bugge, Reg., iii, 43
Builli, fam., *see* Bovil
Bulkeley (Bulkley), Ann, iii, 212; Edw., iii, 69; Joan, iii, 241; Jno., iii, 212; Pet., i, 337; iii, 69; Rob., iii, 212, 241; Rog., iii, 241; Will., iii, 212; *see also* Burdelys
Bulkeleys, man., *see* Burdelys
Bulkley, fam., *see* Bulkeley
Bull, Jas., ii, 101
Bulle, Thos., ii, 151
Bullen, Rev. Hen. St. J., ii, 259 Sarah, ii, 259
Buller, Mary, iii, 332
Bullisdon, Thos., iii, 250
Bullok (Bullock), Eliz., ii, 224; Jno., ii, 224; iii, 91; Kath., ii, 224; Rob., ii, 224

Bulstrode, Edm. (de), i, 326 *n*; iii, 436 *n*; Rich., iii, 278 *n*
Bulthan, Judith, ii, 289
Buly, fam., *see* Bovil
Bunbury, Sir Chas., ii, 192, 193
Buncer's Farm, *see* Caddington
Bunion (Buniun), fam., *see* Bunyan
Bunker, Rich., iii, 375
Bunting, Rev. Edw. S., iii, 179
Buntingford (Herts), ii, 359
Bunyan, Eliz., iii, 207; Hen., ii, 376, 377 *n*, 380; Jno., i, 103, 340-5; ii, 47, 49, 59-60, 374, 377 *n*; iii, 5, 7, 8, 22, 32, 179, 207, 279, 282, 290, 316, 379, 451; Thos., iii, 279, 290; Will., iii, 279; fam., ii, 376, 377
Bunyan Institute, Bedford, iii, 32
Burcester (Oxon), man., i, 360
Burdelys, man. (Gt. Barford), iii, 182-3
Burdelys, man. (Stagsden), iii, 97
Burdelys, Eliz. de, iii, 98; Geoff. de, iii 98, 98 *n*, 182; Hugh de, iii, 182; Joan de, iii, 98; Jno. de, iii, 97, 98, 182; Will. de, iii, 182; *see also* Bulkeley
Burdett (Burdet), Mich., ii, 227; Nich., ii, 238; Will., ii, 238
Burdon (Cambs), i, 364; iii, 247
Burdun, Walt., iii, 129
Bures (Essex), Rom. rem., ii, 13
Bures, Andr. de, iii, 453; Kath. de, iii, 453
Burford, barons of, iii, 317
Burgam, Sir Rog., ii, 191
Burgend Close (Bedford), iii, 32
Burgess, Jno., iii, 442; Thos., iii, 442
Burgh, Beatrix de, iii, 339; Hawise de, iii, 339; Hubert de, i, 319; ii, 27-9; iii, 70, 339, 340, 342; *see also* Kent, earl of; Isabel de, iii, 70; Jno. de, iii, 339; Marg. de, iii, 339; Matilda de, *see* Ulster, ctss. of; Ralph, ii, 374; Rob. de, iii, 276
Burghersh, Sir Barth. (de), iii, 129, 426; Barth. (de), iii, 129, 426; Hen. de, iii, 426-7; Maud, iii, 429; —, bp., *see* Lincoln, bps. of
Burghley, Dorothy, Lady, *see* Exeter, ctss. of; Ld., iii, 13, 459; Thos. Ld., *see* Exeter, earl of
Burghope, Rev. Geo., iii, 432
Burgoyne (Burgoine), Constance, ii, 241, 250; Eliz., ii, 250; Sir Jno., ii, 42, 44, 45, 66 *n*, 68 *n*, 70, 197, 248, 250; iii, 201, 201 *n*; Jno., ii, 39, 40, 220, 222, 228, 238, 239, 244, 245, 248, 250; iii, 329; Sir Jno. M., ii, 66 *n*, 246; Marg., iii, 329; Montague, ii, 250; Sir Montague R., ii, 256; Rich., ii, 238, 239; iii, 329; Rob., ii, 244, 347; Sir Rog., ii, 44, 62, 239, 248, 250; Thos., ii, 220, 238, 239, 248, 250; Thos. J., ii, 241; Will., iii, 21, 329; fam., ii, 44, 66, 249
Burials and burial urns, i, 159, 160, 163, 168, 183, 184, 185, 187-89, 270, 296, 297, 350; ii, 1-14; iii, 402, 448
Burke, Edm., iii, 54
Burlee, Will., iii, 259
Burley Farm (Stevington), iii, 102
Burnaby, Jno. de, iii, 129; Rev. J. B., iii, 323
Burnard, Felicia, ii, 227; Hen., ii, 263; Nich., ii, 227; Odo, ii, 227, 262; Rog., ii, 226, 262; Steph., ii, 262; —, ii, 261, 263; *see also* Barnard and Bernard
Burne, Jno., i, 380; iii, 22
Burneham Mead, ii, 266
Burnel (Burnell), Phil., iii, 118, 119 *n*, 122, 159; Sir Rob., iii, 122; Rob., iii, 118; fam., iii, 283
Burnet, Phil., iii, 55
Burr (Burre), Agnes, iii, 444; Rob., i, 387; Will., iii, 444
Burret, iii, 139, 142
Burreth, Thos., i, 402
Burrland, Rich., iii, 374
Burroughs, Rev. Lynch, ii, 310; Sarah, ii, 310
Burr's Estate (Dunstable), iii, 368
Burt, Thos., iii, 64
Burton, Alex. J., iii, 145; Marg., i, 393; Mrs., iii, 145
Bury, Frances, iii, 340; Fran., iii, 340; Geo., iii, 278, 286; Hadwisa, iii, 190, 192; Jno. de, iii, 190, 192; Rich., iii, 407, 443
Bury End (Shillington), ii, 294; chap., ii, 299
Bury End (Stagsden), iii, 96
Bury Farm (Goldington), iii, 202
Bury Farm (Houghton Conquest), iii, 289
Buryfield (Houghton Regis), Rom. pottery, ii, 8
Bury Hatley, man., *see* Cockayne Hatley
Bury Hill (Thurleigh), earthworks, i, 287
Bury St. Edmunds (Suffolk), i, 328; abbot of, iii, 228, 229
Buryssteede (Salphobury), man., iii, 215 *n*
Busard (Buzzard), fam., iii, 401
Busby, Will., iii, 162
Bush, Eleanor, ii, 362; Ralph, ii, 362
Bushey (Herts), i, 360
Bushmead Priory, i, 349, 350, 385-7; ii, 149, 150; iii, 24, 137, 166, 180, 184, 187, 188, 189, 190, 193, 194, 197-9, 225, 292; ch., i, 386; earthworks, i, 307; man., iii, 198; priors, i, 328, 385-7; ii, 23; iii, 137, 166, 194; sch., ii, 149
Bushmead Wood (Eaton Socon), iii, 189
Bushycommon Wood (Potsgrove), iii, 421
Bussey (Bussy), Andr., iii, 237; Barth. de, i, 362 *n*; ii, 230 *n*; Cecily (Cecilia) de, i, 361 *n*; ii, 230; iii, 255; Cecill, iii, 237; Eliz., iii, 237; Hadwisa de, ii, 230; iii, 252; Joan, ii, 232; Jno., iii, 237; Maud de, i, 361 *n*; ii, 230, 231, 233; iii, 255; Will. de, i, 361 *n*, 362 *n*; ii, 230, 233; iii, 252, 255; fam., iii, 237
Busshey Close (Renhold), iii, 215
Bussy, fam., *see* Bussey
Butcher, Frances E., iii, 210; Rich., ii, 162; Rev. Rob. H., iii, 210
Bute, earls of, ii, 61, 307, 353, 355; mqs. of, i, 330; ii, 61 *n*, 349 *n*, 353, 356, 358, 366, 374; iii, 257
Bute Hosp. (Luton), ii, 375
Butler, Ld. Will., ii, 347; Anne, Lady, iii, 105; Anne, ii, 347; Audrey, ii, 347; Beckingham, ii, 206, 301; Sir Edw., ii, 345, 381; Edw., ii, 206, 215, 301, 302, 345; iii, 126, 385; Eliz., ii, 345; Florence, ii, 289; Geo., ii, 40, 301; Hawise (Hadwisa), ii, 345, 381; Helen, ii, 347; Hen., ii, 347; Jane, ii, 345, 347; Joan, ii, 215, 289; Sir Jno., ii, 345, 347; Jno., ii, 165, 166, 289, 290, 292, 345, 347, 359, 382; iii,
Butler, (*cont.*)
46; Kath., ii, 292; Mary, ii, 347; Nich., ii, 345; Olive, ii, 347; Sir Oliver, iii, 105, 331; Oliver, iii, 21; Sir Phil., ii, 345, 381, 382; iii, 105; Phil., ii, 345; Ralph, ii, 345, 346, 381; iii, 46; Sir Rob., ii, 345; Rob., ii, 382; Sam., iii, 238; Thos., ii, 165, 345, 359; iii, 244, 278, 432; Sir Will., iii, 21; Will., ii, 59, 345, 359, 382; iii, 38; Maj., ii, 54, 55; fam., ii, 330; *see also* Boteler
Butler's Farm (Northill), *see* Cook's Farm
Butt, Sir Will., iii, 134
Butt Close Park, iii, 394
Butter, Will., iii, 374 *n*
Butterfield, W. R., i, 111, 114
Butterflies, *see* Rhopalocera
Butterworth, Mrs., iii, 122
Button, Rich., iii, 331, 332
Butts, Little (Dunstable), ii, 7
Butvillein, Alice, iii, 84 *n*; Eliz., iii, 84 *n*; Joan, iii, 84; Juliana, iii, 58, 84; Nichola, iii, 84; Rob., iii, 84; Will., iii, 58, 84
Buzum, fam., *see* Bosom
Bycham, *see* Beauchamp
Byddik, Ant., ii, 321; Christina, ii, 321; Jno. de, ii, 322
Bygod, *see* Bigod
Bykeleswade, *see* Biggleswade
Bylindon, *see* Billington
Byng, Sir Geo., ii, 60, 61, 64 *n*; iii, 246, 253, 258, 261; *see also* Torrington, vsct.; Adm. Jno., ii, 61; iii, 260; Jno., iii, 246; Pattee, ii, 62, 291; Sarah, ii, 60
Byng of Southill, baron, iii, 258
Geo., baron, ii, 61
Bynnion, Sir Geo., ii, 43
Byrche, Hen., ii, 387; Will., ii, 387
Byrling, Alex., iii, 293; Alice, iii, 293; Jno., iii, 293
Byscote, *see* Biscott
Byssopesdon, Will. de, iii, 231 *n*
Bytham Castle (Lincs), iii, 144

Cabbin Ground (Bromham), iii, 44
Cadbury, man., iii, 193, 194, 197, 198 *n*
Caddington, i, 258, 338; ii, 71, 89, 306, 314, 316, 320; iii, 367; adv., ii, 319, 320; Buncer's Farm, ii, 314; Bury Farm, ii, 315; char., ii, 320; ch., i, 151, 312; ii, 6, 314, 318, 319, 320; Five Horse Shoes Inn, ii, 318; man., i, 312; ii. 314; mill, ii, 315; Nonconf., ii, 320; iii, 367; place-names, ii, 314; pop., ii, 114; prebends of, i, 312, 324; pre-hist. rem., i, 145-6, 151, 154-8, 163, 166, 172, 174; ii, 314 Rom. rem., ii, 6; sch., ii, 181; vicarage, i, 317
Caddington, Gt., man., ii, 315; prebend, ii, 315; Prebendal Farm, ii, 315
Caddington, Little, man., ii, 315; vicarage, ii, 315
Caddington, Rich. de, ii, 309, 310 Sibyl de, ii, 309, 310; Walt. of, i, 384
Caddington Bury, ii, 315
Caddington Green, sch., ii, 181
Caddington Hall, ii, 316, 318
Caddington Hills, i, 151
Caddington Minor, prebend of, ii, 315
Cade, Jack, rebellion of, iii, 359
Cadendone, *see* Caddington

INDEX

Cadenton, *see* Caddington
Cadwell (Holwell), ii, 286
Cadyndone, *see* Caddington
Caen, Paul of, *see* St. Albans, abbot of
Caesar, Sir Julius, ii, 159
Caesar's Camp (Sandy), A.S. rem., i, 184, 242; Rom. rem., i, 271, 272, 273, 274; ii, 9, 10
Cainhoe, ii, 30, 76; chap., i, 318, 351 *n*, 352; ii, 324-5; land value of, ii, 91; man., ii, 80, 322, 323, 325; iii, 273; mills, ii, 323, 324; place-names, ii, 321
Cainhoe, bar., ii, 277, 329, 376, 377, 379, 382 *n*, 383; iii, 50, 51, 54, 60, 113, 146, 236, 237, 286, 309, 346, 379, 396, 435-6
Cainhoe, hon., ii, 321
Cainhoe, Lady Isabel of, ii, 32
Cainhoe, Pet., iii, 278
Cainhoe Castle (Clophill), i, 291-2, 297; ii, 321, 324
Cainhoe Farm (Clophill), ii, 321
Caisneto, *see* Cheney
Caisot, Caissot, *see* Keysoe
Caius Coll. (Camb.), i, 342; ii, 162, 165; iii, 179
Calcutt Farm (Houghton Regis), *see* Carcutt
Caldecote, man. (Herts), i, 386
Caldecote, man. (Houghton Regis), iii, 392
Caldecote, Lower, iii, 242, 246, 251
Caldecote, Upper, iii, 242, 246; chap., iii, 250; ch., iii, 242; man., iii, 246, 247; Rom. rem., ii, 9
Caldecote (Caldecot), Amice de, iii, 138; John, iii, 125
Caldecote Lodge (Northill), iii, 242
Caldwell, i, 315 *n*, 316 *n*; man., iii, 21
Caldwell, John of, i, 353
Caldwell Priory, i, 317 *n*, 322, 325, 328, 349, 374, 379, 382-7, 398 *n*; ii, 244-5; iii, 11, 21, 38, 47, 48, 92, 107, 147, 221, 225, 286, 302, 333, 377; seal, i, 385
Calfe, Susannah, iii, 408
Calhoun, Will., ii, 64, 65; iii, 20
California (Dunstable), i, 160
Callopp, Reg., ii, 379; Thos., ii, 379
Calverly (Calvely), Agnes, Lady, ii, 234; iii, 72, 384; Sir Geo., ii, 234; iii, 72, 384; Mary de, iii, 220; Oliver (de), iii, 219, 220
Calvinist Baptists, *see* Baptists
Cam, riv., ii, 71
Cambleton, *see* Campton
Cambridge, ii, 20, 25 *n*, 48, 50, 51, 79, 138, 199; iii, 1, 10
Cambridge, Maud, ctss. of, iii, 13; earl of, iii, 13
Cambridgeshire, ii, 19, 25, 71, 91, 117
Camden, Lady, ii, 180, 235
Camelton, *see* Campton
Camera, Rob. de, iii, 147
Camestone, *see* Kempston
Camoys, man., *see* Honydon
Camoys, Hugh, iii, 194; Joan, iii, 84; John, iii, 194; Marg., iii, 194; Sir Ralph, iii, 84; Rich., iii, 194; Sir Thos., iii, 194
Campbell, Amabel, ii, 327; Jemima, ii, 327; iii, 65; Sir John, iii, 19; Rob., iii, 293
Campden (Gloucs.), ii, 224
Campion, Andr., iii, 392; Maj. Coventry, iii, 451, 453; Edw., iii, 51; Sir Hen., ii, 42; Hen., iii, 42; Rev. J. W. C., iii, 453; Mrs., iii, 453; —, iii, 125
Campion's Hill (Wootton), iii, 331
Campton, ii, 260, 266-76; iii, 77, 259, 278; adv., ii, 270; Bury Farm, ii, 270; char., ii, 270; ch., i, 315 *n*; ii, 266, 269-70; common, ii, 97; Grange, ii, 266; Highland Farm, ii, 266; mans., ii, 267, 268, 271; man.-house, ii, 268; mkts. and fairs, ii, 268; mills, ii, 266, 268-9; Nonconf., ii, 270; pop., ii, 113; rectory, ii, 266; R.C., ii, 266; sch., ii, 181, 266
Campton-cum-Shefford, *see* Campton
Campton House, ii, 266
Canal Close (Ampthill), iii, 274
Canals, ii, 108; iii, 363, 400
Cane, *see* Kane
Cannon, Tom, ii, 194
Canons (Cannons), man., iii, 329, 331-2
Canons Ashby Priory, ii, 326; iii, 85, 87, 104, 108, 109, 126
Canons (Cannons) Hill (Wootton), iii, 331 *n*
Cantelow(e), *see* Cantilupe
Canterbury, A.S. rem., i, 184; sch., ii, 152
Canterbury, archbps. of, i, 190, 322, 333, 346, 353 *n*, 357 *n*, 372, 374, 375, 389 *n*, 399, 399 *n*, 400; ii, 35, 154, 159, 203, 210, 219, 293, 312, 335, 359; iii, 14, 46, 70, 72, 89, 133, 140, 182, 260, 270 *n*, 272 *n*, 293, 317, 372, 403 *n*
Cantia, Cecily de, i, 390; Laura de, i, 360; *see also* Kancia
Cantilupe (Cantlow, Cantelow), Agnes de, ii, 251; Geo. (de), ii, 32; iii, 118, 370, 448; Hen., iii, 456; Joan de, iii, 229, 370; John, iii, 456; Mascelin de, iii, 370; Millicent (de), ii, 225, 282; iii, 118, 370; Rich., iii, 456; Rog. de, ii, 251, 253; Thos., ii, 32; Walt., *see* Worcester, bp. of; Will. (de), i, 320, 325 *n*; ii, 27, 32, 225, 282; iii, 118, 359, 370, 372, 374, 391, 430, 448, 455-6; fam., ii, 28, 224
Cantlow, *see* Cantilupe
Capel, Ld., ii, 43, 45, 53, 54
Capel (Capell), Sir Arth., iii, 254; Eliz., iii, 254, 427
Capella, Hen., iii, 339
Caperon, Agnes, iii, 74; Ralph, iii, 74; Sybil, iii, 74
Capon, John, iii, 407
Carcutt Calcutt Farm (Houghton Regis), iii, 390, 392
Cardington, ii, 21, 44, 66, 92, 255; iii, 31, 33, 45, 166, 197 *n*, 216, 233, 281, 292; adv., iii, 237; agriculture, ii, 134; bridge, iii, 235 *n*; char., iii, 238; ch., i, 315 *n*, 380; iii, 233, 235 *n*, 236-7; cross, iii, 234; man., i, 381; ii, 299; iii, 13, 15, 234-5; man. farm, iii, 233; man.-house, i, 306; mills, iii, 234-5; Nonconf., iii, 234; pop., ii, 116; prehist. rem., i, 145, 174; iii, 234; sch., ii, 181; vicarage, i, 316 *n*
Cardington Brook, iii, 233, 235 *n*
Cardington Cotton End, man., iii, 236
Cardington Priors, man., *see* Fenlake Barns
Cardington with Eastcotts, iii, 233-8
Cardun, Isabella (de), iii, 119, 122
Cardyngton, *see* Cardington
Carew (Carewe), Eleanor, Lady, ii, 355; Eliz., iii, 424; Jas., iii, 427; Marg., iii, 427; Nich., iii, 427; Sir Rich., ii, 355
Carewrike, Will., iii, 306
Carey, Adolphus, iii, 405; Anne, iii, 405; Eliz., ii, 229; Hen., *see* Hunsdon, Ld.; Walt., ii, 228, 229
Carldon, *see* Carlton
Carlentone, *see* Carlton
Carleton, *see* Carlton
Carlisle, Honoria, ctss. of, iii, 330; Jas., earl of, iii, 330
Carlisle (Carlyll), Alice, iii, 411; Joan, ii, 269; Nich., ii, 161; Rich., ii, 269; iii, 221
Carlton, ii, 115, 145; iii, 34, 49, 50, 51, 76, 77, 100, 114; adv., iii, 51, 54-5; ch., ii, 92; iii, 49, 52-4, 56; man., iii, 49-51, 54-5, 224 *n*; place-names, iii, 49; rectory, iii, 56; sch., ii, 181
Carlton (Carldon, Carleton, Karleton), Geoff., iii, 52; Geo., iii, 304; Godf. de, iii, 55; Rich., ii, 230; iii, 443; *see also* Charleton
Carlton Hall, man., iii, 51-2
Carlyles, man. (Roxton), iii, 221
Carlyll, *see* Carlisle
Carmino, Joan de, iii, 246; John de, iii, 246; Ralph de, iii, 246; Walt. de, iii, 246
Carminos, *see* Caldecote, Lower
Carnarvon, Anna S., ctss. of, iii, 427; Eliz., ctss. of, iii, 427; earls of, ii, 50; Chas., iii, 427; Rob., iii, 427
Carnivora, i, 139
Caron, *see* Carun
Carpenter, Edwin O., ii, 190; John i, 402; Mrs., iii, 297
Carr, Will., ii, 180
Cart, Jane, ii, 179; iii, 351, 367-8
Carter, Anne, iii, 305; Edw., iii, 191; Geo., ii, 188; Howard, ii, 263; H., ii, 261; Ralph le, iii, 333; Thos., iii, 117, 302; Will. (le), iii, 274, 302, 304, 333
Carteret, Lds., ii, 133, 146, 210; iii, 328; Geo., iii, 29; Hen., iii, 326; Hen. F., ii, 60, 341, 343; John, ii, 60, 341; iii, 132, 326
Carteret, Sir Geo., ii, 60, 339, 341; iii, 14; Jemima, Lady, ii, 341 *n*; Sir Phil., ii, 341
Cartwick, Will., ii, 322
Cartwright, Edm., ii, 281 *n*; Hugh, iii, 258-9; Rich., ii, 255; iii, 393; Will., iii, 258-9; Dr., ii, 135
Carun (Caron, Karun), Agnes de, ii, 251; Amice (Amicia) de, ii, 253, 276 *n*; Eliz. de, ii, 276; Flandrina, iii, 66; Hugh de, ii, 276; Joanna de, ii, 251; John de, ii, 251, 276; Lucy de, ii, 276; Margery de, ii, 276; Miles de, ii, 276 *n*; Osbert de, iii, 196 *n*; Ralph de, iii, 66; Rob. de, ii, 251, 253; iii, 76; Walt. de, ii, 251, 252, 253; iii, 196; Will. de (le), ii, 251, 252, 253, 275 *n*, 276-8; iii, 259-60
Caryer, John, ii, 241
Cason, Edw., iii, 314 *n*; Jane, ii, 347; John, iii, 236; Julian, ii, 347
Castelacre, Will. de, iii, 194
Castell, Edw., ii, 167; Mary, iii, 205; Rob., iii, 205; Dr., ii, 347
Castle Ashby, ii, 41; iii, 293
Castle Close (Goldington), iii, 206
Castle Hill (Bedford), iii, 33
Castle Hill (Eaton Socon), iii, 189
Castle House (Berkhampstead), ii, 317
Castle Mill (Goldington), iii, 206
Castor (Northants), iii, 300
Castre, Will. de, iii, 168

Catelayne, Lady, i, 335 *n*; *see also* Catlin
Cater, Anne, iii, 301; Beckford K., iii, 301; Edw., iii, 301; Frances K., iii, 301; John, iii, 301; John K., iii, 301; Marg. K., iii, 301; Mary, iii, 301; May K., iii, 301; Sir Rob. K., iii, 301; Sam., iii, 301; Sophia K., iii, 301; Will., iii, 300, 305; fam., iii, 303; *see also* Cator
Catesby, man., i, 376
Catesby (Catesbie), Ant., ii, 359; iii, 177 *n*, 310; Bridg., iii, 310; Clifton, iii, 310; Dorothy, iii, 177 *n*; Geo., ii, 359; iii, 310; Humph., ii, 359; iii, 310; Sir John, iii, 310; John, ii, 40, 359; Thos., ii, 359, 363, 365; iii, 310; Will., iii, 173
Cates Close (Wootton), iii, 331 *n*
Cateswood (Eaton Socon), iii, 189, 194
Catherine (of Aragon), (queen), i, 374, 376; ii, 38, 122, 123; iii, 270, 296, 353
Catherine (of Braganza), (queen), iii, 227
Catherine, St., ii, 38 *n*, 122, 123
Catlin, Eliz., ii, 257; John, ii, 257; Mary, ii, 232, 243; Sir Rob., ii, 232, 243; *see also* Catelayne
Caton, Dan., ii, 281
Cator, Edw., ii, 54 *n*, 55; —, ii, 44; *see also* Cater
Catuvellauni, ii, 1
Catworth, Gt. (Hunts), iii, 136
Catyeuchlani, *see* Catuvellauni
Cauceys, Geoff. de, i, 372 *n*
Cauf, Will. le, iii, 444
Caulcott (Marston Moretaine), iii, 307; brick kilns, iii, 308; char., iii, 313
Cauldwell, crown property in, iii, 271; price of land, ii, 91
Cauntelow, *see* Cantilupe
Caurel, Pierre, ii, 358
Causeway End (Wilshamstead), iii, 328
Causum, *see* Caversham
Cauvin, — (of Bedford), iii, 102
Cauz (Caus), Jas. de, i, 326 *n*; ii, 382, 384; Nichola, iii, 104; Rich. de, ii, 382; Rog. de, iii, 104
Cavendish, Alice, ii, 334; iii, 429; Chas., ii, 45 *n*; Frances, iii, 43; Geo., iii, 429; John, ii, 334; Thos., iii, 429; Will., iii, 43
Caversham (Causum), ii, 51
Cawne, —, iii, 19-20
Cawse, R. J., i, 134
Cealhgnefaw, *see* Chalgrave
Cecil, Dav., *see* Exeter, earl of; Lady Diana, iii, 315; Dorothy, Lady, *see* Exeter, ctss. of; Hen., *see* Exeter, marquess of; Mary, iii, 330; Sir Thos., *see* Exeter, earl of; Thos., iii, 285, 288; Will., iii, 14
Celestine III, pope, iii, 116
Celgrave, *see* Chalgrave
Cella, John de, ii, 361
Cell Dene (Caddington), ii, 318
Cement and lime works, ii, 117, 261, 384; iii, 447
Cemeteries, A.S., i, 175-90; iii, 402; Bronze Age, iii, 448; Rom., i, 187; ii, 5, 9, 11; Rom. Brit., ii, 266
Cerlentone, *see* Charlton
Cernes, Nich. de, ii, 252, 253; Thos. de, ii, 253
Chad, —, iii, 415
Chadwell End (Pertenhall), iii, 153
Chainhalle, *see* Channels End
Chaisot, *see* Keysoe
Chalenor, Rog., iii, 300; Thos., iii, 300
Chalfont St. Peter (Bucks), ii, 120
Chalgrave, i, 376, 402; ii, 43, 318, 353, 375; iii, 89, 336, 344, 383; adv., iii, 346, 348, 349; chant., i, 325 *n*, 329; iii, 349; char., ii, 181 *n*; iii, 349; ch., i, 311 *n*, 315 *n*, 318, 325 *n*, 371 *n*; iii, 345, 347, 348, 349; ind., iii, 345; man., ii, 22; iii, 345, 346, 347, 380 *n*; Manor Farm, iii, 345; Nonconf., iii, 345; 'Old Orchard,' iii, 349; place-names, iii, 345; pop., ii, 114; rectory, iii, 346, 348, 349; schs., ii, 181; iii, 345, 349; Shoulder of Mutton Inn, iii, 345; vicarage, i, 316 *n*; iii, 345, 348
Chalgrave Hockliffe, *see* Hockliffe
Chalk, —, iii, 226; fam., iii, 224
Chalk Hill, *see* Puddle Hill
Challeye, Sim., ii, 89
Chalmers, —, iii, 125
Chalton, iii, 227, 228, 230, 231, 362, 394, 439, 440, 442; chap., iii, 446 *n*; man., iii, 231, 442, 443, 444
Chalton, Ann, iii, 175
Chalton Cross Farm (Toddington), iii, 439
Chalverston, i, 384
Cham, John, iii, 187; Odo le, iii, 187; Reg. le, iii, 187; Rich., iii, 187; Rob. le, iii, 187; Sabina le, iii, 187; Sim. iii, 187
Chamber, Edw. atte, iii, 182; Gilb. atte, iii, 98; Joan atte, iii, 98
Chamberlain (Chamberlin), Amabel, iii, 152; Amphyllis, iii, 315; Aubrey, iii, 406; Dray, iii, 277; Edw., iii, 433; Eliz., iii, 433; Geoff., ii, 219, 221; Hugh, ii, 219; Joan, iii, 150, 406; John, iii, 112, 406; Sir Leonard, iii, 361; Marg., iii, 406, 433; Sir Rich., iii, 152, 406, 433; Rich., iii, 225, 406, 433; Rob., ii, 219; Sim., iii, 446 *n*; Sybil, iii, 433; Thos., iii, 406; Turstin, iii, 77; Will. (the), ii, 221, 356, 373; iii, 393, 423, 433, 449; fam., iii, 409
Chamberlains Bury, man., ii, 220
Chambers, —, ii, 162
Champion, Rich., iii, 286, 307, 333
Chancellor, Thos. the, i, 366 *n*
Chancellor, the Ld., ii, 170, 173, 175
Chandler, Anne iii, 183; Ant., iii, 393, 454; Dav., iii, 183; Geo., iii, 374, 414; John, iii, 152, 156; Rich., ii, 209, 254, 269, 332, 335; iii, 29, 208, 250, 268, 319, 388, 414, 420; —, iii, 226, 431, 446, 450
Chandos, Cassandra, dchss. of, iii, 255; Jas., dk. of, iii, 255
Chanewe, Will., i, 387
Channels End (Colmworth), iii, 180, 186
Chantrey, Sir Fran., iii, 418
Chantries, i, 325, 326, 329, 383, 397; ii, 155, 156, 242, 299, 318, 325, 326, 330, 332, 333, 335, 368, 369, 374, 381, 382, 384; iii, 30, 40, 43, 49, 92 *n*, 94, 118, 126, 136, 153, 201, 209, 216, 233, 244, 249, 250, 251, 255, 266, 274, 281 *n*, 284, 304, 305, 328, 335, 342, 349, 367, 374, 375, 382, 386, 391, 394, 415, 421, 423, 428, 432, 438, 446, 453, 454, 455; foundation, i, 325; suppression, i, 331; ii, 151, 155
Chantry Farm (Sharpenhoe), ii, 313, 384
Chapel End (Cardington), iii, 234
Chapel End (Colmworth), iii, 186
Chapel End (Houghton Conquest), iii, 289
Chapel End (Wilshamstead), iii, 326
Chapel Herne, iii, 21, 22
Chapel Hill (Hinwick), iii, 81
Chapel of Saint Macutes (St. Machutus, St. Makes, St. Marks), man., ii, 342
Chapels, anct., ii, 269, 320, 343, 365, 368, 369, 370, 372, 373; iii, 49, 255, 283, 304, 313, 349, 365, 374, 430, 443, 446, 459, 461
Chapman, Rebecca, iii, 330; Shuckburgh, iii, 72 *n*; Thos., iii, 330; Walt. le, iii, 358 *n*
Chapman & Mears, ii, 245, 319
Chappell's Groundes (Leighton Buzzard), iii, 404
Charles I, ii, 41, 47, 50-3, 56, 161, 201, 210, 261, 327, 353; iii, 41, 45, 123, 172, 180, 197, 227, 253, 270, 273, 292, 322, 355, 458
Charles II, i, 343; ii, 53, 56, 57, 61, 111, 147, 239, 341; iii, 14, 197, 206, 227, 270, 272, 317, 322, 379, 404, 417, 434, 440
Charles, —, iii, 125
Charlet, Rob., i, 370
Charleton, Eliz., Lady, ii, 231; Rich., ii, 231; Sir Thos., ii, 231; Thos., ii, 231; *see also* Carlton
Charlewood (Studham), ii, 145 iii, 429
Charlewood (Woburn), iii, 461
Charnock, *see* Chernock
Charterhouse, London, ii, 159
Chase, C. E., ii, 200; Steph., iii, 133; Thos., i, 402
Chastellon, John, iii, 422; Marg., iii, 422
Chaucer, Alice, iii, 403, 429; Maud, iii, 429; Thos., iii, 403, 429
Chaucombe, prior, iii, 184
Chaugrave, *see* Chalgrave
Chaul End (Caddington), ii, 314, 374
Chaumbre, *see* Chamber
Chauncey, Eliz., iii, 387
Chaurugge, Will. de, iii, 408
Chaworth, bar., iii, 443
Chaworth, hon., iii, 162
Chaworth, Matilda de, iii, 439; Pat. de, iii, 162, 439; Payn de, iii, 162, 439, 446
Chawston, i, 384; iii, 180, 201, 218, 219; beagles, ii, 190; man., iii, 219, 220; man.-house, i, 305
Chawston, Walt. of, i, 381
Cheddington, John of, i, 373, 377
Cheeke (Cheke), Frances, iii, 281; Hen., iii, 8, 281; Thos., iii, 281
Cheetwood, *see* Chetwood
Cheiroptera, i, 138
Cheisley, —, ii, 53
Cheke, *see* Cheeke
Chelbert, iii, 52
Cheletone, Rob. de, iii, 427
Chellington, iii, 34, 54-6, 59, 63, 85, 175; adv., iii, 51, 55, 56; char., iii, 56; ch., i, 324 *n*; iii, 53, 54, 55, 56; man., iii, 51, 54, 55, 56; pop., ii, 115; rectory, iii, 54, 56; sch., ii, 181
Chellington Hill, iii, 54
Chellington-with-Hinwick, iii, 175
Chelmarsh (Salop), ii, 351
Chelvinton, *see* Chellington
Chelvynton, *see* Chellington
Chelyngton, *see* Chellington
Chenemondewiche (Biggleswade) ii, 201

INDEX

Cheney, Lady Jane, iii, 382, 440, 447; Ld., iii, 439; Ld. Hen., iii, 440 *n*
Cheney, Alex. de, iii, 133; Anne, Lady, iii, 346, 436; Anne, iii, 445; Barth. de, iii, 133; Eliz., ii, 243, 345, 363; iii, 51, 77; Geo., ii, 359; Sir Hen., iii, 440, 445; Hen., iii, 311, 346; Jane, Lady, ii, 377; iii, 445; Jane, iii, 346; Sir John, ii, 321; iii, 191, 272; John (de), iii, 66, 133, 458; Kath., *see* Pabenham; Lawr., ii, 243, 345, 382; iii, 77, 191; Margery, ii, 385 *n*; Mary, ii, 363; Rob. (de), ii, 359, 363, 366; Sir Thos., ii, 377, 385; iii, 51, 77, 311, 346, 380, 381, 436, 440; Thos., ii, 40, 359, 363, 385, 387; iii, 191, 231, 286; Walt. ii, 144; Sir Will., iii, 191; Will., iii, 77
Cheneys, man., iii, 77, 78
Cherleton, *see* Charleton
Cherlewude, West, *see* Charlewood (Studham)
Cherneton, *see* Cardington
Chernock (Charnock(e), Charnok), Sir Boteler, ii, 60 *n*, 62, 323; iii, 387; Eliz., iii, 387; Helen, iii, 387; Sir John, ii, 325; John, i, 335 *n*; ii, 323; Sir Pynsent, ii, 58 *n*, 323; iii, 37, 387, 436; Rich., i, 335 *n*, 377; ii, 40, 323; iii, 377, 386, 387, 388; Sir Rob., iii, 387; Rob., ii, 323; iii, 387, 388; Sir St. John, ii, 323; iii, 387; Sir Villiers, ii, 58, 59, 323; iii, 387, 388, 425; Mrs., iii, 388; fam., ii, 60; iii, 338
Chesham (Bucks), adv., i, 366; ch., i, 319, 366, 370, 371 *n*
Chesney, Robt., *see* Lincoln, bps. of; *see also* Cheney
Chester, earls of, ii, 28, 29; iii, 9, 10
Chester, Sir Ant., ii, 58, 59; iii, 216, 306, 434; Ant., ii, 295; Sir Chas., iii, 434; Chas., iii, 58; Sir Chas. B., iii, 434; Dorothea, iii, 434; Frances, Lady, iii, 434; Sir Hen., iii, 434; Hen., ii, 41, 54 *n*, 295; H. M., iii, 58; Sir John, iii, 307, 434; Judith, Lady, iii, 434; Rob., iii, 434; Sir Will., iii, 434; —, iii, 433; fam., ii, 58; iii, 435
Chesterfield (Sandy), Rom. rem., i, 271, 273, 274; ii, 9, 10
Chesterfield, Eliz., ctss. of, iii, 427; Phil., earl of, iii, 427
Chetel, iii, 51
Chetewood, *see* Chetwood
Chetham, Sons & Biffen, ii, 200
Chetwode, *see* Chetwood
Chetwood, Agnes, ii, 234; iii, 384; Anne, ii, 234; Crewe, iii, 72 *n*; Dorothy, iii, 73; Eliz., iii, 71, 384; Guy, iii, 384; John, iii, 72 *n*, 384; Jonathan, iii, 72; Knightley, iii, 72; Lucy, Lady, iii, 384; Nich., iii, 384; Sir Rich., iii, 70, 72, 73; Rich., ii, 234, 328; iii, 72; Sir Rob., iii, 384; Sir Thos., iii, 71; Thos., iii, 384; Valentine, iii, 72
Chetwood-Aiken, Constantia E., iii, 72; John C., iii, 72, 73
Chew, Thos., iii, 351; Will., ii, 179; iii, 351; fam., iii, 355
Cheyne, *see* Cheney
Cheyney, *see* Cheney
Chibnall, Thos., iii, 246; *see also* Chubnoll
Chicheley, Hen., ii, 157; iii, 92, 182, 317, 424; Thos. iii, 182
Chichesane, *see* Chicksands
Chichester, Audrey, ctss. of, ii, 347, 382; Fran., earl of, ii, 347, 382
Chichester, Ralph de, iii, 458
Chickessaund, *see* Chicksands
Chicksands (Chichesane, Cudessane, Chikesond, Chickessaund), ii, 43, 260, 266, 271; iii, 227 *n*; char., ii, 276; ch., i, 315 *n*, 324, 392, 393 *n*; ii, 273-4, 276; mans., i, 393; ii, 271, 273, 275, 342, 344; mills, ii, 271; pop., ii, 113; vicarage, i, 316 *n*
Chicksands Priory, i, 313, 318 *n*, 349, 356, 365 *n*, 378 *n*, 389, 390-93, 395 *n*; ii, 83, 152, 197, 203, 206, 244, 266, 267-9, 271-8, 288, 289, 293, 302, 303, 305, 336, 341, 343; iii, 24, 137, 139, 166, 168, 169, 240, 242, 260, 293; chap., ii, 273, 274, 275; Dayre House farm, ii, 275; mills, ii, 275; ii, 274; priors of, i, 314, 393; ii, 203, 244, 343; iii, 258; seal of, i, 393; 'Warming Pan Bed' in, ii, 275
Chigwell Hall (Essex), iii, 146 *n*
Chikesond, *see* Chicksands
Child, Hen., i, 319 *n*; John, iii, 9, 90, 91, 258; Marg., iii, 82, 86; Rich., iii, 82, 83, 86, 119; Rob. le, iii, 91, 221; Thos., iii, 184, 221; Will. le, iii, 91
Chillington, *see* Chellington
Chiltern, Eliz., i, 390
Chiltern Green, ii, 348, 374
Chiltern Hills, i, 175, 188, 189; iii, 383; earthworks, i, 269
Chinale, Will., iii, 118
Chinnor (Oxon.), ii, 45
Chippenham, man. (Suff.), i, 393
Chishull, Barth., ii, 220; John, ii, 220
Cholmeley, Christiana, Lady, iii, 430; Sir Rog., iii, 430
Christadelphians, iii, 31
Christ Church Coll. (Oxf.), ii, 332; iii, 242
Christendome, Andrew, ii, 323
Christie (Christy, Chrysty), Alice, iii, 25; Anne, iii, 25; R. N., ii, 198; Thos., ii, 58, 59; iii, 25, 29, 32, 33; —, ii, 10; iii, 20
Christine, St., i, 358
Christmas, Rob., iii, 403, 429
Christ's Hosp. (London), ii, 290; iii, 301
Christy, *see* Christie
Chrysty, *see* Christie
Chubnoll, Alice, iii, 116; John. iii, 116; *see also* Chibnall
Church, John, iii, 122; Kath., iii, 332; Will., iii, 332
Church Close (Podington), iii, 82
Church End (Barton-in-the-Clay), ii, 308
Church End (Biddenham), iii, 36
Church End (Colmworth), iii, 186
Church End (Eversholt), iii, 375
Church End (Flitwick), iii, 284
Church End (Haynes), ii, 338
Church End (Knotting), iii, 139
Church End (Milton Bryant), 418
Church End (Old Warden), iii, 251
Church End (Ravensden), iii, 209
Church End (Renhold), iii, 214
Church End (Studham), iii, 426
Church End (Wilden), iii, 226
Church End (Wootton), iii, 331
Church End Farm (Eversholt), iii, 375
Church End Farm (Wilden), iii, 223
Church endowments, i, 324, 332
Church Farm (Podington), iii, 80
Churchill, Eleanor, iii, 128; Fleetwood, iii, 125, 127; Jos., iii, 125; Mrs., iii, 125
Church Panel (Shillington), earthworks, i, 276; ii, 294 *n*
Cimmay, Gilb. de, i, 315 *n*; ii, 356
Cioches, Gunfrei, iii, 85
Cirencester, Bert. of, ii, 6; Rich. of, ii, 6
Cistercians, i, 322, 349, 351, 361-72, 382, 383, 392, 395 *n*, 399 *n*; iii, 318, 459
Civil War, i, 314, 342; ii, 41-54, 340; iii, 4
Claidich, John de, ii, 263; Warin de, ii, 263
Clanfield (Oxon), i, 357
Clanricarde, Ld., ii, 194
Clapham, ii, 21, 43, 52; iii, 123, 126, 147, 150, 151, 183, 279, 297; adv., i, 384; iii, 131, 132; chap., i, 315 *n*, 318, 347 *n*, 382, 383; char., ii, 182 *n*; iii, 132; ch., iii, 131, 132, 152, 153; deanery, i, 347; Fox and Hounds Inn, iii, 128; ind., iii, 128; man., iii, 128, 129, 183; man.-house, iii, 128; Nonconf., iii, 128; place-names, iii, 128; pop., ii, 115; iii, 132; sch., ii, 182; sundial, iii, 128; vicarage, iii, 132
Clapham, Mabel de, iii, 302
Clapham Greenacres (Fitzjeffry's), man., iii, 129, 130, 131, 152; mills, iii, 130
Clapham Pk. (Bedford), ii, 66 *n*, 194, 195; iii, 128
Clare, Gilb. de, ii, 384; iii, 36; *see also* Glouc., earl of; Isabel de, ii, 306, 351, 352, 353, 384; John de, iii, 173; Marg. de, ii, 284, 384; iii, 36; Rich. de, i, 394; ii, 384; iii, 36, 135, 198; Rog. de, *see* Hertford, earl of; Thos. de, ii, 384; Will. de, i, 315 *n*; de, fam., i, 315; iii, 78
Clare Coll. or Hall (Camb.), i, 184; ii, 228, 229
Claremont, Alice de, i, 394
Clarence, Geo., duke of, iii, 16
Clarke (Clark), Anne, ii, 281, 286; iii, 159; Chris., iii, 293; Dorothy, iii, 293, 376; Edm., iii, 126; Edw., iii, 293; Ernest, ii, 140; Sir Fran., iii, 293; F. A., iii, 29; Rev. Hamlet, i, 71; Jane, iii, 215; John, ii, 281, 285; iii, 57, 288, 318; Judith, ii, 281; Nich., iii, 376; Paine, ii, 55; Sibella, ii, 281; Thos., ii, 281; iii, 250, 293, 456; Will., iii, 217, 311, 331 *n*, 335; —, Miss, iii, 57; *see also* Clerke
Clavel, Walt., i, 390 *n*
Claver, Thos., i, 338 *n*
Clavering, Ada, ii, 238; Rob., *see* Peterborough, bp. of
Claybrookes, man. (Harrold), iii, 67
Clayton, Anne, ii, 385; Eliz., ii, 385; Frances, ii, 385; John., ii, 385; Marg., ii, 385; Will., *see* Sundon Ld.; —, Miss, iii, 255 *n*
Cleat Hill, ii, 194; iii, 209, 210
Cleat r (Cleyture) (Cumb.), ii, 160
Cleck, Rob. le, iii, 76
Clement, St., ii, 38 *n*
Clements, —, iii, 18
Clerke (Clerk), Anne, iii, 295; Columba, iii, 29; Eliz., iii, 58; Sir Fran., ii, 41, 180, 182 *n*; iii, 292, 295-6, 332; Fran., iii, 326, 332; Gilb., iii, 43; John., ii, 40, 316; John D., iii, 58; Julia, iii, 29; Ralph, iii, 29; Thos., iii, 128; Will., ii, 20; *see also* Clarke
Clermont, earl of, ii, 192, 193
Clermont, Alice (Alicia) de, iii, 90, 95, 135, 142, 143, 157, 160

Cleveland, earls of, iii, 381, 438; Thos., ii, 42, 43, 56, 261; iii, 337, 346, 440, 441, 445; Thos., Ld., iii, 380 *n*
Cley, Eliz., iii, 443
Cleyture (Cumb.), *see* Cleator
Clifford, Isabel de, ii, 231, 232; Rob. de, ii, 231; Rog. de, ii, 231, 232
Clifton (Clistone), ii, 260, 266, 270, 276; adv., ii, 279, 280; almshouses, ii, 280; assessment, ii, 261; char., ii, 280; Chicksands Priory lands, ii, 266; ch., ii, 278, 279; coins, i, 173; mans., ii, 276, 277, 280, 305, 323, 362; iii, 260, 318; mills, ii, 276, 278, 280; iii, 258; Nonconf., ii, 280; pop., ii, 113; Rom. rem., ii, 6; schs., ii, 182, 280; ship-money, ii, 261
Clifton, hund., ii, 18, 72, 113, 260-305, 308
Clipsham, Will., iii, 427
Clipstone (Clipston), iii, 400; chap., iii, 414; man., iii, 403
Clipstone Brook, iii, 383, 399, 421
Clistone, *see* Clifton
Clopeham, *see* Clapham
Clopelle, *see* Clophill
Clopham, *see* Clapham
Clophill (Clopelle), i, 352, 397; ii, 66, 76, 306, 320-5, 329, 342; iii, 50, 113, 313, 318, 351, 352; adv., ii, 324, 325; Beadlow Farm, ii, 321; Brickwall Farm, ii, 320; chant., ii, 325; char., ii, 325; chs., i, 315 *n*, 318, 334, 351 *n*, 352; ii, 320, 324, 325; earthworks, i, 291-2, 297; ii, 321; fishery, ii, 323; Flying Horse Inn, ii, 320; man., ii, 321-4; iii, 273; mills, ii, 320; Nonconf., ii, 325; pop., ii, 114; rectory, i, 352; sch., ii, 182; vicarage, i, 316 *n*, 352; ii, 325
Clophill Agricultural Societies, ii, 142
Clopton, Avice de, iii, 440 *n*; Steph., ii, 335 *n*; Will. de, iii, 440 *n*
Clothworkers Co. (Lond.), ii, 299
Clutterbuck, Rev. Hen., iii, 304; —, ii, 4
Clynton, Ld., iii, 422
Clynton, Joan de, ii, 360; Sir John de, iii, 285; John de, ii, 360
Clyve, Steph. atte, iii, 458
Clyve, forest, iii, 63 *n*
Cnut, king, ii, 20, 21
Coal, i, 2, 27; iii, 5
Cobbe (Cobb), Agnes, iii, 119; Anne, iii, 91; Eliz., iii, 91; Geo., iii, 91, 94; Rev. H., ii, 18 *n*; John., iii, 91; Paul, ii, 58, 59; iii, 91, 94; Rebecca, iii, 91; Thos., iii, 91, 94-5, 119; Will., iii, 91, 94; Dr., ii, 169, 170; —, ii, 356, 382
Cobbitt, Nich., iii, 316
Cobden, Rich., ii, 65
Cobham, Joan, baroness, ii, 227; Lds., ii, 224 *n*; iii, 188, 363; Geo., iii, 140, 187, 208, 230, 236; Hen., iii, 208; John Brook, iii, 140, 187, 230 *n*; Thos., iii, 140; Will., iii, 187, 208
Cobham, Joan de, ii, 227; Reg. de, iii, 221; fam., ii, 262
Cochepol, *see* Cople
Cockayne (Cokayne, Cokkyne), Anne iii, 452; Beatrice, ii, 354; Chad, ii, 216; Edm., ii, 216, 354; Edw., ii, 218; Eliz., ii, 206, 216, 218; iii, 129; Frances, ii, 355, 356; Hen., iii, 129; Humph., ii, 216;
Cockayne (*cont.*)
Joan, ii, 354; Sir John, ii, 218; John, ii, 215, 216, 218, 354; iii, 137; Judith, ii, 216; Kath., iii, 247; Lewis, ii, 216; Marg., ii, 216 *n*; Reg., ii, 216, 354; Rich., ii, 216; Sam., ii, 216; iii, 247; Susan, ii, 216; Thos., ii, 206; Sir Will., iii, 452; Will., ii, 216, 218, 355, 356; fam., ii, 44, 218
Cockayne-Cust, Fran., ii, 218; Hen. F., ii, 66 *n*
Cockayne Hatley (Bury Hatley, Hatley Port), ii, 96, 197, 201, 215-18, 257; adv., ii, 216 *n*, 218; char., ii, 218; ch., i, 315 *n*; ii, 216; Hill House, ii, 216 *n*; man., ii, 215, 216, 256; mills, ii, 215, 216; pop., ii, 113
Cocke (Koc), Eliz., iii, 100; John, iii, 100; Rich. iii, 98
Cockeswall, man., iii, 370
Cockett, *see* Cokett
Cocks, Jas., iii, 368; Thos. S. V., iii, 368
Coddenham, Eliz., iii, 177; Hen., iii, 177
Codicote (Herts), ii, 232 *n*
Codington, John de, ii, 224 *n*
Codon, Eliz., iii, 248; Rob., iii, 248
Coembestunae, *see* Kempston
Coffins, iii, 116, 266, 327, 334, 411, 420, 425, 434, 446
Cogan, Ann, iii, 198; Ant., iii, 198; Kath., iii, 198; Sara, iii, 198
Coggepole, *see* Cople
Coins, i, 190, 270; ii, 73, 261; iii, 2, 132, 275; A.S., i, 190; Brit., i, 170, 173, 174; ii, 210, 234, 237, 242, 261, 304, 326, 348; Rom., i, 173, 269, 273, 274; ii, 2, 5-11, 13-15; iii, 175, 238, 390, 448
Cokerel (Cokrel), Pet., ii, 278; Rob., iii, 196
Coker Way (Leighton Buzzard), iii, 405
Cokett (Cockett, Coket), Ant., iii, 165, 184, 197; Hen., iii, 201
Cokkyne, *see* Cockayne
Cokrel, *see* Cokerel
Colbeck, Bridg., ii, 253; John, ii, 253
Colburn, Hen., ii, 86
Colby, Dorothy, iii, 236; Thos., iii, 236
Colchester, Brit. coins, i, 173
Coldbatch, Eliz., Lady, iii, 132; Sir John, iii, 132
Cold Brayfield (Bucks), iii, 109, 281, 304
Cold Harbour (Dagnall), Rom. rem., ii, 6
Coldnorton, man., i, 374
Cole, Eliz., ii, 385; Isabella, iii, 461; Mich., iii, 335 *n*; Rob., iii, 461; Sim., iii, 233, 461; —, iii, 375
Coleman, fam., iii, 277
Coleoptera, i, 71-78
Coles (Cranfield), iii, 278
Colesden, iii, 219; man., iii, 220
Colesden, Jordan de, iii, 221; Sim. de, i, 386; Will. de, iii, 221
Coleshill (Warws.), i, 360
Colestone, Will., i, 402
Colfox, Rich., iii, 59
Colhoun, *see* Calhoun
College manor (Northill), iii, 250
Colleton, Chas. G., iii, 66; Mrs., iii, 66
Collie, Miss, ii, 177
Colling, *see* Collins
Colling End Green (Harlington), iii, 381 *n*
Collins (Colling), Ann, iii, 31, 209; Barwell, ii, 252; iii, 209; Eliz., iii, 209; Sir John, ii, 59; Rob., iii, 209; Sam., iii, 57; Thos., iii, 113
Collison, John, ii, 281 *n*
Collop, Ann, iii, 287; Reg., iii, 287
Colmeworde, *see* Colmworth
Colmorde, *see* Colmworth
Colmorthe, *see* Colmworth
Colmworth, ii, 44, 133; iii, 31, 34, 165, 180, 186-9, 205, 271; adv., ii, 187, 189; char., iii, 189; ch., i, 385; iii, 186, 188, 189; earthworks, i, 305; man., iii, 181, 186-7, 189, 199; man. farm, iii, 186; Nonconf., iii, 186; place-names, iii, 186; pop., ii, 113; sch., ii, 182
Colmworth, Will. of, i, 385; *see also* Compworth
Colne, riv., i, 151
Colne, Will., ii, 224
Colnworth, *see* Colmworth
Colt, fam., iii, 247
Colville, Sir Chas., ii, 68; Joan, iii, 191, 194; John, iii, 247; Maud, iii, 247; Sir Will., iii, 191; Will., iii, 194
Colworth (Sharnbrook), iii, 88, 92, 94; man., iii, 92, 95; pk., iii, 89
Colworth House, iii, 88, 92, 94
Colworth Thicket, iii, 94
Coly, Eleanor, iii, 97-8
Colyn, John, ii, 227
Combe Park (Lidlington), iii, 305
Combes Park (Ampthill), ii, 145
Common Farm (Lidlington), iii, 305
Comond, *see* Colmworth
Compass Inn (Ampthill), iii, 268
Compton, Eliz., Lady, iii, 208; Ld. Alwyne F., ii, 70; Will., Ld., *see* Northampton, earl of
Compton, Sir Hen., ii, 336; Jas., iii, 208; John, ii, 291; Spencer, iii, 208; Sir Will., ii, 267, 322; fam., iii, 205
Compton Grove (Willington), iii, 264
Compworth, Thos., iii, 133; *see also* Colmworth
Comyn, Eliz., ii, 223; Joan, iii, 193
Conger Hill (Toddington), earthwork, i, 286, 287
Congregationalists, ii, 241, 258, 270, 271, 299, 374, 375; iii, 30, 64, 68, 96, 132, 202, 218, 279, 367, 383, 415, 458
Coningsby, Eliz., ii, 360; Hen., ii, 347 *n*; John, ii, 360
Conington (Hunts), ii, 214
Connolly, Lady Anne, ii, 277, 278; iii, 441; Lady Louisa, iii, 446; Thos., iii, 346, 441, 446
Conquest, Alice, iii, 291; Benedict, iii, 291; Benj., ii, 59; Sir Edm., ii, 339; iii, 291; Edm., ii, 329, 332; iii, 291; Eleanor, ii, 331; Eliz., iii, 291, 295; Geoff., iii, 290; Hen., iii, 291; Isabel, iii, 295; Joan, ii, 329; John, iii, 129 *n*, 290, 291, 294 *n*, 295; John T., iii, 291; Lewis, iii, 292; Mary, iii, 292 *n*; Miles, iii, 291 *n*; Sir Rich., ii, 180; iii, 291; Rich., ii, 43, 54; iii, 270, 291, 295, 296; Rog., iii, 291; fam., iii, 289
Conquest Bury, man., *see* Houghton Conquest
Constable, Chas., iii, 255; Dorothy, ii, 233
Constable Lands (Gilden), iii, 179
Conygrave, Joan, ii, 282; Reg., ii, 282
Conyngestone, Nich., ii, 296 *n*

INDEX

Cooke (Cook), Alice, iii, 375; Ant., iii, 168; Hugh, ii, 385; iii, 375; Jas., iii, 311; John, iii, 248; Jos., i, 169; Nich., iii, 246; Rich., ii, 271; Thos. J., iii, 394; Rev. —, ii, 133; fam., iii, 361
Cook's Farm (Northill), iii, 246
Cook's Lane (Southill), iii, 261
Cookson, Thos., iii, 261; Dr., i, 342 *n*
Cooper, Anne, ii, 385; Maj. Cooper, i, 185; ii, 8; Eliz., iii, 441; Eliz. C., iii, 446; Eliz. G., iii, 441; John, iii, 60, 441; Judith, iii, 60; Rev. Oliver St. J., ii, 97, 98; iii, 60, 69; Sam., iii, 33, 109; Tomkinson, ii, 385; Will., iii, 441, 446; Will D., iii, 444
Cooper's Hill (Ampthill), iii, 269
Coops (Battlesden), iii, 343
Cope, Sir Walt., iii, 72 *n*
Cople, ii, 44, 66, 96, 196, 197, 340; iii, 32, 182, 193, 227, 238; adv., i, 393; iii, 242; char., iii, 242; ch., i, 315 *n*, 392; ii, 92; iii, 238, 239, 240 *n*, 241, 242; man., iii, 240; pop., ii, 116; Rom. rem., ii, 5, 6; iii, 238; sch., ii, 182; vicarage, i, 316 *n*, 341; iii, 238
Cople (Copley), Anne, ii, 355; Edw., ii, 267; Humph., ii, 179; Rog., ii, 355; Thos., i, 384; fam., iii, 197
Cople House, ii, 66 *n*; iii, 238
Cople Woodend, ii, 42
Copley, *see* Cople
Copmanford, Jos. of, i, 386
Coppin, Anne, ii, 317; Sir Geo., ii, 317; John, ii, 317, 319, 320, 377-80; John R., ii, 317; Martha, ii, 320; Sam., ii, 317; Thos., ii, 317, 320; fam., ii, 377
Coppinger, Walt., iii, 244
Copple-cum-Keone, man., ii, 145
Coprolites, i, 39; ii, 117
Copt Hill land (Heath and Reach), iii, 417
Corbet (Corbett), Sir Andr., iii, 416, 422 *n*; Andr., iii, 405; Anne, iii, 405; Eliz., iii, 405, 422; Sir Rich., iii, 405; Rich., iii, 405; Rog., iii, 405; Sir Vincent, iii, 405 *n*
Corker, John, iii, 245
Corn, price of, iii, 3
Corner, Anora, iii, 220; John, iii, 220
Cornewayle, *see* Cornwall
Cornish, Sir Sam., iii, 90, 95, 331
Cornwall, earls of, iii, 362; Edm., iii, 154, 362; Rich., i, 362; iii, 291, 362, 383
Cornwall, Constance de, i, 388 *n*; Sir Geoff. de, iii, 317; Sir John (de), ii, 35, 36, 324; iii, 270, 272, 273, 292, 296, 310, 317, 318, 319, 326, 437; Phil. de, i, 388 *n*
Cornwallis, Eliz., ii, 289; iii, 97; John, iii, 22, 348; Lucy, iii, 46, 96; Sir Will., iii, 14, 97; Will., ii, 289; iii, 46, 96
Coronation almoner, iii, 12, 13, 14, 15
Corpus Christi Coll. (Oxf.), iii, 154, 167
Corpus Christi gild (Eaton Socon), iii, 201
Corpus Christi gild (Leighton Buzzard), iii, 415
Corston, —, ii, 121
Cosen (Cosyn), Edm., iii, 211; Edw., ii, 244; Rich., ii, 211
Costentin, Geoff. de, ii, 248; Hen. de, ii, 248
Costin, John, iii, 32
Coston, —, ii, 170
Cosyn, *see* Cosen
Cotes, man., *see* Cardington Cotton End
Cotes, Gilb. de, iii, 315
Cotgrave, Thos. de, ii, 275
Cothemannesholme (Oakley), iii, 150
Cotherstoke, Will. de, iii, 30
Cotton, man., *see* Cardington Cotton End
Cotton (Coton), Eliz., Lady, iii, 286; Eliz., iii, 286; Frances, iii, 286; Hen., iii, 101; Jane, iii, 286; Sir John, ii, 180, 211, 214, 215; iii, 286; John, i, 396; ii, 45 *n*; iii, 149; Mary, ii, 332; iii, 286; Philadelphia, Lady, ii, 357; Sir Rob., ii, 45 *n*, 211 *n*; Sam., iii, 83; Sir Thos., ii, 45 *n*, 357
Cotton End, iii, 32, 227, 234, 238; man. house, i, 306; iii, 234; Nonconf., iii, 234; sch., iii, 234
Couci, Ingelram de, *see* Bedford, earl of; Isabella de, ii, 39
Coulthirst, Nich., ii, 316
Councell, Hugh, ii, 270
County Council, ii, 141, 142; iii, 320
Coupol, *see* Cople
Courtney, Alice, iii, 436, 437; Edw., iii, 436
Court Place (Wymington), iii, 119
Coutances, bps. of, i, 313; iii, 54, 85, 90, 95, 110, 114, 119, 125, 133, 139, 142, 157, 162, 175
Couture, La, abbey of (Le Mans), i, 315 *n*; iii, 439, 444, 446
Coventry, Hen., ii, 195, 254
Coventry and Lichfield, bp. of, Walt. de Langton, ii, 224, 225, 227, 228, 238, 262, 263
Covington, ii, 72; iii, 31
Covington (Covyngton), A., i, 107-143; Hugh, iii, 64; John, iii, 213; Nich. de, iii, 154 *n*
Covington Fee, man., *see* Howe and Pertenhall
Cowe, John de, iii, 55
Cowepyll, *see* Cople
Cowper, ctss, ii, 182 *n*; Anne, ii, 327; Katrina C., iii, 233; earls, ii, 142, 146, 176, 327; iii, 229, 233
Cowper, John, ii, 151, 156, 263; Mich., ii, 263; Will., ii, 314; *see also* Cooper
Cowslade, John, iii, 407, 430; Thos., iii, 407, 430
Cox, Jas., ii, 101; —, ii, 333; iii, 444
Coxed, —, warden of Bedford College, ii, 172
Coynte, Alice (le), ii, 297, 334; iii, 252; Joan de, iii, 252; Margery de, iii, 252; Will. (le), ii, 297, 334; iii, 252; fam., iii, 253
Cozens, John, iii, 250
Crabbe, Helen, i, 390
Cracheley, John de, i, 320, 321, 325
Cracroft, Rich., iii, 196
Cradock's Field (Leighton Buzzard), iii, 402
Cramavilla, Hen. de, ii, 223, 224
Cranesle, John, ii, 316 *n*
Cranfield (Crangfeld, Cranfelde), ii, 21, 25, 66, 77, 78, 81, 90, 187, 268; iii, 40, 267, 275-79, 297; adv., iii, 278; agric., ii, 82, 84, 99; Black Death, ii, 88; char., iii, 278, 279; ch., i, 313; iii, 277; man., i, 312, 313; ii, 79, 80, 87, 91, 143; iii, 276; Nonconf., iii, 275, 279; pk., iii, 276; pop., ii, 115; priests' stipend, i, 336; Rom. rem., ii, 6; iii, 275; sch., ii, 182; iii, 278
Cranfield (Craunfeld, Craunfield), Jas., iii, 276; Sir Lionel, iii, 276; Rich. de, iii, 246; Will. de, iii, 276
Cranfield Court, iii, 276
Cranfield Mead (Tingrith), iii, 382 438
Cranford Mead, ii, 376 *n*
Crangfeld, *see* Cranfield
Cranmer, Thos., ii, 38
Cransley (Northants), i, 181 *n*
Cratford, Chris., iii, 212
Craunfeld (Craunfield), *see* Cranfield
Cravenherst, *see* Gravenhurst
Crawelai, *see* Husborne Crawley
Crawley, brook, ii, 71
Crawley, man., *see* Husborne Crawley
Crawley, Arth., ii, 349 *n*; Dionisia de, iii, 396 *n*; Edw., ii, 346 *n*, 375; Sir Fran., ii, 43, 364, 373; Fran., ii, 147, 197, 346, 356-9, 361-2, 373-4; iii, 105, 109, 137, 177; Joan, ii, 364; John, ii, 40, 349 *n*, 358-9, 361-3, 366; iii, 105, 177; John S., ii, 66 *n*, 319; Judith, iii, 105; Rich., ii, 40, 356-7, 361, 364; Sam., ii, 66 *n*; Susannah, iii, 177; Thos., ii, 312, 346 *n*, 356, 358-9, 373, 375; T. S., ii, 356, 357, 374 *n*; Will., ii, 358, 364, 375; —, ii, 358; iii, 21; fam., ii, 66; iii, 361
Crawley House (Husborne Crawley), iii, 394
Crawley Park Farm (Husborne Crawley), iii, 394
Crayford, Sir Will., ii, 40; iii, 322
Creaker (Creuker), Geoff., iii, 182; John, iii, 257
Creakers (Crewkers, Westende), man., iii, 181, 183, 184
Creakers, The (Gt. Barford), earthwork, i, 303
Crendon (Bucks), man., ii, 253
Crespinges, Eliz. de, ii, 276; Will. de, ii, 276
Cressy (Cressie), Isabel de, iii, 426; John, ii, 307, 351 *n*, 352, 355, 359; Rog. de, iii, 426; Thos., ii, 352; Val., iii, 414
Creuker, *see* Creaker
Crevecoeur (Crevequer), Agnes de, iii, 452; Anne, iii, 183; Eleanor de, iii, 452; Geoff. de, iii, 183; Hamon de, iii, 452; Isolda, iii, 452; Jas. de. iii, 183; John de, iii, 183, 211; Mabel de, iii, 452; Matilda de, iii, 452; Rob. de, iii, 183; Steph., iii, 183, 211, 212; Will. de, iii, 452
Crewe, Lds., iii, 73 *n*; John, ii, 341
Crewe, Temperance, ii, 341 *n*; iii, 73 *n*; Sir Thos., ii, 341
Crewkers, man., *see* Creakers
Crichton, Rob., iii, 311
Crispe (Crisp), Anne, iii, 145; John, iii, 145
Crispin, Miles, iii, 105, 129, 147, 150
Croft (Crofte), John, iii, 128; Hugh de, iii, 173; Will., ii, 161
Crofts, Arabella, ii, 377, 379; Briers, Lady, ii, 377, 379; Edw., iii, 347; Sir Hen., ii, 377; Sir John, ii, 377; iii, 346; Marg., Lady, iii, 346; Sam., iii, 346
Croiser, *see* Croyser
Croisores, *see* Croyser
Crokebarowe, Agnes, iii, 281
Crokedayke, Alex. de, ii, 256, 257; Isabel de, ii, 257 *n*; John de, ii, 257; Juliana, ii, 257
Crompton, Eliz., iii, 283; John, ii, 291; Lovetus, iii, 283; Rob., iii, 283; Thos., iii, 283
Cromwell, Ralph, Ld., iii, 272

Cromwell, Anne, iii, 193; Ida de, ii, 231; John de, ii, 231; Mary, iii, 155; Sir Oliver, iii, 155; Oliver, ii, 45-7, 49-52, 54-5, 179, 271, 275; iii, 4, 64, 349; Rich., ii, 55, 228
Crook, John, i, 341, 345
Crools Farm (Willington), iii, 262
Crophill, Ralph, iii, 285
Croson, Eliz., iii, 274
Crosse (Cross), Hammond, ii, 363; Hen., ii, 200; John, ii, 363; iii, 269, 275; Thos., ii, 363
Crosse Ash (Ridgmont), iii, 321
Crosseland Fosse (Kempston), iii, 297
Crosses, i, 373 *n*; iii, 47, 54, 76, 100, 108, 127, 142, 148, 152, 234, 279, 314, 315, 351, 353, 399, 458
Crosshall Farm (Eaton Socon), iii, 190
Cross Meadow (Wilshamstead), iii, 328
Croswayte, Agnes, ii, 363
Crouche (Crouch, Crowch, Crowche), Edm., ii, 378; Mary, ii, 346; Nich., ii, 380; Rob., iii, 54, 242; Sam., ii, 346
Crowe, Gerard, iii, 231; Nich., iii, 231
Crowhill Farm (Wilden), iii, 223
Crowmarsh, ii, 25
Croxton, Dan., i, 367 *n*, 368 *n*; John de, iii, 162, 164; Rich. de, iii, 162
Croyser (Croiser, Croisores), Anne, iii, 78; Eliz., iii, 78; Ellen, iii, 67; John, iii, 85; Nich., iii, 85; Sim., iii, 67, 85; Sir Will., ii, 256; iii, 158; Will., ii, 90, 354; iii, 77, 78
Crustaceans, i, 91-7
Cruys, Gamaliel, iii, 456
Cryptogams, i, 55-67
Cryscyan, John, ii, 319
Cublington (Bucks), ch., i, 371 *n*, 376
Cudessane, *see* Chicksands
Cufaude, Anne, iii, 220; John, iii, 220
Cukkowe, John, ii, 205
Cullebere, John, iii, 20
Culverden, Will., ii, 269
Culy, man. (Wootton), iii, 331
Culy Green (Wootton), iii, 329
Cumming, Will. C., ii, 252
Cunningry Close (Clapham), iii, 132
Cuppe, Rob., i, 399
Cursson, *see* Curzon
Curtis (Curteys, Curtius), Adolph, iii, 206; Aubrey, iii, 118; Hugh, iii, 118, 122; Jas., ii, 265; John, iii, 118, 120; Matilda, iii, 436; Thos., iii, 436; Sir Will., iii, 206; Will., iii, 94
Curzon, Agnes, iii, 452; Greg., iii, 140; Mary, iii, 452; Thos., iii, 452
Cust, Eliz., ii, 216; Fran., ii, 216; Hen., ii, 216; Hen. F., ii, 216, 257; John H., *see* Alford, vsct.; Lucy, ii, 216; Sir Rich., ii, 216; Saville, ii, 216; fam., ii, 66
Cutha, *see* Cuthwulf
Cuthbert, —, ii, 385; fam., iii, 286
Cuthwulf (Cutha), i, 269 *n*; ii, 18, 349 *n*; iii, 1, 401
Cutts, Chas., iii, 51
Cycle Works, ii, 127

D'Abernon, Eliz., iii, 78; Gilb., iii, 78; John, iii, 78, 79; Will., iii, 78
Dacre, Thos., Ld., iii, 192
Dacre, Anne, iii, 192; Eliz., iii, 192; Geo., iii, 192; Mary, iii, 192
Dacre and Greystock, Thos., Ld., iii, 192; Will., Ld., iii, 192
Dacres, Annabella, iii, 133; Edw., iii, 133; Geo., iii, 182; Rob., iii, 92, 133, 182, 302; Sir Thos., iii, 133
Dagnel (Dagnoll), Margery, ii, 275; Pet, ii, 275; Sam., iii, 449
Daie, *see* Day
Daintone, *see* Dunton
Daintry Wood (Tingrith), iii, 435
Dairy farming, ii, 136
Dakeney, Alice, ii, 322; Joan, ii, 321, 322, 323; Sir John, ii, 322; John, ii, 321, 322; Mary, ii, 322; Rob., ii, 321; Sir Rog., ii, 321, 322; Rog., ii, 321-3; Walt., ii, 322
Dalbier, Col., ii, 53
Dalderby, John, bp., *see* Lincoln, bps. of
Dale, Anne, ii, 207, 253; Isabel de la, ii, 207; Joan, ii, 227; John, ii, 207, 228, 252; Maud, iii, 329; Thos., le, ii, 207, 208, 227, 252; Will., ii, 207, 227, 252, 253; —, iii, 329
Dallow (Dollow), man., ii, 350, 356, 357, 358, 362, 366; man.-house, ii, 356; mill, ii, 366; prehist. rem., i, 145, 174; ii, 348
Dallow Farm (Luton), ii, 357
Dalton, Capt. Rob. F., iii, 171; —, iii, 132
Dalyell, Col. J. T., ii, 70
Dam Acre (Northill), iii, 248
Dame Ellensbury, man., iii, 270 *n*, 291, 292
Dame Ellensbury Park, ii, 147
Dame Margaret's Holme, *see* Dam Acre
Dammartin, Reg. de, ii, 255
Danes, i, 281, 310; ii, 18, 19, 20, 73; iii, 1
Daneswood (Woburn Sands), iii, 338
Daniell (Daniel, Danyell), John, iii, 56, 385; Edw., ii, 329, 333, 335; Eliz., ii, 329; John, iii, 438; Rich., ii, 329; Steph., ii, 329; Thos., ii, 329; Will., ii, 329, 333
Danish place-names, i, 297
Dansey, —, ii, 188
Dansie, Jas., ii, 385
Danver, Eliz., *see* Neville; Sir John, iii, 14
Danvers, Burnaby, iii, 364; John, iii, 193; Sam., iii, 193
Danyell, *see* Daniell
Dapifer, Eudo, ii, 207, 208, 243, 244, 251, 277, 278; iii, 190, 191, 199, 219, 229 *n*, 260, 386 *n*
D'Arcy, Sir Conyers, ii, 295
Darell, Anastasia, iii, 154; Beatrice, iii, 154; Isabel, iii, 154; John, iii, 154; Julian, iii, 154; Marg., iii, 154; Thos., iii, 154; fam., iii, 166
Darkland (Ridgmont), iii, 321
Darley (Derb.), abbot of, i, 372 *n*
Darling (Derling), Sir Rob., iii, 54; Thos., iii, 101
Dartford (Kent), prioress of, i, 403
Dartiguenave, Anne, iii, 197
Darwin, Bern., ii, 198
Datchet (Bucks), man., iii, 436
Daubeney, Giles, Ld., ii, 267, 322
Daubeney (Albini, Albingi), Alice, iii, 298; Amicia, iii, 237; Ascelina (Asseline, Azeline) de, iii, 236, 271, 317; Cecilia, iii, 148; Cecily, i, 352, 377 *n*; iii, 237; Christina, ii, 321; iii, 271; Eleanor, iii, 298; Eliz., iii, 298; Sir Giles, iii, 298; Giles, iii, 299; Hen. (de), i, 351; ii, 263, 267, 281, 321, 322; iii, 237, 273; Isabel, ii, 211, 321; iii, 236, 271, 317, 318; Joan, ii, 321, 322; iii, 236, 268, 271, 272; John, iii, 298; Marg., iii, 298, 299; Nigel (de), 143, ii, 211, 263, 277, 281, 283, 309, 321, 324, 329, 376, 383; iii, 50, 51, 60, 113, 146, 196, 199, 236, 260, 271, 286, 309, 315, 317, 326, 379, 396, 435; Philippa, iii, 298; Ralph, iii, 298; Rob., i, 318 *n*, 350, 351, 352, 366, ii, 26, 263, 270, 281, 321, 322, 324, 325, 342, 344; iii, 148, 236, 237, 271, 317, 318; Sim., ii, 321; Will., ii, 32, 321, 322, 383; iii, 112, 271, 298; fam., i, 372 *n*; ii, 30, 323, 324; iii, 273
Daubeney, bar. of, i, 292; ii, 30 *n*, 324
Daubeny, hon., iii, 112
Daventry, Isabella de, iii, 436; Joan de, iii, 436, 437; Matilda de, iii, 436; Rob. de, iii, 436; Thos. de, iii, 436, 437; Walt. de, iii, 436; fam., iii, 286
Davey, *see* Davy
David I, king of Scotland, i, 388; iii, 9, 65
David Ashby, man., ii, 350
Davie, *see* Davy
Davies, Oliver, iii, 212; Thos., iii, 278 *n*
Davis, H. W. C., ii, 26 *n*; Kendrick, iii, 385; Stanley P., ii, 190
Davis's Spinney (Turvey), iii, 110
Davy, Eliz., iii, 115; Sir Humph., ii, 135; John, ii, 40
Dawe, Rob., iii, 385
Dawkins, Rev. Edw. H., iii, 233; E. H. F., ii, 183 *n*; F., iii, 231; —, Mrs., iii, 233; fam., iii, 231
Daws, Sir Thos., iii, 314
Dawson, John, iii, 145
Day (Daye, Dey, Deye), Benj., ii, 360; Edm., iii, 108, 221; Frank, iii, 191; Gilb., iii, 96; John H., iii, 191; Marg. le, iii, 159; Sim. le, iii, 159; Thos., i, 383, 385; Walt. iii, 159; Will., ii, 360; —, iii, 175
Deacons (Deacon), Edw., iii, 282; Mary, iii, 282; Thos., iii, 282, 288, 438
Deacon's charity, iii, 416
Dead-man's Slode (Slade) (Leighton Buzzard), A.S. rem., i, 187
Dean (Dena, Dene), ii, 96; iii, 123, 132-36, 142, 165, 170, 174; adv., iii, 135; chant., iii, 136; char., iii, 136; ch., i, 315 *n*, 325 *n*, 394; iii, 134; mans., *see* Overdean and Netherdean; Man. House Farm, iii, 132; mills, iii, 132; Nonconf., iii, 132, 136; place-names, iii, 132; pop., ii, 115; Rectory Farm, iii, 132; sch., ii, 182; treasure trove at, iii, 132; value of land, iii, 134
Dean, Nether (Lower), iii, 132
Dean, Upper, iii, 132, 160
Dean (Deane, Dene), Anstis (Anastasia), i, 355, 357; Chris., ii, 289; Jas., iii, 102; —, iii, 155; *see also* Den
Deane Hills Park, iii, 394
Deaneries, rural, i, 313, 323, 347
Dean Hall, iii, 132
Dean House, iii, 132
Dearman, Edw., ii, 325; Thos., ii, 324

INDEX

Debenham, Gilb., iii, 371
Decker, Sir Matth., iii, 255
Decons (Decon, Dekene, Dycons), Eliz., iii, 306, 309; Rich., ii, 328; iii, 306, 309; Thos. (le), iii, 306, 364 *n*, 407; fam., iii, 313
Deep Hall (Oxf.), iii, 275
Deer Pk. (Husborne Crawley), iii, 394
De Grey of Wrest, *see* Grey (of Wrest) de
Dekene, *see* Decons
Delamere, Thos., i, 363
De Lanie, *see* Delaune
Delap, Jas. B., iii, 219; Rev. Rob., iii, 219; fam., iii, 183
Delaune (de Lanie), Gideon, iii, 183, 219; Will., iii, 184, 219
Delavere, Hester, iii, 134; Kinnaird, iii, 134
De la Warr, Joan, iii, 339; John, iii, 339
Delawne, *see* Delaune
Dell, Dr. Humph., iii, 286; Will., i, 342; iii, 179; —, iii, 64
Delmé, Anne, ii, 286
Den, Gilb. de, iii, 324-5; Will. de, iii, 324-5; *see also* Dean
Dena, *see* Dean
Dendon, Agnes, i, 398; Rob., i, 398
Dene, *see* Dean
Denel End (Dunhill), iii, 284
Denel (Dennel) End (Flitwick), iii, 288, 438
Denham, Hen., ii, 357
Denis, *see* Dennis
Denison, Sam., ii, 204; Rev. Will. H., iii, 54, 56
Denman, Sir Thos., iii, 72
Dennis (Denis, Dennys) Andr., iii, 25; Eliz., iii, 298, 304; John, iii, 298; Mary, iii, 298, 304; Matth., iii, 298, 304; Rob., iii, 277, 298; Will., iii, 298, 304
Denny (Cambs), iii, 40; nuns of, i, 326
Denny, Ant., iii, 302; Edw., *see* Norwich, earl of; Honoria, iii, 330; John, iii, 302; Thos., iii, 302
Dennys, *see* Dennis
Denshire, Geo., iii, 155 *n*
Denston Hall (Suff.), iii, 243
Denton (Lincs.), ch., ii, 217
Denton, Nich., ii, 40; Rich., iii, 361
Derby, sch., ii, 155
Derby, Alice, ctss. of, iii, 102; Isabel, ctss. of, ii, 351; earls of, iii, 139; Edw., iii, 119; Ferd., iii, 102; Hen., ii, 247; iii, 119; Thos., iii, 102, 119, 283; Will., ii, 351; iii, 78, 230
Derby, John de, iii, 30; Ralph of, i, 384; Rich., i, 384; Will. de, iii, 357 *n*
Dere, Godwin, iii, 134
Derling, *see* Darling
Dert House (Eaton Socon), iii, 190
Despenser, Anne le, ii, 231; Edw. le, ii, 230, 231, 232; Eleanor le, ii, 300, 339, 362, 384; Hugh (le), ii, 31, 231, 300, 339, 362, 384; iii, 262; Rob. le, ii, 291; Will. iii, 95
Deule, Alwin, i, 297 *n*; ii, 276; iii, 155
Devenish, Eliz., ii, 355; Rich., ii, 355
Devereux, Will., iii, 18
Devilhoe, *see* Duloe
Devil's Jumps, *see* Yarlswood
Devil's Spinney, *see* Doctor's Corner
Devon, Christian, ctss. of, iii, 290
Devonshire, lace ind., ii, 123
Devotion, Thos., *see* Dyer
Dey, Deye, *see* Day
Deyville, Joan, ii, 238; John, ii, 238; iii, 190 *n*
Dickens, Eleanor, iii, 380; Thos., iii, 380
Dickenson, —, iii, 117
Dickinson, Capt. John Marche, ii, 69
Dickson, John, iii, 173
Dier, *see* Dyer
Digby, Beatrice, iii, 45; Sir John, iii, 45, 49; John, iii, 46; Sir Kenelm, ii, 275
Dilewick, man., *see* Dylywyk
Dillingham (Dyllingham), Brampton G., iii, 162; Fran., iii, 195, 226; Theophilus, iii, 162, 164
Dillon, Col. Rob. V., iii, 328
Dilly, Chas., iii, 257; Edw., iii, 257; John, iii, 257
Dimmock, *see* Dymoke
Dingwall, bar., ii, 327
Diocese, i, 332, 346-47
Dionisia, iii, 419
Distaff Lane (Lond.), ii, 214
Ditchfield, Edw., ii, 310, 312; iii, 253, 285, 292, 306, 321, 326, 332
Dive, Dives, *see* Dyve
Dix, Will., iii, 80
Dixse, Hughe, iii, 200
Dixwells, man., iii, 435, 438
Dobbe, Frances, iii, 67; John, iii, 67
Dobbin Spinney (Turvey), iii, 110
Dobbs, Phil., iii, 51; Will., iii, 194
Dobson, Frances, ii, 94; iii, 456; John, iii, 456; Miles, iii, 456; Will., iii, 200, 456; —, ii, 169
Dockra, *see* Docwra
Doctor's Corner (Clapham), i, 116
Docwra, Edw., ii, 359, 365; Thos., ii, 59, 365; Capt., ii, 69
Dodd (Dod), Jas., ii, 296; Kath., ii, 378; Rev. Will., ii, 102; iii, 345; Will., ii, 378, 383
Dodsworth, Eliz., iii, 322
Dodwell, —, ii, 296
Doe, Jolland le, ii, 255
Doffevill, Hugh, iii, 257; Isabel, iii, 257
Doggett, —, iii, 415
D'Oilli, *see* Doyley
Dokesworth, Hugh de, iii, 98; John de, iii, 98
Doket, *see* Duckett
Dolby, —, ii, 177
Dolling, Rev. —, iii, 128
Dollow, man., *see* Dallow, man.
Dolt, Rich., iii, 385; Thos., iii, 385
Domesday Survey, i, 191-266
Dominican monks, *see* Friars, Black
Dominican nuns, i, 396 *n*
Domnic, iii, 229 *n*
Doncaster, Jas., vsct., *see* Carlisle, earl of
Donne (Done), Dinah, iii, 146; Jas., iii, 293; John, i, 342; iii, 146, 233; Rog. de, iii, 137
Donton (Dontone), *see* Dunton
Dorchester (Oxon), bpric., i, 311, 313, 347; ii, 18, 153; bps., ii, 20, 21, 294, 309; iii, 84, 408, 414; St. Peter's Abbey, i, 388 *n*
Dormer, Dorothy, iii, 177 *n*; Edw., ii, 319; Eliz., iii, 427; John, ii, 360, 362; iii, 277; Mary, *see* Sydney; Sir Rob., ii, 40; iii, 407, 427, 429; Rob., ii, 354; iii, 177, 406; Susanna, iii, 427; Sir Will., iii, 427; Will, iii, 177, 427
Dorset, Cecily, mchnss. of, iii, 380; mqs. of. iii, 381; Hen., iii, 89, 380; Thos., iii, 89, 230, 248
Dorset, Rich. of, i, 402
Douglas, Rev. Jas., i, 182
Dounton, *see* Dunton
Dove House Farm (Kensworth), iii, 368
Dover (Kent), hosp., iii, 395
Dover, hon., iii, 50
Dover, Hen., earl of, iii, 314; John, earl of, ii, 342 *n*
Dover (Dovre), John de, ii, 283; Junian de, ii, 351 *n*; Phil. de, ii, 283; Rich. de, ii, 283
Dovey, John, i, 398
Downe, Will., earl of, iii, 140
Downes, Lt.-Col. Chas. V., iii, 387; Mrs. C. V. S., iii, 338; fam., ii, 293
Downham, Hen., ii, 358
Downing, Edw., ii, 221; iii, 29, 392, 425; Sir Geo., ii, 256, 257; Sir Jacob G., ii, 256, 257; Marg., ii, 256
Downing College (Camb.), ii, 257
Downshire, mchnss. of, ii, 330; mqs. of, iii, 376
Doyle, Col., ii, 67
Doyley, Cath., iii, 188; John, iii, 188; Rob., iii, 107, 129, 147, 153 *n*
Drake, Eliz., iii, 198; Helen, Lady, ii, 347, 382; Sir John, ii, 347, 382; Thos., iii, 198; —, Capt., iii, 276
Drakelowe, Ankareta, iii, 424; Emma, i, 389, 390; Thos., iii, 424
Draper, Gabriel, iii, 407; John, ii, 89, 234; Will., iii, 407
Draycot, Ant., i, 334
Dray's Ditches (Limbury), earthworks, i, 280; ii, 348
Drayton (Bucks), i, 370
Drayton, Ada, iii, 300; Eliz., iii, 299; Geoff. de, ii, 252; Isabel, iii, 299; Joan, iii, 299; Joanna de, ii, 251; John, iii, 299; Miles de, ii, 251-3; Nich., iii, 299
Drayton Parslow, ii, 254, 332
Drayton's Manor (Kempston), *see* Brucebury
Drayton's Manor (Tempsford), ii, 251-3
Drew's Wood (Northill), iii, 245
Drinking Bush Hill (Stevington), iii, 101
Drivval (Drival), Godf. de, iii, 12; Will., iii, 223 *n*
Drover's Way Field (Northill), iii, 251
Droxford (Hants), A.S. rem., i, 183 *n*
Dru, Will., iii, 247
Druce, Edric, ii, 141
Druel, Amice, iii, 92; Giles, iii, 92; John, iii, 92; Will., iii, 90; fam., iii, 91
Druet, Ralph, iii, 74; Sampson, iii, 74
Dryden, Sir Hen., i, 187 *n*; ii, 7
Drye, Sim., ii, 379
Duberly, Sir Jas., iii, 125
Dublin, archbp. of, iii, 119
Duck End (Maulden), iii, 275, 314, 316
Duck End (Wilshamstead), iii, 326
Duckett (Doket), Ann, ii, 377, 378, 379; Noah, ii, 377; Pet., ii, 377, 378; Rob. ii, 341
Duckford, man., *see* Duxworth
Duck's Cross (Colmworth), iii, 186
Dudley, Alice, iii, 112; Anne, iii, 112; Aug., iii, 112; Edw., iii, 112; Eliz., iii, 57, 112; Fran., iii, 112; Gamaliel, iii, 112; Joan, iii, 112; Rich., iii, 112; Sir Rob., iii, 310; Rob., iii, 112; *see also* Leicester, earl of; Thos., iii, 57, 112; —, iii, 416

Dudley Castle, ii, 364
Dudleys, man. (Turvey), iii, 112, 113, 114
Dudswell (Herts), ii, 375
Duffyn, John, i, 354 *n*
Dugdale, J. H., ii, 141; Sir Will., iii, 355
Duke, Warin, iii, 95
Duloe (Devilhoe), i, 297; iii, 193, 197-8, 202; farm-houses, iii, 190
Duloe, brook (Eaton Socon), iii, 189
Dun, *see* Dunn
Duncombe, Anne, iii, 407; Brandreth, iii, 407; Sir Edw., iii, 344, 383, 422; Edw., iii, 385; Eliz., iii, 330, 345, 405; Ellen, iii, 344, 423; Fran., iii, 51, 330; Sir John, iii, 345; John, iii, 344; Thos., iii, 330, 408; Will., ii, 40, 44; iii, 344, 345, 367, 405, 407, 415, 422 *n*, 423; fam., iii, 415, 422
Dundin, John, iii, 220
Dungewood (Dungee Wood), iii, 64, 67
Dunhill, *see* Denel End
Dunn (Dun), Tom, ii, 198; iii, 350
Dunrigge, man. (Caddington), ii, 315
Dunstable (Durocobrivae, Dunstaple), i, 320, 328 *n*, 376, 394, 400, 401; ii, 1, 3, 23, 28-31, 34, 37, 43, 45, 53, 105, 178; iii, 11, 18, 290, 294 *n*, 336, 337, 349, 355-7, 360, 361, 389, 400; adv., i, 378; iii, 366; agric., ii, 83-5, 129, 132, 133, 136; almshouses, iii, 351, 367-8; A.S. rem., i, 175, 184, 189; assize of bread and ale, iii, 358; Brotherhood House, iii, 367; chants., i, 326; ii, 179; iii, 367; char., ii, 179, 182 *n*; iii, 367-8; ch., i, 17, 315 *n*, 321, 328, 335 *n*, 350, 373, 378, 396 *n*; iii, 285, 351, 360, 364-6, 368-9; Civil War, ii, 47; coins, i, 173; ii, 2, 6, 7; council at, i, 373; crosses, i, 373 *n*; iii, 351, 353; crown property, iii, 271; deanery, i, 347, 351, 404; disputes with prior, i, 319, 320; iii, 358-60, 366; earthwork, i, 166, 269, 270; ii, 9; Five Knolls, i, 169, 270; forestry, ii, 144; gaol, iii, 358; gilds, i, 330; iii, 360, 366-7; gipsies, iii, 352; highway robberies, ii, 99, 102; hosps., i, 349; ind., ii, 119-22, 349; iii, 350-1, 363; inns, iii, 351, 352, 355, 364, 368, 394; Jews, iii, 363; Katharine of Aragon's trial, ii, 38; Ladies' Lodge, iii, 351, 368; lepers, i, 401; man., i, 376; iii, 361; mkts. and fairs, ii, 46, 87, 88, 102; iii, 351, 361-3; mayor, ii, 35, 89; iii, 360; mills, i, 320; iii, 351; miracle play, iii, 350; Mount Pleasant, i, 160; Nonconf., iii, 367; pk., iii, 350, 351; parl. repre., iii, 361; peasants' revolt, i, 373; place-names, iii, 350-1; poor house, iii, 352; pop., ii, 114; prehist. rem., i, 150, 159-70, 174, 269, 270; iii, 350; races, ii, 191; rectory, iii, 366; roads, i, 176, 269; ii, 4; iii, 354; Rom. rem., i, 293, 294; ii, 2, 3, 6, 7; royal visits, i, 372; ii, 24, 27; iii, 352, 353, 355; schs., i, 351; ii, 149, 178-9, 199; iii, 350, 351, 356, 367; sheriff, iii, 361; squatters, iii, 352; tolls, iii, 362; tournaments, ii, 30, 33; iii, 353, 354; town hall, iii, 351; value of land, ii, 92; vicarage, i, 316 *n*; wells, ii, 2; iii, 349
Dunstable, Gilb. of Tingrith, dean of, i, 321
Dunstable, Matth. of, i, 325 *n*; iii, 49
Dunstable Downs, ii, 7, 198, 199; iii, 349, 363, 369, 447
Dunstable larks, iii, 363
Dunstable Priory, i, 313, 317 *n*, 319, 321-3, 325, 332, 349, 350-1, 353, 362, 366, 371, 374-5, 382, 391, 394-6, 400-1; ii, 17, 23, 31-2, 84-5, 87, 91, 144-5, 149, 178, 332, 353, 357, 360, 376-7, 380, 384; iii, 29, 107, 285, 286, 288, 320-3, 325, 346, 348-52, 356, 359, 361, 362-4, 372, 377, 382, 384, 390, 392, 395, 397-8, 408, 428, 430-2, 442, 448-51, 456; episcopal visits, i, 374, 375; lay brothers, i, 374, 403 *n*; priors, i, 314, 320, 328, 353 *n*, 377, 378, 379 *n*; ii, 33, 83-6, 318, 328, 350; iii, 89, 342, 344, 358, 390-1, 395-6, 427; sub-priors, i, 382, 384 *n*
Dunstan, St., ii, 154, 217
Dunton, i, 323, 335 *n*, 344 *n*; ii, 201, 218, 233; adv., ii, 220, 222; char., ii, 222; ch., i, 315 *n*; ii, 221; forestry, ii, 146; man., ii, 221; Nonconf., ii, 222; pop., ii, 113; sch., ii, 182; vicarage, i, 316
Dunton Chamberlain (Newtonbury), man., ii, 219, 220, 221; earthwork, i, 307
Dunton Fen, ii, 222
Dunton Goyes, man., ii, 220
Duport, —, iii, 415
Durant, *see* Durrant
Durham, bpric. of, i, 312; ii, 220, 262
Durham, Margery, iii, 344; Col., iii, 286
Durrant, (Durant, Duraunt), Eleanor, iii, 285; John, i, 375, 394; iii, 285, 350, 354 *n*
Dusburgh, Matilda, iii, 437; Ralph, iii, 437
Duxworth, man., iii, 98
Dycons, *see* Decons
Dyer (Dier), Cath., iii, 188; Edw., iii, 385; Hen., iii, 188; Sir Jas., iii, 187; John, ii, 229, 292; iii, 127, 131, 315, 393, 438; Sir Lewis, iii, 156, 189, 366; Sir Lodovick, ii, 44; iii, 187, 188; Sir Rich., iii, 156, 187, 366; Thos., iii, 311; Sir Will., iii, 156, 187, 188, 366; Will., iii, 189
Dyers Hall Farm (Harlington), iii, 379
Dyllingham, *see* Dillingham
Dylywyk (Stagsden), man., iii, 13, 96-7, 212
Dylywyk, Hen. de, iii, 98
Dymoke, Isabel, iii, 129; John, iii, 129
Dymond, Mrs., iii, 338
Dynevor, Ld., iii, 47, 96; Geo., Ld., iii, 45
Dynevor House (Ampthill), iii, 268
Dyson, Eliz., iii, 427; Jas., iii, 195; Jer., iii, 427
Dyve (Dive, Dives, Dyves), Beatrice, iii, 45; Edm., iii, 391; Sir Fran., iii, 45; Fran., iii, 104; Hen., iii, 46; Isabella, iii, 48; Sir John, i, 395 *n*; iii, 45, 48, 391; John, iii, 46, 311, 355; Sir Lewis, ii, 43-6, 48; iii, 4, 45-9, 104, 271, 391; Lewis, iii, 48, 311, 391; Mary, iii, 48; Theophila, iii, 104; Will., ii, 150; iii, 46, 391, 394; fam., ii, 58, 60; iii, 37

Eadwig, mint of, iii, 2
Eagles, Marianne, iii, 275
Eakring (Notts), ch., i, 394
Ealdred, iii, 345
Eames, Jas., ii, 344
Earl Marshal, the, ii, 223, 261, 262, 301 *n*
Early Close, Gt. (Renhold), iii, 215
Early Close, Little, iii, 215
Early Man, i, 145-74
Earthworks, i, 267-308; ii, 73, 210, 242, 251, 261, 288, 294 *n*, 321, 324, 344, 348, 365; iii, 64, 102, 104, 176, 202, 206, 207, 210, 212, 215, 252, 262, 284, 320, 321, 402, 439, 447; Brit., ii, 8; Rom., ii, 5, 9, 10
East Anglia, Helen, ctss. of, iii, 297; Gurth, earl of, iii, 297; John le Scot, earl of, iii, 297
Eastcotts, ii, 116; iii, 31, 227, 234, 279; man., iii, 237; sch., ii, 182
East End (Cranfield), iii, 275
East End (Flitwick), iii, 284
Easf End (Harlington), iii, 379
East End (Wilden), iii, 223, 226
East End Moor (Flitwick), iii, 288
Eastern Association, the, ii, 43, 44, 46, 47, 51
Easton (Flitwick), *see* East End
Easton (Hunts), iii, 123, 136
Easton (Northants), iii, 247
Easton Maudit (Northants), iii, 110
Easton Mill (Flitwick), iii, 287
Eaton, bar., i, 386, 403; ii, 208, 243 *n*, 251, 253, 277, 281; iii, 190-4, 197, 219, 246, 258, 260, 424 *n*
Eaton, Gerard of, i, 399; Sim. of, i, 372, 377; Ulmar of, ii, 207, 208, 243, 251; iii, 248; Wildeboef of, i, 385
Eaton Beauchamp, iii, 193
Eaton Bray (Eitona, Eytona), i, 320, 325 *n*, 373; iii, 336, 369; adv., iii, 374; Bellows Mill, iii, 370; cast., i, 305; ii, 28; iii, 369, 370; chants., iii, 375; char., iii, 375; ch., i, 315 *n*; iii, 369, 373; ind., iii, 369; man., iii, 370-2, 456; mkts. and fairs, iii, 369; mills, iii, 307, 370, 372; pk., iii, 371; Peverell's fee, iii, 372; place-names, iii, 370; pop., ii, 114; iii, 374; Rye cottage, iii, 369; sch., ii, 182; vicarage, i, 316 *n*, 317; iii, 369, 374
Eaton-cum-Soka, *see* Eaton Socon
Eaton Ford, iii, 189, 190; bridge, ii, 53
Eaton Green (Eaton Bray), iii, 369
Eaton Socon, i, 326 *n*; ii, 43, 71, 76, 86, 277; iii, 96 *n*, 180, 189; adv., iii, 200; agric., ii, 136; Begwary Farm, iii, 190; cast., iii, 191; chant., i, 329 *n*; char., iii, 201, 202; ch., i, 315 *n*, 325 *n*, 394; ii, 208; iii, 199; deanery, i, 347; earthworks, i, 297, 298, 299; gild, i, 330; inclosures, ii, 97; mans., i, 394; iii, 190, 191, 195, 198, 199, 201, 258; mkt., iii, 199; mill, i, 298; iii, 189; Nonconf., iii, 190; Oakley Club meet, ii, 189; pk., i, 386; iii, 197; place-names, iii, 190; pop., ii, 113; prehist. rem., i, 145; priory lands, iii, 197; rectory, iii, 201; sch., ii, 182
Eaton Soken, *see* Eaton Socon
Eayre, J. and J., bellfounders, ii, 236, 245, 285, 292, 373; iii, 29, 63, 68, 116, 138, 152, 164, 167, 179, 200, 242
Ebrington, Edw., iii, 40
Ebroinus, ii, 78
Eccles, Rich., iii, 392

INDEX

Eccleshale, Ralph de, ii, 360
Ecclesiastical divisions, i, 346
Ecclesiastical history, i, 309-48
Eccleye, *see* Oakley
Echam, *see* Higham Gobion
Edeston, ii, 364
Edgar, king, ii, 19, 21, 286, 294; iii, 338
Edgcumbe, Sir Rob. P., ii, 242, 244
Edgebury (Aspley Guise), iii, 338
Edington, Will. de, i, 402
Edith, queen, ii, 21
Edlesborough (Bucks), i, 384, 404; ii, 71; iii, 336, 432; ch., iii, 372
Edlesborough Hill, iii, 369, 370
Edlesborough Mill, iii, 370
Edmund, king, ii, 19, 20
Edmunds, Islip, iii, 143; —, iii, 148
Edred, king, i, 311 *n*
Edward (the Elder), i, 281; ii, 18, 19, 21, 251; iii, 1, 345, 401
Edward I, iii, 353, 362
Edward II, iii, 281, 362, 428
Edward III, iii, 353, 354
Edward VI, ii, 210, 275
Edward (the Black Prince), iii, 101
Edward, Hen., iii, 311
Edwards, Anne, ii, 281 *n*; Eleanor, ii, 244 *n*; Eliz., ii, 282; Frances, ii, 282; Geo., ii, 69, 207, 262, 280, 281, 282, 285; Geo. N., ii, 285; Hen., ii, 40; Jasper, ii, 207, 244, 247; Rich., ii, 55 *n*, 244, 262, 265, 282; Sam. B., ii, 262, 263; Will., i, 399; ii, 185 *n*; iii, 328; Will. B., ii, 262; Will. G., iii, 122; fam., ii, 281, 285
Edwin, ii, 314, 361
Edwinsmede (Turvey), iii, 113
Edworth, ii, 113, 201, 218, 220, 223-26, 248, 261, 262, 357 *n*; adv., ii, 226; char., ii, 226; ch., i, 315 *n*; ii, 223, 225, 302; ch. farm, ii, 223; man., ii, 223, 224, 225; moat, ii, 223; place-names, ii, 223; Rom. rem., ii, 7, 223; sundial, ii, 225
Edworth, Steph. de, ii, 263
Efelmus, ii, 215; Affa, w. of, ii, 215
Egerton, Hume (Cust), ii, 66 *n*; John, *see* Bridgewater, earl of; Sir Thos., *see* Ellesmere, baron; Thos., *see* Ellesmere, earl of; Miss, iii, 286
Eggington (Ekenden), John de, iii, 419 *n*
Eggington (Ekendon), iii, 368, 399, 400, 402; chap., i, 341; ii, 114; iii, 414, 417; ch., iii, 400, 412; man., iii, 408; Nonconf., iii, 415; vicarage, iii, 414
Eggington House, iii, 400
Eglemond, John de, iii, 448
Eglemunt's quarry, iii, 448
Eglinton, Ld., ii, 192
Egremont, Sir John, iii, 298, 299
Egton (Northants), man., i, 365
Eitona, *see* Eaton Bray
Ejected clergy, i, 338
Ekelston, Kath., iii, 106; Rob., iii, 106
Ekenden, *see* Eggington
Ekendon, *see* Eggington
Elbone, Rob., ii, 160
Eldred, John, iii, 110, 175 *n*, 247, 253, 331
Eldridge, John, iii, 327
Eleanor, queen, i, 373 *n*; iii, 16, 351, 353, 370; sister of Hen. III., ii, 306, 350, 439
Elgin, Diana, ctss. of, iii, 314, 315; earls of, ii, 44, 49, 55 *n*, 267, 325; iii, 315, 324; Rob., ii, 147, 268; Thos., iii, 290, 314, 316; Ld., iii, 270
Elizabeth, queen, ii, 295, 310; iii, 42, 252, 276, 339, 353, 376, 459
Elkin, Mary, iii, 408
Ell, Will., ii, 94 *n*
Ellenborough, Ld., ii, 65
Ellesmere, Ld., iii, 102; Thos., earl of, iii, 448
Ellingham, Dan., iii, 413, 414; Eliz., iii, 413; Thos., iii, 407
Elliot (Elliott), Florence, iii, 126; Rob., iii, 126
Ellis, Thos., iii, 243
Elmele, Gawin, iii, 453
Elmes, Ann, iii, 159; Edm., iii, 158; Thos., iii, 158, 159; Will., iii, 159
Elmore (Gloucs.), iii, 339
Elmore, —, ii, 326
Elms Farm (Goldington), iii, 202
Elnestow, *see* Elstow
Elrichton, Will. de, i, 402
Elstow (Elnestow), i, 120, 353, 356; ii, 58, 115, 190, 197; iii, 2, 41, 205, 226, 267, 279-84, 384; Abbey House, iii, 281; adv., i, 326; iii, 281, 283; chant., i, 326; iii, 284; chap., iii, 283-4; char., iii, 284; ch., i, 315 *n*, 325 *n*, 326, 353, 354, 355 *n*; iii, 279, 282-3; crown property, iii, 271; earthworks, i, 305; fairs, iii, 281; inds., iii, 280; inns, iii, 280; man., i, 313; iii, 280, 281; mkt. cross, iii, 279; moot hall, iii, 279; place-names, iii, 279, 280; prebend, iii, 284 *n*; rectory, iii, 284; Rom. rem., iii, 280; Samian ware, ii, 7; sch., i, 350, 355; ii, 150, 177-8, 182; vicarage, i, 317 *n*, 327
Elstow, Grace, iii, 25; John, iii, 25
Elstow Abbey, i, 313, 314, 315 *n*, 316 *n*, 326, 332, 349, 353, 355-8, 362, 364, 383, 398; ii, 332, 333, 338, 380; iii, 23, 237, 282, 284, 304, 314, 315, 326, 328, 353, 438, 454; abbesses, i, 357, 380 *n*; ii, 296 *n*; seal, i, 361
Eltesdon (Eltesdone, Eltesden), John de, iii, 428, 429, 430, 449; Marg. de, iii, 428; Walt. de, iii, 428; Will. de, i, 325 *n*, 326 *n*; iii, 428, 455, 432, 449
Elton, John de, ii, 289
Elvendone, iii, 123
Elwes, Dudley Cary, ii, 25 *n*; Geoff., iii, 393
Elwyn, Rich., i, 399
Ely, bps. of, i, 314 *n*, 400; ii, 214, 312, 332, 374, 380; iii, 29, 30, 117, 165, 209, 214, 219, 304, 366; John de Kyrkeby, iii, 39
Ely, diocese, i, 347
Ely, Isle of, ii, 25, 31-32
Emerton (Emmerton), Will., ii, 292, 335; iii, 378, 414; —, ii, 324; iii, 39, 315, 328, 334, 348, 398, 435
Emery, Eliz., ii, 289, 293; iii, 274; Florence, ii, 262; Hen., i, 363-5; Rich., ii, 281, 289; Sarah, ii, 289, 293; iii, 274; Thos., ii, 262
Emmanuel College (Camb.), ii, 163, 167, 168
Enderbies man. (Sutton), ii, 248
Enderby, Alice, ii, 211, 224; Eleanor, ii, 211, 221, 224, 248; iii, 230, 248; John, ii, 36, 204, 210, 211, 212, 214, 220, 224; iii, 230; Maud, ii, 204, 211, 214, 224; iii, 230; Rich., ii, 204, 210, 211, 224; iii, 230
Enfield, Barth. de, iii, 168, 172
Engayne, Clarice, iii, 211; Eliz. d', ii, 243; iii, 191; Joan d', iii, 191, 194; John, i, 325 *n*, 361, 385; ii, 243, 245; iii, 191, 194, 201; Joyce d', ii, 243; iii, 191, 194; Kath., ii, 243; Mary d', ii, 243; iii, 191; Nich., iii, 211; Sim., iii, 211; Thos. d', ii, 243; iii, 191; Will., iii, 214; fam., iii, 210, 211, 331
Engelar, ii, 305
Engelram, iii, 370
Engineering works, ii, 125
Engleys, Will. le, iii, 162
Englysshe, Hen., iii, 220; Marg., iii, 220; Thos., iii, 220
Enveyse, *see* L'Enveise
Episcopacy, pet. for abolition, i, 337
Eppeho Wood, iii, 442
Erchtdehene, Isabel la, iii, 168
Erfast, ii, 263, 281, 283; iii, 309
Erneys, Edw., iii, 144; Elinor, iii, 144; John, iii, 144, 147; Phil., iii, 144; Rog., iii, 144; Walt., iii, 144; Will., iii, 144
Ernuin (Ernui), i, 312; iii, 37, 237
Eseltone, *see* Shelton
Espaigne, Thos. d', ii, 227
Espec, *see* Spech
Esperun, Thos., ii, 253
Esseby, Dav. de, iii, 314; Hugh de, iii, 314; Rob., iii, 67
Essex, assessment, ii, 48 *n*; ealdormanry, ii, 19; peasants' revolt, ii, 35; straw-plait. ind., ii, 121
Essex, Roais, ct. of, *see* Beauchamp, Rohesia de; earls of, ii, 45, 46, 47, 53, 354; iii, 111; Geoff., 390; iii, 9, 70, 169, 171; Hen., ii, 295; Humphrey de Bohun, ii, 223 *n*; Rob., ii, 339; Will., ii, 154; iii, 173
Estcotes, *see* Eastcotts
Estfeld (Riseley), iii, 157 *n*
Esthaddon, Ralph of, i, 402
Estodham, *see* Studham
Eston, Christina, ii, 212; John, ii, 59; iii, 8; Ralph de, i, 401; Rich., ii, 212; Thos., ii, 212; fam., ii, 55
Estons, man. (Holme), ii, 212
Estwick, Anne, iii, 418, 419; Chris., ii, 40; iii, 384, 418, 419; Marion, iii, 419
Ethelfled, ii, 18
Ethelred, earl, iii, 345
Ethelred II, iii, 345, 383
Eton, par. *see* Eaton Socon
Eton (Etone), John de, iii, 201; Laur., ii, 295; Nich. de, iii, 188; Ulmar of, i, 300; ii, 271 *n*, 277, 304
Etonbury, earthwork (Arlesey), i, 278-80; ii, 261
Etonbury, man. (Arlesey), ii, 223 *n*, 234, 261, 262, 263, 265; mkt., ii, 261, 263; mill, ii, 261
Eton Coll. (Bucks), i, 404; ii, 157; iii, 47, 48, 49, 152, 401, 403
Etrick, Ant., ii, 359; Eliz., ii, 359
Eu, Ralph de Issoudun, earl of, ii, 223 *n*
Eu, Alice d', ii, 223 *n*; Will. d', ii, 211, 223, 261, 263, 383 *n*, 384
Eudo, iii, 211, 246, 248
Eugenius IV, pope, i, 352
Eureton, *see* Everton
Eustace, count, iii, 74, 90, 96 *n*, 111; sheriff of Hunts., iii, 168, 169
Evans, Dr. Arth., i, 170, 177; Sir John, i, 145, 151, 157, 158 *n*, 159, 161, 162, 166, 169, 170, 173 *n*, 174, 190, 269
Evelyn, Geo., iii, 392
Everard, Edm., iii, 423; Hen., iii, 248; fam., iii, 422
Evereshawe, *see* Eversholt

Evereshont, *see* Eversholt
Evereshot, *see* Eversholt
Everitt, Sir John, iii, 453; John, iii, 453
Eversden Parva (Cambs), i, 360
Eversend, Will, iii, 383
Eversholt, ii, 84, 85, 114; iii, 336, 375, 458, 459; adv., iii, 376, 378; char., iii, 378; ch., i, 315 *n*; iii, 375, 377, 378; crown property, iii, 271; man., i, 370; iii, 23, 375, 376, 377; Nonconf., iii, 375; parson, i, 323; rectory, iii, 375; sch., ii, 182
Eversholt, Alice de, iii, 429; John de, iii, 375, 377; Miles de, iii, 375; Paulinus de, iii, 376; Rich. de, iii, 377, 419, 429
Eversolt, *see* Eversholt
Everton, ii, 71, 96, 113, 201, 226-30, 242, 255, 262; iii, 8; adv., ii, 229; char., ii, 229, 230; ch., i, 345; ii, 228; man., ii, 226, 227, 228, 238; man.-house, ii, 226; mkts. and fairs, ii, 227, 228; place-names, ii, 226; sch., ii, 182
Everton Biggin, man., ii, 228
Everton Norsbury, man., ii, 227, 228
Eveshall, Rich. de, iii, 362
Evretune, *see* Everton
Evreux, Almaric, ct. of, iii, 390; Millicent, ctss. of, iii, 390
Evyesholt, *see* Eversholt
Ewell (Surrey), Roman well, ii, 6
Ewelme (Oxon), ii, 157
Ewen, Rich., ii, 318
Exeter, bps. of, i, 315 *n*; iii, 142; Bartholomew, iii, 143; Hen. Phillpotts, ii, 175
Exeter, Dorothy, ctss. of, iii, 235, 330; Anne, dchss. of, iii, 102; dks. of, iii, 272; Hen., iii, 102, 272; earls of, iii, 13, 15; iii, 236; Brownlow, iii, 14; David, iii, 14, 235; John, iii, 14, 101, 102; Thos., iii, 14, 235, 330; Will., iii, 235; Hen., mqs. of, iii, 14
Exeter Wood (Cardington), iii, 235
Exmore, Edw., i, 399
Exmouth, Clementia de, iii, 120; John de, iii, 120
Eye (Eya), ii, 336, 337; man., ii, 333
Eymewe, Thos., ii, 332
Eyr, Le, Will., iii, 116 *n*; fam., iii, 113
Eyre, Mrs., ii, 374
Eythorne (Kent), i, 389 *n*
Eytona, *see* Eaton Bray
Eyworth (Aieworde, Aisseworde), ii, 113, 201, 219, 230-33; iii, 106; adv., i, 362 *n*; ii, 233; char., ii, 233; ch., i, 315, 333 362; ii, 230, 231; field-names, ii, 230; mans., ii, 143, 230-3; vicarage, i, 327; windmill, ii, 232
Eywurth, *see* Eyworth

Faber, Will., iii, 95
Facey, John, iii, 458
Fâfiton, Rob., ii, 328
Fage, John, iii, 220, 222
Fagg, Anne, ii, 235; Sir John, ii, 235
Fairclough, John, iii, 204, 205; Mary, iii, 204; Sam., i, 342
Fairfax, Sir Thos., ii, 48, 49, 50, 54; iii, 35, 227
Fairfield (Biggleswade), i, 110
Fairie, *see* Fayrey
Fairs, ii, 263, 330, 349, 350, 351 *n*, 353 *n*; iii, 16, 17, 21, 35, 64, 69
Falbe, Mme. de, ii, 353
Falconer's Hall, man., *see* Greathampstead, man.
Falconer's Hall Farm (Luton), ii, 358
Faldo, ii, 345; man., ii, 346
Faldo (Faldoe, Faldho), Agnes, iii, 39; Amphyllis, iii, 315; Anne, iii, 315; Cecilia, ii, 346; John, ii, 164 *n*; iii, 39; Paul, iii, 27; Rich., iii, 151, 315; Rob., ii, 164, 357; iii, 315, 351; Thos., iii, 18; Will. (de), ii, 346, 377, 379; iii, 39, 146, 315
Faldo Farm (Faldo), ii, 344, 346
Falkland, Lucius Chas., vsct., iii, 332; Sarah, vsctss., iii, 332
Fancott (Toddington), iii, 439; almshouses, iii, 439
Fane, Mrs. V., iii, 231, 233; Will., iii, 368; —, iii, 231
Fanhope, Geoff., baron, iii, 317; John, Ld., iii, 272, 285; *see also* Cornwall, Sir John
Fanshawe, Fred., ii, 174, 175; Kath., ii, 317; Sir Thos., ii, 317; Thos., ii, 317
Farele, Will., iii, 294 *n*
Farleigh (Hants), iii, 405
Farley, ii, 342; hermitage, i, 400; hosps., i, 349, 400; ii, 357; man., ii, 350, 357, 358, 360, 361 *n*
Farmer, Anne, Lady, iii, 452; Eliz., Lady, iii, 452; Sir Geo., iii, 452; Sir Halton, iii, 452; Joanna, iii, 115; Mary, Lady, iii, 452, 454; Rich., ii, 44; Sir Will., iii, 452; Will., Ld. Leominster, *see* Leominster
Farm House (Eaton Socon), iii, 193
Farndish, ii, 115; iii, 34, 57; adv., iii, 58; bronze ornaments, i, 189, 190; char., iii, 58; ch., iii, 58; man., iii, 57,; Manor Farm., iii, 57; Rectory Farm, iii, 57
Farndissche, *see* Farndish
Farnedis, *see* Farndish
Farnham, John, iii, 23
Farrer (Farrar), Anne, iii, 66; Rev. C. F., ii, 178; Denis, iii, 187, 281, 304; Eliz., iii, 281, 304; Eliz., iii, 304; Farrer G. S., iii, 304; Frances, iii, 304; Fran., ii, 40; iii, 66; Geo., iii, 68; Helen, iii, 66; Jenny, iii, 304; Mary, iii, 37, 66; Ralph, iii, 66; Thos., iii, 66; Will., ii, 168; iii, 20, 37, 66, 68, 304; fam., ii, 59; *see also* Ferrers
Farwell, John, ii, 262
Faryndysh, *see* Farndish
Fatt, Mrs., ii, 314
Fauconer, Thos., ii, 295, 310
Fawcett, John, ii, 335
Fawkeswell, Marg., i, 360 *n*
Fayrey, Agnes, iii, 367; Hen., ii, 40; iii, 367; John, iii, 367; Mary, iii, 367; Thos., iii, 133
Fayrey pall, iii, 367
Fécamp, Aubrée de, i, 357
Feery, Mary, ii, 256
Feevell, Will., iii, 244
Feilde, *see* Field
Feke, Jas., iii, 300
Felbrigge, Sim., ii, 382
Feldemerishull (Studham), iii, 426, 428
Fell, Dr., iii, 275
Felmersham (Flammersham), i, 324; ii, 115, 138; iii, 34, 54, 59-63, 68, 73; adv., iii, 63; bridge, iii, 59; char., iii, 63; ch., i, 315 *n*, 318, 326; iii, 59, 61, 80; deanery, i, 347; inclosure of land, ii, 97, 98; man., iii, 60; mill, iii, 59; sch., ii, 182; vicarage, i, 326 *n*, 327
Felmersham, John (of), i, 400; iii, 173
Felmersham Hardwick, iii, 59
Felmersham Mead, ii, 92
Fenlake, i, 380; iii, 227, 234; prehist. rem., i, 145, iii, 234
Fenlake Barns (Cardington Priors, Regine), man., iii, 236
Fenlake Mead, ii, 92
Fennels Grove, man., ii, 350, 352 *n*, 358; mill, ii, 358, 366
Fenner, Joan, iii, 392
Fenny Stratford (Bucks), ii, 3 *n* 71; iii, 383, 402
Fens, the, ii, 61 *n*
Fenton (Fentoun), Thos., vsct., ii, 267, 310, 322; iii, 271, 331
Fenwick, Rev. Chas., iii, 304
Feoffee (Charity) Estate (Ampthill), iii, 275
Feoffee Farm (Fancott), iii, 439
Fermbaud, Alice, iii, 384; Amabilia, iii, 386; Eliz., iii, 343 *n*; John, iii, 36, 386; Kath., iii, 386; Nich., iii, 36, 46, 343, 386, 387; Thos., iii, 343, 384, 386
Fermor (Fermour), Jer., ii, 355; Rich., ii, 329, 355, 357, 359, 378 *n*
Fernadis, *see* Farndish
Fernedis, *see* Farndish
Ferneslie (Verneslie), —, iii, 244
Ferns, i, 55-6
Farrell, Rev. Maur., iii, 238, 313; Will., iii, 28
Ferrers (Ferrars), Agatha de, ii, 351; Anne, ii, 231, 317; Edw., ii, 212, 237, 297; Eleanor, ii, 351; Eliz., ii, 316; Geo., ii, 316, 317, 318; Hen., *see* Groby, Ld. de; Isabel de, ii, 351; Joan de, ii, 351; iii, 452; Sir John, ii, 317; Julius, ii, 317; Kath., ii, 317; Knighton, ii, 317; Maud de, ii, 351; Rob. (de), iii, 427, 452; Sybil de, ii, 351; Thos., ii, 316; Will. de, iii, 212; *see also* Derby, earl of, and Groby, Ld. de; fam., iii, 139; *see also* Farrer
Fettiplace, Alex., ii, 253; Anne, ii, 207, 253; Sir Edm., ii, 253; Edm., ii, 207; John, ii, 207; Will., ii, 207; —, ii, 44
ffitche, John L., ii, 268; *see also* Fitch
Field (Feilde), Anne, ii, 342; Chas., ii, 69; Sir Chas. V., ii, 268; Eliz., iii, 278; Geo., ii, 361; Henrietta, ii, 268; Hen., iii, 421; Jas., ii, 361; John, ii, 268; Susan, ii, 216; Thos., ii, 342, 361; iii, 37 *n*; Will., ii, 304; iii, 277
Fielden, Hannah, ii, 358; Rich., ii, 358
Fielder, R., iii, 273
Fields-Clarke, G. T., ii, 147 *n*
Fiennes, Edw., *see* Clynton, Ld.
Finaunce (Fynaunce), Agnes, iii, 97, 396; Jas., iii, 97; John, iii, 97, 396
Finch, Rich., iii, 367
Finderne, *see* Fynderne
Finlinson, A. W., ii, 200
Fiott, John, iii, 92
Firegod, Rob., iii, 76
Fish (Fishe), Sir Edw., iii, 260; Geo., iii, 227, 246, 259, 260; Humph., iii, 245, 261; Sir John, iii, 260; John, ii, 281, 285, 342 *n*; Marg., iii, 245
Fisher (Fyssher), Agnes, Lady, iii, 257; Agnes, ii, 277, 323; iii, 41, 194, 396; Ann, iii, 286; Geo., ii, 322, 323; Hen., ii, 322, 323;

Fisher (*cont.*)
Jasper, iii, 226; Jeffrey, iii, 61, 286; Sir John, ii, 276, 277, 280, 323; iii, 194, 257; John, i, 365 *n*; ii, 277, 279; iii, 50, 130, 194, 259, 299, 392; Sir Mich., ii, 277, 278, 279; iii, 41, 61, 257, 259, 305, 396; Mich., ii, 323; iii, 154, 194; Nath., iii, 431; Rich., iii, 208; Susan, iii, 156; Thos., i, 399; ii, 165; iii, 146
Fisheries, ii, 212, 323, 351, 366; iii, 11, 38, 44 *n*, 47, 55, 59, 60, 65, 66, 73, 74, 78, 79, 91, 102, 114, 125, 129, 130, 143, 144, 146, 147, 149, 184, 196, 199, 244, 259, 299, 301, 387, 453
Fisher's Grange (Southall), iii, 257
Fishes, i, 98-101
Fishponds, ii, 288; iii, 205, 280, 343, 354 *n*, 370 *n*, 372, 406
Fitch, Rev. S. E., i, 176, 177; *see also* ffitch
Fitz, Alice, ii, 329; Eliz., ii, 329; Geo., ii, 378, 381; Joan, ii, 329, 330; John, iii, 231; Sim., ii, 329, 377, 378, 384; Susan, ii, 329, 378; Will., ii, 329, 377; iii, 249, 250
Fitzakerly, John, ii, 303
Fitz Brian, Thos., iii, 176 *n*
Fitz Geoffrey (Fitz Geffrey, Fitz Jeffery, Fitz Jeffry), Edw., iii, 146; Elinor, iii, 144; Eliz., iii, 105, 144, 146, 183; Fran., iii, 129, 132, 184, 220; Geo., iii, 105, 146, 183, 212, 214; Gerard, iii, 213; Jane, iii, 183; Joan, iii, 183, 422; John, iii, 105, 106 *n*, 129, 146, 147, 183, 185, 220; Judith, iii, 146, 183; Leonard, iii, 129; Will., iii, 105, 146, 183, 212; —, w. of John, iii, 129
Fitzgerald, Rev. W. G., iii, 29
Fitz Herbert, Edm., ii, 352; Reg., ii, 351
Fitz Hugh, Anne, iii, 193; Joan, iii, 106; John, ii, 383; iii, 106; Mary, iii, 193; Nich., iii, 195; Rich., iii, 196, 197, 282; Rob., iii, 193; Thos., ii, 329, 330; iii, 193; Will., iii, 196
Fitz James, Rich., i, 399
Fitz Jeffery, Fitz Jeffry, *see* Fitz Geoffrey
Fitzjeffry's, man., *see* Clapham Greenacres
Fitz Jocelin, Nich., iii, 133
Fitz Lewis, Eleanor, iii, 115
Fitz Neel, Grace, ii, 358; Rob., ii, 358
Fitz Otho, Beatrice, iii, 12, 13, 46, 330; Maud, iii, 13, 46, 330; Thos., iii, 12, 13, 46
Fitz Patrick, John, *see* Upper Ossory, earl of; Mary, *see* Fox; Rich., ii, 61; W. E., iii, 128; W. L., ii, 189
Fitz Payn (Fitz Payne), Ela, iii, 426; Rob., iii, 426
Fitz Peter, Sim., i, 378; ii, 26
Fitz Piers (Peter), Geoff., ii, 144; *see also* Essex, earl of; Hen., ii, 306; Joan, ii, 351; Reg., ii, 351; —, w. of Geoff., i, 391
Fitz Ralph, Rich., iii, 21
Fitz Richard, Alice, ii, 346; Emma, ii, 329 *n*; Gilb., iii, 142 *n*; Hugh, ii, 326; Ralph, ii, 329, 330, 332, 346
Fitz Robert, Rob., iii, 145
Fitzroy, Anne, ii, 379; Geo., ii, 378 *n*, 379
Fitz Salomon, Gilb., i, 296 *n*
Fitz Walter, Rob., ii, 361, 362
Fitz Warin (Fitz Warine), Agnes, iii, 70; Fulk, ii, 29; Hugh, ii, 362; Pet., ii, 362; Will., ii, 362; iii, 69, 70, 74
Fitzwilliam, earl, iii, 31; Ld., ii, 61; iii, 272
Fitz William, Alice, iii, 300; Eliz., ii, 323; iii, 192, 244; Fran., iii, 300; Geoff., ii, 144; Humph., ii, 40; iii, 300, 398; Jane, Lady, iii, 300; Joan, Lady, ii, 323, 325; iii, 244, 250; Sir John, iii, 300; John, iii, 162, 192; Kath., ii, 323; iii, 244; Mabel, ii, 323; iii, 244; Ralph, iii, 191 *n*, 192; Rob., iii, 192; Thos., iii, 300, 305; Sir Will., ii, 323, 325; iii, 244, 250, 251, 300; Will., ii, 252; iii, 300; fam., iii, 303
Fitz Wirnart, Sim., ii, 145
Five Knolls (Dunstable Downs), prehist. rem., i, 169, 270; iii, 448; Rom. rem., ii, 3
Flamstead (Herts), ii, 314, 375
Flamvill (Flamville), Alice, iii, 293; Hamo, iii, 216; Hen., iii, 206, 216, 293; Jas., iii, 216; John, iii, 216, 293; Matilda, iii, 293; Rob. de, ii, 341; iii, 293, 216; fam., iii, 216
Flamwelles (Flamwells, Flavells), man., iii, 216, 291, 293
Flannel manufactory, iii, 4
Flaun, Ad., i, 325
Flavells, man., *see* Flamwelles, **man.**
Fleet, riv., *see* Flitt
Fleet, Ralph, i, 364 *n*; w. of Ralph, i, 364 *n*
Fleete, deanery, i, 347, 351
Fleetwood, Gen. Chas., iii, 125; Hen., iii, 104; Smith, iii, 125; Sir Will., iii, 125, 456; —, ii, 51; iii, 125
Fleming, Hugh le, iii, 82, 84, 92, 104; Saer, ii, 234; iii, 70; Sim., ii, 234; iii, 70; Sybil le, ii, 235; iii, 70; Walt., ii, 143, 204, 205, 210 *n*, 211, 234, 235, 282-3, 309, 326; iii, 69, 70, 73, 82, 92, 104, 113, 118, 119, 146, 260
Flemish colony, iii, 268
Fletcher, Will., ii, 204; W., ii, 199
Flewton End (Milton Ernest), iii, 144
Flichtam, *see* Flitton-cum-Silsoe
Flietewicke, *see* Flitwick
Flint implements, i, 269; ii, 5
Flints, Thos., iii, 429 *n*
Flit, riv., *see* Flitt
Flitcroft, Hen., iii, 459, 460
Flitt, hund., ii, 113 *n*, 114, 261, 293, 306-87, bailiff of, ii, 383
Flitt (Flit, Fleet), riv., i, 286; ii, 138, 320; iii, 284, 286, 313, 438
Flitton, *see* Flitton-cum-Silsoe
Flitton, Pet. de, ii, 328; Phil. de, ii, 328; Will. of, i, 366
Flitton-cum-Silsoe, i, 174, 325 *n*, 352, 357; ii, 36, 114, 139, 283, 290, 305-6, 325-34, 336, 376, 378, 451; iii, 316; adv., ii, 332; chap., i, 315 *n*; char., ii, 333; ch., i, 314 *n*, 315 *n*, 318, 357; ii, 36, 331; crops, ii, 326; Lock-Up tower, ii, 326; man., ii, 328; mausoleum, ii, 327; minister's stipend, i, 341; Rom. burials, ii, 1, 7; vicarage, i, 316 *n*; ii, 326
Flitton Greenfield, ii, 182
Flitton Moor, ii, 326
Flitwick, i, 145, 286; ii, 85, 115, 135, 138, 139, 145; iii, 61, 267, 274, 284-88, 435; adv., iii, 288; chalybeate springs, ii, 118; iii,
Flitwick (*cont.*)
284; char., ii, 214; iii, 288; ch., i, 286, 326, 371 *n*; iii, 287, 347; coins, ii, 2; crown property in, iii, 271; inclosures, ii, 97; ind., ii, 117; irrigation, ii, 135; man., i, 377; ii, 197; iii, 284-6; man.-house, iii, 284; mill, iii, 286-7; Nonconf., iii, 284; place-names, iii, 284; Rom. rem., ii, 7; sch., ii, 182
Flitwick, Ad. de, iii, 285; Amabel de, iii, 285; Barth. de, ii, 378; iii, 395; Dav. de, ii, 378; iii, 285, 395, 398; Dav. R. de, iii, 285; Eleanor de, iii, 285; Joan de, iii, 285
Flitwick Moor, ii, 118, 326; iii, 284; Rom. implements, ii, 7
Flitwick Park, ii, 146
Flitwick Plantation (Steppingley), iii, 324
Flower, A. D., ii, 200
Flower-culture, ii, 139; iii, 369
Floyer, Pet., iii, 104; —, ii, 357
Flythewick, *see* Flitwick
Foliot (Foliott), Alice, ii, 346; Margery, ii, 247; Mary, iii, 106; Rog. ii, 346; Rich., i, 385-6; ii, 247; iii, 106; Rob., ii, 247; iii, 70
Folly Pit (Caddington), i, 151
Fontaine, *see* Fountain
Fontevraud Abbey, *see* Fontevrault
Fontevrault Abbey (France), i, 319 *n*, 370, 402-4; iii, 370, 401-4, 408, 429
Fonts, ii, 209, 213, 218, 222, 225, 229, 241, 245, 250, 254, 258, 265, 269, 279, 285, 292, 303, 312, 319, 338, 347, 372, 380, 383, 384, 387; iii, 25, 26, 27, 28, 39, 43, 53, 56, 58, 63, 68, 75, 80, 87, 94, 99, 103, 108, 116, 121, 127, 131, 135, 138, 141, 148, 152, 156, 160, 164, 167, 170, 178, 184, 188, 200, 208, 214, 217, 218, 222, 226, 233, 237, 254, 261, 265, 273, 275, 283, 288, 294, 303, 312, 323, 333, 340, 345, 347, 365, 374, 378, 382, 385, 387, 393, 398, 410, 411, 412, 413, 420, 423, 434, 438, 445, 450, 454
Ford (Fort), ii, 153, 154; iii, 198
Forde, John atte, iii, 376
Ford End (Biddenham), *see* Kirtons
Ford End (Eaton Socon), iii, 191
Forder, B. J., & Sons, iii, 329
Fordham, Geo., ii, 194; Rupert, iii, 256
Foreigners, fines for, iii, 17
Forester, *see* Forster and Foster
Forestry, ii, 143-8
Forrest, friar, i, 331 *n*, 369
Forster (Forester), Diana, ii, 286; Eliz., ii, 330; Giles, i, 334; Thos., ii, 330; *see also* Foster
Fort, Samson le, i, 387, 388, 389; iii, 65; Will. le, *see* Albemarle, earl of
Fortescue, Alice, iii, 112; Fran., ii, 231; Hen., ii, 231; John, ii, 231; iii, 112; Mrs., i, 335 *n*
Forty Foot Lane (Podington), iii, 80
Foscall, Thos., iii, 293
Fossey, F. J., i, 169; fam., ii, 206
Fossils, i, 6-12, 15, 16, 18-21, 23, 26-8, 32-4, 150, 169; iii, 44
Foster, Chas., iii, 236; Edw., J. F., iii, 335; Eliz., iii, 236; Gabriel, iii, 434; Geo., iii, 287; Hen., iii, 236; John, iii, 236, 311; J., ii, 134, 135, 139; J. N., iii, 335; Martha, iii, 236; Mary, ii, 204 *n*; iii, 236; Rebecca, iii, 236; Rog., ii, 204 *n*; Thos., iii, 195, 238;

Foster (*cont.*)
Dr. Will., ii, 59, 167; —, ii, 97, 131, 133; iii, 195, 329; fam., ii, 243; *see also* Forster
Foster's Hill, iii, 5
Fotherby, Dr., iii, 22
Fotheringay, Agnes de, iii, 110 *n*; Thos. de, iii, 110 *n*
Fotheringhay, college, ii, 235
Foucault, Daniel, iii, 212
Foule, John, ii, 296
Foulislea, (Ampthill), iii, 268
Foullerton, Dav., ii, 320; *see also* Fullerton
Fountain (Fontaine), Sir Erasmus, ii, 180, 212, 235; John, ii, 235 *n*; iii, 462; Kath., iii, 307; Rob., iii, 307
Fountains, Rog. of, i, 370
Fountains Abbey (Yorks), i, 366, 367 *n*
Fourneys, John de, ii, 220
Fowler, Edw., iii, 433; Fran., ii, 285; Gabriel, iii, 433, 435; Dr. G. H., iii, 338; Sir Rich., iii, 433; Rich., iii, 406, 434; Sybil, iii, 433; Villiers, ii, 344; Mrs. Villiers, iii, 296; Dr., i, 342 *n*
Fox, Geo., i, 341, 343, 345; Georgina, iii, 320; John, iii, 136; Mary, ii, 61; iii, 136; Rich., iii, 158, 167; Steph., ii, 61; iii, 317
Fox Burrow (Foxborough Hill, Toddington), i, 185; Rom. rem., ii, 14
Frambolt (Frampolt), Godwin, iii, 52, 83, 119
Franchenat, Isabel, iii, 347; Sim., iii, 347
Franchevaler, Sim., iii, 442
Francis, Ad., ii, 231; Eliz., ii, 231; Jonathan, ii, 180; Sim., ii, 286; —, ii, 194; *see also* Fraunceys
Franciscan Friars, *see* Friars, Grey
Franck, *see* Frank
Francklin, *see* Franklin
Francroft Wood (Sharnbrook), iii, 89
Frank (Franck), Anne, ii, 316; Thos., ii, 316; iii, 278; Walt., iii, 278 *n*
Franklin (Francklin, Franklyn), Dorothy, iii, 127; Edm., iii, 208 *n*, 212; Eliz., ii, 295; Geo., ii, 184 *n*, 266; iii, 109, 182, 204, 208 *n*, 212; Sir John, ii, 295, iii, 182; John, ii, 69, 220, 342, 361; iii, 127, 182; Rev. John, 361; iii, 80, 126, 182, 208 *n*, 212, 407; John L., iii, 126, 182; Jos., ii, 69; iii, 80; Lucretia, iii, 80; Nich., ii, 220; Rich., ii, 295, 361; iii, 182, 185; Sir Will., ii, 56; iii, 20; Will., i, 398; — (parson of Haynes), ii, 343; fam., iii, 149
Franklins, man. (Haynes), ii, 339, 342
Fraunceys, John, i, 365; Will. le, i, 381; *see also* Francis
Fray, John, iii, 195; Kath., iii, 195
Freeman, Thos., i, 335; —, ii, 69, 165
Freemonger, Humph., ii, 44
Frenches, man., *see* Buddenho
Frenches, Will., iii, 247
Frere, Rev. E. B., ii, 214
Frereman, Rich., iii, 22
Frere's Wood, ii, 187
Fresshyng, Annora, ii, 243 *n*; John, ii, 243 *n*
Freston, Alan de, i, 401
Friaries, i, 395-6
Friars, Black, i, 322, 323, 349, 359, 363, 374 *n*, 395-6
Friars, Grey, i, 322, 395; ii, 91, 239; iii, 22
Friar's Grove (Goldington), iii, 208 *n*
Friars Observants, i, 395
Friends, Society of, i, 341, 344, 345; iii, 9, 275, 279, 338, 414, 458
Frilford (Berks), i, 178, 188
Froghole Farm (Flitwick), iii, 288
Froissart, Will, iii, 418
Frowick, Eliz., ii, 360; Hen., ii, 360
Fruel, Will., iii, 92
Fruit, Will., iii, 278
Fruit-growing, ii, 139, 296
Fulbert, ii, 267 *n*
Fuller, Hen., iii, 449; John, ii, 253; Will., iii, 111; —, iii, 116
Fuller's earth, i, 12, 31; ii, 117; iii, 338
Fullerton, John, ii, 317; *see also* Foullerton
Fulthorpe (le Dale), Thos., ii, 227, 252
Fulwood, Charlotte, ii, 289; Thos., ii, 289
Fungi, i, 61-6
Furness, Martha, iii, 32; Rich., iii, 32
Furnival, Christina de, ii, 247; Gerard de, ii, 247
Furtho, Alice, ii, 224; Eliz., ii, 224; Will., ii, 224, 226
Fyler, Col., ii, 263
Fynaunce, *see* Finaunce
Fynderne, Alice, ii, 221; Mich., ii, 221; Will., ii, 212
Fyret, Joan de, i, 360 *n*
Fysshepenny, iii, 105
Fyssher, *see* Fisher
Fyson, G., ii, 198

Gadbury, Marg., ii, 233; Sir Rich., ii, 233
Gaddesden, Gt. (Herts), iii, 429
Gaddesden, Little, iii, 426
Gaddesden, fam., *see* Gatesden
Gadsey Brook, iii, 214, 215
Gale, Hen., iii, 167
Galing, fam., ii, 124
Galley Hill Camp, i, 273, 280; ii, 9, 10, 242
Galloway, Marg., Lady, iii, 297; Alan, Ld., iii, 297
Galloway, Devorgilla, iii, 297
Galoys, Joan, iii, 403; Walt., iii, 403
Galsey Wood (Bletsoe), iii, 40
Gambier, Rob., iii, 90, 331; Will., iii, 66; Mrs., iii, 66; fam., iii, 95
Gamble, John, ii, 171; Rev. J., ii, 209
Gannoch's Castle (The Gannichs), Tempsford, i, 282; ii, 251
Gaols, ii, 103
Garden Wood (Eaton Socon), iii, 189
Gardiner, Sir Edm., ii, 59; John, iii, 258
Gardner, Dan., ii, 163, 164; John, iii, 408; Kirkman, iii, 428
Garnault, Anne, iii, 21
Garners Close (Wootton), iii, 332
Garnons, Ant., iii, 196; Christina, iii, 196
Garrard, John, ii, 377; *see also* Gerard
Garstin, Lt.-Col. R., ii, 70
Garth, Jas., iii, 66
Garway, Hen., iii, 293; Thos., iii, 293
Gascelin, *see* Gastlyn
Gascoigne (Gascoyne, Gascoyn), Agnes, i, 358, 380 *n*, 390; Dorothy, iii, 15, 235; Eliz., iii, 231, 235; Geo., ii, 167, 342; iii, 231; Humph., i, 398; Jas., iii, 15, 235; Sir John, ii, 342; iii, 166, 184, 197, 235-6, 284; John, ii, 166; iii, 235; Marg., ii, 342; iii, 235; Sir Will., ii, 39; iii, 24, 137, 166, 181, 184, 187, 197, 235, 237, 270 *n*, 292; Will., iii, 97, 230
Gascon, Will. le, iii, 155
Gastlings (Southill), iii, 256
Gastlyn (Gascelin), Alice, iii, 257-8; Edm., iii, 257; Sir Geoff., iii, 257; Geoff., iii, 257-8; Joan, iii, 258; John, iii, 257-8; fam., iii, 211
Gastlyns (Gastlynbury), man. (Southill), iii, 257, 258; mkts., iii, 258
Gate-houses, iii, 1, 4, 7, 100, 432
Gatesden (Gaddesden), Aubrey, Lady, iii, 406; Audufus de, iii, 406; Joan de, iii, 406; Sir John, iii, 406; John de, iii, 406, 409; Marg. de, iii, 406; Pet. de, iii, 406; Will. de, iii, 406
Gateways, ii, 364, 365; iii, 25, 84, 279, 297, 351, 400, 439
Gaunt, John of, ii, 248; iii, 102
Gayer's Hill (Toddington), iii, 439
Gayhurst, ii, 187
Gearman, John, iii, 416
Gedney, John, ii, 365
Gell, Thos., iii, 91
Gemys, man. (Stagsden), iii, 97
Gemys, Christine, iii, 97; Eleanor, iii, 97; John, iii, 97; Rob. de, iii, 97; Will. de, iii, 97
Geoffrey, ii, 190; abbot of St. Albans, i, 359; ii, 178
Geology, i, 1-32, 45, 59, 62, 63
George, Agnes, iii, 375; Cuth., iii, 372
Gerard (Gerhard), Ann, iii, 392; Judith, ii, 281; Justus, iii, 392; Will., ii, 281
Gerey, *see* Gery
Gerhard, *see* Gerard
Germund, ii, 275
Gery, Alan, iii, 197 *n*; Anne, iii, 197; Chas., iii, 198; Geo., ii, 43; iii, 166; Hester, iii, 198; Rev. H. W., iii, 128; Rebecca, iii, 165, 301; Sir Rich., ii, 41; Rich., iii, 137, 165, 195, 197-8; Thos., iii, 166 *n*, 197 *n*; Walt., ii, 22; Will., ii, 22, 23, 43, 66 *n*; iii, 137, 155, 165, 166, 193, 195, 197, 198, 301; fam., ii, 66; iii, 194; *see also* Wade-Gery
Gibbard, John, iii, 94; L. S., iii, 91; Will., iii, 94; —, iii, 91
Gibbins, Rob., iii, 145
Gibbs, Sam., iii, 18 *n*; Thos., ii, 55
Giffard (Gifard), Agatha, i, 354; Geo., iii, 459; Kath., ii, 283; Walt., i, 354; ii, 210 *n*, 220, 221, 267, 269, 275; iii, 310, 314, 343, 459; *see also* Buckingham, earl of; Will., ii, 283; fam., ii, 71
Gilbert, earl, ii, 350; iii, 196
Gilbert, Sir Hen., ii, 140; Hen., ii, 262; Rich., iii, 80
Gilbertine order, i, 390-3
Gildesburgh, Rog. de, ii, 358
Gilds, i, 329-31; ii, 179, 214, 374; iii, 15-17, 201, 250, 268, 278, 347, 360, 366, 367, 415
Giles, A. J., ii, 198
Gill, Eliz., ii, 252; Fran., ii, 252; Marg., ii, 211
Gillingham, Rog., ii, 295, 374; iii, 238
Gilman, Rebecca, ii, 257; Rich., ii, 257

INDEX

Gilpin, Agnes, iii, 385; Esther, iii, 385; Kath., iii, 385; Margery, iii, 385; Pet., iii, 385; Pet. V., iii, 346; P. P., iii, 392, 417; Sir Rich., ii, 70; Rich., iii, 346, 348, 385, 392; Rich. T., ii, 66 *n*; iii, 407, 443; Rob., iii, 385; Col. R. T., ii, 69; Thos., iii, 348, 385; fam., ii, 66; iii, 386
Girtford, i, 173; ii, 201, 242; coins, ii, 242; man., ii, 244; Nonconf., ii, 242, 246; Rom. rd., ii, 4
Girton, Alice, ii, 182 *n*; iii, 278; John, ii, 99-100
Gisby, Rich., iii, 156
Gladley, iii, 336, 408; Grange mill, iii, 409; man., i, 376; iii, 405, 409, 422
Gladley Wood (Leighton Buzzard), iii, 408
Glasgow, ii, 139
Glass, i, 184, 299; ii, 217, 222, 226, 233, 258, 273, 303, 308, 312, 324, 326, 338, 372; iii, 6, 25-6, 47, 56, 59, 68, 76, 80, 108, 110, 121, 126, 135, 147, 151, 152, 156, 167, 169, 174, 188, 198, 202, 208, 217, 218, 226, 287, 295, 312, 344, 365, 423, 450; Rom., ii, 9, 12, 14
Glassbrook, Ann, iii, 195
Glatton (Hunts), ii, 214
Glaykyn, Will., iii, 297
Gledly, *see* Gladley
Glen, iii, 119
Glenister, Thos., iii, 320
Glintells (Bolnhurst), iii, 126
Gloucester, bp. of, i, 342 *n*
Gloucester, hon., iii, 36, 39, 54, 76, 78, 85, 110, 157, 175, 176, 219, 343, 387, 405, 421, 422
Gloucester, Isabel, ctss. of, iii, 390 *n*; dk. of, iii, 118; Thos., dk. of, iii, 156, 171; earls of, ii, 29, 30, 31, 32; iii, 36 *n*, 176 *n*, 390 *n*; Gilb., iii, 176, 362, 422; Rich., ii, 384; Rob., i, 314, 315 *n*; ii, 24, 350, 356, 393; Will., ii, 350, 356; iii, 393
Gloucester, Hugh of, iii, 446; Will. of, ii, 310
Gobion, Agnes, i, 359, 360; Eliz. de, ii, 381; Hawise, ii, 345, 381; Hugh (de), ii, 30, 345, 381; iii, 65; Isabel, i, 360; Kath., ii, 345, 381; Marg., ii, 345; Maud, ii, 345; iii, 65; Rich. (de), ii, 345, 346, 381
Godarvill, Joan de, iii, 257; Walt. de, iii, 257
Goddard, A. R., ii, 19 *n*; Joan, iii, 53, 60; Vincent, iii, 50, 60; Will., iii, 50, 60
Goddington (Oxon), ch. i, 357
Goderich, Hen. Grey, vsct., *see* Kent, dk. of
Goderiche, Eleanor, iii, 285; John, iii, 285; Rob., iii, 285; Will., iii, 285
Godfrey, ii, 341 *n*; iii, 133, 159, 278
Godfrey, Eliz., iii, 243, 246; Frances, ii, 378; Hen., ii, 241, 289; iii, 243, 244, 246; Jer. iii, 328; Joan, ii, 289; iii, 243; John, ii, 378; iii, 29, 198; Jos., iii, 91; Marg., i, 358; Mary, iii, 198; Nich., iii, 211; Rebecca, iii, 91; Rich., ii, 204, 289; iii, 243-4
Godmar, Mary, iii, 346; Walt., iii, 346
Godric, iii, 133
Godwer, Rich., iii, 451
Godwin (Godwine), iii, 78, 150, 248
Godwin, Will., ii, 248; Mrs., ii, 333; *see also* Goodwin
Goff, John, iii, 68
Gold Close (Pulloxhill), ii, 376
Goldentone, *see* Goldington
Golderon, iii, 51
Goldington, i, 296, 297 *n*, 324, 365, 380; ii, 94 *n*, 113, 154, 199, 200; iii, 31, 34, 109, 180, 202-09; adv., iii, 208; Bury Farm, iii, 205; char., iii, 209; ch., i, 315 *n*, 380; iii, 202, 207; inns, iii, 202; man., iii, 203-6; mills, i, 296, 297 *n*; iii, 206-7; Nonconf., iii, 202; place-names, iii, 202; sch., ii, 182; sheep, ii, 130; vicarage, i, 316 *n*, 341; iii, 202, 205, 208
Goldington, man. (Eaton Socon), iii, 191, 194
Goldington, Christiana de, iii, 205; Edwin de, iii, 206; Joan de, iii, 205; John (de), ii, 243; iii, 191, 194, 272, 306, 422; Joyce de, ii, 243; iii, 194; Mich. of, i, 381; Ralph de, iii, 205; Rog. (de), iii, 205, 206; Thos. de, iii, 206, 306; Wigain de, iii, 206; Will. (de), iii, 205-6, 306, 307
Goldington Bury, iii, 202; man., iii, 204, 205
Goldington Grange, iii, 202
Goldington Hall, iii, 202
Goldinton, *see* Goldington
Gold mine (Pulloxhill), i, 31; ii, 376
Goldsmith, Dan., ii, 270; Eliz., iii, 444; John, i, 398; Mary, iii, 444; Oliver, iii, 19; Rob., ii, 224; Thos., iii, 444; Will., ii, 382; iii, 259, 444
Goldstone (Goldston), Geoff., iii, 98; John, iii, 98; Pet., iii, 98; Rich., iii, 98; Thos., ii, 376; iii, 98
Goldyngton, *see* Goldington
Gonville and Caius Coll. (Camb), iii, 453
Good, Rich., ii, 157
Goodfellow, John, iii, 133
Goodman, Jas., iii, 275, 279; John, iii, 200
Goodwich Farm (Eaton Socon), iii, 190, 196
Goodwich, man., *see* Begwary
Goodwin, Edw., iii, 183; Florence, ii, 262; Geo., iii, 408; Hen., ii, 262; Thos., iii, 408; *see also* Godwin
Gooseberry-bush Hill (Luton), i, 173
Goosey, John, iii, 84, 119; J. G., iii, 119; Will., iii, 87, 122; W. G., iii, 119
Goosey Lodge (Wymington), iii, 117
Gore, Thos., ii, 63; —, iii, 20
Gorerong Woods (Podington), iii, 80
Gorges, Edw., Ld., iii, 83
Gorges, Sir Rob., iii, 83
Gorham, Geoff. of, iii, 350, 356 *n*
Gormanston, Chris., vsct., ii, 323; iii, 244; Kath., vsctss., ii, 323; iii, 244
Gosfield (Essex), iii, 266
Gosling End Green (Harlington), iii, 381
Gossard's Green (Cranfield), iii, 275
Gostwick, Alice, i, 335 *n*; Anne, iii, 21, 263, 266, 302; Dorothy, iii, 258; Chas., iii, 266; Sir Edw., iii, 203, 240, 264, 266; Edw., iii, 215, 258, 259; Eliz., iii, 203; Geo., iii, 240; Jane, iii, 203; Joan, Lady, iii, 247, 266; Joan, iii, 15, 22, 203, 204, 210, 212, 214, 296; Sir John, i, 331 *n*, 364; iii, 215, 216, 240, 247, 262, 263, 264, 266; John, i, 365; ii, 219, 220, 221, 266, 267; iii, 15, 22,
Gostwick (*cont.*)
37, 38, 184, 203, 204, 206, 207, 210, 212, 214, 225, 237, 263, 264, 296; Marg., iii, 203; Rob., iii, 253, 263, 266; Sir Will., ii, 59, 60 *n*; iii, 203, 210, 211, 239, 240, 263, 265, 266, 311; Will., ii, 219, 220; iii, 13, 15, 21, 203, 204, 212, 216, 253, 258, 263, 264, 266, 302, 311; fam., ii, 60; iii, 212, 213
Goswell End (Harlington), iii, 379
Goswood, John, ii, 333
Goude, Hen. C., iii, 368
Gould, T. C., i, 281; —, i, 306
Goushill, Eliz., ii, 340; Hadwisa de, ii, 355; Rich. de, ii, 231 *n*; Sir Rob., ii, 340
Gower, Ld., ii, 192
Gowran, Lady, ii, 61; iii, 272
Goyes (Goyz), Andr. le, ii, 220; John le, ii, 220; Thos. le, ii, 220; Will. de, iii, 299
Grace, John, i, 367 *n*
Grafton, Alex., ii, 127
Graham, Rich., iii, 32; W. B., i, 91
Graie, *see* Gray and Grey
Graies Bury (Henlow), ii, 281 *n*, 282
Grandim, Hugh, ii, 294
Grandison, Geo. V., vsct., ii, 347; John, vsct., ii, 347; Frances, vsctss., ii, 347; Mary, vsctss., ii, 347
Grange, Rich., iii, 278
Grange Farm (Colesden), iii, 219
Grange Farm-house (Haynes), ii, 342
Grantesden, Sim. of, i, 387
Grantham, Mary, baroness, ii, 332; Ld., ii, 327, 329
Grantmesnil (Grentmeisnil, Grantmaisnil), Adeliza, iii, 230, 231; Hugh de, ii, 21 *n*; iii, 144, 230, 293; Parnel, iii, 293
Granville, ctss., ii, 60 *n*; John, earl, ii, 341; Rob., earl, ii, 210, 341; iii, 293, 326
Grassineau, Jas., iii, 195
Graunson, fam., iii, 43
Graunt, John le, iii, 159
Grave, La, *see* Grovebury Priory
Gravel Pit Hill (Houghton Regis), ii, 8
Gravenel, Joan, ii, 230, 232; John, ii, 230, 232; Thos. de, ii, 230
Gravenhurst, Lower, ii, 41, 114, 306, 333-4, 336-8; adv., ii, 338; char., ii, 338; ch., i, 315 *n*, 380; ii, 337; man., ii, 334, 336; iii, 286, 418 *n*; ship-money, ii, 337
Gravenhurst, Upper, ii, 76, 114, 266, 306, 333-6; adv., ii, 335; chant., ii, 335; chap., i, 324; char., ii, 335; ch., i, 324 *n*, 331; ii, 334; man., ii, 333; iii, 286; Nonconf., ii, 335; sch., ii, 182
Gravenhurst, Elias of, ii, 336; Rog. of, i, 377
Graves (Greve, Greves, Greyves), Agnes, iii, 146; Edw., iii, 340; Rich., iii, 146; Thos., iii, 450; Walt., ii, 242, 244
Gravesend, bp., *see* Lincoln, bps. of
Gray (Graie, Graye), Ant., ii, 257; Chris., ii, 209, 229, 250, 343; iii, 58, 131, 218, 283, 325, 425, 438; F. H., iii, 386; Harry, ii, 332; Sir Hen., iii, 233; H. J. S., iii, 386; John, iii, 122; Mary, Lady, iii, 233; Miles, ii, 233, 254, 285, 303, 335; iii, 167, 200, 288, 378; Pet., iii, 321-2; Sibella, ii, 281; Walt., ii, 281; —, Mrs., iii, 386; *see also* Grey

Graynger, Marg., i, 393
Grazehill End (Ravensden), iii, 209
Great Englands field (Dunstable), iii, 350
Greathampstead, man. (Luton), ii, 350, 352 *n*, 358
Greathampstead Farm (Luton), ii, 358
Greathampstead Someries, man. (Luton), ii, 358, 364
Great Hayes Close (Wootton), iii, 332
Green (Greene, Grene), Andr. P., iii, 211; Edm., ii, 156, 160, 162; Edw., ii, 317; Edw. W. S., iii, 211; Eliz., iii, 462; Fran., iii, 19, 28; Sir Hen., iii, 443; Hen., ii, 316 *n*; iii, 92; H. H., ii, 138; John, ii, 266; iii, 92, 443; Jos., iii, 194; J. R., ii, 18 *n*; Kath., iii, 92; Sir Ralph, iii, 92; Ralph, iii, 92, 443; Rev. Rob., ii, 229; Rob., iii, 387; Rudd, iii, 181; Sir Thos., iii, 92; Thos., i, 403; iii, 92, 443
Greenacre, Isabel, iii, 129; John, iii, 129; Rich., iii, 129
Greene, *see* Green
Green End (Gt. Barford), iii, 181
Green End (Little Staughton), iii, 165
Green End Farm-house (Gt. Barford), iii, 181
Greene's Closes (Maulden), iii, 275
Greenfield (Grenfield), ii, 139, 326, 376; man., i, 370; ii, 376; mill, ii, 376; Nonconf., ii, 333
Greenfield (Grenefield), Sir Rich., iii, 340; Thos., i, 402; W. B., ii, 338; —, ii, 197
Greenlane, John, iii, 248
Greensbury (Grymsbury) Farm (Bolnhurst), iii, 124
Green Way (Dunstable), iii, 350
Greenway, Rich., iii, 361
Gregory, pope, ii, 29; iii, 278
Gregory, John, ii, 41; Rich., iii, 257
Grendon, Rob., iii, 126; Rog., iii, 126; Thos., iii, 126; Walt., iii, 126
Grene, *see* Green
Grenfield (Grenefield), *see* Greenfield
Grentmeisnil, *see* Grantmesnil
Grenville, Sir Bern., ii, 339; Sir Bevil, ii, 339; Sir John, ii, 339; Sir Rich., ii, 338
Gresham, Will. R., ii, 271
Gresley, Frances, Lady, iii, 282; Hawise de, iii, 339; Joan de, iii, 339; Rob. de, iii, 339; Sir Thos., iii, 282
Gretton (Northants), iii, 57
Greve, Greves, *see* Graves
Grey, Chas., earl, ii, 64 *n*; Ladies, ii, 380; Amabel, ii, 327; *see also* Grey of Wrest, ctss.; Eliz., ii, 267; Susanna, iii, 228 *n*; Lds. de, ii, 130, 231 *n*; Hen., iii, 144; Reg., ii, 283; Rich., ii, 267; Jemima, mchnss. de, ii, 327, 332; Hen., mqs. de, *see* Kent, duke of
Grey (of [de] Groby), Lds., ii, 44; iii, 248; Hen., ii, 231; Will., iii, 230
Grey (de Rougemont), Thos., Ld., ii, 37
Grey (of [de] Ruthyn), Lds., i, 352; ii, 35, 36, 147, 334; iii, 65; Edm., ii, 37, 327; Edw., ii, 323; Reg., ii, 327, 331; iii, 13; Rog., ii, 327
Grey (of [de] Wilton), Lds., i, 330; iii, 377; Arth., iii, 253; Hen., ii, 327; John, ii, 328; Reg., ii, 327
Grey (of Wrest), Amabel, ctss. de, ii, 61, 323, 327, 332, 377, 380; earls de, iii, 52; Thos. P., ii, 325, 332
Grey, Agnes de, ii, 326; iii, 105; Amabel de, ii, 332; Anne (de), ii, 290, 332, 334; iii, 300; Anne S. de, ii, 332; Ant., ii, 219; Cecilia, iii, 89; Chas., ii, 290, 332; Sir Edm., ii, 215; iii, 272; *see also* Kent, earl of; Eleanor, ii, 208, 283, 328; Eliz., iii, 78, 300; Florence de, ii, 328; Fran. T. de, ii, 327; Henrietta de, ii, 332; Sir Hen., ii, 290, 305, 327, 329, 333, 334; iii, 82, 272, 286, 310; Hen. (de), ii, 85, 263, 290, 327, 332, 335; iii, 64, 147, 443; *see also* Dorset, mqs. of; Humph., iii, 443; Jas., iii, 444, 446; Jane, iii, 443; Jemima de, ii, 332; Sir John de, i, 325 *n*, 326, 388, 390 *n*; John (de), ii, 30, 256 *n*, 263, 281 *n*, 283, 326, 327, 330, 332; iii, 51, 65, 66, 67, 78, 82, 85, 105, 147, 321, 326, 377, 444, 446; Pet., ii, 342; iii, 201, 259, 349, 367, 377, 443; Sir Reg. de, ii, 33, 281 *n*; iii, 2, 360; Reg. de, ii, 32, 208, 263, 267, 283, 322, 326, 328, 329, 336; iii, 51, 71 *n*, 82, 106, 229, 292, 300, 322, 396, 397; *see also* Grey (of (de) Ruthyn), Reg., Ld.; Sir Reynold de, i, 328; Rich. (de), ii, 263, 330; iii, 272; *see also* Kent, earl of; Sir Rog. de, iii, 396; Rog. de, ii, 146, 329, 331; iii, 65, 322 *n*; Simeon, iii, 156; Sim., iii, 154; Sophia de, ii, 332; Susan, ii, 290; iii, 156; Thos., iii, 300; *see also* Dorset, mqs. of; Will., iii, 444, 446; Zachery, iii, 296; —, bp., *see* Lincoln, bps. of; —, Lady, i, 330; ii, 37; fam., ii, 56, 146, 330, 331, 332, 377; iii, 144, 321
Grey Friars, *see* Friars, Grey
Greystock, Eliz., baroness, iii, 192; John, Ld., iii, 192; Ralph, Ld., iii, 192
Greystock, Alice de, iii, 192; Ralph de, iii, 192; Sir Rob., iii, 192; Will. de, iii, 192
Greyves, *see* Graves
Gribble, Geo., ii, 282, 283 *n*; G. F., ii, 285; G. J., ii, 281
Griffin, Thos., iii, 307; Walt., i, 336 *n*
Grigg, Alice, ii, 449; Geo., ii, 383, 449; Mich., ii, 43; iii, 315; Rich., ii, 383; Rob., iii, 425; Thos., iii, 311, 425
Grimbald, iii, 395
Grimbaud, *see* Grymbaud
Grimscote, man., i, 376
Grindall, archbp., ii, 159
Grivell, John, ii, 224
Grocers' Company (London), i, 329; iii, 40, 49
Groome, John, iii, 385; Will., iii, 385
Groos, Oliver, iii, 424
Gros, Will., iii, 219
Grossetête, bp., *see* Lincoln, bps. of
Grosvenor, earl, ii, 192
Grove, man., *see* Britens
Grovebury (La Grave, La Grove), man., iii, 404; farm, ii, 77, 80, 82, 83
Grovebury Priory (La Grave, La Grove), i, 319 *n*, 374 *n*, 403; iii, 10, 402, 429, 430
Groves, man., *see* Britens
Grovesfield, New (Bolnhurst), iii, 128
Grubb's Wood, ii, 187
Grym, Alice, iii, 125; Jas., iii, 125; Margery, iii, 125; Rob., iii, 125
Grymbaud, Joan, iii, 220; Mabel, iii, 39, 219, 220; Nich., iii, 220; Rob., iii, 220; Will., iii, 220
Grymsbury, man. (Bolnhurst), iii, 125, 126
Grymsbury Farm, *see* Greensbury
Grymstede, John, ii, 219; Kath., ii, 219; Rich. de, ii, 219; Thos. de, ii, 219
Gudmunt, iii, 125
Guînes, Bald., count of, i, 388; iii, 47, 74, 101, 103-4
Guînes, Rob., de, iii, 101
Guise, Rog., iii, 385; *see also* Gyse
Gullet Wood (Turvey), iii, 110
Gully Hill (Luton), rem., i, 172
Gullyng, Nich., iii, 7
Gunter, abbot, iii, 179
Gurdon, Ad., ii, 31
Gurdun, Geoff. de, iii, 133
Gurney, bar., iii, 390
Gurney (Gurnay), Hugh de, iii, 370, 372, 390, 391; Millicent de, iii, 370, 390, 391; Thos., iii, 304, 406, 458; —, ii, 234; iii, 349
Gustard, Falk, iii, 206; Rob., iii, 206; Will., iii, 206
Gutch, Will., ii, 93
Guthrum, iii, 345
Gutteridge, Rich., iii, 443
Gweldene, *see* Yelden
Gwyn, John, i, 338
Gwynneth, John, i, 333
Gylberd, *see* Gilbert
Gylys, Thos., i, 377
Gynwell, bp., *see* Lincoln, bps. of
Gyrth, earl, ii, 21 *n*
Gyrwa, South, i, 190
Gyse, Anselm (de), iii, 339, 340, 342; Beatrix de, iii, 339; Cath., iii, 339; John (de), iii, 339, 342; Marg. de, iii, 339; Reg. de, iii, 339; fam., iii, 340; *see also* Guise

Hacche, Le (Barton), ii, 309
Hacet, Ralph, iii, 343
Hache (Northill), *see* Hatch
Hackett (Hacket), Eliz., iii, 425; John, i, 338 *n*, 343; John A., i, 341; Nich., iii, 424; Rog., iii, 307; Thos., iii, 424, 425
Hacklete, Rich., ii, 255
Hadden, Harriet, iii, 281; Capt. Jas., iii, 281
Haddon, Will., iii, 427
Hagar, Eliz., ii, 252
Hagenes, *see* Haynes
Haighton, Rev. Rich., iii, 128
Hail Weston (Hunts), ii, 71; iii, 222
Haine, *see* Haynes
Hainton (Lincs), iii, 206
Hairum, John, ii, 78
Hakeneye, Kath. de, ii, 378; Rob. de, ii, 378
Haldenby, John, iii, 456; Margery, iii, 456
Hale, Bernard, ii, 357; Frances, ii, 385; Helen, ii, 95; John, ii, 224; iii, 159; Pain, ii, 224; Rich., ii, 224, 296; Rowland, ii, 224; Sir Will. de, ii, 309; Will, ii, 224, 296, 383; Will. E. B., ii, 224
Hales, Sir Jas., iii, 456; Marg., Lady, iii, 456
Halfhide, Geo., iii, 282; Mary, iii, 282

INDEX

Halford, Anne, iii, 57; Edw., iii, 57
Halfpenny, Bernard, ii, 346; Mary, ii, 346; Thos., ii, 346, 380
Halibred, Agnes, iii, 114; Rich., iii, 114 *n*; Will. iii, 114
Halifax, Geo., earl of, ii, 275; Geo., mqss. of, iii, 427
Haliwell, fam., *see* Halliwell
Haliwell Priory, i, 315 *n*, 323
Hall, C. P., ii, 146 *n*; Edw., iii, 374; Rev. Edw., iii, 342; E., iii, 457; Ralph, ii, 266; Rob., i, 370; Will., iii, 284
Hallaton (Leics.), Rom. rem., ii, 12
Hall End (Maulden), iii, 313, 314
Halliwell (Haliwell), Anne, iii, 373; Jane, ii 340; iii, 373; Rich., ii, 340, 373; fam., iii, 373
Halsal, *see* Halsoll
Halsey, Hen., ii, 360; Will., iii, 423
Halsey's Farm (Studham), iii, 429
Halsey Wood (Sharnbrook), iii, 89
Halsoll (Halsal), Hen., iii, 183; Jas., ii, 254
Halstead, Rob., iii, 115
Halsted, Alice, ii, 213; Isabel, ii, 213; Will., ii, 213
Halton, Eliz., iii, 97; John, iii, 97
Halton-super-Humber (Lincs), i, 353, 357
Halyday, Clarice, iii, 22 *n*; Maurice, iii, 22 *n*
Halydayes (Bedford), iii, 22
Hamelyn, Eliz., ii. 346; Ralph, ii, 346
Hamilton, duke of, ii, 54
Hammond, John, ii, 314
Hamo, iii, 67
Hampden, vsct., ii, 60; iii, 96; John, vsct., iii, 45; Thos., vsct., iii, 55
Hampden, Barbara, iii, 177; Edm., iii, 177; John, ii, 57 *n*; iii, 112, 177; Rich., ii, 57; Thos., iii, 177
Hampson, Leonard, iii, 432, 456; Nich., iii, 277; Rich., ii, 262
Hampton, Thos., iii, 300
Hamsey (Sussex), ii, 163
Hancock, Matth., iii, 133; Rev. Rob., iii, 251
Handborough (Sussex), ii, 162
Handforth (Ches.), ii, 340
Hanefeld, iii, 123
Hanger Wood (Stagsden), iii, 96
Hankin, Will., ii, 241
Hanley, Eliz., iii, 140
Hanmer, Col. H., iii, 401, 404; Sir W. E., iii, 404; fam., iii, 406, 407
Hannot, Sam., ii, 357
Hanscombe, Jas., ii, 299; Matth., ii, 40; Reg., ii, 297; Rob., ii, 297; Will., ii, 295; —, ii, 295
Hanscombe End, ii, 297
Hanscombe Lee, ii, 295 *n*
Hanslape, Rob., i, 385
Hanslope (Bucks), ii, 27, 28
Harcourt, Arabella de, iii, 231 *n*; Celia de, iii, 231; Hen. de, iii, 231; John de, iii, 122; Rich. (de), iii, 120, 231; Will. (de), iii, 120, 231
Harding (Hardinge, Herdyng), Anne, iii, 250; Cecilia, iii, 253; Eliz., iii, 243, 301; Hen., iii, 301; John, ii, 157, 315; iii, 253; Lewis, iii, 243; Rich., ii, 40; iii, 243, 250; Thos., ii, 266; Will., iii, 380
Hardings Place (Harlington), iii, 380
Hardingstone (Northants), i, 183 *n*
Hardwick (Kempston), iii, 302
Hardwick (Keysoe), iii, 136
Hardwick (Tilbrook), iii, 171, 172
Hardwick (Herdewyk, Herdwick, Herdwyk), Pet. de, iii, 168, 169 *n*, 172; Rich. of, i, 384; Will., iii, 92
Hardwicke, Phil., earl of, ii, 61, 327, 332
Hardwicke Bridge, iii, 329
Hare, i, 370; iii, 347
Hare, John, iii, 285; Marg., ii, 216 *n*
Harewelle, *see* Harrold
Harewode, *see* Harrold
Harewold, *see* Harrold
Hargrave (Northants), i, 393, 394
Hargrave, Edw., iii, 415
Harington, Isabel, Lady, iii, 89; John, Ld., iii, 89; Rob., Ld., iii, 89; Will., Ld., iii, 89
Harington, Cecilia, iii, 89; Eliz., iii, 89
Harringworth (Northants), i, 357
Harison, *see* Harrison
Harker, Prof., ii, 141
Harkett, Mary, iii, 294; Nich., iii, 294
Harleston, Ivo de, ii, 219; John de, ii, 219
Harlew, Ad., iii, 98
Harlewin, iii, 182 *n*
Harley, Edw., Ld., iii, 137
Harlington, i, 327 *n*, 366, 370; ii, 30 *n*, 43, 114, 133, 410; iii, 336, 379; adv., iii, 382; chants., iii, 382; char., iii, 382; ch., i, 185, 315 *n*, 333, 371 *n*, 372; iii, 381; crown property, iii, 271; deer pk., iii, 381; man., i, 377; iii, 379-81; mills, ii, 278; iii, 379-80; 'Rising Sun' inn, iii, 379; sch., ii, 182; vicarage, i, 327
Harlington, Dionisia de, iii, 419; John de, iii, 419; Rob. de, iii, 419; Walt. de, iii, 419
Harlington East End, iii, 381
Harlington Grange Farm (Streatley), iii, 379
Harlington Wood, iii, 381
Harlington Wood End, iii, 379, 380, 381
Harman (Herman), Fran. A., iii, 146; Joan, iii, 106; John, iii, 106
Harmer (Hermer), John, iii, 310, 313
Harne Chapel, *see* Chapel Herne
Harneys, Rog., iii, 427
Harpar, *see* Harper
Harpeden, Sir John, ii, 227 *n*
Harpenden, ii, 310
Harper, Alice, ii, 152, 158, 159, 172; Joan, ii, 161; John, iii, 171; Marg., ii, 156, 161; iii, 25; Margery, ii, 161; Rich., ii, 161; Sir Will., ii, 152, 156-62, 166, 172, 181 *n*; iii, 3, 19 *n*, 25, 31; Will., ii, 157, 360, 362; iii, 8, 22
Harpur, *see* Harper
Harris, Eliz., ii, 257; Fran., ii, 383; Hen., iii, 162; John, ii, 257; Mary, ii, 257; Rebecca, ii, 257; Sarah, ii, 257; Thos., ii, 383; iii, 162
Harrison (Harison), Alice, ii, 160; John, ii, 347; Rich., ii, 347; Will., ii, 279
Harrold, i, 305, 315 *n*, 316 *n*, 382, 394; ii, 92, 115, 133, 144, 147, 154; iii, 34, 49, 54, 63, 73, 114; adv., i, 388; iii, 66, 68; bridge, iii, 55, 63, 65, 74; char., iii, 68; coins, Rom., ii, 2; ch., i, 315 *n*, 317, 324 *n*, 344, 388; iii, 64, 67; hounds, ii, 188; ind., ii, 125; iii, 64; man., iii, 64-8; mkt. and
Harrold (*cont.*)
fairs, ii, 88; iii, 35, 64; mills, iii, 65; pk., ii, 147; iii, 65; place-names, iii, 64; Rom. rem., ii, 8; sch., ii, 182; iii, 64; vicar of, i, 317; woods, ii, 145; yeomanry, ii, 70
Harrold, Ralf of, i, 365
Harrold Hall, ii, 188; iii, 64, 66-7
Harrold Priory, i, 315 *n*, 349, 387-90, 395; ii, 91; iii, 24, 38, 52, 64-8, 101, 103, 333; prioresses, i, 317; iii, 22, 74, 113
Harrowden, i, 308, 312; ii, 153, 324; iii, 33, 51, 227, 234, 236, 237, 279; prehist. rem., i, 33, 145; iii, 234
Harrowden, Ernest, Ld., iii, 78; Thos., Ld., ii, 354; Will., Ld., iii, 201
Harston Club, ii, 191
Hart, Lady Jane, ii, 332; Rob., iii, 271 *n*
Harte (Hert), Will., iii, 30, 212
Harter, J. F. H., iii, 276; J. H., iii, 278; Steph. J. H., iii, 279; Walt. G., iii, 297; Walt. G. H., iii, 301
Harteshorne, fam., *see* Hertshorne
Harthill, ii, 375
Hartley, Will., ii, 296
Hartop, Chas., iii, 212
Hartshorne, man., *see* Caldecote, Upper
Hartshorne, fam., *see* Hertshorne
Hartshorne Farm (Ickwell), iii, 247
Hartwell (Hertewell), Abra., iii, 435; John de, iii, 144, 147; Rich., iii, 278
Hartwell Ground (Leighton Buzzard), iii, 415
Harvies Manor (Riseley), iii, 158, 159
Harvey, *see* Hervey
Haryson, *see* Harrison
Haselden, Alice, iii, 204; Anne, ii, 252; iii, 205; Benj., iii, 205, 208, 209; Cath., iii, 146, 205; Constance, iii, 208 *n*; Dorothy, iii, 205; Eliz., i, 357; iii, 146, 205, 209; Hugh, iii, 182, 204-6, 216; Jas., iii, 209; John, iii, 205; Marg., iii, 205; Mary, iii, 204, 205; Rob., ii, 252; iii, 204, 205, 208 *n*, 209; Thos., iii, 204; Will. iii, 204; fam., iii, 204
Haselfoote, Thos., iii, 255; Will., iii, 255
Haselhod (Sharnbrook), iii, 91
Hasells (Sandy), ii, 197
Hasilden, *see* Haselden
Hasleden, *see* Haselden
Haslewood, Edm., iii, 406; Joan, iii, 406-7; John, iii, 406
Haslingfield (Cambs), i, 179 *n*, 180
Hasselden, *see* Haselden
Hastings, Ada, ii, 211, 238; iii, 300; Anne de, iii, 229; Sir Hen. de, iii, 229; Hen. de, ii, 30, 31, 211; iii, 229, 300, 370; Isabella, iii, 48; Joan de, iii, 370; John de, ii, 238; iii, 229, 233; John Baron, iii, 300; Laur. de, *see* Pembroke, earl of; Sir Ralph, iii, 48, 51, 130, 229; Will. (de), iii, 229; fam., ii, 30; iii, 48
Hasuldene, *see* Haselden
Haswell, Sewel de, ii, 212
Hasylden, *see* Haselden
Hat and bonnet ind., ii, 101, 118-22
Hatch (Northill), iii, 242, 248, 250
Hatecrist, Will., iii, 58
Hather (Lincs), iii, 237
Hatley, Agnes of, ii, 215; Anne, iii, 182; Ellen of, ii, 215; Godf., iii,

Hatley (*cont.*)
240; John, iii, 182; Rob., iii, 182, 204, 208; Will., iii, 240
Hatley Port, *see* Cockayne Hatley
Hatton, Anne, iii, 381; Sir Chris., iii, 8, 109 *n*, 160, 220 *n*, 281 *n*, 303; Chris., i, 346; iii, 294; Jane, iii, 86; Jonas, iii, 381; Rich., iii, 349; Sir Thos., iii, 86
Haughton, *see* Houghton
Haukes, Cath., iii, 402
Haulsey, Will., ii, 222, 226
Haunce, *see* Haynes
Haunes, *see* Haynes
Haveningham, Will., iii, 404
Havering, John de, ii, 359; Lucy de, ii, 359; Rich. de, ii, 359
Haverings, man., ii, 350, 355 *n*, 359-60, 364 *n*, 366
Haveryngs, *see* Haverings
Hawburth, Will., i, 370
Haw End (Houghton Conquest), iii, 289
Hawes, John, ii, 40; Thos., iii, 25, 31-3
Hawkins, Anne, iii, 205, 209; Geoff., ii, 347; Geo., ii, 170; Isaac, iii, 306; Rev. John, ii, 347; John S., iii, 209; Mary, ii, 347; Rebecca, iii, 172; Rob., iii, 205, 209; Will., iii, 172, 173, 366
Hawksley, Rev. J. W., iii, 95, 142
Hawle, John, iii, 427
Hawnes, *see* Haynes
Hawnes Grange, *see* Haynes Grange
Hawte, Marg., Lady, iii, 456; Sir Will., iii, 456
Hawtt, Eliz., ii, 319; John, ii, 319
Haye (Hay), Jas., iii, 330; John (de la), ii, 359, 373; iii, 231; Matilda de la, ii, 309, 310, 359, 379; Nich. de la, ii, 359; Reg. de la, ii, 359; Rog. de la, ii, 359; Walt. de la, ii, 309, 310, 379
Hayes, man. (Luton), ii, 350, 359
Hayes, Gt. (Podington), iii, 80
Hayes, Little (Podington), iii, 80
Hayes, Will., iii, 140, 302
Hayes-Millar, R. C., ii, 199
Haynes, i, 318 *n*, 351 *n*, 352; ii, 42, 44, 66, 114, 306, 314, 338-44; iii, 289; adv., ii, 343; anct. pottery, ii, 8; chap., ii, 342; char., ii, 344; ch., i, 315 *n*, 378 *n*, 391-2; ii, 289 *n*, 343; iii, 289; deanery, i, 347; man., ii, 339-41; iii, 12; mill, ii, 341; Nonconf., ii, 344; poorhouse, ii, 104; sch., ii, 182; vicarage, i, 316 *n*; woods, i, 391
Haynes, Maj., iii, 383
Haynes Grange, man., i, 391-2; ii, 290, 341-3
Haynes Park, ii, 60, 147, 197, 338, 341, 344
Hays, *see* Hayes
Hayter, Anne, iii, 57; Will., iii, 57
Hayward, Tyler & Co., ii, 127
Haywood (Eversholt), iii, 375
Hazeldean, wood, i, 352
Hazelrigg, Sir Art., ii, 190, 191
Healing, J., ii, 199
Hearne (Chalgrave), iii, 347
Heath and Reach, ii, 117; iii, 336, 399, 400, 402, 417; chap., i, 341; iii, 414; char., ii, 182 *n*; ch., iii, 412; man., iii, 405; Nonconf., iii, 415; pop., ii, 114; sch., ii, 182; vicarage, iii, 414
Hecham, *see* Higham Gobion
Heghham, *see* Higham Gobion
Heldemar of Tournay, i, 388 *n*
Helder, Rob., iii, 282 *n*
Hele, John, iii, 189; Rev. Rob. H. S., iii, 125, 189; Thos., iii, 343
Helwell, Marg., iii, 386
Hemiestowe, iii, 120
Hemingford (Hemyngford), John de, iii, 137, 166, 194
Hemp, Alice, iii, 84; John, iii, 84
Hemp Land (Maulden), iii, 316
Hemyngford, *see* Hemingford
Hende, Joan, iii, 231
Hendon (Middlesex), ii, 375
Heneage, Anne, ii, 262; John, ii, 262; Geo., iii, 206; Geo. F., iii, 206, 209; Thos., ii, 262, 263, 265, 282
Henlow, ii, 97, 113, 225, 256, 260, 261, 268, 276, 280, 283, 285, 294, 304, 324, 326; iii, 69; adv., ii, 106, 285; char., ii, 285; ch., ii, 283; fishery, ii, 283; man., ii, 204 *n*, 283; mills, ii, 283; prehist. rems., i, 174; ii, 281; sch., ii, 182; vicarage, i, 316
Henlow End, i, 281
Henlow Grange, ii, 281
Henlow Grey, man., ii, 282, 283
Henlow Lanthony, man., ii, 281, 285
Henlow Warden, ii, 271, 281, 282, 283, 285
Henlow Zouches, ii, 225, 282
Henneage, *see* Heneage
Hennes, Will., iii, 134
Henry I, i, 349, 371; ii, 23, 88, 143; iii, 350, 352, 355, 356
Henry VIII, ii, 38-9
Henshaw, Hen., iii, 348
Hensman, Hen., iii, 57; Martha, iii, 57
Herbert, iii, 114, 233, 377, 423, 461
Herbert, Ld., iii, 173
Herbert, Auberon, *see* Lucas and Dingwall, Ld.; Florence, ii, 328; Geo., ii, 214; Rich., iii, 173 *n*; Sir Will., iii, 173, 364; Will., ii, 99
Herdewick, *see* Hardwick
Herdwick, *see* Hardwick
Herdyng, *see* Harding
Hereford, earls of, iii, 155, 166, 173; Humph., iii, 153, 156, 168, 171, 172; Ralph, iii, 276; Will., iii, 171
Hereford, Rob., bp. of, i, 371 *n*; Thos. Cantilupe, bp. of, ii, 32
Hereford, Cicely, ii, 257, 258; Eleanor de, ii, 257; Imbert de, ii, 257, 258; John de, ii, 257; Juliana, ii, 257; Margery of, i, 390; Reg. de, ii, 257; Rob. de, ii, 257
Hereford's Manor (Wrestlingworth), ii, 256, 257
Hereward the Wake, ii, 22
Herghetone, *see* Harrowden
Herle, Sir Will. de, ii, 334; iii, 276
Herlingdone, *see* Harlington
Herlyng, John, iii, 384
Herlyngdon, *see* Harlington
Herman, *see* Harman
Hermer, *see* Harmer
Hermits and anchorets, i, 349
Herne (Herne Grange, Herne Manor), iii, 438, 439, 442, 443
Herne (Heron), Frances, iii, 443; Fran., ii, 63, 307, 353; Hen., iii, 206, 209; Humph. de, iii, 442
Herne Farm, iii, 438, 439, 447
Heron, *see* Herne
Herrick, Thos., iii, 361
Herring's Green (Eastcotts), iii, 326
Hert, *see* Harte
Hertewell, *see* Hartwell
Hertford, Rich., earl of, iii, 135; Rog., earl of, i, 394
Hertford, Rich. of, i, 353
Hertshorne (Harteshorne), Eliz., iii, 84, 85; John, iii, 211; Kath.,
Hertshorne (*cont.*)
iii, 85; Thos., iii, 84; fam., iii, 247
Hervey (Harvey, Hervy), Ad., iii, 106; Agnes, iii, 158; Barbara, iii, 387; Charlotte, iii, 387; Dorothy, Lady, iii, 235, 237; Edm., iii, 281, 283, 302, 304, 328; Edw., iii, 387; Eliz., i, 358; iii, 107, 283, 388, 425; Rev. F. M., ii, 181 *n*; iii, 128; Sir Geo., iii, 15; Geo., ii, 289; iii, 97, 107, 158, 187; Sir Gerard, iii, 235, 237; Gerard, iii, 158 *n*, 187, 335; Helen, iii, 387; Hen., iii, 106; Isabel, iii, 154, 281, 283, 304; Sir Jarrate, iii, 237; Joan, iii, 106; John, ii, 54 *n*, 59, 66 *n*, 69; iii, 60, 107, 109, 147, 155, 158, 159, 187, 244, 245, 247, 250, 283, 331; Maj. John, ii, 70; John E. A., iii, 244-7; Marg., iii, 97, 283; Margery, iii, 283; Mary, ii, 289; iii, 106; Sir Nich., iii, 273; Nich., iii, 106; Oliver, iii, 107, 331; Osbert, iii, 106; Sim., iii, 154; Steph., iii, 107; Susannah, iii, 250; Will., iii, 106; Will. M., iii, 128; —, iii, 202; fam., ii, 66; iii, 104, 237, 283, 338
Hervy, *see* Hervey
Hesding (Hesdin), Ernulf de, i, 287 *n*; iii, 347, 439; Matilda de, iii, 439; Sibel de, iii, 439
Hesriche, Reg. de, iii, 428
Hesse, Anne, iii, 61; Jas., iii, 61
Heton, John, iii, 106, 173; Rich., iii, 173; Will., iii, 106, 173
Hettenlaia, *see* Cockayne Hatley
Hevingham, Lady Mary, ii, 342 *n*
Hewet (Hewett, Huet, Huett), Sir John, ii, 44; Marg., iii, 281; Margery, iii, 285; Mary, iii, 319; Rob., iii, 285, 286, 288; Thos., ii, 257; iii, 281; Will., iii, 286, 319; —, i, 335 *n*
Hewyns, Will., ii, 323
Hexton (Herts), ii, 72, 308, 313
Heydon, Ralf, iii, 221
Heydon Hall (Marston Moretaine), iii, 308
Heydon Hill (Marston Moretaine), iii, 308
Heyham, *see* Higham Gobion
Heyhoe, Thos., iii, 206, 209
Heyne, John, iii, 179
Heyward, Nich. le, i, 400
Heyworth, *see* Eyworth
Hibbert, Rob., ii, 357, 375
Hibernia, Walt. de, *see* Ireland, Walt. de
Hibbins, Rev. —, iii, 444
Hicchecok, Agnes, iii, 273; Will., iii, 273
Hicks, Mrs., iii, 446; — (vicar of Wrestlingworth), i, 345, 346
Hide, *see* Hyde
Higgins, Anna M., iii, 117; Chas., iii, 111, 114, 117; Chas. L., iii, 115, 117; C., ii, 193; F. C., iii, 102; F. G., iii, 104; Hen. L., iii, 111, 115 *n*; Gustavus F., iii, 51, 111, 116; John, ii, 60 *n*; iii, 109, 111; T. C., iii, 111, 116; Lt.-Col. Will. B., iii, 117; W. F., i, 135; Col., ii, 185 *n*; Miss, ii, 185 *n*; —, ii, 194; iii, 12, 117
Higham, John de, iii, 139 *n*; Nich. de, iii, 408
Higham Bury, ii, 376
Higham Ferrers (Northants), ii, 189; iii, 40, 128, 139, 143, 160, 171, 182

INDEX

Higham Ferrers College, iii, 92, 133, 181, 182
Higham Gobion, ii, 114, 306, 326; iii, 46; adv., i, 360, 376; ii, 347; char., ii, 347; ch., i, 315 *n*; ii, 346, 371 *n*; earthworks, i, 276, 277, 278; ii, 344; man., ii, 330, 344; mills, ii, 345, 346; Rom. rems., ii, 8, 344; vineyard, ii, 345
Higher Berry End (Eversholt), iii, 375
Higher Rads End (Eversholt), iii, 375
Highfield (Goldington), iii, 202, 208 *n*
Highlord, John, iii, 285, 292
Highwood (Luton), ii, 361
Hilier, John le, iii, 114; Margery le, iii, 114; Rob. le, iii, 114
Hill (Warden), ii, 43; iii, 254; chap., iii, 255; man., iii, 253
Hill (Hille, Hilles), Ad., iii, 159; Alice, ii, 331; iii, 315; Edw., iii, 315; Eliz., ii, 102, 330; Joan, iii, 167; John, ii, 257; iii, 315; Martin, iii, 342; Mary, iii, 315; Maud atte, iii, 428; Rich. (atte), ii, 159; iii, 220, 315, 428; Rog., ii, 330; Sarah, ii, 257; Thos. (atte), ii, 331; iii, 428; Will., ii, 331
Hillersdon, Anne, iii, 281; Dennis F., iii, 189, 281; Eliz., iii, 187, 205, 281, 304, 376; Guy, ii, 364; iii, 302; Harriet, iii, 281; John iii, 283; Marg., iii, 281; Mary iii, 283; Mich., iii, 302; Rich., iii, 187, 189, 205; Sarah, iii, 281; Sir Thos., iii, 376, 377, 386; Thos., iii, 187, 279, 281, 283, 376, 384; Will., ii, 170; iii, 187, 281, 304, 376; —, iii, 20
Hilles, *see* Hill
Hill Farm (Houghton Conquest), iii, 289
Hill Farm (Old Warden), iii, 253
Hill Foot End (Shillington), ii, 293
Hillgreen Farm (Cranfield), iii, 275
Hillingdon, Rog. de, iii, 220
Hillings, the (Eaton Socon), i, 297
Hills, the, earthworks (Meppershall), ii, 288
Hillsdown, Will., *see* Hillersdon, Will.
Hills End (Eversholt), iii, 375
Hills Plantation (Tingrith), iii, 435
Hilsden, —, ii, 44
Hilton, Ad., iii, 366
Hinchenbrook, Ld., ii, 64 *n*
Hind, John, ii, 180
Hinde, Morgan, ii, 337
Hindley, Mary, ii, 304
Hinton, Alice, ii, 363 *n*; Geo., ii, 363 *n*; iii, 325; Thos., iii, 325, 377; Walt., iii, 377
Hinwick, iii, 57, 80-85, 176; Rom. rem., iii, 82
Hinwick Hall (Hinwick Manor), iii, 83-5, 146
Hinwick House, ii, 122; iii, 81, 82
Hinwick Lodge, iii, 82
Hinxworth (Herts), ii, 214, 223, 225
Hipwell, Dan., iii, 80; fam., ii, 124
History, political, ii, 17-72; social and economic, ii, 73-116
Hitchin (Herts), ii, 53, 67, 72, 266, 276, 280, 286, 288, 304, 334, 348; ch., i, 356; iii, 454; Rom. rem., ii, 5, 9
Hithe, John, iii, 251
Hiz, riv., i, 28, 145; ii, 261, 280, 286
Hoare, Sir Hen., ii, 190
Hobard, Sim., ii, 296 *n*; Thos., ii, 296
Hobart, Sir Hen., ii, 295, 322; Hen., iii, 293
Hobbes (Hobbs), Alice, iii, 355; Eliz., ii, 281; Jane, ii, 281; John, ii, 281; iii, 359; Mary, ii, 281; Rich., iii, 386; Rob., i, 367, 369 *n*, 370; Thos., ii, 35, 89; iii, 355, 360; Will., iii, 119
Hobbes Edes (Shillington), ii, 295 *n*
Hobcote, Will., iii, 245
Hocclive, *see* Hockliffe
Hoccon, Walt. de, i, 401
Hocgganclife, man., *see* Hockliffe
Hocheleia, *see* Hockliffe
Hockeclyff, *see* Hockliffe
Hockley (Hockley in the Hole), *see* Hockliffe
Hockley, John, iii, 392
Hockliffe, i, 305, 400; ii, 40, 47, 66, 114; iii, 336, 344, 345, 348, 349, 368, 383, 384, 385, 421; adv., i, 401; iii, 385; chants., iii, 386; char., iii, 386; ch., i, 401; iii, 385; Hosp. of St. John, i, 349, 401, 402; inns, iii, 383, 435; man., iii, 383; Nonconf., iii, 383; place-names, iii, 383; Rom. rd., ii, 3; sch., ii, 182
Hockliffe Grange, ii, 66 *n*; iii, 383, 385
Hockliffe House, iii, 383
Hocton, *see* Houghton
Hoddesdon (Hoddesden), Sir Chris., iii, 403, 404, 405, 408, 411, 416; Ursula, iii, 404, 411; fam., iii, 414
Hodgkins, John, i, 332
Hodgson (Hogeson), John, ii, 204; Rob., iii, 436, 438; Thos., i, 370; —, ii, 170
Hodson, John, iii, 56, 68, 80, 103, 278
Hogens, John, ii, 325
Hogeson, *see* Hodgson
Hogg, Maj., ii, 188
Holand, John de, *see* Huntingdon, earl of, Sim. de, iii, 20; Thos. de, *see* Kent, earl of; *see also* Holland
Holbeche, Hen., bp., *see* Lincoln, bps. of
Holborn, ii, 159, 163, 165, 172
Holcot, i, 370; ii, 96, 114; iii, 175, 176, 321, 336, 386, 436; adv., iii, 388; char., iii, 388; ch., i, 315 *n*, 332 *n*; iii, 388; crown property, iii, 271; man., iii, 386; mills, iii, 386, 387; sch., ii, 184
Holcote, Joan de, iii, 173; Rich. de, iii, 173; Steph. de, iii, 153; Walt. de, ii, 334
Holcot Marston (Bucks), ii, 146
Holcot Mill Pond (Aspley Guise), iii, 338
Holcot Moor, house, iii, 386
Holcot Moors, iii, 386
Holcot Wood, iii, 386
Holcotwood Farm (Holcot), iii, 386
Holcrofte, —, iii, 326
Holcutt, *see* Holcot, Holcote
Holden, Thos., i, 340
Holderness, earl of, ii, 295
Holecote, *see* Holcot, Holcote
Holesgrove, Ellen M., ii, 285
Holewell, *see* Holwell
Holgyll, Will., iii, 158
Holland, earl of, ii, 53; Lady, iii, 269; Lady Mary, iii, 317; Lds., ii, 61; iii, 272, 291, 317, 318, 320; Steph., iii, 317
Holland, Sir John, iii, 427; Maud, ii, 328; Rob. de, ii, 328; *see also* Holand
Holloway, Benj., ii, 170
Holme, i, 308; ii, 201, 209, 211, 214, 215, 235, 248, 324; iii, 69, 260; chap., ii, 179; earthworks, ii, 210; mans., ii, 210, 234
Holme, Nichola de, iii, 260; Thos. de, iii, 260
Holme Mill Grange, iii, 259
Holme Mills, ii, 209; iii, 260
Holme-with-Langford, man., ii, 211, 234
Holt, Anne, Lady, iii, 411; Sir John, iii, 107; Rowland, iii, 107; Sir Thos., iii, 411; Thos., iii, 107;
Holwell (Great Holwell), i, 384; ii, 25, 113, 260, 261, 286, 297. adv., ii, 287; char., ii, 287; ch., i, 312; ii, 287; man., i, 312; ii, 286
Holwell, Little (Nether), ii, 260, 293, 294; man., ii, 296; mill., ii, 297
Holwell (Holewell), John de, ii, 296; Nich. de, ii, 296, 297; Pet. de, ii, 276 *n*; iii, 231 *n*; Rob. de, iii, 231; Sim. de, ii, 296; iii, 112, 113; Steph. de, ii, 296, 305; Walt. de, ii, 296; Will. of, ii, 296
Holwell Bury, i, 307; ii, 286, 296
Holwells, man., *see* South Mills
Holy Sepulchre, order of the, i, 349, 382
Holy Trinity, brotherhood of the, iii, 30
Holy Trinity, hosp. of (Northants), iii, 40, 43
Holy Trinity in the Wood, priory of the, *see* Markyate Priory
Holywell (Clapham), iii, 130
Holywell Priory (Midd.), ii, 221, 222
Home, Hen., i, 26 *n*
Home Wood (Eaton Socon), iii, 189
Honeydon, *see* Honydon
Honeywood, Matth., iii, 286; Rob., iii, 286
Honiton lace ind., ii, 123
Honnor (Honner, Honour), Hen., iii, 407, 413, 430; Jas., ii, 281 *n*; Jane, iii, 413; John, iii, 430; Mary, ii, 281 *n*; Thos., iii, 430
Honydon (Honeydon, Camoys), ii, 86; iii, 193, 197; farms, iii, 190, 195
Hoo, man., (Pertenhall), iii, 154, 155
Hoo, The (Kempston), iii, 297
Hoo, The (Wootton), iii, 328
Hoo, Thos., Ld., ii, 34 *n*
Hoo, Anne de, ii, 355; Eleanor de, ii, 355; Eliz. de, ii, 355; Isabella, ii, 355; Nich. de, ii, 289 *n*; Ralph de la, iii, 74; Rob. de, ii, 355, 360, 365; iii, 314, 315; Sir Thos., i, 400; ii, 36, 355; Thos. de la (atte), ii, 34, 35, 355, 365; iii, 315; Walt. de, ii, 289 *n*; Will. de, ii, 355
Hooburne, man., *see* Hayes
Hoobury, man .(Renhold), iii, 215, 216
Hoobury (Horbury), Eliz., iii, 14, 45, 215, 330; John de, iii, 14, 215
Hood, Anne, iii, 135; Rich., iii, 135
Hoo Farm (Wootton), iii, 329
Hoo Hill (Clifton), ii, 276
Hook, John, ii, 173
Hooks, the (Westoning), iii, 455
Hook Wood (Eaton Socon), iii, 189
Hope, Sir John, ii, 67
Hopton, Eleanor, iii, 422; Eliz., iii, 405, 422; Walt., iii, 405, 422
Hopworth, Dan. R., i, 368 *n*
Horbury, *see* Hoobury

Hordelhide, ii, 152
Hore, Thos., i, 398
Horepol, Rob. de, ii, 22
Horim, Alwin, ii, 328
Horle, Eva de, ii, 81 ; Rob., ii, 81
Horley, Rev. Edw., iii, 201
Horne, Anne, iii, 61 ; Thos., i, 398 ; Will., iii, 61 ; —, ii, 63 *n* ; 64
Horne Lane (Bed.), Angl.-Sax. rem., i, 186 ; Rom.-Brit. rem., ii, 5
Horsehill Farm (Harlington), iii, 379
Horsetails (Equisetaceae), i, 56
Horsley, iii, 63
Horthornes (Woburn), iii, 461
Horwodys (Cople), iii, 240
Hospitallers (Knights of St. John), i, 314 *n*, 315 *n*, 349, 373, 394, 396-8 400, 401, 402, 403 ; ii, 144, 204, 235, 277, 278, 288, 290, 305, 330, 362, 377, 379 ; iii, 23, 24, 31, 64, 75, 85, 90, 95, 107, 114, 135, 142, 143, 147, 154, 157, 158, 160, 165, 167, 176, 184, 190 *n*, 198, 200, 201, 212, 240, 245, 246, 258, 260, 264, 286, 302, 315, 318, 324, 332, 350, 376, 378, 383, 384, 385, 396, 420, 437, 444, 446
Hospitals, i, 396-403 ; iii, 6, 149
Hotofts, man. (Cople), iii, 240
Hotot, Isabel (de), ii, 321 ; iii, 271, 290 ; Joan, iii, 112 ; Juliana, iii, 112 ; Rob., iii, 98, 112 ; Thos., iii, 112 ; Will (de), ii, 321 ; iii, 112, 113 *n*, 271
Houghton, Ad., iii, 385 ; Hugh of, iii, 362 ; Isabel de, ii, 321, 324 ; iii, 271, 317 ; John, i, 319, 320, 348 ; ii, 29 ; Rebecca, iii, 385 ; Rob., i, 384 ; Will. de, ii, 321 ; iii, 271, 317
Houghton, brook, iii, 329
Houghton Conquest, ii, 66, 115 ; iii, 14, 267, 270 *n*, 288-96, 373, 389, 393 ; adv., iii, 295 ; char., ii, 180 ; iii, 296 ; ch., iii, 273, 294, 381 ; crown property, iii, 271 ; hayward of, ii, 86 ; man., ii, 147 ; iii, 290 ; man.-house, iii, 289 ; mills, iii, 289 ; Nonconf., iii, 296 ; pk., ii, 147 ; iii, 290 ; place-names, iii, 290 ; poorhouse, ii, 104 ; sch., ii, 180, 182
Houghton Franchise, iii, 295, 296
Houghton Gildable, iii, 295, 296
Houghton Grange, man., iii, 291, 293
Houghton Hall, iii, 367, 368, 389
Houghton House ii, 61, 64 ; iii, 289, 290
Houghton Lodge, ii, 41
Houghton Regis, i, 174 ; ii, 102, 114, 151, 314 ; iii, 336, 337, 350, 351, 352, 355, 368, 372, 389-93 ; adv., i, 314 ; iii, 393 ; chant., i, 329 ; ii, 150, 151 ; iii, 391, 394 ; char., iii, 394 ; ch., i, 311, 314, 315 *n*, 329 *n*, 332 ; ii, 150, 151 ; iii, 392 ; gild, i, 330 ; grange, iii, 394 ; hayward of, ii, 86 ; hound money, ii, 143 *n* ; ind., iii, 390 ; man., ii, 23, 150, 178 ; iii, 370, 371, 390 ; mills, iii, 389 ; Nonconf., iii, 389 ; place-names, iii, 390 ; prehist. rem., i, 146 ; Rom. rems., ii, 8 ; schs., ii, 150, 151, 156, 182 ; iii, 394 ; springs, i, 19 ; vicarage, i, 316 *n*, 341
Houghton Regis, ldship. of, i, 371, 372, 376
Houghton Regis, Upper, iii, 352, 389
Houlden, Rev. —, iii, 29 *n*
Hour-glass, iii, 47, 266
Houston, R., ii, 265
Houstone, *see* Houghton Conquest and Houghton Regis
Houton, *see* Houghton Regis
Hoveden, Rob., iii, 424
Hovell, Le, close (Wootton), iii, 331 *n*
Howard, Lady Lucy, iii, 441 ; Lady Mary, ii, 347, 382 ; Edw., Ld., ii, 347, 382
Howard, Chas., ii, 138 ; Sir Fred., ii, 66 *n* ; iii, 6 ; Geoff., ii, 66 *n* ; Harrold, ii, 66 *n* ; Jas., ii, 66 *n*, 126 ; iii, 9, 128, 130 ; Jas. H., iii, 297 ; John, ii, 65, 66 *n*, 103, 108, 125, 126 ; iii, 5, 7, 8, 20, 30, 87, 233, 234, 238, 285, 383 ; *see also* Norfolk, duke of ; John C., iii, 238 ; Lucy, ii, 277 ; Marg., ii, 340 ; Phil., iii, 192 ; Sir Rob., ii, 340 ; Thos., *see* Surrey, earl of, and Norfolk, dk. of ; Will., *see* Stafford, visct.
Howard Villa (Cardington), iii, 233
Howbury Hall (Renhold), ii, 65, 66 *n* ; iii, 214, 215, 216
Howe, vsct., iii, 444
Howe, Will., iii, 313 ; —, ii, 15
Howe and Pertenhall, man. (Pertenhall), iii, 154, 155
Howell, Jos., ii, 317, 319
How End, man. (Houghton Conquest), iii, 293
Howgill, Rob., iii, 266
Howland, John, ii, 359
Howlett, —, ii, 25 *n*
How Wood (Stagsden), iii, 96
Hubald, Hugh, iii, 138, 159
Huckell, Agnes, ii, 285 *n*
Huddleston, Sir John, ii, 382 ; Will., ii, 382
Hudibras' Hole (Cople), iii, 238
Hudnall, man. (Studham), iii, 427
Hudson, John, ii, 204 ; Will., ii, 204
Huet, Huett, *see* Hewet
Hugate, Will de, i, 391, 393
Hugeford, *see* Huggeford
Hugesson, Sir Will., iii, 219
Huggeford (Hugeford), Alice, iii, 224 ; Margery, iii, 50, 211, 224, 330 ; Sir Will., iii, 50, 330 ; Will., iii, 50, 211, 224
Huggyns, Jane, ii, 359 *n* ; Will., ii, 359 *n*
Hugh, St., *see* Lincoln, Hugh of Avalon, bp. of
Hugh, ii, 282, 283, 326, 383 *n* ; iii, 46, 113, 223 ; archd. of Beds, i, 313 ; monk, i, 364 *n*
Hughes, Isaac, iii, 372
Hulcote, *see* Holcot
Hulier, Pet., iii, 146
Hull, Rev. Rich., ii, 305 ; Will., iii, 156
Hulls (Pegsdon), ii, 295 *n*
Huls, Will., ii, 305
Hulston, John, ii, 245
Humberdale, iii, 60, 144, 146
Humbershoe, ii, 114, 314, 318 ; iii, 362 ; chap., i, 318 *n*, 326 *n* ; man., ii, 318
Humbrichesho, *see* Humbershoe
Hume, Sir Patrick, ii, 217, 218
Humphrey, iii, 90
Humphrey, Anne, ii, 385 ; John, iii, 427 ; Matilda, iii, 427
Humphreys, Rev. —, ii, 168 ; —, ii, 257
Hunderigg (Bucks), chap., i, 318
Hunderigg, Thurstan of, i, 371 *n*
Hundon, Thos., ii, 236
Hunesdone, *see* Hunsdon
Hungate, Thos., iii, 454
Hunger, John, iii, 95
Hungerhill (Marston Moretaine), iii, 308
Hungerhill Spinney (Podington), iii, 80
Hunsdon (Hunesdone), ii, 154
Hunsdon, Lds., Geo., iii, 314 ; Hen., iii, 314 ; John, iii, 314
Hunstanton Convalescent Home, ii, 246
Hunt (Hunte), Anne, iii, 220 ; Eliz., iii, 220 *n* ; Jane, iii, 416 ; Mary, iii, 220 ; Rog. (or Rob.), iii, 220 ; Thos., ii, 327 *n* ; iii, 220 ; Will., iii, 220, 448
Hunter, Geo., i, 334
Huntercombe, Ellen, ii, 255 ; Walt., ii, 255 ; Will. de, ii, 255
Huntingdon, i, 294 *n*
Huntingdon, hon., i, 387 ; ii, 30, 210, 226, 238, 246, 247 *n*, 255 ; iii, 23, 42, 46, 59, 61, 64, 126, 134, 150, 166, 195, 234 *n*, 240, 260, 280, 290, 297, 314, 326
Huntingdon, archds., i, 324, 334 *n*, 397 ; priors, ii, 219 ; iii, 134, 168, 169
Huntingdon, ctsses. of, ii, 36 ; Constance, i, 388 *n* ; Judith, wife of Earl Waltheof, *see* Judith, ctss. ; Maud, ii, 237 ; earls of, iii, 16 *n*, 74 ; David, iii, 195 ; Hen., i, 388 ; iii, 102 ; John, ii, 210, 237, 238 ; iii, 101, 102 ; Sim., ii, 255 ; Tosti, ii, 237 ; Waltheof, ii, 21 *n*, 22, 155, 237 ; iii, 280, 338, 408
Huntingdon, Christine of, i, 358, 359 ; Hen. of, i, 313 ; ii, 24 *n* ; Rob. de, iii, 194
Huntingdonshire, lace ind., ii, 123 ; land measurement, ii, 77 ; wool ind., ii, 91
Huntingfold, Godf. de, iii, 247 ; Hen. de, iii, 247 ; Joan de, iii, 247 ; Sibil de, iii, 176 *n* ; Walt. de, iii, 247
Hurdlow (Derb.), i, 181 *n*
Hurley, John, Ld., iii, 441
Hurley, Thos., iii, 293
Hurst, Will. de, i, 386 *n*
Husborne Crawley, ii, 114, 324 ; iii, 308, 320, 394-99, 458 ; adv., i, 376 ; iii, 398 ; char., iii, 398 ; ch., i, 315 *n*, 332 *n*, 371 *n* ; iii, 397 ; crown property, iii, 271 ; man., i, 377 ; iii, 395 ; mills, iii, 394 ; sch., ii, 183 ; treasure trove, iii, 395 ; vicarage, i, 316 *n*
Huse, Geoff. de la, iii, 57 ; Godf. de la, iii, 58 ; Thos. de la, iii, 57, 85
Huskey, J. R. T., iii, 146 ; Rich., iii, 146
Husseburne Crawel, *see* Husborne Crawley
Husy, Sir John, iii, 272 *n*
Hutchinson, Eliz., iii, 251 ; John, iii, 12 ; —, ii, 207
Hut-circles, i, 270
Hutton, Will., iii, 276
Huxley, Eliz., iii, 376 ; Jas., iii, 281 ; Sir John, iii, 371 ; John, iii, 371, 372, 376, 407 ; Sarah, iii, 408 ; Thos., iii, 372 ; Will., ii, 158
Hyde, East and West, ii, 306, 308, 348, 349, 350, 359, 360, 374 ; chs., i, 346 ; ii, 374 ; mans., ii, 350, 357, 363 ; mill, ii, 366
Hyde, La, man. (Upper Gravenhurst), ii, 334
Hyde, The, man. (Studham), iii, 427-9

INDEX

Hyde (Hide), Agnes de la, ii, 357; Alan de, ii, 357; Aylward de la, ii, 357 *n*; Fulk de la, ii, 357; Hawisia de, iii, 429; Hen. de la, ii, 357; John, ii, 310; iii, 374 *n*; Maude, iii, 287; Petronilla, ii, 357 *n*; Rog. de la, ii, 357; Thos. de la, ii, 357, 359; Walt. de, ii, 357; Will., iii, 118, 429
Hyde Aynel, West, man., ii, 350, 360
Hyde mill (Luton), ii, 357 *n*, 366
Hydewood (Studham), iii, 429
Hylston (Ilvestone), Rich., i, 398
Hyndeman (Hyneman), Rich., i, 398, 399; ii, 332
Hynton, *see* Hinton

Ibbot, —, iii, 104
Iberians, i, 158-9
Iceni, the, iii, 176 *n*
Ickleford (Herts), ii, 287, 304
Icknield Way, i, 159, 161, 173, 176, 269, 280; ii, 3, 7, 17, 18, 23, 314; iii, 350, 351, 356, 390, 448
Ickwell, i, 394; iii, 245, 246; fair, iii, 246; man., i, 394; iii, 245
Ickwell Bury, ii, 66 *n*; iii, 242, 244, 246
Ickwell Green, iii, 245
Ickwell House (Northill), iii, 242, 245
Idell, John, ii, 281, 281 *n*
Ilefeulde, Will. de, iii, 173
Illyngworth, Geo., iii, 6; Rich., iii, 6
Ilvestone, *see* Hylston
Impey (Impie, Ympie), Sam., iii, 385; Thos., ii, 40; iii, 346, 348, 385
Implements, bronze age, i, 169; Celtic, i, 170; ii, 4; neolithic, i, 30, 31, 161-167; ii, 308; iii, 350; palæolithic, i, 29, 30, 145-6, 151-159, 171; ii, 251, 314, 348; iii, 36, 234, 297, 350; post-glacial, i, 28; Rom., i, 172; ii, 7, 12-15
Incent, John, ii, 157
Inclosures, ii, 96
Industries, ii, 117-27
Inge, Edw., ii, 315; Fremund, iii, 452; Isolda, iii, 452, 453; Joan, ii, 336; iii, 449, 452; Marg., iii, 452; Rich., ii, 316; Thos., iii, 252, 430, 449; Sir Will., ii, 285; Will., i, 325 *n*; ii, 336; iii, 437, 449, 452, 453, 454
Ingewar, ii, 226
Ingleton, Geo., iii, 91; Joan, iii, 91; Rob., iii, 91
Inglis, Cath., iii, 418; Mary, iii, 421; Sir Hugh, iii, 418; Hugh, iii, 417; Mary L., iii, 421; Sir Rob., ii, 66; Sir Rob. H., iii, 421, 423; Rob. H., iii, 419; —, Lady, iii, 419
Ingram, Rob., iii, 154
Inlonde (Southill), *see* Ireland
Inns, John, ii, 224
Inscriptions, ii, 218, 233, 254 *n*, 266, 273 *n*, 275, 287, 299, 324, 331, 332, 338, 343, 359, 372, 373; iii, 25, 27, 28, 39, 47, 53, 75, 76, 86, 103, 120, 127, 135, 138, 143, 149, 179, 185, 188, 193, 235 *n*, 241, 250, 266, 273, 289, 295, 307, 319, 328, 340, 351, 366, 373, 388, 411, 425, 434, 438, 450; Roman, ii, 6, 7
Insectivora, i, 139
Insects, i, 71-88
Inskip, Thos., ii, 11, 13, 14
Inwards, R. W., iii, 306
Inwen, Sarah, iii, 332; Thos., iii, 332
Inwode, close (Ravensden man.), iii, 210
Inwood (Haynes), ii, 341, 342
Ion, *see* Gravenhurst, Lower
Ion House (Lower Gravenhurst), ii, 337
Irchester (Northants), i, 184
Ireland (Southill), iii, 256
Ireland, Walt., i, 325 *n*; iii, 132, 136
Iremonger, Frances, iii, 406; Humph., iii, 406; John, iii, 406; Judith, iii, 406; Marg., iii, 406; Martha, iii, 406; Thos., iii, 368, 406; Will., iii, 406, 409
Ireton, Col., ii, 51, 52; iii, 4
Iron Age, i, 170, 182; interments, i, 182; vases, i, 170, 174
Isaac, Edw., iii, 207
Isabella, dau. of Edw. III, ii, 39; queen, ii, 33; iii, 16, 353
Isabella 'inclusa', i, 350
Isham, John, iii, 416
Islip (Islep), Sim. de, iii, 125; Will., iii, 91, 92
Ispannia, Rob. de, ii, 267
Issoudun, Alice, ii, 233 *n*; Maud, ii, 223 *n*; Ralph de, ii, 223 *n*
Ivel, canal, ii, 276
Ivel, riv., i, 28; ii, 71
Ivell, Thos., iii, 248
Ivinghoe (Bucks), iii, 368
Ivo, iii, 144
Ivory, John, ii, 286; Rob., ii, 286; Will., ii, 286
Ivota, i, 354 *n*; iii, 283
Ivri, Acard de, iii, 338; Ralph de, iii, 339; Reg. de, iii, 339

Jackman, Clem., iii, 406; Eliz., iii, 407; Gabriel, iii, 407; John, iii, 406; Reg., iii, 407; Rob., iii, 155; Will., iii, 406, 407, 411
Jackman's Farm (Goldington), iii, 202
Jack's Lane (Turvey), iii, 114 *n*
Jackson, John, ii, 262; Rob., ii, 204; Lt.-Col. S., ii, 70; Rev. Will. H., iii, 100
Jacob, iii, 363
Jacobs, R., ii, 198
Jakes, Thos., iii, 448
James I, king, ii, 40; iii, 42, 107, 289, 290
James, Giles, ii, 163, 164; —, ii, 120
Janaway, Thos., ii, 241
Janyns, *see* Jennings
Jarman, Eliz., iii, 428; Will., iii, 429; *see also* Jermayn
Jarpenville, Will., iii, 137
Jeeves, Messrs., ii, 118
Jefferies (Jeffries), John, ii, 255; iii, 109; Rob., iii, 109; Thos., iii, 109
Jempsis, man., *see* Gemys
Jenkin (Jenkyn), John, iii, 335; Rob., ii, 310
Jenkins, —, ii, 194; iii, 202
Jenkinson, Ant., iii, 332
Jenkyn, *see* Jenkin
Jenney, Edm., ii, 296
Jennings (Janyns), John, iii, 442; John W., iii, 381; Sir Steph., ii, 159; —, ii, 133
Jermayn, Thos., iii, 154; *see also* Jarman
Jermye (Jermy), Eliz., ii, 323; iii, 244; Fran., ii, 323; iii, 244
Jervis, Eliz., iii, 384; Will., iii, 384
Jessop (Jessopp), Thos., i, 342
Jeune (Jeuene, Juvene, Juveni, Juvenis), Agnes le, ii, 318; Barth. le, ii, 32, 318; Giles le, ii, 318; Isabella, ii, 318; John de, ii, 232; iii, 358, 457; Rich., ii, 318; iii, 362; Thos. de, ii, 232
Jewelsbury Manor, *see* Gravenhurst, Upper
Jews, i, 321; iii, 338, 363
Jobson, Sara, ii, 358; Stafford, ii, 358
Joce, John, iii, 248; Rob., iii, 248; Walt., iii, 286; Will., iii, 248; *see also* Joyce
John, king, iii, 352
John, parson of Haynes, ii, 289 *n*; the smith, iii, 383
John of Gaunt's Hill (Sutton Park), i, 300
Johns, Phil., ii, 40
Johnson, Anne, ii, 277; iii, 441; Cath., iii, 418; Fran., ii, 99; Geo., iii, 325; Sir Hen., ii, 277; iii, 441; Hen., iii, 418; Dr. Jas., iii, 87, 328; Jerome, ii, 335; John, ii, 156; Jos., iii, 418; Martin, ii, 118, 349 *n*; Mary, ii, 378; Rich., iii, 442, 454; Rob., iii, 424; Sam., iii, 257; Thos., ii, 378; iii, 307, 418, 448; Will., ii, 39; iii, 408, 418; —, iii, 125, 323
Jolliffe (Joliffe), Ann, iii, 66, 68
Jones, A. O., ii, 199, 200; Chas., iii, 307; Griffith, iii, 202; Rich., iii, 307, 415; Rowland, ii, 199
Jordan, iii, 155
Joyce, Rob., ii, 316; R., ii, 199; Thos., ii, 43, 344; *see also* Joce
Joye (Joy), Will., ii, 155; iii, 30, 215 *n*
Judd, Sir Andr., ii, 157
Judith, ctss., i, 313, 353; ii, 153, 210, 211, 216, 226, 237, 239, 246, 247, 277; iii, 42, 46, 47, 59, 61, 64, 92, 96 *n*, 126, 150, 195, 229, 234 *n*, 236, 240, 260, 280, 297, 302
Julyan, Thos., ii, 377; iii, 126; Rich., iii, 126
Jurden (Jurdon), Hen., iii, 226; Will., iii, 121, 325
Juvene (Juveni, Juvenis), *see* Jeune

Kadington, *see* Caddington
Kancia, Jas. de, iii, 246; Thos. (de) (of), iii, 246, 248; *see also* Cantia
Kane (Cane), Barbara, ii, 289; Rich. de, ii, 321
Kantia, *see* Cantia
Karleton, *see* Carlton
Karun, fam., *see* Carun
Kateden, *see* Caddington
Katherine, *see* Catherine
Kaye, Cecil W., ii, 177
Keale, Sybil, iii, 144
Keaynsham, *see* Keynsham
Keblewhite, John, iii, 376 *n*
Kebyle, Will., ii, 226
Keeble, Geo., iii, 264, 266; Jas., iii, 264; Messrs., iii, 240
Keeley (Wootton), iii, 328, 329, 331
Keeling (Kelyng), Antelminelly, ii, 270; Sir John, iii, 258, 261; John, ii, 270; iii, 261; Serjeant, ii, 55, 56
Keene, Jas., iii, 76, 241, 242, 414, 420; John, ii, 229; iii, 283, 288; —, iii, 334
Kelway, Rob., ii, 151
Kelyng(e), *see* Keeling
Kemble, J. M., i, 184
Kemhestun, *see* Kempston
Kemmeston, *see* Kempston
Kempston, i, 354; ii, 21, 30, 44, 70, 96, 115; iii, 21 *n*, 23 *n*, 251, 267, 284, 290, 296, 302, 308, 326, 333,

Kempston (*cont.*)
335; adv., iii, 304; A.S. rems., i, 176, 177, 178, 179, 180, 181, 183, 184, 185, 188, 189; iii, 297; char., iii, 305; ch., i, 315 *n*, 357; iii, 297, 303, 304; man., ii, 21 *n*; iii, 297; manuf., ii, 127; mill, iii, 297; Nonconf., iii, 297; palæolithic implements, i, 145, 162, 165, 174; iii, 297; Rom. rems., ii, 8; iii, 297; sch., ii, 183; iii, 297, 305; vicarage, i, 316 *n*
Kempston, Geo., iii, 216; Will. (of), iii, 23, 216
Kempston Borne, iii, 304
Kempston-Daubeny, man., iii, 297, 298, 299, 304
Kempston Greys, man., *see* Kempston Hastingsbury
Kempston Hardwick, iii, 297, 299, 300, 301
Kempston Hastingsbury, iii, 300, 301; mill, iii, 303
Kempston Wood, iii, 329
Kempton, ii, 139
Kendale, Beatrix de, ii, 256 *n*, 354; Edw. de, ii, 256, 354, 357; Eliz. de, ii, 256; Isabella de, ii, 256 *n*; Jordan de, ii, 356; Marg., ii, 255, 256; Rob. de, ii, 255, 328, 354, 356; Thos., ii, 354
Kendall, Anne, iii, 301; Rob., iii, 301
Kendals man. (Wrestlingworth), ii, 255, 256, 257; mill, ii, 256 *n*
Kenninghall (Norf.), i, 183, 189
Kensington, iii, 368
Kensworth, ii, 3, 71, 314; iii, 367, 368, 390 *n*, 426; man., ii, 23; prehist. rem., i, 166; Rom.-Brit. rem., ii, 1, 8; sch., ii, 183
Kensworth Lynch, ii, 3
Kent, ctsses. of, ii, 327; Amabel, ii, 322, 324, 345; Arabella, ii, 332; Eliz., ii, 261; Joan, iii, 101; Marg. iii, 339; Mary, ii, 332; Susan, iii, 232; Jemima, dchss. of, iii, 66; dks. of, ii, 62, 337, 376 *n*, 377, 378, 379, 380; iii, 66, 68; Hen. Grey, ii, 327, 332; earls of, i, 335 *n*; ii, 44, 324; iii, 16 *n*, 65, 290, 321, 323, 326; Ant., ii, 56, 290, 325, 327; Chas., ii, 327, 330, 337; iii, 228, 232; Edm., ii, 37, 283, 327, 331; iii, 3, 101, 272; Geo. ii, 37, 267, 296 *n*, 327, 332; Hen., ii, 61, 261, 283, 305, 327, 329, 330, 332, 334, 337; iii, 65, 105, 229, 396; Hub. de Burgh, ii, 283; Reg., ii, 327; Rich., ii, 37, 266, 322, 323, 327; iii, 396, 436; Thos. de Holand, iii, 101
Kent, Edw., ii, 285; iii, 243; Eliz., iii, 243; Thos., ii, 285, 378, 379, 380; fam., iii, 194
Kentish, Thos., ii, 270
Kentwode, Reg., iii, 230
Kerdinton, *see* Cardington
Kerdyngton, *see* Cardington
Kersey, Joan de, iii, 292; Rich. de, iii, 292
Kershaw, J. C., ii, 198
Keston, Thos. de, ii, 355
Ketenho, ii, 357 *n*
Kettell, John, iii, 340
Keynes, Alice, ii, 346, 379; Christina, ii, 346, 379; Eleanor de, iii, 272; Emma, ii, 346, 379; Joan de, ii, 346; Margery de, ii, 346, 379; Will. de, ii, 346, 378 *n*, 379
Keynsham, Anne, ii, 252; Eliz., ii, 252; Geo., ii, 40, 252, 253
Keyrun, *see* Carun
Keysoe, i, 297, 308; ii, 115, 246; iii, 123, 128, 136-139, 153; adv., iii, 139; char., iii, 139; ch., i, 315 *n*, 392; iii, 138; earthworks, i, 305, 306; iii, 136; man., iii, 14, 136; mill, iii, 136; rectory, i, 393; sch., ii, 183; vicarage, i, 316 *n*
Keysoe Bury (Berrysted), man., iii, 136, 137, 138
Keysoe Grange, man., iii, 137
Keysoe Park Farm, iii, 136
Keysoe Row, iii, 136
Killbere, Sim., iii, 3
Kim, riv., ii, 71; iii, 153
Kimbolton (Hunts), ii, 39, 71, 200; iii, 40, 124, 136, 157, 160, 171, 202, 209; Catherine of Aragon at, ii, 38; man., iii, 168, 171
Kimbolton, hon., iii, 153, 155, 166, 171, 172, 173, 296
Kimpton, Edm., ii, 204; Eliz., ii, 204; Geo., ii, 203, 204; Lucy, ii, 204; Will., ii, 342 *n*; fam., iii, 406
Kimptons, man. (Stanbridge), iii, 406, 407
King (Kinge, Kynges), Eliz., iii, 157; Eulalia, iii, 157 *n*; John, i, 402; ii, 385; iii, 157; John E., ii, 176; Smith, iii, 255; Thos., i, 398; ii, 379; iii, 278; Will., ii, 381
King John's Well (Odell), iii, 74
Kingsbury (Dunstable), i, 360; ii, 23; iii, 351, 352, 356
Kingsbury, Thos., i, 353 *n*
Kingsbury House (Dunstable), iii, 351, 368, 416
King's Coll. (Camb.), i, 400; ii, 357, 358
King's Ditch (Bedford), i, 281; iii, 1, 6, 8, 9
King's Hall (Camb.), i, 326 *n*; iii, 61, 63
Kings Langley (Herts), priory, i, 376 *n*
Kingsley, Eliz., iii, 166; Hen., iii. 166; Heylock, ii, 244; iii, 166
Kingsmead (Bedford), iii, 8
King's Way (Ridgmont), iii, 321
Kingswood (Chamois Park) (Eaton Socon), man., iii, 195
King's Woods (Leighton Buzzard), iii, 400, 405
Kinnardseye, John de, ii, 247
Kippest, Rob., iii, 201
Kiriel, Bertram de, iii, 452; Eleanor de, iii, 452
Kirke (Kyrke), Alex., iii, 437; Rich., ii, 301; Will., iii, 437
Kirkeby (Kirkby, Kyrkeby), Christine de, iii, 40, 194, 219; John, i, 402; *see* Ely, bps. of; Mabel, iii, 219, 220; Marg. de, iii, 194; Rob. de, ii, 337; Will. de, i, 326 *n*, 353; iii, 40, 194, 219, 220
Kirton, Alan de, iii, 37; Grace de, iii, 37; fam., iii, 39
Kirtons (Biddenham), *see* Ford End
Kitchen, man. (Pulloxhill), ii, 378
Kitchen End Farm (Pulloxhill), ii, 376, 378
Kitson (Kytson), Eliz., ii, 277; Hen., ii, 277; Marg., ii, 277; iii, 318; Sir Thos., ii, 277; —, iii, 355
Knapp, Constance, iii, 208 *n*; John, iii, 208
Knight, Dan., ii, 373; Hen., ii, 364; John, ii, 343; iii, 376, 377; Jos., iii, 431; Rich., iii, 376, 377; Sim., iii, 363
Knightley, Anne, ii, 234; Sir John, iii, 367; Sir Valentine, ii, 234
Knighton, Anne, ii, 317; Sir Geo., ii, 317; Thos., iii, 415
Knights Templars, *see* Templars
Knoll, the (Aspley Guise), iii, 338;
Knotting, ii, 96, 115; iii, 123, 139-142; adv., iii, 142; chap., i, 318; iii, 142; char., iii, 142; ch., i, 315 *n*; iii, 139; inclosure, ii, 97; man., iii, 95, 139-142, 401; sch., ii, 183
Knotting Green, iii, 139
Knottyngges, *see* Knotting
Knowles, Thos., ii, 99
Koc, *see* Cocke
Kym, riv., *see* Kim
Kyme, Maud (Matilda), de, ii, 351, 352, 352 *n*, 355, 366; Will. de, ii, 351
Kympton, *see* Kimpton
Kynaston, Edw., ii, 262
Kynbell, Nich., ii, 296 *n*
Kynges, *see* King
Kyrke, *see* Kirke
Kyrkeby, *see* Kirkeby
Kyrkham, Amicia de, ii, 287; Amy (Anne), iii, 429; John (de), ii, 287; iii, 429
Kytson, *see* Kitson

Lace-making, ii, 38 *n*, 108, 122-124, 213; iii, 5, 35, 64, 69, 82, 89, 94, 96, 100, 117, 124, 128, 149, 157, 234, 280, 297, 305, 309, 435, 458
Lachebury, Will., i, 400
Lacies, man. (Clifton), ii, 277
Lacu, John de, i, 384
Lacy, Agatha (Alice) de, iii, 182; Hen. de, ii, 277; John de, ii, 277, 378; Sir Rich. de, iii, 182; Roland, iii, 119
Lady Mary's Well, *see* Ladywell
Ladysgrove (Soulsbury), iii, 415
Ladywell (Turvey), iii, 114 *n*
La Hyde, man. (Upper Gravenhurst), *see* Hyde
Lake, Sir Thos., iii, 201; Thos., ii, 256; Will., iii, 167
Lalega, Lalegh, La Leye, *see* Thurleigh
Lalleford, man. (Luton), ii, 350, 363
Lamar, John, ii, 373
Lamb (Lambe), Barbara, iii, 440, 445; Hen., iii, 451; Sir John, iii, 440; John, iii, 451
Lambert, Jane, ii, 318; John, ii, 318; —, ii, 318
Lambert's Spinney (Stagsden), iii, 96
Lamb's Farm (Renhold), iii, 218
Lameleye, Rog. de, iii, 244
Lampslandes, le (Renhold), iii, 217 *n*
Lancaster, duchy of, ii, 238, 250, 256, 257; iii, 371
Lancaster, earldom of, ii, 21 *n*
Lancaster, John of Gaunt, dk. of, ii, 248; iii, 102; Hen., earl of, ii, 33; iii, 3, 101; Thos., earl, ii, 247, 300, 339, 384; iii, 2, 12
Landas, Juliana de, iii, 456; Nich. de, iii, 449; Valentina de, iii, 449; Will. de, iii, 449
Landimareswell, *see* Ladywell
Landon, Rog., iii, 54, 315, 425
Landpark Wood (Totternhoe), iii, 448
Lane, Mich. in le, iii, 95; Sir Ralph, iii, 98; Ralph, ii, 295; Rich., ii, 281 *n*; Rob., ii, 295; iii, 98; Will., iii, 17; Mrs., iii, 228
Langbain, —, ii, 170
Langdate, John, iii, 209
Langeho (Gt. Barford), iii, 182 *n*

INDEX

Langeley, *see* Langley
Langenhoe, Sim. de, iii, 147
Langetot, Ralph (de), ii, 220, 221, 267, 275
Langford, ii, 75, 113, 138, 201, 209, 211, 234, 282 *n*, 326 *n*; iii, 69; adv., ii, 237; Brit. coins, i, 173; ii, 234; char., ii, 237; ch., i, 315 *n*, 324 *n*, 349, 394 *n*; ii, 234, 236; iii, 70; man., i, 394; ii, 143, 204, 210 *n*, 211, 216, 234; iii, 258; mills, ii, 235; poor-house, ii, 104; prehist. impls., i, 145; ii, 234; sch., ii, 183; vicarage, i, 316 *n*
Langford, Christian, iii, 425; John, iii, 425; Ralf de, i, 358; Rob., iii, 425; fam., iii, 424
Langford End (Tempsford), ii, 251
Langford Rectory, man. (Langford), ii, 234, 235, 237; mill, ii., 235
Langhill (Gt. Barford), iii, 182 *n*
Langhorne, Dan., ii, 165; Eliz., iii, 22; Thos., iii, 102; Will., iii, 22
Langley, Edw., iii, 329; John, i, 330; Rich., iii, 277; Sir Rog., ii, 345; Sir Will., ii., 345
Langleys, man. (Luton), ii, 350, 363
Langston, Thos., iii, 377
Langton, John de, iii, 91; Thos. de, iii, 91; Walt. (de), bp., *see* Coventry and Lichfield, bps. of
Langtons, man. (Sharnbrook), iii, 90, 91
Lanie, de, *see* Delaune
Lant, iii, 118, 120
Lanthony, man. (Arlesey), ii, 203, 262, 263
Lanthony Henlow, *see* Henlow Lanthony
Lanthony Priory (Glouc.), ii, 155, 263, 281, 285; mills, ii, 283
Lanti vase, iii, 460
Lanvaley, Gunnora de, ii, 243; Hadwisa de, iii, 190; Will. de, ii, 243; iii, 190
Lark-catching ind., iii, 363
Latimer, bar., ii, 203 *n*; iii, 14
Latimer, Eliz., Lady, ii, 203, 238; iii, 13; Lds., iii, 12, 77, 96; John, iii, 46, 235, 330; Rich., ii, 203; Will., iii, 13
Latimer (Latymer), Alice, ii, 238, 247, 248, 250; iii, 193, 194, 198 *n*; Edith, iii, 116; Eliz., ii, 203, 211, 247, 256, 275; iii, 13, 114, 216; Nich. le, ii, 247; iii, 194; Will. le, i, 382; ii, 203, 211, 238, 239, 247, 250, 256, 257, 275; iii, 3, 21, 96, 194; fam., ii, 235; iii, 181, 212, 215, 383
Latton, John, iii, 103
Lauderdale, earl of, ii, 53
Launcelayns, man., *see* Wood End, Cople
Launcelyn, Anne, iii, 239, 241; John, iii, 241; Marg., iii, 239, 241; Rich., iii, 239; Walt., iii, 239, 247
Laundres, Emery de, iii, 59; Rob. de, iii, 59; Steph. de, iii, 59
Laurence, archd. of Beds, i, 313
Laurence (Lawrence), Anne, iii, 381; Edw., ii, 281 *n*; iii, 67; Geoff., iii, 67; Hen., iii, 67; Jane, ii, 281 *n*; Joan, ii, 305; Joanna, ii, 305; John, ii, 224 *n*; iii, 381, 392; Marg., ii, 305; Nich., iii, 67; Rich., ii, 358; iii, 67; Will., iii, 158
Laurence Place, *see* Sokes, man.
Lavendon (Bucks), iii, 31, 63, 117
Lawe, Ant., iii, 254
Lawford, Dr. Edw., i, 187; Edw., iii, 416
Lawley, Agnes, ii, 352 *n*; Thos., ii, 295, 352, 358; Will., ii, 352 *n*
Lawrence, man. (Risley), iii, 158, 160
Lawrence, fam., *see* Laurence
Lawson, Geo., iii, 319; John, iii, 106; Nath., iii, 294; Nich., iii, 294; Theodosia, iii, 106
Layton, *see* Leighton Buzzard
Layton, Dr., i, 356, 389, 392
Lea, riv., i, 53, 98, 269; ii, 18 *n*
Leach, Joan, ii, 305; John, iii, 60; Judith, iii, 60; May, iii, 60; Sam., ii, 305; Thos., ii, 305; Will., iii, 60
Leachland, Thos., iii, 416
Leader, Frances, Lady, iii, 167; Sir Oliver, iii, 167; Oliver, iii, 204
Leadwell, *see* Ladywell
Leagrave, ii, 306, 348-50, 374; Brit. coins, i, 173, 174; ii, 348; chaps., ii, 374; kilns, ii, 2; neolithic rem., i, 164, 166; ii, 348; Rom.-Brit. rem., ii, 8
Leagrave Marsh, i, 269
Leaper, Kath., ii, 342; Peregrine, ii, 342; Sim., ii, 342; Thos., ii, 342
Leather, Marg., *see* Harper, Marg.
Leather-dressing, iii, 64, 69
Lecton, *see* Leighton Buzzard
Ledet (Ledit), Christina, i, 361; ii, 237, 247, 250; Margery, i, 361 *n*; ii, 237, 247; iii, 253; Wischard (Wiscard, Wyschard), i, 361, 364; ii, 237, 247; iii, 195, 253
Lee (Podington), ii, 326
Lee, Anne, iii, 340; Hen., ii, 385; John, ii, 377; iii, 122, 377; Joyce, ii, 362; Kath., iii, 377; Marg., Lady, iii, 340; Philip de, ii, 312; Rob., ii, 362; Rob. C., ii, 347; Rog., ii, 376; iii, 443; Sir Rich., iii, 237, 339, 340; Thos., ii, 69; Will., ii, 385; —, iii, 22; *see also* Leigh
Lee-Antonie, Will., iii, 92
Leedare, Marg., *see* Harper, Marg.
Leeds, dk. of, iii, 453
Lefstan, ii, 341 *n*
Lega, par., *see* Thurleigh
Lega, fam., *see* Leigh
Leget, John, i, 399
Legh, Legha, *see* Leigh
Leghton, *see* Leighton Buzzard
Lehton, *see* Leighton Buzzard
Leicester, diocese, ii, 18
Leicester, hon., iii, 144, 231, 294
Leicester, Parnel, ctss. of, iii, 293; earls of, iii, 144; Rob., ii, 232; iii, 246, 294; Sim. de Montfort, ii, 351; iii, 439
Leicester, Will., iii. 377
Leigh, Lady Mary, iii, 404, 429 *n*; Thos., lord, i, 341; ii, 44, 54; iii, 277, 401, 402, 404, 408, 411, 414, 429 *n*
Leigh (Lega, Legh, Legha, Leya, Leye), Agnes de, i, 385; Alicia, iii, 411; Andr. de la, ii, 105, 326; Anne (Anna), iii, 302, 411, 415; Barth., iii, 104; Basile de la, i, 389; Chas., ii, 59, 62; iii, 277, 411, 415, 416; Dionisia, iii, 105; Eliz., iii, 411; Gerard, ii, 353; Gerinus, iii, 51, 54; Goddard, iii, 292; Hen., iii, 51; Hugh de (la), ii, 326; iii, 85, 104, 108; Sir John, iii, 404; John (de la), iii, 21, 104, 105, 147, 277, 334, 411; John G., ii, 353; John S., ii, 353, 356, 366; Lewis, iii, 21, 277, 335; Lucy, iii, 277; Mary, iii, 292-5 *n*,
Leigh (*cont.*)
411; Nichola, iii, 104; Rog. de la, ii, 253; Sim. (de la), iii, 24, 104; Steph. (la), iii, 85, 87, 104, 108; Sir Thos., *see* Leigh, Thos., Ld.; Thos., ii, 158; iii, 21, 277, 300, 302; Ursula, iii, 411; Will., iii, 24, 104, 146; Dr. —, i, 363, 368; fam., iii, 82; *see also* Lee
Leighton, Baldwyn, ii, 286; Rog. de, iii, 356, 357, 358
Leighton Buzzard, i, 319, 324, 327, 349; ii, 44, 45 *n*, 47, 54, 55, 62, 67, 71, 102, 114, 116 *n*, 133, 189, 190, 348, 349; iii, 320, 336, 367, 368, 383, 399; adv. i, 317, 341; iii, 414; A.S. rem., i, 176, 181, 187, 189; bridge, iii, 402; chant., iii, 415; chaps., i, 346; char., iii, 368, 415; chs., i, 311, 312, 324 *n*, 329; iii, 400, 402, 409-414; Danes in, iii, 401; fire, iii, 402; gild, iii, 415; Hermitage, the, iii, 409; hound money, ii, 143 *n*; inns, iii, 399, 400, 415; liberty, iii, 337; mans., i, 319 *n*, 403; iii, 100 *n*, 337, 402-9; market cross, ii, 100; iii, 399; mkts. and fairs, ii, 76, 88; iii, 401; mills, iii, 400, 408, 409; Nonconf., ii, 375; iii, 414; place-names, iii, 402, 408; prebendal estate, iii, 408; prehist. rem., i, 145, 162, 173, 174; racing, ii, 190, 191; rectory, i, 341; Rom. rem., ii, 1, 8, 9; iii, 402; sand ind., ii, 117; schs., ii, 183; iii, 416; wheat-growing experiments, ii, 134; witchcraft, ii, 100; iii, 402
Leighton Heath, i, 187
Leighton prebendal (rectorial), man., iii, 408
Leith, Rev. Alex., iii, 33; Martha, iii, 32, 33
Leiton, *see* Leighton Buzzard
Lekeburn, Pet. de, iii, 172
Le Mesurier, Rev. H. C., ii, 174
Lenborough (Bucks), ii, 18 *n*, 349 *n*; iii, 401
Lenham, Isolda de, iii, 452; John de, iii, 452
Lennox, Marg., ctss. of, ii, 339
Lenton Priory, i, 315 *n*,; ii, 288, 292, 293; iii, 63, 80
L'Enveise (Enveyse), Agatha (Alice), iii, 181, 182; Jordan, iii, 125, 181; Walt., iii, 181; Will., iii, 125
Leofnoth, ii, 326
Leofwin (Leofwine, Lewin), i, 296 *n*, 347; ii, 21 *n*, 204, 234, 278, 288; iii, 70, 248
Leominster, Sophia, Lady, iii, 453; Thos., Ld., iii, 453; Will., Ld., iii, 452
Lepidoptera, i, 78-88
Lepine, Maria, iii, 444
Lestrange (Lestraunge), Geo., Ld., iii, 140
Lestrange (Lestraunge, L'Strange, De Extraneis), Joan, iii, 119; Matilda, ii, 268 *n*; iii, 16 *n*; Maud, ii, 300 *n*; iii, 44, 215, 329; Rob., i, 379 *n*; iii, 137, 150; Sir Rog., iii, 44; Rog., ii, 300 *n*, 339, 341; iii, 12, 52, 97, 215, 262, 329; Thos., iii, 150
Lessy, Phil., iii, 294 *n*
Lester and Pack, bell-makers, ii, 338; iii, 25
Lestone, *see* Leighton Buzzard
Lethers, Marg., *see* Harper, Marg.; Rich., ii, 160
Lethom, Will. de, i, 401
Letitia, ii, 376

Leuiet, *see* Leviet
Leutton, *see* Luton
Levenot, iii, 70, 113, 118
Leventhorpe, Ann, ii, 289; Eliz., ii, 289, 291; Geo., ii, 289; Joan, ii, 289; John, ii, 289; Thos., ii, 289, 291
Leverington, Ad. of, i, 387
Leveson-Gower, Gertrude, ii, 62 *n*
Leveva, iii, 338
Leviet (Leuiet), i, 312 *n*; priest, iii, 37, 107
Levinz, Sir Creswell, iii, 150, 159; Creswell, iii, 83, 105; Will., iii, 105
Levret, iii, 120
Levric, iii, 105
Lewelyck, Denise, i, 360
Lewen, Rich., iii, 146
Lewes (Pegsdon), ii, 295 *n*
Lewin, *see* Leofwin
Lewis, Jas., iii, 446; Will. V., iii, 404
Lewknor, Cath., iii, 195; Eleanor, iii, 194, 195; Rog., iii, 194, 195
Lewsey, man. (Luton), ii, 350, 363
Leyburne, Eleanor de, ii, 351, 353, 354; Ida, ii, 230, 232; Idonea de, ii, 230 *n*; Rog., ii, 231, 232, 351
Leyghton, *see* Leighton Buzzard
Leyham, Isabel de, ii, 207; John de, ii, 208; Matth., de, ii, 207; Oliver de, ii, 207 *n*; Pet. de, ii, 207, 208
Lichens (Lichenes), i, 60-1
Lichfield and Coventry, bps. of, i, 343; ii, 224
Lidlington, ii, 66; iii, 4, 267, 305, 422; adv., i, 321 *n*, 322; iii, 307; char., iii, 307; ch., i, 313, 322; iii, 305, 306, 307; crown property, iii, 271; farms, ii, 131, 134; iii, 305; inclosures, ii, 97; inds., iii, 305; man., i, 312; iii, 272, 305, 306; Nonconf., iii, 305, 307; rents, ii, 132; schs., ii, 183; iii, 307; spring, iii, 308; vicarage, i, 329 *n*; iii, 307; workhouse, ii, 104
Lidlington, Agnes de, iii, 325; Thos., iii, 307; Will. of, i, 387
Lightgrave, *see* Leagrave
Lightgrave, man., *see* Woodcroft
Lilincletone, *see* Lidlington
Lillingestan, *see* Lidlington
Lilly, Hen., iii, 150
Limbury, i, 173, 175, 269, 269 *n*, 280; ii, 18 *n*, 306, 308, 348, 349, 362 *n*, 374, 384; iii, 401; mans., ii, 350, 360, 366; mill, ii, 360; Nonconf., ii, 374; Rom. rem., ii, 8
Limbury (Lymbury), Joan de, ii, 360; Phil. de, ii, 360; Ralph de, ii, 329; Rich. de, ii, 360
Limersey Grange, *see* Lymbotsey
Limestone quarries, iii, 96, 448
Lincelade (Bucks), iii, 12, 14, 46
Lincoln, ii, 24, 33; ii, 153
Lincoln, cathedral ch. of, i, 376 *n*, 383; ii, 154; iii, 21, 346, 408; endowment, i, 311; ii, 210; library, ii, 152; prebends, ii, 214; iii, 284 *n*
Lincoln, diocese of, i, 346, 347, 379
Lincoln, archds. of, ii, 154; iii, 359
Lincoln, bps. of, i, 311, 315 *n*, 321 *n*, 327, 328, 330, 339, 340 *n*, 354, 358, 360, 361, 375, 378, 379, 387 *n*, 396, 400; ii, 38, 88, 97, 149, 154, 178, 206, 208, 210, 212, 214, 230 *n*, 252, 253, 258, 296, 312, 319, 343, 356, 374, 380; iii, 22, 29, 37, 69, 116, 133, 155,
Lincoln, bps. of (*cont.*)
159, 185 *n*, 250, 264, 272, 284, 334, 342, 348, 349, 359, 364, 374 *n*, 398, 408, 414, 431, 432, 437; Alexander, ii, 210; Barlow, i, 339 *n*; Beaufort, i, 328, 397; iii, 414; Buckingham, i, 330, 355, 375, 379; ii, 178, 296; Burghersh, i, 360, 375; ii, 149, 297; iii, 49; Chesney, i, 313; Dalderby, i, 359, 362, 375, 383, 389, 395, 397, 398, 401; ii, 209; Gravesend, i, 317, 322, 351, 354, 374; iii, 148, 334; Grey, i, 329, 360, 376, 380, 383; ii, 179; iii, 414; Grossetête, i, 317, 322, 366, 374, 379, 382, 383, 385, 400 *n*, 401; iii, 208; Gynwell, i, 355, 362, 375, 389; Holbeche, ii, 210; Hugh of Avalon, i, 313, 388; ii, 150, 212, 299 *n*, 312, 335; iii, 142; Hugh de Wells, i, 316, 317 *n*, 322, 372, 396; ii, 332, iii, 208, 214, 304, 334, 348, 364, 398, 414; Longland, i, 356, 376, 383, 384, 396; Montaigne, i, 339 *n*; Remigius, i, 311, 312, 347 *n*; ii, 153, 154, 275 *n*, 276; iii, 22, 414; Repingdon, i, 355, 356 *n*, 383, 388 *n*; ii, 384; iii, 170; Rotherham, ii, 352; iii, 299; Sutton, i, 317 *n*, 322, 323, 325 *n*, 354 *n*, 359, 374, 375, 389, 395, 398, 401; ii, 212
Lincoln, deans of, i, 320; iii, 22, 384 *n*
Lincoln, Edw., earl of, iii, 94, 382
Lincoln, Alured of, iii, 119, 122
Lincoln College (Oxf.), ii, 176, 178
Lindon, hon., iii, 247
Linford (Bucks), iii, 271
Linley, John de, iii, 456
Linslade (Bucks), i, 392; iii, 399, 400, 401, 415; man., iii, 405 *n*; rectory, i, 393
Lisle (de Insula, L'Isle, Lyle), Alice de, ii, 267; John (de), i, 393; ii, 224 *n*, 267; iii, 285, 395; Maud (de), ii, 267; Ralph de, ii, 210, 211, 212; Rob. (de), ii, 267, 268; iii, 70, 285, 395; Rose, *see* Wahull; Warine de, ii, 267, 268; Sir Will. de, ii, 267; Will. de, iii, 122
Lismore, Rob., bp. of, ii, 379, 380; iii, 431
Lister, Lady, iii, 203
Litchfield, Hen., iii, 380 *n*
Litgrave, *see* Leagrave
Little, H., ii, 250
Little England's, field (Dunstable), iii, 350
Littlewood Farm (Clapham), iii, 128
Littleworth (Wilshamstead), iii, 326
Litton (Litten, Lytton), Agnes, iii, 220; Anne, ii, 301; John R., ii, 301; Judith, ii, 301; Rowland, ii, 239, 241, 301; iii, 281; Thos., iii, 146; Will., ii, 301; iii, 220
Livesay, Eliz., iii, 83, 87; Jane, iii, 84; John, iii, 83; Maj.-Gen. John, iii, 83, 119; Paradine, iii, 83; St. Andr., iii, 83; Will., iii, 83
Livesey (Norfolk), man., i, 360
Livius, Geo., iii, 21, 304
Liz, Muriel le, iii, 60; Robt. le, iii, 60
Llanthony, *see* Lanthony
Lloyd, Will., iii, 184
Loccles (Locels), Will. de, ii, 344, 381, 383
Lock, Mary, ii, 363
Lockington, Mary, iii, 367, 368
Lockwood, fam., iii, 57
Lodge, Alice, iii, 430; Ellen, iii, 430; Hen., ii, 40; iii, 430; Mich., iii, 430
Lodington (Lodynton), John, iii, 273; Thos., iii, 423
Loitone, *see* Luton
Lollards, the, i, 330
Lomax, Caleb, iii, 332; F. G., ii, 218; Joshua, iii, 332; Ruth, iii, 332; —, ii, 216, 257
Londe, Walt. de la, iii, 137
London, ii, 365, 370, 392; ii, 135, 163; Beds property, ii, 310; iii, 253, 285, 292, 321, 326, 332; riot, ii, 30
London, bps. of, i, 329, 332, 400; ii, 38, 320; iii, 194, 349
London, ld. mayor of, ii, 158; iii, 25, 372
London, Augustine, i, 365; Dan. T., i, 363, 364; John, of, i, 377; Sim. de, iii, 16
London End (Keysoe), iii, 136
London End (Milton Ernest), iii, 144
Lone Close (Goldington), iii, 208 *n*
Loney, Sir Rich., iii, 286
Long (Longe), Cecil, iii, 301; Dorothy, iii, 302, 376; Eliz., ii, 330; iii, 302, 376; Hen., ii, 330; iii, 230, 376; Marg., Lady, iii, 318; Sir Rich., ii, 277, 330, 379; iii, 23, 213, 240, 260, 264, 302, 315, 318, 324, 332, 376, 437; Steph., ii, 155; Thos., ii, 374; Sir Will., iii, 303, 305; Will., iii, 301
Longbridge (Warws), i, 181
Longdon, Hen., ii, 248
Longe, *see* Long
Longespée, Will., *see* Salisbury, earl of
Longeville, *see* Longueville
Longford, ctss. of, ii, 181 *n*
Longland, bp., *see* Lincoln, bps. of
Longley plantation (Podington), iii, 80
Longney (Gloucs), iii, 251
Long Stowe (Cambs.), iii, 415
Long Tag Wood (Stevington), iii, 100
Longueville, Anne, ii, 290, 295 *n*; Chas. G., ii, 290; Frances, ii, 295; Grey, ii, 290, 295; Hen., ii, 290, 295 *n*; Isabella de, iii, 189; John de, iii, 187, 199; Lucy, ii, 290; Marg. (de), ii, 295; iii, 184, 187; Sir Michael G., ii, 290; iii, 228 *n*, 232; Susan, ii, 290; iii, 232; Susanna, Lady, iii, 228 *n*
Longworth, John, ii, 166, 167, 168
Lord, John, ii, 277; Obadiah, ii, 385
Lord lieut., ii, 56, 59, 61, 62 *n*, 175
Loring (Lorenge, Loryng), Dav., iii, 331; Isabel, iii, 89; John (de), ii, 252, 356 *n*, 357; Marg., iii, 346, 440; Sir Nigel (Neel), i, 325, 329; ii, 353; iii, 89, 346, 348, 349, 440; Pet. (de), ii, 318; iii, 89, 346, 347, 349, 367; Rob., iii, 345; Rog., i, 371 *n*; iii, 89, 348; Will., ii, 318, 353, 356 *n*, 357
Lorings, man. (Sharnbrook), iii, 89
Lorraine, Alb. of, ii, 22; iii, 89, 329, 332, 345, 346
Loryng, *see* Loring
Lotrell, Hugh, ii, 227
Lovat, riv., *see* Ouzel
Loveday, Anne, i, 384 *n*
Lovelace, Anne, Lady, iii, 441
Lovell (Lovel), Fran., ii, 210; H., iii, 278; Sir John, ii, 316; John, iii, 422; Pet. H., ii, 210; Phil., iii, 422; Will., iii, 231

INDEX

Lovells (Lovells Bury), man. (Potsgrove), iii, 422
Lovett (Lovet), Rob., ii, 291 ; iii, 283, 339 ; Will., iii, 284, 286, 395
Lowe, Fran., iii, 322 ; John, iii, 396 ; Will. D., iii, 133
Lower Berry End (Eversholt), iii, 375
Lower End Farm (Lidlington), iii, 305
Lower Rads End (Eversholt), iii, 375
Lowick (Luffewyche) (Northants), iii, 92 *n*
Lowndes (Lownde), Eliz., iii, 330 ; Kath., iii, 285 ; Marg., iii, 285 ; Rich., iii, 330 ; Thos., iii, 285 ; Rev. Will., iii, 330 ; Will., iii, 330 ; Will. L., iii, 330
Lubenham, Rob. of, i, 386, 402
Lucas, Ladies, iii, 66, 228 ; Amabel, *see* Grey of Wrest, ctss. of ; Anne, ii, 327 ; Ld., ii, 142, 197, 200, 325, 327, 334 ; iii, 64 ; *see also* Grey, Lds., and Kent, dks., etc.
Lucas, Rob., ii, 270
Lucas and Dingwall, Ld., ii, 283, 290, 305, 322, 323, 325, 332, 333, 337, 345, 377, 379, 380 ; iii, 52, 65, 68 ; Auberon Herbert, Ld., ii, 328
Lucy (Luci), Alice, iii, 224 ; Anne, iii, 427, 429 ; Sir Edm., iii, 230 ; Edm., iii, 50 ; Eleanor, Lady, iii, 230, 248 ; Eleanor de, ii, 354, 422 ; Eliz., iii, 50 ; Emery de, ii, 354 ; Fran., iii, 330 ; Geoff. de, ii, 30 *n*, 354 ; iii, 405, 409, 422 ; Geo., ii, 204 *n* ; Joan, ii, 204 *n* ; John, iii, 286 ; Juliana de, iii, 422 ; Marg., ii, 354, 429 ; Maud, iii, 422 ; Rebecca, iii, 330 ; Reg. de, ii, 354 ; Sir Rich., iii, 181 *n* ; Rich. (de), ii, 26 *n* ; iii, 330 ; Sir Thos., iii, 224, 330 ; Thos., iii, 50, 211, 224 ; Walt. de, ii, 354 ; Sir Will., iii, 405, 422 ; Will. de, ii, 354 ; iii, 50, 427, 429
Ludgershall (Bucks), i, 400 ; iii, 175, 176 *n*
Ludlow, Ld., ii, 187
Ludlow, fam., ii, 66
Ludsop, John, ii, 36
Luffewyche (Northants), *see* Lowick
Lufwyk, Rob. de, i, 382 *n*
Luke, St., relics of, i, 400
Luke, Anne, ii, 262 ; Cecily (Cecyle), Lady, iii, 193, 241 ; Eliz., ii, 216, 340 ; Frances, iii, 195 ; Sir John, iii, 193, 239 ; John, ii, 262, 263, 282 ; iii, 193, 198 ; Sir Nich., ii, 216 ; iii, 158 *n*, 193, 239, 241 ; Nich., ii, 262, 282, 342, 382 ; iii, 29, 146, 193, 197, 209, 212 ; Sir Oliver, ii, 42, 44, 282, 339, 340, 342 ; iii, 29, 193, 239 ; Oliver, ii, 262, 282, 340, 341 *n*, 382 ; iii, 29, 195 ; Paul, ii, 235 ; iii, 198 ; Sir Sam., ii, 41, 42, 44, 45, 46, 47, 48, 49, 54, 55, 340, 343 *n* ; iii, 227, 238, 239, 404, 456 ; Sir Walt., iii, 239, 241 ; Walt., ii, 40 ; iii, 197 ; Will., iii, 197 ; fam., ii, 44, 60 ; iii, 238, 342, 343
Lunde, la, wood (Little Staughton), iii, 165
Lupton, Rog., ii, 157
Lusignan, Guy de, ii, 29
Luthmere, Thos., iii, 125
Lutlingeton, Lutlyngton, *see* Lidlington
Luton, ii, 18, 67, 100, 114, 120, 147, 295, 305, 306, 314, 321, 326, 333, 338, 342, 344, 348-75 ; iii, 10, 105, 317 *n*, 325 ; adv., i, 314, 317, 336, 341 ; ii, 373 ; iii, 393 ; almshouses, ii, 375 ; chant., ii, 374, 381 ; char., ii, 374 ; iii, 238 ; ch., i, 310, 311, 314, 315 *n*, 324, 346, 372 *n*, 400 ; ii, 349, 356, 368, 381 ; courts, ii, 308, 366 ; deanery, i, 347 ; fairs and mkts., ii, 76, 88, 349, 351, 352, 353 *n*, 360 ; fire, ii, 85, 366 ; gilds, i, 330 ; ii, 92, 149, 374, 381 ; hosps., i, 349, 399, 400 ; ii, 375 ; hound money, ii, 143 *n* ; inds., ii, 109, 119, 121, 122, 126, 127, 349, 350 ; inns, ii, 348 ; mans., i, 315 *n* ; ii, 143, 306-8, 349-60, 362 *n*, 364, 366, 374, 383 ; mills, i, 311 ; ii, 351, 357, 366 ; neolithic impls., i, 174 ; Nonconf., i, 344 ; ii, 374, 375 ; place-names, ii, 348 ; plait halls, ii, 119, 121 ; Rom. Cath., ii, 374 ; Rom. coins, ii, 9 ; schs., ii, 149, 180, 183, 375 ; vicar, i, 316, 324 *n*, 327 *n*, 333, 395 *n*, 400 ; Witan at, ii, 350 *n*
Luton (Leutton, Lutton), Ad. of, i, 370 ; Alice de, ii, 357 ; John, iii, 233 ; Mary, iii, 312 ; Maud of, i, 360 ; Rob. de, ii, 276 *n* ; Rog. de, ii, 357
Luton Castle, ii, 350
Luton Downs, ii, 198
Luton Hoo, man., ii, 61, 119, 197, 257, 348, 350, 353 *n*, 355, 357, 361, 365, 373, 375 ; mill, ii, 366 ; Rom. coins, ii, 9
Luton Hoo Park, ii, 147, 348, 355, 360
Lutune, *see* Luton
Luvholt, Godf. de, ii, 376 ; Mabel de, ii, 376
Lycett, Inskip & Co., ii, 262, 263
Lydall, Rich., iii, 261
Lyde, Hen., iii, 198
Lye, Rev. Thos., ii, 375
Lyencourt, Will. de, i, 403, 404
Lygetune, *see* Leighton Buzzard and Luton
Lygon, Mary, iii, 430 ; Rich., iii, 430
Lyle, *see* Lisle
Lylebone, Sir John de, ii, 378 ; Sibyl de, ii, 378
Lymbotsey (Limersey) Grange (Ampthill), iii, 273
Lymbotseye, John de, iii, 292
Lymbury, *see* Limbury
Lyner, Godf. de, iii, 314
Lyne-Stephens, Mrs., ii, 270
Lynford mill, ii, 283
Lynn (Norfolk), ii, 91
Lynom, Thos., iii, 92
Lysons, Mary, iii, 28
Lytlington, *see* Lidlington
Lytton, *see* Litton

Mabel, Abbess of Elstow, i, 355
Macan, —, ii, 189, 190
McDowall, —, ii, 177
Machell, John, ii, 158 ; Capt., ii, 194
Machinery manufacture, ii, 125-7
Mackenzie, Sir Geo. S., ii, 197, 251
Maclear, Basil, ii, 200
Macnamara, Anne, ii, 318 ; iii, 372 ; Arth., ii, 318 ; iii, 372 ; John, ii, 318 ; iii, 372, 455 ; Sophia, iii, 400
MacQueen, Dr. Malcolm, iii, 293, 322 ; T. Potter, iii, 322 ; Dr., ii, 133
Madan Castle, *see* Maiden Bower
Maddison, Col., iii, 361
Madin-boure, *see* Maiden Bower
Madning-bowre, *see* Maiden Bower
Maenfinin, ii, 23
Maggotts Moor (Ampthill), iii, 274
Magiovinum (Bucks), *see* Brickhill, Little
Magniac, Chas., iii, 90, 92, 94, 95, 140, 142 ; Hollingworth, ii, 188 ; iii, 92 ; H. R., iii, 142 ; Vernon, iii, 94, 95
Magpie Hall Farm (Marston Moretaine), iii, 313
Maidbury, man. (Elstow), iii, 281, 282
Maidbury (Maydebury), Thos., iii, 282
Maiden Bower (Dunstable), Rom.-Brit. rem., i, 160, 163, 164, 166, 169, 170, 174, 269, 294 ; ii, 2, 7, 9 ; iii, 390
Maidwell, Cutts, iii, 57 ; Godf., ii, 345 ; Thos., iii, 57 ; Will. L., iii, 57
Maister, *see* Master
Makehams Close (Steppingley), iii, 325
Malcolm IV, king of Scotland, i, 361, 388 ; iii, 23, 65
Maldon, battle of, ii, 20
Malens, man., *see* Maryons
Malens, fam., *see* Malyns
Malet, Hugh, i, 370
Malherbe, Geoff., iii, 293 ; Joan, iii, 292 ; John, i, 401 ; iii, 52, 292, 383 ; Lucy, iii, 384 ; Pain, iii, 52, 293 ; Rob., iii, 291, 383, 385 ; Will., iii, 44 *n*, 52
Malory, Alice, ii, 286 ; Anketin, iii, 162 ; Bertram, ii, 286 ; Eleanor, ii, 286 ; Fran., iii, 162, 164 ; John, ii, 286 ; Pet., iii, 162 ; Ralph, iii, 162 ; Rob., ii, 286 ; Sim., ii, 286 ; Thos., iii, 162 ; Sir Will., iii, 162 ; Will., iii, 162
Malyns (Malens), John, iii, 183, 211, 212, 229, 231 ; Thos., iii, 183, 231
Mammals, i, 138-43
Man, *see* Mann
Mancels Grove (Turvey), iii, 114
Manchester, Chas., dk. of, iii, 169 ; Hen., earl of, iii, 168
Mandeville, Geoff. de, i, 378 *n*, 390 ; ii, 25 ; *see also* Essex, earl of ; Hen., iii, 171 ; Isabel (de), iii, 70 ; Rohese de, *see* Beauchamp ; Walt. de, ii, 354 ; Will. de, iii, 171 ; *see also* Essex, earl of
Manepeny, Will., i, 370
Maney, Hugh, ii, 332, 333
Mangehoo, man. (Marston Moretaine), iii, 311
Maningham, *see* Manningham
Manley, John, iii, 326 ; Pet. de, iii, 223, 224
Mann (Man, Manne), John, ii, 327 *n*, 378 ; iii, 408 ; Mary, iii, 408 ; Will., iii, 408 ; Mrs., iii, 383, 384
Manning, Rev. —, iii, 162
Manningham (Maningham), Sir John, ii, 220, 257 ; John, ii, 219 ; iii, 231 ; Kath., ii, 257 ; Sir Will., ii, 257
Manor Farm (Goldington), iii, 202
Manshead, hund. of, ii, 95, 114, 116 ; iii, 70, 336, 337 ; assessment, iii, 391
Mantell (Mauntel), Hen., iii, 366 ; Marg., iii, 456 ; Thos., iii, 456 ; Walt., iii, 456
Manyngham, *see* Manningham
Marborowe, Hen., iii, 155 ; Thos., iii, 155 ; *see also* Marlborough
Marbury (Marbery), Edw., ii, 307 ; Eliz., iii, 255 ; John, iii, 255 ;

Marbury (*cont.*)
Lewis, ii, 307; Thos., iii, 255, 261, 393
March, earls of, ii, 191, 192, 328; Edm., ii, 328; Rog., ii, 33, 327; iii, 229, 281
Marche, Will. de la, iii, 286; *see also* Marsh
Mareis, Adeliza (de), i, 392; ii, 267; Walt. de, ii, 267; *see also* Marsh
Mareschal, *see* Marshal
Margets, Thos., ii, 55, 212
Market gardening, i, 39; ii, 118, 130, 138-9, 213; iii, 181, 189, 218, 242, 256, 284, 369
Markets and Fairs, ii, 46, 87, 88, 102, 105, 121, 140, 237, 239, 242, 261, 263, 266, 268, 330, 348, 349, 351, 352, 353 *n*, 360, 385; iii, 16, 17, 21, 35, 64, 69, 73, 142, 199, 229, 246, 254, 258, 268, 269, 271, 276, 281, 311, 317, 340, 355, 361, 362, 363, 401, 441, 453, 459
Market Street (Herts), *see* Markyate Street (Herts)
Markham, Ad., ii, 356 *n*; Alice iii, 85; Frances, ii, 355, 356; Gervase, i, 374, 377; iii, 361; John, ii, 355, 356, 357; iii, 85, 285; Kath., iii, 85; Thos., iii, 85; Will., ii, 355, 356; iii, 395, 398
Markyate, Christine of, i, 350; Rog. of, i, 350
Markyate Cell (Caddington), ii, 317
Markyate Priory, i, 315 *n*, 316 *n*, 349, 351, 358-61, 395; ii, 316, 347, 383, 387
Markyate (Market) Street (Herts), ii, 71, 92, 314, 316-20, 377, 380; iii, 337, 455; A.S. rem., i, 146; char., ii, 320; ch., ii, 319; Five Horse Shoes Inn, ii, 318; man., ii, 316, 317; Nonconf., ii, 320; Rom. rem., ii, 3, 7; sch., ii, 317, 320
Marlborough, Jane, ctss. of, ii, 347, 382; dchss. of, iii, 211, 240; Sarah, dchss. of, iii, 104, 203, 213, 214, 224, 264, 306, 309; earl of, iii, 4; Jas., earl of, ii, 347, 382
Marlborough, Marg., iii, 98; Thos., ii, 295 *n*; iii, 98; *see also* Marborowe
Marlie, Will., iii, 363
Marmyon, Sir Will., iii, 162
Marsh (Marshe), Blandina, iii, 367, 368, 416; Dan., iii, 368; Hen., ii, 316; John, iii, 60; Rich., ii, 316; iii, 332; Rotherham, ii, 316; Thos., ii, 316; Ursula, iii, 60
Marshal (Mareschal, Marshall), Alina, iii, 426; Anselm, *see* Pembroke, earl of; Edm., iii, 442; Ela, iii, 426; Eliz., iii, 98, 445; Hawisia, iii, 426; John (le), iii, 147, 329, 391, 426; Maud, ii, 220; iii, 329, 439; Rog., i, 382; iii, 329; Sarah, iii, 329; Thos., i, 325, 373, 375, 376, 377; ii, 178; iii, 98, 329; Walt., ii, 81, 220, 267; Will., ii, 27, 341, 350, 351 *n*, 362 *n*, 366; iii, 426; *see also* Pembroke, earl of; —, ii, 382
Marsh Wood (Renhold), iii, 215
Marsiliaceae, i, 56
Marsland, Clem., iii, 251
Marston (Northants), i, 182 *n*
Marston, North (Bucks), ch., i, 371 *n*, 373, 376 *n*
Marston Moretaine (Morteyne), i, 324; ii, 66, 115, 250, 324; iii, 11, 13, 132, 267, 277, 298, 307-13, 321, 333; adv., iii, 313; char., iii, 313; ch., i, 318; iii, 308, 311-13;
Marston Moretaine (*cont.*)
farms in, iii, 307; inclosures, ii, 97; mans., iii, 309; mkts. and fairs, ii, 88; iii, 311; Nonconf., iii, 308, 313; schs., ii, 183
Marston Park Farm (Marston Moretaine), iii, 308
Marston Pillinge (Marston Moretaine), iii, 308, 313
Marston Thrift (Marston Moretaine), ii, 187; iii, 308
Marsworth (Bucks), ch., i, 382-4
Martel, Osbert, iii, 370
Martin, papal nuncio, ii, 29
Martyn (Marten, Martin), Dr. Edw. i, 339-40, 343; Eliz., iii, 330; Eulalia, iii, 157 *n*; Gilb., iii, 203; John, ii, 227; iii, 145; John K., iii, 154, 157; Thos., iii, 157, 220
Marvin, Rev. —, ii, 347
Marwen, *see* Morwen
Mary, princess (dau. of Edw. I), i, 404
Mary I, queen (of England), ii, 377
Mary, queen (of Scots), ii, 119, 349
Maryon, Isabel, iii, 240; Thos., iii, 240
Maryons (Malens), man., (Cople), iii, 240
Mason, Bartlett, ii, 289
Massey, Eliz., Lady, iii, 443; Jane, iii, 402; Sir Walt., iii, 443
Massingberd, —, iii, 422 *n*
Master (Maister), Marg., iii, 145; Streynsham, iii, 145; Thos., ii, 310; iii, 216; Will., ii, 334
Mather, Will., iii, 9
Mathers, John, iii, 311
Matilda, *see* Maud
Mat industry, *see* Rush-matting ind.
Matthew (Mathew), John, iii, 333; Mary, iii, 191; Sarah, iii, 333; Will., iii, 333
Matthews, Millicent, iii, 368
Mattock, Eliz., ii, 363
Maud (Matilda), ctss., ii, 237; iii, 302, 304
Mauder, Harry, iii, 183
Mauduit, Arth. iii, 443; Eliz., iii, 443; Maria, iii, 443; Sarah, iii, 443; Will., *see* Warwick, earl of
Maulac, Lavaric de, ii, 27
Maulaye, Alice, iii, 233; Rich., iii, 233
Maulden (Meldone), i, 313, 353-4, 356; ii, 66, 115, 135, 321, 324; iii, 267, 273, 275, 286, 313-316; adv., iii, 315; char., iii, 316; ch., i, 315 *n*, 357; iii, 314, 315; inclosure in, ii, 97; inns, iii, 313; man., iii, 314; mills, iii, 314; Nonconf., iii, 314, 316; place-names in, iii, 314; poorhouse at, ii, 104; sch., ii, 183
Maulden Moor, Rom. rem. at, ii, 9
Maulden Wood, iii, 313
Maultby, —, iii, 416
Maunsell, Sampson, iii, 113; Will., iii, 113
Mauntel, *see* Mantell
Mavorn (Maverns, Mavourn, Glintells), man. (Bolnhurst); iii, 126; earthworks, i, 306; iii, 124
Mawcase Field (Wilden), iii, 226
Mawditt, *see* Mauduit
Maxey, —, ii, 97
Maxie, Edw., ii, 161
May, John, iii, 159
Maydebury, *see* Maidbury
Maydenford, Pet. of, i, 352
Mayfield Farm-house (Markyate), ii, 314
Mayhew, Rev. Geo., ii, 206, 265
Mayn, John, iii, 133
Maynard, Will., Ld., ii, 241
Maynard, John, ii, 342, 344, 353; iii, 132, 147, 261, 408
Mays, Rich., ii, 232
Mead (Meade), Ann, Lady, iii, 68; Jas., ii, 271, 293; John, iii, 449; Rich., ii, 383; iii, 404; Rob., iii, 432; Rev. T. W., iii, 428; Will., iii, 451; Dr. —, iii, 66
Mears, bell-founders, ii, 218, 222, 236, 241, 250, 254, 287, 319, 347, 380, 383; iii, 116, 214, 255, 278, 295, 307, 315, 411, 423, 446, 454
Mears & Stainbank, bell-founders, ii, 229, 245; iii, 116, 261, 266, 411, 461, 462
Measures, Benj., iii, 171
Medbury Farm (Elstow), iii, 282
Medgate, Jos., iii, 392; Thos., iii, 392
Medland, Will., iii, 60
Medlicott, Thos., ii, 281
Medmenham, man. (Bucks), i, 366, 370
Meech, John, ii, 317
Meen, Eliz., ii, 215
Meisil, Rob. de, iii, 192
Melchbourne (Melceburne), i, 349; ii, 107, 115, 146, 197; iii, 59 *n*, 95, 123, 132, 142-143, 154; adv., iii, 143; chap., iii, 143; ch., i, 314 *n*, 315 *n*, 318, 394; iii, 143; man., i, 394; iii, 142; mkts. and fairs, ii, 88; iii, 142; mills, iii, 142, 143; priest's stipend, i, 336; sch., ii, 183
Melchbourne, Rich. de, iii, 137
Melchbourne Park, ii, 147; iii, 41, 142, 168
Melchbourne Preceptory, i, 315 *n*, 394; ii, 147; iii, 95, 142, 143, 154, 165, 198
Meldone, *see* Maulden
Melebroc, *see* Millbrook
Mellents, fam., ii, 21 *n*
Melton Mowbray, man., iii, 346
Mendham, Rev. John, ii, 325
Mentmore (Bucks), i, 402
Mentmore, Hugh de, iii, 376; Miles de, ii, 333
Meppershall (Mepartyshall, Meperbeshale, Mepertesale, Meppersal), ii, 72, 113, 260, 266, 270, 275, 276, 288-293, 304, 305, 341; adv., ii, 292; chap., ii, 293; Chapel Farm, ii, 288; char., ii, 293; ch., i, 315 *n*, 332 *n*; ii, 291, 296; earthworks, i, 296; ii, 24, 288; mans., i, 296 *n*, 391, 393; ii, 288; moat, ii, 288; place-names, ii, 288; rectory, ii, 288; sch., ii, 183
Meppershall (Meptyshall), Gilb. de, ii, 290, 291, 293 *n*; iii, 63; Joan de, ii, 289, 290; iii, 243; John of, ii, 288, 289, 290, 292, 293 *n*, 296 *n*, 334; iii, 243; Kath. de, ii, 289, 292; Nich., ii, 275, 289; Ranulf of, ii, 289; Rob. de, ii, 288, 289, 292; iii, 59, 63; Sarah de, ii, 289; Will. de, ii, 288; iii, 63
Meptyshall, *see* Meppershall
Mercer, Col. Algernon, ii, 147; iii, 228, 231, 233, 439; Isabella, *see* Cardun; Rich., iii, 231, 233; Will. le, iii, 119
Mercers Co. (London), iii, 347
Merchant Taylors Co. (London), ii, 158, 159, 160, 161
Mercia, ii, 18-21; bps. of, i, 346; earldom of, ii, 20
Mercstun, *see* Marston Moretaine
Mere, John de, ii, 322

INDEX

Merefield, Ralph, ii, 357
Meriet, John de, ii, 306; Mary (de), ii, 306, 351
Merlyn, John, iii, 154
Merry, Rich., iii, 352; Will., iii, 417
Mershtone, *see* Marston Moretaine
Merston, John de, iii, 310; Nigel de, iii, 310; Ralf de, iii, 310; Rich. de, iii, 310
Merstone, *see* Marston Moretaine
Merton Priory (Surrey), i, 371 *n*; ii, 154, 291, 305; iii, 29, 374, 418 *n*, 419, 421
Merwe, Maud, iii, 329; Walt., iii, 329
Meryng, Idonia de, ii, 290; John de, ii, 290; Thos. de, ii, 290
Meschin, Will., iii, 133
Mesurier, Le, *see* Le Mesurier
Metcalfe (Metcalf), Chas. J., iii, 219; Chris., iii, 206, 209; Ellen, iii, 206; Jas., iii, 219; Thos., iii, 118; Will., iii, 219; fam., iii, 183, 220
Methodists, i, 345; ii, 186, 214, 234, 242, 246, 265, 299, 303, 312, 320, 325, 374; iii, 31, 100, 132, 153, 186, 190, 289, 297, 305, 308, 314, 324, 338, 345, 367, 375, 383, 389, 394, 414, 415, 421, 432, 451, 455; *see also* Wesleyans
Meyhec, Joan, iii, 76
Michael House (Cambs.), iii, 63
Michel, Michell, *see* Mitchell
Middeltone (Middletone Ernys), *see* Milton Ernest
Middle English, i, 189
Middleho, man. (Hunts), i, 364, 365
Middlesex, Jas., earl of, iii, 276; Lionel, earl of, iii, 276
Middleton, *see* Milton Bryant and Milton Ernest
Middleton, Erasmus, iii, 116; Mary, iii, 301
Midland Association, ii, 44
Milbrook (Milbroke), *see* Millbrook
Mildentone, *see* Milton Ernest
Mildmay, Rob., iii, 236; Sir Walt., ii, 151
Miles, Rev. Hen. H., ii, 280; H., ii, 280
Militia, ii, 67
Mill (Mille), Cath., iii, 195; John, iii, 195; Lewknor, iii, 195; Will. atte, i, 402; W., ii, 197
Mill-Bank, barrow (Dunstable), i, 159
Millbrook, ii, 66, 84, 97, 115, 136, 324; iii, 252, 267, 275, 308, 316-320; adv., iii, 319; char., iii, 319, ch., i, 315 *n*, 352; iii, 318; crown property, iii, 271; man., iii, 317, 326; mkts. and fairs, iii, 317; mills, iii, 316; place-names, iii, 317; sch., ii, 183; vicarage, i, 316 *n*
Millbrook, Geoff., Ld., iii, 317; John, Ld., iii, 317
Millbrook (Milbrook), Walt., iii, 147
Millbrook Warren (Millbrook), ii, 146; iii, 317
Mill Close (Goldington), iii, 206
Miller, Amicia, iii, 198; Maj. John, ii, 70; John, ii, 358, 363; J. B., ii, 189; Will. the, iii, 198
Miller, Conquest & Haynes, iii, 202
Miller's Bog (Pavenham), prehist. rem., iii, 76
Mill Farm (Eversholt), iii, 375
Mill Hill (Eversholt), iii, 375
Milligan, Dr., ii, 99 *n*
Millo (Dunton), ii, 201, 218, 219; man., i, 312; ii, 220, 267
Millowbury (Dunton), ii, 219
Millowbury Farm (Dunton), ii, 218
Millow Hall Farm (Dunton), ii, 219
Mill Race, riv., iii, 399
Mills, Thos., iii, 293; J. T., iii, 404, 405, 407; —, iii, 401
Mills, ii, 74, 118, 212, 261, 262, 263, 266, 268, 269, 275, 276, 278, 283, 297, 300, 301 *n*, 302, 310, 320, 323, 324, 336, 341, 345, 346, 351, 354 *n*, 355, 356, 357, 358, 360, 366, 376, 381 *n*, 385; iii, 11, 23, 24, 30 *n*, 37, 38, 42, 44, 47, 51, 59, 60, 64, 65, 66, 69, 73, 74, 78, 82, 85, 89, 91, 96, 100, 105, 112, 114, 119, 124, 130, 132, 133, 136, 138, 142, 143, 144, 147, 149, 150, 157, 171, 176, 181, 184, 186, 189, 199, 202, 204, 206, 213, 216, 221, 228, 231, 235, 244, 245, 247, 254, 256, 259, 260, 271 *n*, 275, 284, 286, 287, 289, 297, 302, 303, 307, 314, 316, 325, 326, 340, 351, 370, 372, 375, 379, 380, 386, 387, 389, 394, 395, 400, 408, 409, 418, 453
Mills Farm (Dunton), ii, 222
Milneho (hamlet), *see* Millo
Milnho, Rich. de, ii, 211; iii, 260; Rog. de, ii, 211; iii, 260
Milreth, Beatrice, ii, 354; Will., ii, 354
Milton, Sir John, ii, 254; Thos., iii, 60
Milton Bryant (Milton, Milton Bryan), i, 370; ii, 66, 106, 114; iii, 336, 343, 377, 417-21; adv., iii, 421; char., iii, 421; ch., i, 315 *n*; iii, 420; crown property, iii, 271; Leys Farm, iii, 418; man., iii, 418, 419; Nonconf., iii, 418; parson, i, 330; place-names, iii, 418; schs., ii, 183; iii, 418, 421
Milton Ernest, i, 324, 336 *n*, 384; ii, 115, 189; iii, 34, 76, 123, 125 *n*, 143-49, 154 *n*, 183, 224; adv., iii, 148; char., iii, 144, 149; ch., i, 315 *n*, 351, 352; iii, 147. land rents, ii, 132; man., iii, 144; Manor Farm, iii, 144; mills, iii, 130, 144, 147, 149; Nonconf., iii, 144; Oakley Hunt kennels, iii, 144; printing press, iii, 144
Milton Ernest Hall, iii, 144, 149
Milton Grange (Milton Bryant), iii, 419
Milton Harnes, Milton Herneys, *see* Milton Ernest
Milton Hill, iii, 143
Milton House (Castor, Northants), iii, 300
Milward (Mylward), Sir John, i, 331 *n*, 367 *n*, 368, 402; Rich., ii, 326; Will., ii, 334
Mineccan, Phil., iii, 220 *n*
Missenden Abbey (Bucks), i, 388; iii, 107
Mitchell (Michell, Michel), Avery, iii, 195; John, iii, 195, 451; Rich., ii, 357; Rob., ii, 346; Thos., ii, 357; Will., iii, 50; W. C., ii, 190
Mitchener, Mrs., iii, 435
Moat Farm (Cranfield), iii, 275
Moat Farm (Marston Moretaine), iii, 308
Moat Hall (Eaton Bray), iii, 369
Moats, i, 303-8; ii, 226, 256, 288, 308, 325, 329, 362 *n*, 376, 378, 384; iii, 2, 8 *n*, 42, 83, 96, 104, 109, 124, 136, 153-4, 157, 160, 168, 171, 181, 186, 190, 205, 212, 233, 242, 275, 276, 284, 289, 297, 305, 308, 311, 314, 320, 324, 329, 369, 370, 375, 379, 390, 400, 421, 427, 432, 439, 448, 451
Mobbs, E. R., ii, 200
Moddry (Clophill), iii, 316, 318; ch., i, 352; hermitage, i, 351, 352
Moding, iii, 107
Moggerhanger, i, 307, 380; ii, 21, 116, 209; iii, 228; adv., iii, 233; ch., iii, 228, 233; man., iii, 230, 247; sch., ii, 183; woods, ii, 145
Moggerhanger House, iii, 228, 233
Moggerhanger Park, ii, 147
Mohun, Christina, ii, 353; Isabel, ii, 306, 351, 352 *n*; Joan, ii, 351, 353, 356, 360; John de, ii, 306, 351, 353; Mary de, ii, 306, 351; Reg. de, ii, 306, 351; Will. de, ii, 306, 351
Mokehangre, *see* Moggerhanger
Mole, Anne, iii, 438; Will., iii, 438
Moleyns, Ld., iii, 436, 438
Molivers Wood (Bromham), iii, 44
Molluscs, i, 69-70
Molyneux, Ld., ii, 275
Monasteries, advs., i, 314; alien houses, i, 400, 403; dissolution of the, i, 330; feudal service, i, 319; grants to, i, 316; legacies to, i, 325; parish chs. granted to, i, 313, 315; property survey, ii, 91; rights, i, 323
Monchesney (Monchensey), Beatrice, ii, 203; iii, 13, 114; Will. de, iii, 13, 46, 52, 114, 159, 383; Sir Will. de, iii, 97
Money-pit (Totternhoe), earthwork, i, 294
Monkhouse, Rev. W., i, 297; —, iii, 18, 20
Monk's Close (Pulloxhill), ii, 376 *n*
Monmouth, duke of, ii, 58; iii, 441; Chas., earl of, iii, 111
Monoux, Alice, iii, 334; Anne, iii, 329; Eliz., Lady, iii, 423; Eliz., iii, 177, 329; Frances, ii, 243; Geo., iii, 329; Sir Humph., ii, 56, 191, 243; iii, 177, 330, 334, 335; Humph., ii, 41, 44; iii, 329, 331; Lewis, iii, 329; Mary, iii, 330, 335; Sir Phil., ii, 66 *n*, 69, 242, 243, 245; iii, 20, 330, 334, 335, 423; Thos., iii, 329; fam., ii, 66; iii, 276, 331, 334
Montagu, John, marquess of, ii, 39
Montagu (Montague), Chas., *see* Manchester, duke of; Sir Edw., iii, 92; Edw., ii, 339; iii, 155, 169; Geo., ii, 275; Geo. H., iii, 387; Sir Hen., iii, 168; Mary, ii, 295; Rog., iii, 155; Sim., iii, 155; Thos., ii, 295; iii, 126; Will., ii, 341; iii, 387; Ld. Chief Justice, ii, 96
Montaigne, Geo., bp., *see* Lincoln, bps. of
Montalt, John de, iii, 370 *n*; Millicent de, iii, 370 *n*; 448, 449
Montfort, Edm. de, iii, 144; Hen. de, ii, 30; iii, 144; Sim. de, i, 372, 373 *n*; ii, 30, 31, 351; iii, 144, 229, 353; *see also* Leicester, earl of; Thos. de, iii, 144; Will., le, iii, 119 *n*, 122; fam., ii, 21 *n*
Montgomery, Phil., earl of, iii, 290
Montgomery, Jane, iii, 391; Lewis, iii, 391
Monumental effigies, ii, 172, 217, 218, 232, 233, 249, 250, 265, 269, 273, 278, 279, 292, 312, 319, 324, 332, 343, 379; iii, 28, 39, 48, 68, 76, 120, 135, 148, 152, 184, 208, 214, 218, 222, 226, 232, 237, 241, 255, 260, 261, 264-6, 278, 281, 283, 295, 306, 307, 312, 314-16, 317 *n*, 319, 328, 334, 340, 345, 348, 366, 373, 378, 382, 385, 388, 393, 397, 398, 410, 411, 413, 416, 418, 420, 423, 425, 434, 438, 441 *n*, 445-6, 461

Moody, Edm., iii, 340; F., iii, 340; Rob. S., iii, 340; Ursula, iii, 340
Moore (More), Edm., iii, 196; Eliz., i, 336 *n*; Fran., ii, 146; iii, 384; Sir Hen., i, 336 *n*; iii, 198; Sir John, iii, 250; Dr. John, i, 336 *n*; John, iii, 246, 415; Margery de la, ii, 276; Mary, iii, 246; Rich., iii, 201, 449; Rob. le (de la), ii, 251 *n*, 276; Will., iii, 210; Dr., ii, 312
Moor End (Eaton Bray), cemetery, iii, 369; mill, iii, 370
Moor End (Felmersham), iii, 59
Moorland (Kempston), iii, 297
Moote, John, ii, 360; iii, 394
Moravians, i, 344; iii, 4, 9, 31, 153, 157, 171
Morcar, priest, i, 311; ii, 356, 373; iii, 344, 423
Mordaunt, bar., iii, 111
Mordaunt, Lds., i, 331 *n*, 335; iii, 22, 35, 97, 100, 111, 114, 116, 220; Hen., ii, 40; iii, 111, 326, 327; John, iii, 13, 113, 115, 129 *n*, 219, 329, 443; Lewis, iii, 51, 96, 111, 113, 115, 253; John, vsct., ii, 56
Mordaunt, Agnes, iii, 110 *n*; Alice, iii, 110; Anne, iii, 13, 117, 221, 326; Cecilia, iii, 246, 247, 253; Chas., ii, 60; iii, 111, 150; Edm., ii, 382; iii, 13, 110, 113, 114; Eliz., iii, 326, 329; Ellen, iii, 110; Eustace, iii, 60, 110, 112; Geo., iii, 246, 247, 253, 254, 259; Hen., iii, 116, 253; Joan, iii, 97; Joane, Lady, iii, 111; Sir John, iii, 110, 111, 116, 183; John, ii, 53; iii, 97, 98, 110, 231, 247, 253, 332; *see also* Peterborough, earl of; Lewis, ii, 39; iii, 332; Marg., iii, 326; Maud de, iii, 324; Nichola de, iii, 324; Osmund, iii, 60; Rob., iii, 97, 98, 110, 112, 113; Will., ii, 147; iii, 110, 114, 150, 221, 324; W., wife of, i, 335 *n*; fam., i, 335; ii, 56, 293; iii, 55, 109, 116
Mordaunts Manor (Turvey), iii, 110; mill., iii, 114
More, fam., *see* Moore
More Close (Kempston), iii, 302
Morecote, John, iii, 380
Morewood, Frances, iii, 282; Gilb., iii, 282; Grace, iii, 282
Morgan, Anne, ii, 330; Ant., ii, 330; Fran., ii, 330; Rob., ii, 278, 324, 343; Thos., ii, 330, 378; Will., iii, 195, 398; iii, 326
Morice, *see* Morris
Morin (Moryn), John, i, 388; iii, 65; Philippa, iii, 67; Ralf, i, 388, 389 *n*, 390 *n*; iii, 65, 66, 67, 212; fam., iii, 212
Morins, Rich. de, i, 371, 372, 373 *n*, 374, 377, 379, 401 *n*; iii, 363
Morinsbury, man. (Ravensden), iii, 212
Morker, John, iii, 183, 216
Morkere, earl, ii, 22
Morley, Agnes, iii, 106; Hawisia de, iii, 426; Nich., iii, 106; Rob. de, iii, 426; S. K., iii, 157
Morrell, Anne, iii, 407; John, iii, 407
Morrells, man. (Leighton Buzzard), iii, 407
Morris (Morice, Morres), Agnes, ii, 252; iii, 225; Alice, iii, 291; Benj., ii, 359; Fran., iii, 255; Sir John, ii, 227; John, ii, 227, 252, 253, 329; iii, 225; Marg., ii, 329; Thos., iii, 129 *n*, 291; Walt., iii, 443
Morrison, Sir Chas., iii, 253, 302, 376; Dorothy, Lady, iii, 376; Dorothy, iii, 302; Eliz., iii, 254; fam., iii, 324
Morsbury Hill, *see* Mossbury, earthwork
Morteyn, Constance de, iii, 309; Edm. de, iii, 309, 433; Eliz., Lady, iii, 309; Eliz., i, 354, 357; iii, 23, 433; Eustace, iii, 433; Joan, iii, 406, 433; Sir John, iii, 309; John (de), iii, 309, 406, 433; Kath., iii, 386 *n*, 433; Thos., iii, 433; Will., iii, 386 *n*, 433; fam., iii, 311, 313; *see also* Morton
Morteynes man. (Stanbridge), iii, 407
Mortimer, Agatha, ii, 351, 352; Hen., ii, 352; Hugh, ii, 235, 306, 307, 350, 351, 352, 357, 358, 360, 366; Isabel, i, 391 *n*; Joan, ii, 352; John, iii, 405; Marg., ii, 235, 352; iii, 281; Maud, ii, 352 *n*; Petronilla de, ii, 307, 352 *n*; Rog., *see* March, earl of; Will. de, ii, 307, 352
Morton, Ann, iii, 368; John de, iii, 422; *see also* Morteyn
Mortuing, ii, 211
Morwen (Marwen, Morwenna), ii, 153; iii, 37
Moryn, *see* Morin
Mossbury, earthwork (Ravensden), i, 306, 307; iii, 210, 212
Mossbury, man. (Tempsford), ii, 251, 252, 253
Mosses (Musci), i, 56-8
Moths (Heterocera), i, 80-88
Motor-car industry, ii, 127
Moubray, *see* Mowbray
Moulsoe (Bucks), i, 357; iii, 399
Mounds, burial, *see* Burials and Tumuli
Mount Cabourn Camp (Sussex), Rom. rem., ii, 2, 6
Mounteagle, Lady, iii, 192
Mount Hill (Flitwick), earthwork, i, 286; iii, 284
Mountjoy, Ld., ii, 38
Mount Pleasant (Dunstable), prehist. rem., i, 160, 161
Mount Pleasant (Kensworth), prehist. rem., i, 166
Mowbray, Lds., iii, 30, 324; John, ii, 33; Thos., ii, 320; iii, 334
Mowbray (Moubray), Aliva de, ii, 300, 339; iii, 12, 262; Anne de, ii, 301, 340; iii, 13, 263; Eleanor de, ii, 301; Eliz. de, ii, 301, 339; iii, 263, 264; Isabel, ii, 340; Sir John, i, 379; ii, 211 *n*; John de, ii, 300, 301, 339; iii, 12, 13, 44, 137, 262, 263, 264, 329; *see also* Norfolk, dk. of; Maud de, ii, 300, 341; iii, 12, 262, 329; Rog. de, ii, 300, 339, 344; iii, 12, 44, 77, 262, 329; Thos., i, 379; *see also* Norfolk, dk. of; fam., ii, 223, 235; iii, 11, 136 *n*, 205, 215, 433
Mowsbury Hill, *see* Mossbury, earthwork
Moxhill (Willington), iii, 238, 262
Moyne, Fulk le, iii, 248; Juliana le, iii, 195; Rob. le, iii, 248; Will. le, iii, 195
Mudge, Frances, ii, 379; Rob., ii, 379
Muggerhanger, *see* Moggerhanger
Muir, J. & A., ii, 120
Mulcaster, Rich., ii, 159
Mule, Nich. de, iii, 301
Multone, Thos. de, ii, 28
Munchensy, *see* Monchesney
Munt, —, iii, 361
Munt & Brown, iii, 351
Mural paintings, *see* Wall paintings
Murdak, Christine, i, 390; Hen., *see* York, archbps. of
Mursley, man. (Bucks), i, 370
Musgrave, Sir Chris., ii, 295; Edgar, ii, 296; Eliz. (de), ii, 295; iii, 162; Geo., ii, 296; Horace E., ii, 296; Joan de, iii, 162; Jos., ii, 295, 296; Rich. de, iii, 162; Rob. de, iii, 162
Mustard, Christine, i, 386 *n*; Sim., iii, 383
Muswell Hill, *see* Gooseberry-Bush Hill
Mycetozoa (Myxomycetes), i, 66-7
Myddleton, *see* Milton Bryant and Milton Ernest
Mydelton, *see* Milton Bryant and Milton Ernest
Mylton Harneys, *see* Milton Ernest
Mylward, *see* Milward
Myrnut, Walt. de, iii, 85

Nailour, Mary, iii, 235
Napier, Eliz., Lady, ii, 363; Frances, ii, 353; Sir John, ii, 295, 364; John, ii, 353; Penelope, ii, 373; Rich., ii, 307; Sir Rob., ii, 44, 54, 92, 295, 332, 349 *n*, 350, 353, 354, 355, 356, 359, 360, 361, 363, 373, 374, 375; Rob., ii, 307, 356; Sir Theo., ii, 295 *n*; Theo., ii, 353, 375; fam., ii, 119
Nares (Nares Gladley), man., *see* Gladley
Nares Gladley Farm, iii, 409
Neale (Neal, Neele), Bridg., iii, 415; Edm., ii, 360; Eliz., ii, 380; Esther, iii, 385; Hester, iii, 134; John, ii, 54 *n*; iii, 134, 135; Jos., ii, 182 *n*; iii, 136, 165, 170; Noah, iii, 157; Rich., iii, 134, 173; Thos., ii, 377, 378, 380; iii, 134, 173; —, iii, 132 *n*
Needham, Bridg., ii, 338; Eustace, iii, 328; Fran., iii, 198, 294; Geo., iii, 328; Jer., iii, 328; Mary, iii, 198; Maurice, iii, 328
Neele, *see* Neale
Negoose, Thos., ii, 156
Negus, Henry, iii, 103
Nene, riv., i, 189; ii, 71
Neolithic Age, i, 158-67, 174, 269, 270; ii, 348
Netherbury, man. (Gt. Barford), *see* Burdelys
Nether Dean man. (Dean), iii, 133, 134
Nethersted (Colmworth), iii, 186; man. houses, i, 305
Nethertemple (Millbrook), iii, 318
Nevill (Neville), Alan de, ii, 144; Anne, iii, 14; Dorothy, iii, 14, 235, 330; Eliz., ii, 247, 275; iii, 13; Geo., iii, 13; *see also* Bedford, duke of; Hen., iii, 14; Sir John, iii, 215, 235, 330; John (de), ii, 203, 247, 275; iii, 13, 14; Kath., iii, 14; Lucy, iii, 14, 46; Nich. de, ii, 289; iii, 63 *n*; Sir Rich., iii, 46; Rich., iii, 14; fam., iii, 46, 77, 96, 181, 212, 331, 383
New (Luton), ii, 361
Newark, Ad. of, i, 353
Newbottle, man., i, 376, 377
Newbury (Newberry) man. (Silsoe), ii, 329, 330, 332
Newbury Farm Moat (Silsoe), ii, 325
Newby, Thos. de, iii, 276
Newcastle, dk. of, ii, 62 *n*; Will., dk. of, iii, 43; earl of, ii, 345

INDEX

New College (Oxford), ii, 157, 160-75; iii, 324, 425
Newcombe, Steph., iii, 122
Newcome, —, bellfounders, ii, 226, 245, 254, 299, 312; iii, 29, 63, 94, 148, 208, 233, 250, 278, 283, 323, 393, 398
Newdigate, Anne, ii, 322; Ant., ii, 343; Sir John, ii, 190; John, iii, 326; Sir Rich., iii, 289; Sir Rob., ii, 339, 340; Rob., ii, 340, 341; iii, 326; Thos., ii, 322, 323
Newebond, Gunnora, de, ii, 255; Nich. de, ii, 255
Newell (Newill), Gabriel, iii, 280; John, iii, 280; Lucretia, iii, 80
Newenham, Ann, iii, 72; Will., iii, 72
Newes, Pet., iii, 259
Newhouse, abbot of, i, 314, 353
Newill, *see* Newell
Newman, Anne, ii, 235; Barth., iii, 225; Cecilia, iii, 225; Dan., ii, 235; Eliz., ii, 235 *n*; John, iii, 184; Thos., ii, 241; iii, 200
Newmarket, ii, 191
Newmarket Heath, earthworks, i, 176
New Mill End (Luton), ii, 374
Newnham (Goldington), i, 315 *n*, 316 *n*, 362 *n*, 379; iii, 202; A.S. rem., i, 186; man., iii, 205
Newnham, man. (Biddenham), iii, 37
Newnham Priory, i, 303, 305, 313, 314, 315 *n*, 317, 322, 326, 331 *n*, 332, 349, 350, 354, 362, 371 *n*, 372 *n*, 377-85; ii, 145, 153, 154, 215, 257, 258, 301, 338; iii, 2, 11, 12, 16 *n*, 24, 29, 37, 88, 90, 91, 95, 97, 98, 100, 114, 180, 202-6, 208, 210, 212, 214, 216, 221, 235, 236, 237, 258, 261, 264, 266, 331, 334, 335, 342, 353, 378, 406, 424, 425; endowment, i, 350, 380; ii, 218; foundation, i, 377, 391 *n*; mills, i, 305; ii, 155; iii, 206; priors, i, 328, 372 *n*, 381, 391; ii, 154, 155, 218 *n*; iii, 12, 23, 30, 90, 184, 185, 203, 204, 216, 236, 342
Newport, Anne, ctss. of, ii, 347, 382; Mountjoy, earl of, ii, 347, 382
Newport, Mercia, ii, 378 *n*; Will., ii, 378*n*
Newport Pagnell (Bucks), ii, 46, 47, 48, 49, 51; iii, 271
New Rowney Farm (Southill), iii, 259
Newton (Dunton), ii, 218, 219
Newton, Frances, ii, 378; Humph., iii, 21 *n*; John, iii, 21 *n*; Rich. de, i, 401, 402; Will., ii, 378; iii, 21 *n*; —, iii, 31
Newton Blossomville (Bucks), iii, 114
Newton Bromswold (Northants), ii, 71; iii, 123, 175
Newtonbury, man. (Dunton), *see* Dunton Chamberlain
Nichol, *see* Nicoll
Nicholas, archd. of Beds, i, 313, 379 *n*, 390 *n*
Nicholas's Mill (Flitwick), iii, 287
Nicoll (Nichol), Edw., iii, 429; Thos., iii, 429; Will., iii, 31
Nicolls, Mary, iii, 388; Rob., iii, 271; Rog., iii, 73
Noble, Geo., ii, 270
Nodes, Chas., ii, 234; Geo., ii, 234, 286, 287; iii, 39; Helen, iii, 39; John, ii, 382; iii, 261
Noel, Jas., ii, 235; John, ii, 235
No-man's-land Common (Herts), palæolithic impl., i, 150
Nones Stocking Close (Chicksands), ii, 266
Norbury (Norbery), Anne, iii, 78, 373; Sir Hen., iii, 78; Joan, iii, 78; Sir John, iii, 78; Will., iii, 126
Norfolk, assessment of, ii, 48 *n*
Norfolk, ctsses. of, Constance, iii, 12; Marg., i, 351 *n*; Maud, iii, 439; dchsses. of, Eliz., ii, 223, 267, 301, 340; Eleanor, ii, 268, 275; dks. of, i, 363, 364; iii, 166 *n*, 211, 237, 238, 239; iii, 418; John, ii, 220 *n*, 223, 268, 275, 283 *n*, 301; Phil., iii, 192; Thos., ii, 267 *n*, 301, 340; iii, 12, 41, 111, 263; earls, ii, 220, 223, 268; iii, 71 *n*; John, iii, 12; Rog., iii, 439; Thos., ii, 339; iii, 12
Norgewele, *see* Northill
Norman, iii, 247
Norman, Rob., ii, 293 *n*
Norrell, *see* Northill
Norris, Hen., iii, 172; Sir John, ii, 46; Sarah E., iii, 187; Toby, ii, 299; iii, 135
Nortgible, *see* Northill
Nortgivele, *see* Northill
Nortgylle, *see* Northill
North, Chas., iii, 151; Sir Edw., iii, 30; Gilb., iii, 123, 180
Northampton, iii, 10; Hosp. of Holy Trinity, iii, 40
Northampton, earldom of, iii, 408
Northampton, earls of, iii, 209, 428; Sim., i, 387 *n*, 388; ii, 255; Will., iii, 168, 169, 172, 208
Northampton, Rich. of, i, 353
Northamptonshire, lace ind., ii, 122, 123, 124
Northaw Wood, ii, 361 *n*
North End (Stagsden), iii, 96
North End Farm (Odell), iii, 69
Northewell, John de, ii, 362
Northfleet, Thos. de, ii, 214
Northiell, *see* Northill
Northill, i, 331, 365, 403; ii, 6, 43, 95 *n*, 116; iii, 175, 176, 227, 238, 239, 242-51; adv., iii, 250; anct. burials, ii, 1; chant., i, 329; ii, 92; char., iii, 251; chs., i, 331, 349, 403; iii, 249, 273; copyhold at, ii, 90; mans., ii, 77; iii, 243; mills, iii, 247; rectors, i, 403; Rom. rem., ii, 9; iii, 243; schs., ii, 183; iii, 242
Northill College, i, 403; ii, 92, 251; iii, 244, 250
Northill College Farm, iii, 244
Northill College Manor, iii, 244
Northumberland, earldom of, ii, 20, 22
Northumberland, Kath., ctss. of, iii, 114; earls of, ii, 42; Hen., iii, 14; Siward, iii, 168; Tostig, ii, 22; Uhtred, ii, 20
Northwood, man. (Luton), *see* Norwood
Northwood (Northwode), Alice de, ii, 328; Gilb. de, iii, 396 *n*; Hen. de, ii, 328; iii, 320, 323, 396; John de, iii, 323, 396; Rich. de, ii, 328; Sim. de, i, 327; Thos. de, ii, 328
Northwood End (Haynes), ii, 338
Norton, Alice de, iii, 224; Brett, iii, 259; Eliz. de, ii, 322; Sir Geo., ii, 363; Graveley, ii, 382; Hen., ii, 382; Isabella (de), ii, 383; Sir John, ii, 377, 380; John, ii, 312; Lettice, ii, 382 *n*; Luke, ii, 361, 382, 383; Pet. de, ii, 322; Sir Ralph de, ii, 322; Rich., ii, 184 *n*, 310, 312, 360, 377, 383, 384; Rob., ii, 382; Sarah, iii, 259; Thos. (de), ii, 322, 376, 377, 382, 383; Walt., ii, 382, 383; Will. (de), ii, 382, 383; iii, 224; Col., ii, 47

Norton (*cont.*)
Nortyevele, *see* Northill
Norwell, *see* Northill
Norwich, Dr. Tanners, archd. of, ii, 170; Fran. White, bp. of, ii, 162
Norwich, Mary, ctss. of, iii, 330; Edw., earl of, iii, 330
Norwich, Anne, iii, 340; Greg., i, 387; Ralph, iii, 340
Norwood (Ridgmont), iii, 323
Norwood, man. (Luton), ii, 350, 363
Norwood, man. (Silsoe), ii, 328, 329, 332; chant., ii, 333
Norwood, Edm., iii, 326; John, iii, 326; Thos., iii, 326
Notley Grange (Bucks), ii, 385
Notley Priory (Bucks), i, 387 *n*, 388 *n*; ii, 273, 385
Nottinge, *see* Knotting
Nottingham, Anne, ctss. of, ii, 340; John, earl of, ii, 339; iii, 12, 263; Thos., earl of, *see* Norfolk, dk. of; Will., earl of, ii, 301, 340
Nowers, Grace de, ii, 358; Joan, iii, 118; John de, ii, 358; iii, 118; Rich. de, iii, 118; Rog. de, iii, 118, 119, 122
Nunwood (Harrold), iii, 64, 66
Nurse, Will., ii, 342 *n*
Nussa, Terricus de, i, 394
Nutley (Bucks), *see* Notley (Bucks)
Nutley, Luke of, i, 401, 402
Nyandser, John, ii, 385 *n*; Marg., ii, 385 *n*

Oakden, Sim., iii, 165
Oakely, *see* Oakley
Oakes Farm (Kempston), iii, 302
Oaklands (Aspley Guise), iii, 338
Oakley, i, 335 *n*; ii, 115, 166, 188; iii, 76, 123, 128, 130, 131, 149-53; adv., i, 384; iii, 152; bridge, iii, 149, 150; chant., iii, 153; char., iii, 153; ch., i, 315 *n*, 318, 382; iii, 130, 131, 132, 151; fishery, iii, 149; mans., iii, 149; mills, iii, 149, 150; Nonconf., iii, 153; place-names, iii, 149; sch., ii, 183; vicarage, i, 317; witchcraft at, ii, 100; iii, 149
Oakley, Fran., iii, 9; Will., iii, 18 *n*
Oakley Club, ii, 189
Oakley Hill, iii, 149
Oakley House (Oakley), ii, 187; iii, 149
Oakley Hunt, ii, 187-90; iii, 144
Oakley Hunt steeplechases, ii, 194
Oakley Reynes, man. (Oakley), iii, 149
Obness (Bolnhurst), i, 276
Occliffe, *see* Hockliffe
Ocle, *see* Oakley
Ocle-cum-Clapham, man. (Clapham), iii, 130, 150
Octona, *see* Houghton Conquest
Odecroft, hun., iii, 391
Odell, ii, 44, 115; iii, 34, 50, 54, 59, 69-76, 77, 100, 102; adv., iii, 76; ch., i, 300; iii, 75; earthwork, i, 300; fairs and mkts., ii, 88; iii, 35, 69, 73; forest offences, ii, 144; ind., iii, 69; land values, ii, 92; mans., iii, 73-74; mills, i, 300; iii, 59, 73, 74; sch., ii, 184
Odell, bar., i, 300; ii, 30 *n*, 234 *n*, 282, 326, 328; iii, 69, 71-4, 84, 92, 105, 106, 113, 118, 146, 314, 321, 322, 448, 449

Odell, hon. of, ii, 283 ; iii, 82, 159
Odell, Little, man., iii, 69, 73, 74
Odell, Rob. (of), i, 365 ; iii, 46, 311 ; Steph., iii, 31 ; Thos., iii, 311 ; *see also* Wahull
Odell Castle, i, 300 ; iii, 69, 73, 102
Odell woods, iii, 69
Odley, Odyll, *see* Odell
Offa, king of Mercia, i, 190, 309, 310, 315 *n* ; ii, 20, 314, 361 ; iii, 151, 401
Offley (Herts), iii, 349
Offley, John, ii, 63 ; Sir Thos., ii, 161 ; —, iii, 20
Oger, ii, 22
Oilgi, Oilli, de, *see* Doyley
Okele, *see* Oakley
Okey, Thos., iii, 323 ; Col., ii, 55 ; iii, 64, 271, 404
Okley, *see* Oakley
Olaf, priest, ii, 341
Oldfeild, Rich., ii, 229 ; Rob., ii, 299, 373
Oldham, Hugh, i, 399 ; iii, 408 ; Sim., iii, 201
Old Ramerick Farm (Holwell), ii, 286
Old Rowney Farm (Southill), iii, 259
Olive Ground, close (Leighton Buzzard), iii, 404
Oliver, Jas., iii, 154 ; Jane, iii, 203 ; John, ii, 285 *n* ; N. D. T., ii, 199 ; Sim., iii, 154 ; Will., iii, 203
Oliver's Ditch (Clapham), iii, 130
Olivier, Dan. S., ii, 182 *n*, 280 ; Mary A., ii, 280 ; Susanna, ii, 280
Olney (Bucks), ii, 187 ; iii, 418 ; mkt., iii, 69
Olney, Goditha, iii, 219 ; Rob., iii, 219
Ombersley, barons of, ii, 330
O'Neill, Rev. —, ii, 374
Ongley, Lds., ii, 70, 231 ; iii, 253, 254 ; Rob., iii, 253, 257
Ongley, E., ii, 194 ; Frances, ii, 243 ; F., ii, 194 ; R. H., ii, 63, 64 ; Sir Sam., iii, 255 ; Sam., ii, 60, 62, 243
Ordui (Ordwig), iii, 38, 258, 327
Ordway, John, ii, 385
Ordwig, *see* Ordui
Orewell, Alan de, iii, 214
Orford, Edw., earl of, iii, 376
Orkneys, the, straw-hat ind., ii, 120
Orlebar, Rev. A., i, 283 ; Diana, iii, 60, 81, 87 ; Geo., iii, 82, 86, 233 ; Jane, iii, 86 ; John, iii, 82, 85 *n*, 94, 146 ; Judith, iii, 60 ; Marg., iii, 86, 233 ; Rich., ii, 59, 69 ; iii, 81, 82, 83, 86, 87 ; Rich. R. B., iii, 81, 82, 83, 87 ; Thos., iii, 60, 87 ; Ursula, iii, 60 ; Will. A., iii, 84, 87 ; Mrs., ii, 122 ; —, iii, 80
Ormond, dk. of, iii, 4
Ormond, Joan, iii, 191 ; John, iii, 191
Ormsby, Arth., iii, 154 ; Marg., iii, 154
Ornaments, A.S., i, 179, 181, 182, 184, 187, 189, 190 ; ii, 266 ; iii, 57, 402 ; Rom., ii, 6, 10, 14, 15 ; Rom.-Brit., ii, 11, 14
Orwelle Meade (Clifton), ii, 278
Osbaldiston, Dorothy, iii, 236 ; John, iii, 236 ; Rich., iii, 236
Osbern, iii, 42, 52, 92, 195, 207 *n*
Osbert, i, 313 ; iii, 118, 138, 448
Osborn (Osborne), Sir Algernon, ii, 197 ; Sir Algernon K. B., ii, 270, 271, 273, 291, 342, 344 ; Alice, iii, 39 ; Sir Daniel, ii, 270 ; Sir Danvers, ii, 61, 66 *n*, 273 ; Dorothy, ii, 275 ; Sir Edw., iii, 244 ; Edw., iii, 39, 244, 250 ;
Osborn (*cont.*)
Eliz., iii, 244 ; Sir Geo., ii, 63 *n*, 64, 69, 268, 273, 291 ; Sir Geo. R., ii, 66 *n* ; Hen., ii, 271 ; Sir John, ii, 69, 269, 270, 271, 273, 275, 342 ; John, ii, 59, 66 *n*, 276 ; Sir Pet., ii, 43, 271, 273, 344 ; Pet., ii, 271, 275, 276, 342, 344 ; Sarah, ii, 61, 280 ; Thos., ii, 270, 280 ; Mrs., ii, 62, 63 *n*, 64 ; iii, 428
Osborne, Ld. F. G., ii, 193
Oseney Abbey, *see* Osney
Osgodby, Ad. de, iii, 461
Osiet, iii, 46, 248
Oskytel, archbp., *see* York, archbps. of
Osmund, canon, iii, 37
Osney Abbey, i, 383 ; iii, 153 *n*
Ossington (Notts), i, 394
Ossory, earl of, ii, 192
Ossory, Upper, earl of, *see* Upper Ossory
Osulf, iii, 112, 149
Oswulf, iii, 431
Ottobon, ii, 32
Ottway, Rich., iii, 63
Oughtred, Sir Ant., iii, 158
Oundle, ii, 17 *n*
Ouse, man. (Sharnbrook), iii, 91, 92
Ouse, riv., i, 1, 27, 28, 43 ; ii, 71 ; earthworks near, i, 280 ; isls. in, iii, 195, 202 ; Rom.-Brit. settlement near, ii, 5
Ousel (Ouzel or Lovat), riv , ii, 71
Oustone, *see* Houghton Conquest
Over (Cambs.), ii, 241
Overdean, man. (Dean), iii, 133-4 ; mills, iii, 133
Overhey Wood, iii, 43
Overstone (Northants), iii, 122
Ovy, Anne, iii, 97 ; Nich., iii, 97 ; Philippa, iii, 97
Ow, Ailmar d', iii, 258 ; Will. de, ii, 267 *n*
Owen, Jane, iii, 265 ; Hen., iii, 265 ; fam., iii, 266
Owens & Co., ii, 261
Ox Close (Goldington), iii, 208 *n*
Oxenbridge, Frideswide, Lady, iii, 343 ; Sir Thos., iii, 343
Oxenbrigge, John, ii, 299
Oxford, iii, 16, 17 ; siege, ii, 49
Oxford, Isabel, ctss. of, i, 366 *n* ; iii, 314 ; earls of, iii, 310 ; Hugh, iii, 314 ; John, iii, 263 ; Rob., iii, 314, 459 *n*
Oxfordshire, lace ind., ii, 123
Oxhey Chapel, ii, 317
Oyldeboef (Wildeboef), John, i, 386 ; iii, 239, 332 ; Laura, iii, 239, 332 ; Marg. de, iii, 187 ; Ralf de, iii, 186 ; Rich. de, iii, 186 ; Walt., iii, 186, 187 ; Will., iii, 154, 186
Oyley, d', *see* Doyley
Ozingell, i, 181 *n*

Pabenham, par., *see* Pavenham
Pabenham (Pavenham), Agnes, iii, 41 ; Alice, iii, 50 ; Athelina, iii, 50 ; Eleanor, iii, 77 ; Elena de, iii, 223 ; Eliz., ii, 243 ; iii, 57, 77 ; Sir Jas., iii, 211 ; Jas. de, iii, 50, 224, 259, 330 ; Joan, iii, 77, 259 ; Sir John de, iii, 258 ; John de, ii, 145 ; iii, 41, 43, 50, 57, 64, 67, 77, 79, 83, 85, 223, 224, 226, 258 ; Kath., iii, 77, 191 ; Laur. de, ii, 243 ; iii, 64, 77, 191 ; Margery, iii, 50, 211, 224, 330 ; Rich. de, iii, 67 ; Thos., iii, 77, 85, 224
Pack & Chapman, ii, 373 ; iii, 366
Page, Chas., iii, 416 ; Eliz., Lady, iii, 435 ; Eliz., iii, 435 ; Frances,
Page (*cont.*)
ii, 379 ; Sir Greg., iii, 344 ; Hen., iii, 76 ; John, ii, 379, 380 ; Matth., ii, 377 ; Pet., ii, 377 ; iii, 375 ; Sir Rich., iii, 385, 435 ; Rich., ii, 379, 380 ; Will. S., iii, 416
Paget (Pagett), Sir Will., ii, 377 ; iii, 443 ; Rev., —, iii, 154
Page-Turner, Sir Edw., ii, 363, 385 ; F. A., ii, 363, 383, 385, 387 ; iii, 434, 435 ; Sir Greg., ii, 385 ; iii, 343, 344, 422, 434 ; fam., iii, 435
Pakenham Park (Carlton), iii, 50
Pakinton, i, 360
Palace Yard (Splashyard), wood, (Roxton), i, 302
Palæolithic implements, *see* Implements
Palæolithic races, i, 151
Palæolithic rem., i, 145-58
Palæontology, i, 33-35
Palldocke, John, iii, 208
Palmer, Chas., iii, 236, 253 ; Chas. F., ii, 189 ; iii, 245 ; Dorothy, iii, 236 ; Rev. Fran., ii, 246 ; Fran., iii, 14 *n* ; G., ii, 48 ; Hen., ii, 277 ; Hen. F., iii, 245 ; John S., ii, 358 ; Madeline, Lady, iii, 245 ; Rob., iii, 253 ; Sam., iii, 9 ; Sir Thos., iii, 268, 358 *n*, 377, 380 ; Thos., ii, 329 ; iii, 253 ; Sir Will., ii, 43 ; iii, 253 ; Will., iii, 162 ; —, iii, 52
Pannells Grove (Leighton Buzzard), iii, 409
Papiatem (Caddington), ii, 315
Papley, Walt., iii, 312
Paradine, Capell, iii, 25 ; John, iii, 25 ; Martha, iii, 25 ; Mary, iii, 31 ; Rob., iii, 156, 226 ; Sarah, iii, 33 ; Thos., iii, 22, 32 ; *see also* Parentine
Parage, Rob., i, 350 *n*
Parcell (Parsell), Mary, iii, 247 ; Nath., iii, 247 ; Will., ii, 291
Pardoe, Rob., iii, 430
Pare, John, iii, 392
Parentine (Parentin), Ellen de, iii, 91 ; Rob., iii, 74, 90, 91 ; Will., iii, 159 ; fam., iii, 91 ; *see also* Paradine
Parentines, man. (Sharnbrook), iii, 91
Pares, Thos., ii, 296
Paris (Parys), Amicia, ii, 330 ; Fulk of, ii, 211 ; Matth., i, 310, 354, 359 ; Rob. de, i, 396, 397 ; iii, 330 ; Will. de, i, 352
Parke (Park), Sir Jas., iii, 270 ; Rog., ii, 341
Park End (Stevington), iii, 100
Parker, Hen., iii, 349 ; John, iii, 325 ; —, i, 345
Park Farm (Eaton Bray), iii, 369
Park Grange (Old Warden), iii, 254
Park House Farm (Podington), iii, 80
Parkinson, W., iii, 428
Parks, ii, 146-7
Park Wood (Harrold), iii, 64
Parliamentary representation, ii, 33-4
Parr, Eliz., iii, 72 ; Hen., iii, 392 Kath., iii, 14 ; Sir Will., iii, 72 ; —, ii, 194
Parratt, Thos., ii, 40
Parry, —, ii, 121
Parsell, Will., *see* Parcell
Parsonage Close (Leighton Buzzard), iii, 415, 416
Parsonage Farm (Haynes), ii, 342 *n*
Parsons, John, iii, 301 ; Kath., iii, 301 ; Thos., iii, 301 ; Will., iii, 332 ; —, ii, 165

INDEX

Partington, Thos., ii, 299
Partridge, Jos. A., iii, 259, 276; Steph., iii, 151; Wharton, iii, 128; Mrs., ii, 314
Parys, *see* Paris
Paschall, Rob., iii, 451
Passelowe (Passelewe, Passaquam), Alice de, ii, 283; Amicabilia, iii, 36 *n*; Gilb., iii, 36, 37, 44 *n*, 386, 387 *n*; Joan, iii, 46; Ralph, iii, 36, 39, 343, 345, 386; Rob., ii, 283, 382; iii, 339; Thos., iii, 36; Will (de), ii, 283; iii, 36, 38, 39, 46
Paston, Agnes, iii, 60, 107, 158, 187
Patenham, *see* Pavenham
Patersen, John W., iii, 447
Patishull (Pateshull, Pattishall), Agnes de, iii, 41; Alice (de), iii, 45; iii, 136; Isabel, iii, 45; Sir John de, i, 325 *n*; John de, ii, 34 *n*; iii, 15, 41, 42, 45, 46, 52, 61, 71 *n*, 105, 107, 137, 215, 329, 330; Kath. de, iii, 15, 136, 330; Mabel, Lady de, i, 395; Mabel de, iii, 330; Martin, ii, 28; Sibyl de, iii, 41, 136; Sir Sim. de, iii, 45; Sim. de, i, 366, 385; ii, 30; iii, 14, 40, 61, 107, 184, 330; Walt. de, iii, 40; Will. (de), iii, 15, 41, 45, 136, 215, 330, 424; —, Lady, i, 355 *n*; fam., iii, 91, 181, 206, 235
Patnam, *see* Pavenham
Patten, Mary A., iii, 274
Pattishall (Northants), i, 371 *n*, 376, 377
Paulet (Powlett), Agnes, Lady, iii, 384; Anne, iii, 177; Eliz., iii, 177; Sir Will., iii, 277, 384; Will., iii, 177
Pauncefote, Isabel, i, 386 *n*
Paunfort Lodge (Ampthill), iii, 268
Paveley, Joan, iii, 143; Rich., iii, 143
Pavement, Rom., ii, 12, 223
Pavenham, i, 318; ii, 115, 124, 139; iii, 34, 59, 60, 76-80, 100, 104, 143; adv., iii, 80; char., iii, 80; ch., i, 318; iii, 63, 79; inclosure, iii, 80, inds., ii, 124-5; iii, 76; mans., iii, 49, 50, 51 *n*, 57, 76-79, 83, 330; mill, iii, 78; sch., ii, 184
Pavenham, bar., iii, 248 *n*
Pavenham, fam., *see* Pabenham
Pavenham Bury (Pavenham), iii, 76, 145
Pavenham rush matting and wicker basket industries, ii, 124-5
Paxton, Gt. (Hunts), ii, 246
Paxton, Edm., iii, 18; Sir Jos., iii, 343
Payne (Payn), Cath., ii, 242; Sir Chas., ii, 252; Chas., iii, 330; Chas. S., iii, 228; Sir C. G., ii, 66 *n*; Dan., iii, 85, 87; Fran., iii,, 82, 119; Sir Gillies (Gillias), ii, 65, 252; iii, 330, 335; John, iii, 330; Mary, iii, 330, 335; Sir Pet., ii, 66 *n*; Pet., iii, 330 *n*; Phil., iii, 330; Rob. le, iii, 186 *n*; Sybil, iii, 82, 119; Thos., iii, 60, 82; Will., iii, 82, 85, 86, 87, 119; —, ii, 65
Paynel (Paynell), Eliz., ii, 345; Joan, iii, 234, 331; Ralph, ii 345 *n*; iii, 45, 46, 52, 98, 234' 331; Thos., ii, 330, 345; fam.' iii, 206
Peake, Edw., ii, 179, 215, 255
Pearce, Mary, ii, 317
Pearles, Anne, iii, 119
Pearse, —, iii, 277
Pearson, Geo. J. H., ii, 246; *see also* Pierson
Pear Tree Close (Turvey), iii, 114 *n*
Peasants' Rising, ii, 35, 90
Peat, Thos., ii, 185 *n*; iii, 226
Peche, Hugh, iii, 229; Ida, iii, 229
Pechesdone, *see* Pegsdon
Peck, John, ii, 363; iii, 183; R., iii, 218; Will., ii, 36
Peckham, archbp., i, 375
Pecohe, Edw., iii, 156
Peddar (Pedder), Agnes, iii, 366; Alys, iii, 425; John, iii, 366, 425; Marg., iii, 366; Matilda, iii, 366; fam., iii, 424
Pedley, John, ii, 318; Will., iii, 183; W., iii, 185; —, ii, 133; iii, 183; fam., ii, 316; iii, 184
Peel, vsct., ii, 66, 231, 242, 244
Peel, Arth., ii, 231; B. L., ii, 199; Sir Rob., ii, 244; Sir Will., ii, 244
Peers, John, iii, 31
Pegsdon (Shillington), ii, 25, 79, 294, 295 *n*, 296, 299; farm, ii, 82; man., i, 312; ii, 296, 297
Peile, Dr., ii, 374
Pekesdene, *see* Pegsdon
Pelham, Chas. A., *see* Yarborough
Peling, man., *see* Pillage, man.
Pemberton, Goddard, ii, 54, 55; John, iii, 208, 311, 333; Sir Lewis, ii, 268; Mary, ii, 268; Ralph, iii, 333; Rob., iii, 333; Rog., iii, 333
Pembridge, Sir Fulk, iii, 299; Marg., Lady, iii, 299
Pembroke, ctsses. of, iii, 40; Eleanor, ii, 306, 350; Isabel, ii, 384; Joan, ii, 223; Mary, iii, 290; Maud, ii, 223 *n*; earls of, ii, 211, 224, 227; iii, 64, 314; Anselm Marshal, ii, 223, 351; Aymer de Valence, ii, 275; Gilb., ii, 226, 228, 229; John Hastings, ii, 238; Laur. de Hastings, iii, 229; Walt. Marshal, ii, 220, 267; Will. Herbert, iii, 173; Will. Marshal, ii, 306, 350, 356, 384, 439, 441, 442; Will. de Valence, ii, 223
Pembroke Hall (Camb.), iii, 248
Pendrid, Will, ii, 245
Penne, John de la, iii, 133
Penneclose (Wootton), iii, 333
Pennefather, Edw., ii, 380
Pennyfathers Hill (Maulden), iii, 313
Penruddocke, Sir Thos., iii, 196
Penthelyn, John, ii, 373
Penyston, Fran., iii, 442, 454
Penythorn, Will., iii, 145
Perche, count of, ii, 350 *n*; Geoff., iii, 439, 442, 446
Percival, Sir John, ii, 158, 159
Perdington, Maud, iii, 211
Perot, *see* Pirot
Perots (Beeston-Caldecote, Trumpingtons), man. (Northill), iii, 248
Perry Hill Farm (Cranfield), iii, 278
Personal Strongholds, i, 285-303
Pertenhall (Pertenhale), i, 297 *n*; ii, 72, 115; iii, 123, 137, 138, 153-7, 159; adv., iii, 156; char., ii, 184 *n*; iii, 157; ch., i, 337 *n*; iii, 155; man., iii, 153, 154, 166; moats, iii, 153; Nonconf., iii, 153; sch., ii, 184
Pertenhall, Eustace de, iii, 155 *n*; Rich. de, iii, 155
Pertenhall Hoo Farm, iii, 153
Pertesoil, Athelina, iii, 159; Eliz., iii, 159; John, iii, 159; Rob., iii, 159; Rog., iii, 159; Sim., iii, 159; Will., iii, 159
Pertsoills (Pertesoyles), man. (Risley), iii, 159
Perys, Agnes, ii, 209; Thos., ii, 209
Peshall (Peshale), Aliva, ii, 300, 339; Sir Rich., ii, 339; iii, 263
Peterborough, R. Clavering, bp. of, iii, 179
Peterborough, earls of, ii, 40 *n*, 53, 56, 59, 60; iii, 114-17; Chas. H., iii, 111; Hen., ii, 43; iii, 51, 111; John, ii, 293; iii, 51, 111; fam., iii, 37 *n*
Peterborough Abbey, i, 312; iii, 70
Peters, Rich., ii, 357
Petever, Alice, iii, 355; John, iii, 355
Petre, Eliz., iii, 203, 209; Sir John, iii, 203; John, iii, 209; Sir Will., iii, 203, 218 *n*; Dr., i, 367, 368
Pettit, fam., iii, 388
Pever (Peyver, Peyvre), Avice, iii, 440 *n*; Beatrice, iii, 442; John, ii, 328; iii, 153, 440-2, 446 *n*; Marg., i, 402; iii, 346, 366, 440; Maria, iii, 442; Mary, iii, 346, 366, 440, 442; Nich., iii, 137, 153, 440, 442; Paul (Paulinus), i, 325 *n*; iii, 343, 439, 440, 444, 446; Rog., iii, 153, 346, 444; Thos., i, 402; iii, 346, 366, 440-2, 453; fam., iii, 166, 446
Peverel, hon. of, iii, 57, 223, 225, 433
Peverel (Peverell, Peveril), Edm., ii, 224, 227, 263; Isabella, ii, 224 *n*; John, ii, 224, 227; Jordan, iii, 372; Marg., ii, 224; Rob., ii, 309, 310; Will., i, 314; iii, 57, 86, 433; fam. of, ii, 262
Peyncourt, Eglina, iii, 59; Nich., iii, 59; Rich., iii, 59; Walt., iii, 60
Peyton (Payton), Marg., ii, 286; Rob., ii, 286; Thos., ii, 286; Will., iii, 122
Peyver (Peyvre), *see* Pever
Pheasant, —, iii, 18
Philibert, Hugh de, ii, 362
Philip, Alice, Lady, iii, 403, 429; Sir John, iii, 403, 429; Will., iii, 403
Phillips (Philips, Phillipps), Sir Edw., iii, 260; Edw., ii, 332; Fran., ii, 212; iii, 30, 201, 255; Frank, iii, 287; Jos., iii, 325; Thos., iii, 325
Phillpotts, Jas. S., ii, 149, 175, 176, 177; Hen., *see* Exeter, bps. of
Pick, *see* Pyke
Pickering, Dorothy E., iii, 259; Sir Edw., iii, 461; Eliz., Lady, iii, 461; Eliz., iii, 428; Sir Gilb., iii, 461; Helen, iii, 428; Montagu, iii, 461; Thos., iii, 428; *see also* Puckering
Pickford, Thos., ii, 314
Pickle industry, ii, 118
Pickman, Rich., ii, 222; iii, 273
Picks (Pykes), man. (Luton), ii, 350, 355, 363
Pickshill (Stevington), iii, 102
Picot, Ad., iii, 46, 331; Anabella, iii, 46, 331; Bald., iii, 46, 234, 235, 331; Dorothy, iii, 235; Isabel, iii, 235; Joan, iii, 45, 234, 331; John, i, 325 *n*; ii, 381; iii, 46, 234, 235, 330, 331; Laur., iii, 366; Mich., iii, 45, 46, 234, 331; Will., iii, 46; fam., iii, 206; *see also* Pigott
Pictavus, iii, 2
Picts Hill Gorse (Turvey), iii, 110
Pierson, Thos., ii, 385; —, ii, 168; *see also* Pearson

Pigeon, Edm., ii, 377; iii, 375; Walt., iii, 272, 272 *n*
Pigham, Will., iii, 219 *n*
Pigott (Piggot, Pigot, Pygot, Pygott), Anne, ii, 338; Bald., iii, 15, 92, 296; Benj., ii, 338; Bridg., ii, 338; Dorothy, iii, 15; Eleanor, i, 390; ii, 211, 224, 248; iii, 248; Eliz., ii, 224 *n*; Fran., ii, 211, 221, 224, 244, 248; iii, 248, 258, 259, 449; Hen., ii, 179, 180; iii, 292; Jane, ii, 385; Joan, iii, 15, 295; John, ii, 211, 224; iii, 15, 215, 216; Laur., iii, 456; Lewis, ii, 211, 224; Marg., i, 357; ii, 211; Margery, iii, 259; Mary, ii, 338; Mich., ii, 211, 224; iii, 15, 295; Rob., iii, 449; Thos., ii, 211, 224; iii, 227, 248, 258, 259, 432, 449; Will., iii, 449; fam., ii, 204
Pilgrim, W., iii, 441
Pillage, man. (Marston Moretaine), iii, 310
Pillinge field (Wootton), iii, 335
Pilling Grene (Wootton), iii, 329
Pilling-in-Wootton, man. (Wootton), iii, 332
Pilling Rowsberry, man. (Wootton), iii, 332
Pilling Shingay, man., *see* Pilling-in-Wootton
Pilsworth, Edw., ii, 299
Pinch, mill of (Sharnbrook), iii, 91
Pinchgut Farm (Marston), iii, 307
Pinfold Hill (Ampthill), iii, 275
Pink (Pinke), Rob., ii, 162, 163
Pinkney, Agnes, iii, 71; Sir Hen., iii, 71; Hen. de, iii, 396, 436; Isabella de, iii, 436; Rob. de, iii, 436
Piozzi, Hester L., ii, 357 *n*
Pipard, *see* Pippard
Pipewell Abbey (Northants), ii, 275; iii, 24, 84, 219, 221; abbot, i, 367 *n*
Pipon, iii, 446
Pippard (Pipard), Ad., iii, 206; Ralph, iii, 16; Rob., iii, 206; Walt., iii, 206
Pippin Wood (Bletsoe), iii, 40
Pirot, ii, 382 *n*, 383; iii, 196, 199, 246, 247, 248
Pirot (Pyro, Pyrot), Elyas de, ii, 81; John, i, 371 *n*; ii, 380; Ralph, i, 366, 372 *n*; ii, 30, 32, 81, 380; iii, 51, 54, 196, 248, 379, 380, 381, 382; Reg., iii, 379; Rich., i, 372 *n*; iii, 382; Will., i, 371 *n*; ii, 377, 379, 380; fam., ii, 324
Pirot's Manor, *see* Perots
Pirton (Herts), ii, 287
Pisaquila, *see* Puisaquila
Pisen, Rob., ii, 270
Pitchford, Admiral, iii, 90
Pittman-Coppin, Rev. John, ii, 317; iii, 406; John C., ii, 317; Mary, ii, 317; Susan, ii, 317
Pitt-Rivers, General, i, 175; ii, 2
Pitts, John, i, 399; iii, 22
Place, Will., iii, 49
Plantagenet, Anne, iii, 171; Blanche, iii, 101; Edm., *see* Kent, earl of; Eleanor, iii, 171; Hen., *see* Lancaster, earl of; Marg., ii, 223; Rich., *see* York, duke of; Thos., ii, 223; *see also* Gloucester, dk. of
Playdell, Will., iii, 310
Plenties, man. (Luton), ii, 350, 363, 364
Pleshey (Essex), iii, 126
Plomer, John, i, 393; Sir Will., iii, 253; Will., ii, 212; iii, 253
Plumpton (Northants), iii, 70 *n*
Plunket, —, ii, 163
Pocklington, John, i, 337, 338; iii, 179
Podington, i, 305, 336, 337, 394; ii, 71, 115, 326; iii, 34, 57, 69, 80-7, 117, 119, 122; adv., iii, 87; char., iii, 87; ch., i, 315 *n*, 336; iii, 86; farms, iii, 80, 81; man., iii, 82, 87, 105; man.-house, iii, 83; mills, iii, 82, 85; place-names, iii, 82; sch., ii, 184; vicarage, i, 316 *n*
Podington, Lady Emma de, iii, 82
Podintone, *see* Podington
Podio Barsaco, John de, i, 327; iii, 408; Pontius de, i, 327 *n*
Poer, John le, ii, 354
Poinz, Joan, iii, 268, 271; Nich., iii, 268, 271
Pole, Joan de la, ii, 227; John de la, ii, 227; Marg., de la, ii, 224, 227; Cardinal Reg., i, 333, 399; iii, 72; Rob., ii, 310; Will. (de la), ii, 224, 310; iii, 216, 403; fam., ii, 262
Polehanger, man. (Meppershall), ii, 290, 291
Polehanger Farm (Meppershall), ii, 288, 291
Poley, Alice, iii, 246, 247; Fran., ii, 221; iii, 246, 247; John, ii, 204, 221; iii, 246, 247; Prudence, ii, 204; Will., ii, 204 *n*; *see also* Pulley
Poleyn, *see* Pulleyn
Polge, Rebecca, iii, 165; Thos., iii, 165
Polhill (Polhill-Turner), Cecil H., iii, 203, 209, 214, 215, 216; Fred., ii, 66 *n*; iii, 20, 203, 215; Fred. C., ii, 66 *n*; iii, 203, 215; Fred. E. F., iii, 215; John, iii, 203, 215; Nath., iii, 215; Miss, iii, 331; —, ii, 65; fam., ii, 66; iii, 182, 202, 218
Political history, ii, 17-72, 83, 95, 102
Pollard, John, iii, 128
Poll-tax, ii, 90
Polluxhill, *see* Pulloxhill
Polochessele, *see* Pulloxhill
Polwarth, vsct., ii, 327; Amabel, vsctss., *see* Grey (of Wrest), Amabel, ctss. of
Pomfret (Pontefract), Geo., earl of, iii, 453; Thos., earl of, iii, 453
Pomfret, Eliz., ii, 363; John, ii, 363; —, ii, 165
Pond's Close (Whiperley), ii, 361
Pont, Will., iii, 384
Pontefract, earls of, *see* Pomfret, earls of
Poole, Sir Arth., iii, 195; Benj., iii, 57; Joanna, Lady, iii, 195; Marg., iii, 57; Rev. R. B., ii, 177
Pope, Eliz., iii, 140; Sir John, iii, 140; Sir Thos., ii, 374; iii, 140; Thos., ii, 357
Popham, Sir John, iii, 410
Poplar Well (Blunham), iii, 228
Population, table of, ii, 113-16
Port, Ad. de, i, 314 *n*; ii, 215, 218; Will. de, ii, 215, 216, 218
Porteous, Judith, ii, 216 *n*; Rev. Sam., ii, 216 *n*
Porter, Endymion, ii, 347, 382; Olive, ii, 347, 382; Sim., iii, 172; Will., the, iii, 172; Miss, ii, 177
Portland, Jerome, earl of, iii, 277; Rich., earl of, iii, 277
Portland Cement Works, ii, 261
Portmore, Ld., ii, 191, 192
Posthuma, Anne, iii, 198
Potintone, *see* Podington
Potsgrove, i, 370; ii, 30 *n*, 96, 114, 346, 356; iii, 336, 343, 368, 421-3; adv., iii, 423; chant., iii, 423; char., iii, 423; ch., i, 315 *n*; iii, 423; farms, iii, 421; mans., i, 370; iii, 421; Nonconf., iii, 421; sch., ii, 181; iii, 421; vicarage, i, 316 *n*
Pott, John, ii, 378; Kath., ii, 378; Mary, ii, 378; Rog., ii, 378
Potter, John, iii, 293, 372; Capt. Thos., ii, 69; Thos., iii, 293, 322, 372; Will., ii, 241
Pottery, i, 273, 299, 300; ii, 314; iii, 82, 237; A.S., i, 175, 177, 178, 179, 186; British, ii, 8; iii, 82; Bronze Age, i, 168, 169; Celtic, i, 170, 174; Roman, i, 172, 173, 178, 186; ii, 2, 4-15; iii, 175, 280, 390; Rom.-Brit., i, 172, 307; iii, 297
Potteshoe, Hen. of, ii, 289 *n*
Pottingal, fam., iii, 407
Potton (Potone), i, 173, 174, 384; ii, 17, 22, 93, 98, 113, 201, 209, 215, 216, 226, 230, 237-42, 246, 255; iii, 150, 269 *n*; adv., ii, 239, 241; Brit. coins, ii, 237, char., ii, 241; ch., i, 315 *n*, 326; 333; ii, 239; coprolite ind., ii, 117; fire, ii, 239; mans., ii, 226, 237, 247; mkts. and fairs, ii, 88, 239; mill, ii, 237, 239; Nonconf., ii, 241; place-names, ii, 237; racing, ii, 191; reptilian rem., i, 34; sch., ii, 184; Sun Inn, ii, 237; vicar, i, 323, 327 *n*, 341, 342 *n*
Potton, Rob. of, i, 387
Potton Burdetts, man., ii, 210, 238
Potton Much Manured, man., ii, 238; mill, ii, 239
Potton Rectory, man., ii, 238 *n*, 239, 241
Potton Regis, man., ii, 237, 239
Potts, Anna L., iii, 251; John, iii, 348; Nich., iii, 348; Spencer, ii, 43; Thos., ii, 45
Power, Geoff., ii, 248; Florence, iii, 126; Joan, i, 360; Nich., ii, 248; Sir Rich., iii, 126; Rob., ii, 322, 323; Sim., ii, 89
Powlett, *see* Paulet
Powney, fam., iii, 404
Poynder (Poynter), Thos., ii, 289; iii, 427
Poyntells (Arlesey), ii, 263
Poynter, *see* Poynder
Preaux, *see* Priaulx
Pratt, Edwin, ii, 139
Prechier, Hugh le, iii, 364 *n*
Prehistoric antiquities, i, 170, 172, 174, 270; ii, 281, 314; iii, 76, 350, 390, 439, 448, 451
Prentis, Will., iii, 414
Presbyterians, i, 340, 341; ii, 52
Prescott, Horace W., ii, 315; W., iii, 386
Prest, Hugh le, ii, 86; iii, 165
Preston, Chris., iii, 299
Preston Deanery (Northants), ii, 189
Priaulx (Preaux), Drew des, ii, 321; Isabel des, ii, 321; Matth., ii, 169, 170, 171, 172; Mrs., ii, 172
Priest, Eliz., iii, 32, 238
Priestley (Flitwick), ii, 324; iii, 284, 286, 451 *n*, 453; chap., iii, 288; man., iii, 286
Priestley Farm (Flitwick), Rom. coins, ii, 7
Priestley Moor (Flitwick), ii, 135
Priestley Park (Flitwick), iii, 325

Priestley Plantation (Steppingley), iii, 324
Prigdale, iii, 251
Prikeavant, Will., iii, 73
Prior, *see* Pryor
Priory Farm (Harrold), iii, 66
Prisley, *see* Priestley
Proby, Hen., ii, 314
Profit, Miss, ii, 295
Prothero, R.E., iii, 149
Provenden, man. (Caddington), ii, 315
Pryor (Prior), Maj. Hen. M., ii, 277; John, iii, 212, 311; Maj. Ralston de V., ii, 277; Will., iii, 311
Pryors, Le (Le Monkes) man. (Turvey), iii, 113
Puckering (Puckeringe), Sir John, iii, 8; Sir Thos., ii, 226; *see also* Pickering
Puddington, *see* Podington
Puddle (Pudele, Podele), Hill (Houghton Regis), ii, 3, 102; iii, 355, 389, 390
Puisaquila (Pisaquila), John, ii, 289, 290, 341
Pulford, Rev. Joshua, iii, 416
Pulhanger, Ad. de, ii, 268 *n*
Pullan, *see* Pulleyn
Pulley, John, ii, 65; iii, 18; *see also* Poley
Pulleyn (Poleyn, Pullan), John iii, 349; Rob., ii, 244; Walt., i, 404
Pullokeshull, *see* Pulloxhill
Pulloxhill, i, 370, 394; ii, 96, 114, 306, 324, 326, 376-81; adv., ii, 380; char., ii, 381; ch., i, 311 *n*, 314 *n*, 315 *n*, 371 *n*; ii, 332, 379; dean of, i, 347; gold quartz, ii, 376; inclosure, ii, 376; man., i, 370; ii, 376, 378-80; place-names, ii, 376; sch., ii, 184; ship-money, ii, 376; vicarage, i, 316
Pulloxhill, Hen. of, i, 366; Steph. of, i, 366
Pulloxhill and Greenfield, man., ii, 376 *n*, 377; iii, 380
Pulloxhill Grange, ii, 377
Pulpits, ii, 206, 208, 218, 229, 269, 279, 372, 383; iii, 26, 27, 56, 68, 75, 127, 141, 164, 167, 178, 233, 250, 278, 283, 340, 410, 414
Pungiant, Rich., ii, 252, 253; iii, 260
Punters Stockings Close (Eversholt), iii, 377
Purchase, Laur., iii, 236
Purney, John, iii, 134
Purvey, Alys, iii, 366; Eliz., iii, 366; Nich., iii, 366
Pusey, Phil., ii, 126
Putnoe, man., *see* Puttenhoe, man.
Putnoe Farm (Goldington), iii, 202
Puttenham, Mary, iii, 388
Puttenhoe (Putnoe), man. (Goldington), i, 365; iii, 180, 202-4, 207
Puttenhoe Woods (Goldington), iii, 204
Putteridge Bury, ii, 196
Putteridge Park, ii, 359
Puttes, iii, 182 *n*
Pycard, Joan, iii, 204; Marg., i, 390; Will., iii, 204
Pycot, *see* Picot
Pye, Anne, iii, 282; Edm., iii, 140, 282; Hen., iii, 95; Hen. J., iii, 140; Rev. Jas., iii, 136; fam., iii, 95
Pygeon, *see* Pigeon
Pygot, Pygott, *see* Pigott
Pygun, Will., ii, 361 *n*
Pyke (Pick), Ralph, ii, 81; Will., ii, 85
Pykenham, Will., iii, 408
Pykes, man., *see* Picks, man.
Pym, Capt. C. G., ii, 242; Eliz., iii, 166; Lt.-Col. Fran., ii, 70; Fran., ii, 66 *n*, 242, 244; iii, 166; Guy, i, 271; ii, 66*n*, 198; Will., ii, 244; iii, 166, 411; —, ii, 197; fam., ii, 66
Pynders Hill, ii, 151; iii, 394
Pynfold, Marg., iii, 366; Rich., iii, 366
Pyres, Hen., ii, 378
Pyrley, Will. de, ii, 232
Pyro, Pyrot, *see* Pirot

Quadring, Alex., iii, 429; Alice, iii, 429; Marg., iii, 429; Rich., iii, 429
Quakers, *see* Friends, Society of
Quantock, Frances, iii, 443; John, iii, 443
Quarel, Isabella, iii, 120; Ivo, ii, 211; iii, 120 *n*
Quarries, ii, 308, 384; iii, 47, 76, 96, 313, 373, 448
Quatremars, Nich., ii, 238
Queensberry, duke of, ii, 192
Queen's Woods (Ampthill), ii, 145
Queldryck, Ad. de, iii, 418
Quince Hill (Old Warden), *see* Quint's Hill
Quincy, Arabella de, iii, 231 *n*; Eleanor, ii, 351; Hadwisa de, iii, 78, 101; Helen de, iii, 297; Marg. de, iii, 230; Rob. de, iii, 101, 297; Rog. de, i, 361, 388; ii, 351; iii, 101; Saher de, *see* Winchester, earl of
Quinny, John, iii, 434
Quinton (Northants), i, 338
Quint's Hill (Old Warden), i, 270, 271; iii, 252; Rom. encampment, ii, 15

Race, Geo., ii, 190; John, ii, 190
Racing, ii, 190-5
Radcliffe (Radclyff, Ratcliffe), Alice, iii, 429; Delmé, ii, 193; Sir Edw., iii, 281, 304, 328; Edw., iii, 281, 293; Eliz., Lady, iii, 326; Farnaby, Lady, iii, 322; Frances, iii, 281; Fran. D., ii, 286; Fran. P., ii, 286; Hen. D., ii, 286; iii, 321; Sir Humph., iii, 281, 283, 293, 303, 304, 328; Isabel, Lady, iii, 281, 283, 304; Jane, Lady, iii, 304; John, ii, 286, 287; Sir Ralph, ii, 287; Ralph, iii, 321; Rob., iii, 283, 429; Lady, iii, 158
Rademilde, Marg., iii, 194; Ralph, iii, 194; Rob., iii, 194; Will., iii, 194
Radwell (Felmersham), ii, 324; iii, 61; chap., i, 318; iii, 63; man., iii, 60
Radwell (Radewell), Alice de, iii, 60; Beatrice de, iii, 60; Gilb. de, iii, 60; Hen. de, iii, 60; John (de), iii, 60, 61, 220; Marg., iii, 220; Margery, iii, 61; Petronilla of, i, 390; Rob. de, iii, 60; Thos., iii, 61, 220; fam., iii, 59
Radwell Hall (Felmersham), iii, 59
Raghton, Eleanor de, ii, 257; John de, ii, 257; Oliver de, ii, 257
Ragon, Eliz., iii, 106, 195; Sir John, iii, 106, 125, 195, 314; Kath., iii, 106; Reg., iii, 195, 314; Thos., iii, 106
Ragons Manor (Maulden), iii, 314, 315
Rainald, iii, 146
Rainols, Ursula, ii, 94
Rainsborough, Col., ii, 52
Rake, —, iii, 358
Raleigh, John de, iii, 193
Ralph (Ralf), ii, 190; iii, 229, 245, 375, 419; archdeacon, i, 313; count, ii, 21; the hermit, i, 350; the steward, ii, 78
Ramerick, ii, 72
Ramridge End (Luton), i, 146; ii, 348
Ramsay (Ramsey), Rev. Norman, iii, 224, 226; Sir John, iii, 201; Will., ii, 332; Capt., ii, 48, 49
Ramsey Abbey, i, 312, 364; ii, 20, 21, 76, 86, 207, 209, 215, 237, 261, 278, 294, 295, 296, 297, 299, 309, 310, 312, 333, 334, 335; iii, 9, 10, 12, 70, 128, 129, 150, 199, 276, 277, 278, 297, 331
Rand, John, ii, 287; fam., iii, 59
Randall, Alex., iii, 105, 212; Anne, iii, 212; Will., ii, 245; W., ii, 198
Randei, Kath., iii, 61
Randes (Rands, Raundes), Edm., iii, 61; John, ii, 267 *n*; iii, 113; Oliver, iii, 61; Rich., iii, 115, 116
Randolph, Thos., ii, 235 *n*; iii, 248
Rands, *see* Randes
Rannulf, ii, 226, 227
Ransil Spinney (Podington), iii, 80
Ransom, E., iii, 297; W., ii, 5, 8, 11, 13, 14, 41
Ratchford, Nich., iii, 246
Ratcliffe, *see* Radcliffe
Raundes, *see* Randes
Ravan, iii, 248
Raven, Dorothy, ii, 282 *n*; Eliz., ii, 285; John, ii, 282, 285; Margery, iii, 456; Rich., iii, 456
Ravenhill, Agnes, iii, 396; Nich. iii, 97, 396
Ravensden, ii, 113; iii, 180, 183, 209-14; adv., iii, 214; char., ii, 184 *n*; iii, 214; ch., i, 140, 315 *n*; iii, 213; dean of, i, 347; mans., i, 365; iii, 203, 210-12; place-names, iii, 210; sch., ii, 184; vicarage, i, 316 *n*, 317
Ravensden, Nich. de, iii, 210
Ravensden Grange (Manor), iii, 209, 210, 211
Ravensden House, iii, 209
Ravensholt Grange (Old Warden), i, 364; iii, 247, 253
Rawlins (Rawlyns), Agnes, iii, 210; Fran., iii, 211; Gabriel, iii, 407; John, iii, 210, 211; Rob., iii, 211; Steph., iii, 210, 211; Thos., ii, 292; Will., iii, 407
Raworth, Rob., ii, 204 *n*, 286
Ray, Rich., iii, 187
Raymond, Thos., iii, 104
Raynar, iii, 104
Raynsford, Frances, ii, 282; Maj.-Gen. Hanbury, ii, 282, 285; Geo. N., ii, 282; Thos. A., ii, 282, 285; fam., ii, 285
Raynton, Geo., ii, 293 *n*
Reach, man. (Leighton Buzzard), iii, 403
Read (Reade, Rede), Alex., iii, 18, 438; Alice, iii, 246; Eliz., ii, 323; iii, 244; Innocent, ii, 323; iii, 244; Jas., iii, 349; Joanna, iii, 438; Rob., iii, 246; fam., iii, 247
Reading (Berks), A.S. rem, i, 184; sch., ii, 159
Reading Abbey, ii, 23; iii, 289, 294
Readshill Plantation (Maulden), iii, 313
Reckey (Riky), Barth., ii, 289, 290, 341

Rectory Manor (Northill), *see* Northill College Manor
Redbornestoke hund., ii, 115; iii, 267-335
Redburn, Sim. of, i, 386
Reddall, *see* Riddell
Reddings, man., *see* How End
Rede, *see* Read
Redeware, Rob. de, iii, 196
Redinges, Rob. de, iii, 276
Reeve (Reve, Rowe), Agnes le, iii, 114; Alice le, iii, 114; Geo., ii, 164; Hugh, i, 337, 338, 340, 342; iii, 273; Joanna le, iii, 114; John le, iii, 114; Thos., ii, 164, 218; iii, 101, 392
Regine, man. (Cardington), *see* Fenlake Barns
Reincourt, Rich. de, ii, 247
Rekesduna, *see* Roxton
Religious houses, i, 349-404
Relye, *see* Thurleigh
Remigius, bp. of Lincoln, *see* Remy
Rempston, Sir Thos. de, iii, 263
Remy (Remigius), bp., *see* Lincoln bps.
Renhall, *see* Renhold
Renhold, i, 335 *n*, 365; ii, 113, 154; iii, 180, 183, 202, 214-18; adv., iii, 218; Chantrie Close and lands, iii, 217; char., ii, 184 *n*; iii, 218; ch., i, 315 *n*, 325 *n*, 380; iii, 217; earthworks, i, 280, 284, 285; man., iii, 13, 215; Nonconf., iii, 214; place-names, iii, 215; sch., ii, 184; vicarage, i, 316 *n*
Renhold (Ronhale), Rich., iii, 216; Sybil de, iii, 215
Repingdon (Repyngton), Philip, bp., *see* Lincoln bps.; Will., iii, 442
Reptiles, i, 102-3
Reptilian remains, i, 34-5
Repton, G. W. J., iii, 74 *n*
Repyngton, *see* Repingdon
Resby, Will., iii, 250
Restwold, Ralph, iii, 246
Retchford, Nich., ii, 180
Reve (le), *see* Reeve
Rewse, John, ii, 167; *see also* Ros and Rous
Reynal, John, iii, 384; John S. N., iii, 384
Reynardson, Allan, iii, 198; Anne, ii, 317; John, ii, 317
Reyner, Cuth., iii, 259; John, iii, 137
Reynes, man. (Stanbridge), *see* Morteynes
Reynes, Alex. de, i, 362, 365; Amabel, iii, 152; Cecilia, iii, 150; Eliz., iii, 309, 312, 345, 385; Joan, iii, 150; John, iii, 150, 309; Nath., iii, 345; Ralph, iii, 150, 152; Rich., iii, 150, 309; Sibyl de, i, 362 *n*; Sir Thos., iii, 113, 147, 309; Thos., iii, 150, 309, 311, 312, 417; fam., iii, 313
Reynolds (Reynold), Edw., iii, 51; Frances, iii, 51; Fran., iii, 51; John, ii, 245; iii, 233; Walt., iii, 195; —, iii, 414
Rhee, riv., ii, 71, 218, 230
Rhodes, Sam., iii, 287
Rhopalocera, i, 79-80
Rice (Ryce), Geo. R., iii, 45; Will., iii, 106
Rice-Trevor, Elianore M., iii, 49; Miss, ii, 181 *n*; iii, 45
Rich, Sir Thos., ii, 173; Thos., iii, 282
Richard, archd. of Beds., i, 313
Richard I., king, iii, 229
Richard II., king, ii, 211, 235
Richard, king of Germany, ii, 384; iii, 353
Richards, Chas., iii, 274; John, ii, 374, 375; Sam., iii, 160
Richardson, Alice, ii, 329, 330; Rev. John, ii, 220; Pet., ii, 330; Will., ii, 329, 330; Will. S., iii, 326; —, ii, 222
Richborough (Kent), i, 184
Richmond, earls of, iii, 298; Hen., iii, 230; John, iii, 297
Richmond, Pet. de, ii, 234
Richmond and Derby, Marg., ctss. of, ii, 256
Riddell (Reddall, Ridel), Agnes, iii, 223, 224; Amb., ii, 69; iii, 310, 423, 436; Eliz., iii, 423; Jas. B., ii, 383; Jane, ii, 385; Sir John, ii, 385; John, iii, 224; Sir John B., ii, 385; Ralph (Ralf), iii, 219, 223, 224; Thos., iii, 310; —, iii, 375
Riddises Spinney (Lidlington), iii, 307
Ridel, *see* Riddell
Ridgeway, Col., ii, 195
Ridgmont, i, 336; ii, 87, 115, 129, 140, 141, 146, 147; iii, 267, 320-323, 394, 459; adv., iii, 323; char., iii, 323; ch., iii, 323; crown property, iii, 271, 322; man., iii, 321; Nonconf., iii, 320; place-names, iii, 321; Rom. rem., iii, 320; sch., ii, 184; wells, iii, 320
Rievaulx, Sylvan, abbot of, i, 353 *n*
Rigge, Isabella, ii, 224 *n*; Rob., ii, 224 *n*
Riky, *see* Reckey
Ringe, Thos., iii, 277
Ripley, Rev. Thos., ii, 280
Risceby, Alice, ii, 334; John, ii, 334; Will. de, ii, 334
Riselai, *see* Riseley
Riseley, i, 394; ii, 115; iii, 40, 43, 106, 123, 143, 157-61; adv., iii, 161; Cake Bread Close, iii, 161; char., iii, 161; ch., i, 315 *n*, 333, 394; iii, 160; deanery, i, 347; ind., iii, 157; man., iii, 134, 157; mills, iii, 157; moats, iii, 157; Nonconf., iii, 157; place-names, iii, 157; sch., ii, 184; wells, iii, 157
Riseley (Risely, Risley, Rysley), Geoff. de, iii, 158, 159; Hen. de, iii, 159; Hervic de, iii, 106; Jas. iii, 328; John (de), i, 387; iii, 24, 159, 244; Lawr. de, iii, 158; Rich. de, iii, 159; Walt. de, iii, 158; Will. de, iii, 158
Riseley Lodge (Riseley), iii, 157
Riseley Old Domain, earthwork, i, 306
Risinghoe (Goldington), iii, 204, 207
Risinghoe Castle (Goldington), i, 285 *n*, 296, 297; iii, 202, 206, 207
Risley, *see* Riseley
Rivers, earls, iii, 118; Ant., iii, 118
Rivers, Marg., iii, 10; Rich., iii, 92
Rixband, Marg., ii, 211; Will., ii, 211
Roads, Brit., iii, 350; Rom., i, 176, 269, 271, 358, 371; ii, 1-8, 17, 18, 23, 40, 46, 98, 203, 209, 212, 223, 276, 280, 300, 314, 317; iii, 256, 350, 355, 383, 389, 390, 400
Roais, ctss., *see* Beauchamp, Rohesia de
Robbins, *see* Robins
Robert, iii, 92, 238
Robert Bruce (king of Scotland), iii, 299
Roberts, John, ii, 310
Robins (Robbins), E. C., ii, 176; John, ii, 378, 379, 380; iii, 27; Mary, iii, 27; Susanna, iii, 27
Robinson, Dorothea, Lady, iii, 434; Dorothea, iii, 434; Frances, iii, 244; Sir Geo., iii, 434; Gilb., iii, 84; Rev. John, ii, 333; John, ii, 167; iii, 117, 243, 244, 434; Marg., ii, 353; Underhill, iii, 144; Will., ii, 301; iii, 122; Dr., ii, 198; Mrs., iii, 386; —, iii, 355
Roche, fam., iii, 48
Rochechouart, Guy de, ii, 351; Sybil, ii, 351
Roches, John des, ii, 309; iii, 315; Pet. des, bp., *see* Winchester, bps. of
Rochesdon, *see* Roxton
Rochester, bar. of, iii, 377, 419
Rochester, Ansgot of, iii, 376, 377, 419; Paris, archd. of, ii, 320
Rockingham Castle (Northants), ii, 22; iii, 70, 82
Rodentia, i, 141-3
Rodland, *see* Rowland
Roe, Henricus O., ii, 184 *n*, 304; *see also* Reeve and Rowe
Roger, i, 358; ii, 376; iii, 165, 258, 259, 291
Rogers, Alice, iii, 198, 311; Hen., iii, 198; Jas., ii, 380; Rich., i, 387; Rog., ii, 222; Sam., iii, 317; W. H., iii, 207; —, ii, 169, 170
Roherd, iii, 344
Rohrweger, Miss, iii, 329
Rokele, John de la, i, 400
Rokes, Eliz., ii, 329, 330; Rich., ii, 329, 330
Rokesdon, *see* Roxton
Rolffe, Will., iii, 260
Rolland, iii, 247
Rolt (Rolte), Anna, iii, 183; Capt. Edw., iii, 155; Edw., ii, 42; iii, 155; Eliz., iii, 224; Frances, ii, 280; Fran., ii, 280; Sir John, iii, 146; John, iii, 146, 183, 224; Judith, iii, 146, 183; Mary, iii, 155; Sam., iii, 20, 146; Steph., iii, 148; Susannah, iii, 148; Sir Thos., iii, 155; Thos., ii, 44; iii, 145, 146, 148, 154 *n*, 155, 183, 211, 224, 226; Walt., ii, 277, 280; iii, 154 *n*, 155; Will., iii, 146 *n*, 259; —, i, 342 *n*; fam., iii, 149, 156
Romano-British period, ii, 1-15
Roman remains, i, 186, 271, 274; ii, 6, 7, 12-15, 212, 223, 294, 344; iii, 44, 82, 175, 243, 252, 257, 262, 280, 320, 390, 402; *see also* burials, coins, implements, ornaments, pottery
Romylo, Steph., iii, 216
Ronhale, man. (Ravensden), *see* Ravensden, man.
Ronhale, par., *see* Renhold
Rook, Admiral, iii, 4
Rookham, Rob., iii, 396
Rooktree Farm (Holcot), iii, 386
Rookwood, Amb., iii, 354
Roos, *see* Ros
Rootham's Green (Colmworth), iii, 186
Roper, Kath., iii, 443; Will., iii, 443
Ros (Roos), Ralph de, iii, 36; Rob. de, ii, 31 *n*; Serlo de, iii, 36, 37, 44 *n*; Will. de (le), i, 381; iii, 219; fam., iii, 149; *see also* Rewse and Rous
Rose, man. of the (Lond.), ii, 159
Rose, E. P., ii, 209, 222; Thos., i, 333; archd., iii, 295; Mrs., iii, 364

INDEX

Rosewell, Pet., iii, 145
Roses (Rosae), i, 55
Rotherham, college at, ii, 157
Rotherham, Agnes, ii, 363 ; iii, 13, 313 ; Alice, Lady, iii, 292 ; Alice, ii, 295, 299, 300 ; Anne (Ann), ii, 343, 380 ; Eliz., ii, 363, 375 ; Geo., ii, 40 *n*, 295, 305, 342, 343, 353, 356, 357, 358, 361, 363, 372, 380 ; iii, 13, 293, 300, 415, 432 ; Isaac, ii, 343, 380 ; Jane, iii, 443 ; Sir John, ii, 353, 356, 363, 364, 372 ; John, ii, 219, 295, 352, 354 *n*, 356, 359, 363, 374, 380 ; iii, 313 ; Nich., ii, 363 *n* ; Sir Thos., ii, 150, 354, 372 ; iii, 292, 299, 300, 437, 443 ; Thos., ii, 219, 295, 352, 353, 358, 360, 361, 363 ; iii, 299, 437 ; Thos., archbp., *see* York, archbps. of, and Lincoln, bps. of ; —, Lady, ii, 372 ; fam., ii, 307
Roubury, Gilb. de., i, 327
Round Green (Luton), i, 146 ; iii, 348
Round Hill (Roxton), i, 297
Round Wood (Sharnbrook), iii, 89
Roupe, Thos., iii, 436
Rous (Rouse, Rowse), Eliz., iii, 159 ; Geoff. le, iii, 332 ; Joan le, iii, 332 ; Rich. le, iii, 137 ; Rob., i, 397 ; Rodenham, ii, 313, 384 ; Sim. le, iii, 332 ; Thos. le, iii, 162 ; Will., iii, 129, 332 ; Admiral, ii, 194 ; Mrs., iii, 129 ; *see also* Rewse and Ros
Rowe, John, iii, 129 ; Nich., ii, 206 ; Thos., iii, 129, 131, 151 ; *see also* Reeve and Roe
Rowington (Warws), iii, 294 *n*
Rowland (Rodland), Nich., iii, 241 ; Pernel, iii, 241 ; Walt., iii, 241 ; fam., iii, 240
Rowlands, man., (Cople), iii, 182, 240
Rowley, Agnes, ii, 325
Rowney, i, 365 ; iii, 227, 259
Rowney Grange, i, 365 ; iii, 259
Rowney Warren, ii, 147 ; iii, 256
Rowse, *see* Rous
Rowthe, Thos., ii, 157
Roxhill (Wroxhill) (Marston Moretaine), iii, 308 ; ch., i, 318, 331 ; iii, 313 ; man., iii, 310
Roxhill Farm (Marston Moretaine), iii, 310
Roxox, *see* Ruxox
Roxton, ii, 113 ; iii, 175, 176, 180, 186, 193, 198, 218-22, 384 ; adv., iii, 222 ; char., iii, 222 ; ch., i, 315 *n*, 382, 384 ; iii, 221 ; earthwork, i, 297, 302 ; man., iii, 183, 219, 221 ; mill., iii, 221 ; Nonconf., iii, 218 ; sch., ii, 184 ; vicarage, i, 316 *n*
Roxton (Rokesdone), Alice de, iii, 192 *n* ; John (de), i, 377 ; iii, 192 *n*, 364
Roxton Wood End, man., *see* Carlyles
Roys, ctss., *see* Beauchamp, Rohesia
Royston (Herts), iii, 197 *n* ; ii, 191 ; iii, 197 *n*
Rualon (Ruallon), ii, 376 ; iii, 181, 184
Ructona, *see* Roxton
Rudde, Thos., iii, 85 ; Will., iii, 85
Rudge, Susanna, iii, 427
Ruding (Rudyng), Hen., i, 398 ; John, ii, 213
Rudlonds (Rudlandesfelde), man. (Cranfield), iii, 277
Rudyerd, Sir Benj., iii, 427
Rudyng, *see* Ruding
Rufford, Eleanor, iii, 453 ; Joan, iii, 422 ; John, iii, 422, 423, 453 ; Thos., iii, 422, 439, 453
Rufinus, i, 173
Rufus, Agnes, ii, 301 *n* ; Godf., iii, 238 ; John, iii, 238 ; Laura, iii, 239 ; Rob., ii, 301 ; iii, 159, 238 ; Sim., ii, 301 ; iii, 238, 239 ; Will., ii, 301 ; iii, 240
Rugemont Castle (Ridgmont), iii, 321, 322
Ruggerwyk, Margery, iii, 195 ; Thos., iii, 195
Runhale, *see* Renhold
Rupert, Prince, ii, 46, 50 ; iii, 4
Rushden (Northants), i, 376 *n* ; ii, 71 ; iii, 34 *n*, 40, 117
Rush-matting ind., ii, 124-5
Rushmere Lodge (Leighton Buzzard), iii, 400
Russell, Cath., Lady, ii, 277 ; Eliz., Lady, ii, 277 ; iii, 332, 376 ; Marg., Lady, iii, 67 ; Rachel, Lady, ii, 57 *n* ; Lds., iii, 461 ; Chas., ii, 65, 188 ; Chas. J., ii, 187 ; Edw., ii, 61 ; Fran., ii, 244, 277 ; iii, 67, 203, 332 ; *see also* Bedford, earl of ; Geo. W., ii, 65 ; iii, 20 ; John, ii, 39, 65, 66 *n*, 70 ; iii, 266, 459 ; Will., ii, 56, 57, 60, 62, 277 ; iii, 332, 460
Russell (Russel), Arth., *see* Ampthill, Ld. ; Sir Edw., iii, 437 ; Admiral Edw., ii, 60 ; Edw., ii, 43, 54 *n* ; iii, 376 ; Fran., iii, 376 ; Sir Geo., ii, 41 ; Geo., ii, 65 *n* ; Hawise, iii, 449, 456 ; Herbrand A., *see* Bedford, dk. of ; Isabel, iii, 301 ; John, ii, 43, 54 ; iii, 376 ; Letitia, iii, 376 ; Matilda, iii, 301 ; Ralph, iii, 301 ; Sir Thos., iii, 430 ; Thos., ii, 213, 245 ; iii, 37, 143, 156, 200, 218, 233, 315, 334 ; Sir Will., iii, 376, 429 *n* ; Will., iii, 334, 376, 449, 456 ; —, ii, 303, 312 ; iii, 108, 454 ; fam., ii, 56 ; iii, 20, 324, 436, 459
Russell Park (Bedford), i, 186, 190, 285 *n* ; iii, 5
Russell's Close (Ampthill), iii, 275
Ruthyn, Rich, de, iii, 46
Rutland, dk. of, iii, 458
Ruxox (Flitwick), i, 305, 375 ; ii, 83, 85 ; chap., i, 371 *n* ; iii, 284, 286 ; man., iii, 286
Ryce, *see* Rice
Rycroft, —, iii, 195
Ryde, Hen. de, ii, 328 ; Will., ii, 328
Rydemounde, *see* Ridgmont
Ryder, John W., ii, 256 ; Nath., iii, 310 ; Thos., ii, 257
Rye, La, bar., iii, 428
Rye, Agnes de, iii, 426 ; Alina de, iii, 426 ; Hen. de, iii, 426 ; Hubert de, iii, 426 ; Isabel de, iii, 426
Ryggley, Nich., iii, 145
Ryman, Will., ii, 378
Rysley, *see* Riseley

Sabine, Eliz., ii, 337 ; Sir John, ii, 337
Sacchevilla, *see* Sackville
Sacheverell, Rich., iii, 230
Sachynton, Rob. de, iii, 276
Sackville (Sacchevilla), Alex. de, ii, 320 ; Athelina, iii, 159 ; John, iii, 158 ; Thos., iii, 159 *n*, 322 ; iii, 158
Sacombe Park (Herts), iii, 155
Sadleir, Edw., iii, 340 ; Ralph, iii, 340 ; Rich. V., iii, 340 Thos. L., iii, 340 ; Ursula, iii, 340 ; Will., iii, 340
Sadler, Mich., F. iii, 9 ; Ralph, ii, 256 ; Thos., ii, 44
Saffey (Saffrey), Alice, ii, 322 ; Brian, ii, 76, 322 ; Joan, ii, 322 ; Margery, ii, 322 ; Thos., ii, 322
Saher (Seiher), ii, 326 ; iii, 321
St. Albans (Herts.), i, 1, 3, 324 *n*, 372 *n* ; ii, 314, 350, 356, 358, 363 ; iii, 10, 362 ; almshouses, iii, 333 ; battle of, ii, 37, 352 ; sch., ii, 178
St. Albans, Greg. of, i, 353
St. Alban's Abbey, i, 310, 313 *n*, 314, 323, 350-4, 358, 360, 363, 366, 386 ; ii, 23, 35, 270, 321-5, 342, 361, 362, 368, 369, 373, 374, 378, 384 ; iii, 16, 148, 149, 181, 344, 350, 370, 393, 394, 401, 422, 426, 430, 431, 448 ; abbot of, Geoff., i, 351 *n*, 358 ; ii, 178, 361 *n*, 363 ; Paul of Caen, i, 310 ; Rich., ii, 178, 361 ; Rob., i, 359 *n* ; cell of, at Millbrook, iii, 316, 318
St. Amand, bar. of, ii, 324
St. Amand, Eleanor, Lady, ii, 147 ; Eliz., iii, 140, 380 ; Lds., ii, 277 ; iii, 187, 317 ; Almaric, iii, 187 ; Rich., ii, 337 ; iii, 140, 187, 230, 380 ; Will., iii, 230, 380
St. Amand, Almaric (Aimery Aumary), de, i, 352 ; ii, 32, 33, 324, 342, 376, 379 ; iii, 236, 252, 271 *n*, 272, 292, 317, 318, 379, 380, 440 ; Ant., iii, 140 ; Asseline (Azeline), ii, 324 ; iii, 272, 317 ; Eleanor, iii, 272, 292, 317, 379 ; Sir Emery de, iii, 2 ; Emery de, iii, 2, 113, 324 ; Joan de, iii, 236 ; John de, iii, 252, 272, 317, 379 ; Mary de, iii, 440 ; Ralph, ii, 211, 324 ; iii, 236, 237, 272, 317 ; fam., iii, 326
St. Andrew's Priory (Northampton), i, 315 *n* ; iii, 23
St. Anne's Farm (Thorncote), iii, 244
St. Anne's Hill (Luton), ii, 348
St. Bartholomew's Priory (Lond.), iii, 456
St. Briavells, Will. de, iii, 281
St. Bridget's Well (Houghton Regis), iii, 390
St. Clare (St. Clair), Gunnora de, iii, 190 ; Hamo de, iii, 190 ; Jas., iii, 223 ; Marg., iii, 433 ; Phil., iii, 433
St. Croix, Hugh de, ii, 321 iii, 271 ; Isabel, ii, 321 ; iii, 271 ; John de, iii, 272 ; Pet. de, ii, 277, 321, 383 ; iii, 271, 272, 318, 346 ; Rob. de, ii, 321 ; iii, 272, 318 ; Thos. de, iii, 272
St. Edmunds Abbey, i, 312, 362 ; ii, 18, 25 *n* ; Baldwin, abbot of, iii, 38
St. Edward, Alice, iii, 331 ; Hugh, iii, 331, 333 ; Joan, iii, 331 ; John de, iii, 220 *n* ; iii, 331
St. Evroul's Abbey, iii, 294 *n*
St. Faith's Priory (Longueville), iii, 315, 343 *n*
St. Francis's Home (Campton), ii, 266
St. George's Chapel (Oxford), iii, 153 *n*
St. George's Chapel (Windsor), iii, 366, 401, 403, 404, 409, 429
St. Giles Hamstead Priory, iii, 385
St. Giles in the Wood, convent, (Flamstead), i, 315 *n*, 375 ; iii, 435
St. Gilles, Eustace de, iii, 60 *n*

St. Helen's Priory (London), i, 315 *n*; ii, 231, 232, 233
St. James's Abbey (Northampton), iii, 67, 109, 114
St. John, Ladies, iii, 61; Agnes, ii, 243; iii, 257, 396; Arabella, iii, 137; Dorothy, ii, 277; Emma M. E., iii, 143, 160; Frances, iii, 43; Kath., iii, 137; Lds., i, 339; ii, 40, 63 *n*, 70, 130, 146, 147, 183 *n*, 197, 257; iii, 3, 35, 40, 41, 42, 61, 73, 94, 123, 133, 134, 142, 143, 155, 158, 160, 165, 175, 180; Beauchamp M., iii, 41; John, iii, 41, 137, 172, 258, 259; Oliver, ii, 44, 56, 277, 323; iii, 35, 94, 109, 123, 125, 137, 146 *n*, 158, 163, 179, 180, 194, 195, 257, 258; Paulet, iii, 177; Rowland, iii, 41; St. Andrew, iii, 41, 163; St. Andrew B., iii, 163; Will., iii, 41; Will P., ii, 243
St. John, Agnes, ii, 277, 323; iii, 194; Sir Alex., ii, 40; Alice, iii, 343; Anne, ii, 252; Ant., ii, 252; Sir Beauchamp, ii, 41, 42, 44; iii, 163, 172; Rev. Edm. T., iii, 42, 43; Eliz., iii, 73, 343 *n*; Fran., ii, 207; Sir Hen., iii, 163; Hen., i, 396; Sir John, ii, 150, 277; iii, 7, 43, 60, 125, 127, 137, 158, 159 *n*, 168, 197, 343 *n*, 396; John, i, 395, 396; ii, 39, 296; iii, 41, 125, 137; Judith, iii, 395; Marg., ii, 277; iii, 41, 137; Margery, ii, 385 *n*; iii, 343; Mary, ii, 207; iii, 380; Sir Oliver, iii, 41; Oliver, i, 397; ii, 39, 55 *n*, 277, 296, 323, 385 *n*; iii, 137, 143, 146, 160, 177, 194, 395, 396; *see also* Bolingbroke, earl of; Sir Paulet, iii, 41, 137, 163, 177; Pawlett, ii, 56; Sir Rowland, iii, 73; St. Andr., ii, 64; iii, 172; Sir Walt., ii, 207; Will., iii, 74, 380
St. Johns, man. (Kempston), *see* Brucebury
St. John's College (Cambs.), i, 346; ii, 157, 164, 166, 168, 293; iii, 69, 230, 296, 313
St. John's College (Oxford), ii, 159, 250
St. John's Hospital (Bedford), i, 316 *n*, 396-8; iii, 31, 225
St. John's Hospital (Hockliffe), i, 401-2
St. Leonard's Hospital (Bedford), i, 354, 398-9; iii, 31, 237; adv., i, 398; iii, 22; chant., i, 326
St. Macute's Chapel (Haynes), i, 318 *n*, 351 *n*, 352; ii, 344; man., ii, 342-3
St. Macute's Wood (Haynes), ii, 343
St. Martin-le-Grand, ch. (Lond.), i, 364 *n*
St. Mary Colechurch, ch. (Lond.), i, 392
St. Mary de Pré, abbey (Leicester), i, 315 *n*; iii, 94
St. Mary Magdalene's Hosp. (Dunstable), i, 400-1; iii, 364; masters, i, 401
St. Mary Magdalene's Hosp. (Luton) i, 399-400
St. Mary Over (Dunstable), iii, 364
St. Mary's (Dunstable), ii, 7
St. Mary's Abbey (Stratford), *see* Stratford Abbey
St. Maur, Mary, Lady, iii, 440 *n*; Rich., Ld., iii, 440 *n*
St. Maur, Alice, iii, 440 *n*; Ellen de, ii, 328; Nich., ii, 224, 328; *see also* Seymour
St. Mildred, Wallbrook, ch. (Lond.), i, 392
St. Neots (Hunts), ii, 214; iii, 189
St. Neots, Hen. of, i, 353; W. de, i, 327 *n*
St. Neot's Priory (Hunts), i, 314 *n*, 394 *n*; ii, 226, 228, 229, 251, 253, 254, 262; iii, 110, 113, 116, 117, 142, 184, 190 *n*, 196, 221, 231
St. Nicholas' Abbey (Angers), ii, 281
St. Nicholas' Abbey (Arrouaise), i, 387, 388; Gervase, abbot of, i, 387; iii, 65
St. Oswald's Priory (Glouc.), i, 383 *n*
St. Paul's Cathedral (Lond.), i, 312, 317, 324 *n*, 358, 360; ii, 71, 153, 314, 315, 316, 318, 319-20, 351 *n*, 356; iii, 140, 206; deans, ii, 318, 320; iii, 230, 233
St. Peter's Abbey (Dorchester), i, 387 *n*, 388 *n*
Saintpierre, Isolda, iii, 452 *n*
St. Remigius, *see* St. Remy
St. Remy, Agnes de, iii, 223, 224; Cecilia de, iii, 223, 224; Elena de, iii, 223; Rich. de, iii, 223, 225; Rob. de, iii, 126, 223, 224, 225; Will. de, iii, 223
St. Sampson, abbot of, iii, 119 *n*
St. Sampson, Joan de, iii, 119; Ralph de, iii, 119, 163
St. Sepulchre's schs. (Lond.), iii, 368
St. Stephen Jewry, ch. (Lond.), i, 392
St. Thomas's Chapel Manor (Meppershall), i, 391; ii, 288, 289, 290, 305, 341
St. Valery (St. Walery), Aubrey de i, 379; Guy de, i, 379; Reg. de, ii, 283; iii, 339
Salchou, *see* Salphobury
Salden House (Bromham), iii, 45
Sale, Nich. de, iii, 22; Walt. de la, iii, 166
Saleby, Rob. de, iii, 134
Salem (Solemn) Thrift (Bromham), iii, 44
Salford, ii, 45, 114; iii, 336, 388, 424-5; adv., iii, 425; char., ii, 184 *n*; iii, 425; ch., i, 315 *n*, 333, 378 *n*; iii, 424; man., iii, 424; mill, iii, 424; Nonconf., iii, 424; iii, 425; sch., ii, 184; vicarage, i, 316 *n*
Salford, Dan. R., i, 367 *n*, 368, 369; Hugh de, ii, 301; iii, 424; John de, iii, 424; Nigel de, ii, 301; iii, 424, 425; Pet. de, iii, 424; Rog. de, i, 371 *n*, 378, 379
Salinis, Steph. de, ii, 255
Salisbury, Will., earl of, ii, 27, 244; iii, 184, 439 *n*
Salisbury (Salusbury), John, ii, 69; Rev. Lynch, ii, 310; Rog. of, i, 353 *n*; Sarah, ii, 310; Sir Thos., ii, 310; Will., iii, 61
Salmon, Eliz., ii, 292; Thos., ii, 292; —, ii, 133, 134
Salndy, *see* Sandy
Salomon, priest, iii, 107
Salph End (Renhold), iii, 180, 214-16
Salphobury (Salpho), man. (Renhold), i, 380; iii, 210, 216
Salter, Geo., ii, 256
Saltmers, Pet. de, iii, 186
Salusbury, *see* Salisbury
Salvation Army, ii, 214; iii, 31, 367
Salveyn, Gerard, ii, 354
Salvho, *see* Salphobury
Sambrook (Sambroke), Eliz., iii, 177; Sir Jeremy V., ii, 62; iii, 105, 109, 137, 177, 179; Judith, iii, 105, 177; Susannah, iii, 177
Samian pottery, *see* Pottery, Roman
Sampson, Humph., ii, 268; Jas., ii, 268; John, iii, 145; Laur., ii, 268
Samshill (Lower) Farm (Westoning), iii, 451
Samshill (Upper) Farm (Westoning), iii, 451
Samwell, Anne, ii, 346; Ant., ii, 346; Arth., ii, 346; Will., ii, 346
Sandall, Mrs., ii, 222
Sandeia, *see* Sandy
Sanders, *see* Saunders
Sanderson, Anne, iii, 205, 209; John, iii, 205; Thos. A. E., ii, 180; *see also* Saunderson
Sandon, John de, ii, 359
Sandwich, earl of, ii, 64 *n*; Edw. Montagu, earl of, ii, 339.
Sandy, i, 271, 272, 273, 274, 384, 394; ii, 66, 107, 113, 116, 199, 201, 226, 228, 237, 239, 242-6, 248, 255; iii, 190, 227 *n*, 243, 264; adv., i, 383; ii, 245; A.S. rem., i, 184, 189; ii, 242; chant., ii, 245; char., ii, 246; ch., i, 315 *n*, 325 *n*, 332 *n*, 382, 384; ii, 244; coins, i, 173, 174; ii, 2, 11, 242; earthworks, ii, 242; Hasells, the, ii, 242, 244; inclosure, ii, 97; inds., ii, 117, 118; mans., ii, 243; mkt. gardening, ii, 138, 139; mills, ii, 243 *n*, 244; Nonconf., ii, 245; place-names, ii, 242; prehist. rem., i, 166; rectory, ii, 242; rent, ii, 132; Rom. rem., ii, 1, 9-11; sch., ii, 184, 242; stone quarry, ii, 242
Sandy, Hen. of, ii, 279; Hugh of, ii, 279
Sandy Place (Sandy), i, 300; ii, 242
Sandyplane Plantation (Husborne Crawley), iii, 394
Sandys, Ladies, Anne, iii, 376; Kath., iii, 298, 391; Letitia, iii, 376; Lds., ii, 330; iii, 23; Edwin, iii, 376; Sam., iii, 376; Will., ii, 340; iii, 298, 391
Sandys, Sir Edwin, iii, 371, 391; Eliz., iii, 371; Hen., iii, 371; Margery, ii, 340; iii, 371; Mary, iii, 391; Miles, iii, 151, 371, 391; Walt., iii, 371; Sir Will., iii, 371; Will., iii, 371; fam., iii, 324
Sandy Warren (Sandy), ii, 146, 197, 242, 244, 246
Sanes, Cecil de, iii, 372
Sanford, Rob. de, iii, 66; Rog. de, iii, 452
Sankey, Thos., iii, 432
Santingfield Hosp. (Wissant), i, 400; ii, 358
Sanvill (Saunvill), Gilb. de, iii, 285; Osmund de, iii, 398; Osmunda de, iii, 285; Phil. de, i, 371 *n*; iii, 285, 286, 288, 395, 398; *see also* Savile
Sapte, F., ii, 265
Sarnebroc, *see* Sharnbrook
Sarnes, man. (Ravensden), *see* Mossbury, man.
Saunders (Sanders), Abra., ii, 385; Edw., iii, 155; Ellen, iii, 344, 422, 423; Isabel, iii, 423; Jane, ii, 385; Joan, iii, 423; Sir John, iii, 130, 310; John, iii, 310, 451; Marg., iii, 411; Mary, iii, 193; Rich., iii, 310, 409, 411, 423; Thos., iii, 193, 344, 422, 456; Val., iii, 129, 130; Will., iii, 344, 422, 423
Saunderson, John, ii, 252; iii, 209; Judith, ii, 342; Laur., ii, 252; *see also* Sanderson
Saunderson, H. G., & Co., ii, 127

INDEX

Saunderton, Bern., iii, 310; Will., iii, 310, 313
Saundeye, *see* Sandy
Saunvill, *see* Sanvill and Savile
Saurez (Sawrey), Ant., iii, 151, 391
Savage (Sauvage), Alice, iii, 423; Sir Arth., iii, 236; John le, iii, 211; Ralph, iii, 423; Rob., iii, 85, 423; Thos., iii, 236; fam., iii, 210, 211
Savile, Lady Eliz., iii, 427
Sawbridge, alderman, ii, 64; iii, 20
Sawell (Houghton Regis), *see* Sewell
Sawrey, *see* Saurez
Sawtrey Abbey, ii, 228
Sawyer, John, iii, 119
Saxons, i, 188; ii, 18, 73; iii, 350; *see also* Anglo-Saxon
Saye and Sele, Lady, iii, 179; Rich. Fiennes, Ld., ii, 162
Scaccario, Rog. de, iii, 383
Scale-mosses and liverworts (Hepaticae), i, 58
Scanden, Edm., iii, 129
Scarborough, Eliz., iii, 286
Scargill, fam., iii, 237
Schepehoo, man. (Upper Gravenhurst), ii, 334, 335
Schepehoobrade (Upper Gravenhurst), ii, 334
Schools, ii, 149; farm, ii, 142; lace, ii, 124; plaiting, ii, 120
Schutz, John, ii, 262, 265 *n*; Mary, ii, 204, 262; Mrs., ii, 207
Sclater, *see* Slater
Scortegrave, *see* Shortgrave
Scoteny, Beatrice de, i, 357
Scott (Scot), Ada (le), ii, 210, 237; Eliz., ii, 252; iii, 198; Isabel, ii, 237; iii, 299; John le, iii, 297, 299; *see also* Huntingdon, earl of; Marg., ii, 237, 238; iii, 297; Rob., i, 403; ii, 251-3; Rev. R. C. F., ii, 265; Sam., iii, 198; Thos., ii., 352 *n*
Scott's Close (Goldington), iii, 109
Scrivener, —, iii, 439
Scroggs (Skroges), Alex., iii, 203, 218 *n*; Joan, iii, 216; Oliver, i, 335 *n*; ii, 40; iii, 203, 216; Rich., i, 335 *n*; Will., iii, 246
Scroop's Farm (Biggleswade), ii, 209
Scrope, Hen., Ld., ii, 385
Scrope (Scroop), Hen. le, ii, 211, 235; John, ii, 384; Marg. le, ii, 235, 385; Rich., ii, 211, 235, 385; iii, 260; Rog. le, ii, 385; Col., ii, 53
Scudamore, Rich., ii, 356
Seabroke, G., iii, 432
Seayres, Lucy, iii, 415
Sebon, Rog. of, ii, 296 *n*
Seckford (Sekford), Hen., iii, 201; John de, ii, 89
Sedbergh, chant. sch. at, ii, 157
Seddington (Sandy), ii, 242
Sedgwick, Steph., iii, 405; Will., iii, 405
Segenhoe (Segenehou), man. (Ridgmont), i, 297, 377; ii, 76, 81, 83, 84, 87; iii, 267, 320-2; ch., i, 315 *n*, 371 *n*; iii, 320-3; tithes, i, 376; vicarage, i, 316 *n*
Segrave, Marg., Lady, ii, 339; Lds., iii, 12 *n*, 133; John, ii, 339
Segrave, Christina de, ii, 353; Eliz., ii, 339; Sir Hugh de, iii, 299; Ida de, iii, 229; Steph. de, iii, 229
Segresdone, iii, 123
Seiher, *see* Saher
Sekford, *see* Seckford
Sellator, Lambert, iii, 114
Seller, Will., ii, 157
Senhouse (Senhous), Rich., iii, 22, 23; Thos. de, ii, 220
Senior, E. N., ii, 197
Senliz (Senlis), Sim. de, i 315 *n*; ii, 239
Sergeant, Walt. le, iii, 73
Serle, John, iii, 137; Rich., iii, 137
Serviens, Phil., iii, 113
Settle, Elkanah, iii, 355; Josias, iii, 355
Sewell (Houghton Regis), iii, 336, 389; chant., i, 329 *n*; ii, 150, 151; iii, 394; man., iii, 391, 392; prehist. rem., i, 169; well, ii, 6, 7
Sewell (Sewelle), Ad. de, iii, 391; Hen., iii, 391, 433; Joan de, iii, 433; Sir John, iii, 393; John de, iii, 390, 391; Rev. J. E., ii, 156; Matilda, iii, 391 *n*; Nich. de, iii, 391; Walt. de, iii, 391 *n*; Dr., ii, 162 *n*
Sewick End (Wilden), iii, 223, 225
Sewster, Will., ii, 282
Sexton's Manor (Wilden), iii, 224, 225
Seylade, iii, 76
Seymour, Thos., Ld., ii, 270
Seymour, Sir Edw., iii, 158; Jane, iii, 111; *see also* St. Maur
Shaa, Sir Edm., *see* Shaw
Shakerstone (Shackerstone) (Leics.), ch., i, 388, 389; iii, 65
Shafto, —, ii, 192
Shappenho, *see* Sharpenhoe
Sharnbrook, i, 349, 380, 394; ii, 66, 78, 81, 115, 326; iii, 34, 59, 88-94, 105 *n*, 346; adv., i, 317; iii, 94; agric., ii, 83, 134; chant., iii, 94; char., iii, 94; ch., i, 315 *n*; ii, 92; iii, 88, 92; fish-stew, ii, 76; lace ind., iii, 89; mans., iii, 89; mills, iii, 89, 91; Nonconf., iii, 89; place-names, iii, 89; sch., ii, 184; vicarage, iii, 88, 94
Sharnbrook, Hen. de, iii, 52, 91
Sharnbrook Grange, iii, 88
Sharnbrook House, iii, 88
Sharnbrook Meadow, iii, 59
Sharnbrook Summit (Wymington), iii, 117
Sharp (Sharpe), Hen., ii, 333; iii, 56; Rev. Wilfred, iii, 188
Sharpenhoe, i, 297, 306, 308, 313, 345, 381-3; chap., i, 318 *n*, 326 *n*; ii, 384; Chantry Farm, ii, 313, 384; man., ii, 89, 382; man.-house, ii, 384; moat, ii, 384
Sharpenhoo, *see* Sharpenhoe
Sharpin, Rev. F. L., ii, 200
Shathewell, Isabel, iii, 453; John, iii, 453
Shaw (Shaa), Sir Edm., ii, 159
Sheeplane (Potsgrove), iii, 421
Sheeprack Wood (Knotting), iii, 139
Sheepwalk Hill (Toddington), i, 185
Sheepwalk Spinney (Turvey), iii, 110
Sheerhatch Wood (Willington), iii, 264
Sheffield (Sheffeld), Edw., ii, 373; Eliz., ii, 252; Marg., ii, 252, 253; Thos., ii, 252
Shefford, i, 173, 174, 187, 189; ii, 1, 5, 14, 44, 46, 113, 265, 267 *n*, 268, 270, 271, 276, 280, 286, 288, 294, 300, 320, 333; iii, 75 *n*, 313, 326; char., ii, 270; ch., ii, 269, 270, 271; deanery of, i, 347; mkt. ii, 88, 268; iii, 21; Nonconf. ii, 271; Rom. Cath., ii, 270; Rom. rem. at, ii, 2, 11-13, 266; Rom. road, ii, 4; sch., ii, 184; vicarage, ii, 270
Shefford, Sir Geo., i, 402
Shefford Hardwick (Southill), ii, 113; iii, 227, 256; man., iii, 259
Sheldon, Cuth., iii, 286; Prudence, ii, 204; Rich., ii, 204; fam., iii, 286
Sheldwick, Will. de, i, 362, 365
Shele, Thos., iii, 349
Shelley (Shellelond), man. (Wrestlingworth), ii, 256
Shelton, i, 384; ii, 71, 115, 324; iii, 89, 123, 136, 161-5, 193, 302, 313, 332, 333; adv., iii, 164; char., iii, 165; ch., iii, 163, 165; mans., i, 384; iii, 162, 164; ship-money, iii, 162; tithe rent, ii, 106
Shelton, Lower (Marston Moretaine), iii, 308, 313; man., iii, 311
Shelton, Upper, hamlet (Marston Moretaine), iii, 308, 333
Shelton, Upper, man. (Wootton), *see* Wootton Shelton, man.
Shelton Grene (Wootton), iii, 329
Shelton Hall (Shelton), iii, 160
Shelbethorpe, Rob. de, iii, 125
Shelvestrode, Joan de, iii, 252; Walt. de, iii, 252
Shengay Preceptory (Cambs), *see* Shingay Preceptory
Shenkwyn, Thos., i, 399
Shenley Hill (Leighton Buzzard), iii, 400, 415
Shepherd (Sheparde, Sheppard), John, iii, 429; Philippa, iii, 429; Rich., iii, 444; Rob., iii, 411; Sarah, iii, 444; Thos., iii, 316, 385; Will., iii, 383, 384; —, i, 342 *n*; iii, 18, 30
Shepherd's Bush (Dunstable), Rom. rem., ii, 6
Sherard, Geo., iii, 386, 387 *n*; Marg., iii, 386; Rich., iii, 386, 387; Thos., iii, 386
Sherborne (Sherbourne), Ad. of, i, 381; Rob., iii, 301; Sophia, iii, 301; Sir Will., i, 368 *n*, 369
Sheriff, Rich., iii, 446
Sherley, Thos., *see* Shirley
Sherwin, Thos., ii, 299
Shillington, i, 276, 324, 327; ii, 21, 25, 77, 78, 90, 113, 260, 261, 288, 293-9, 304, 308, 333, 344; adv., i, 324; ii, 299; chant., ii, 299; char., ii, 299; ch., i, 313; ii, 78, 293, 297-9, 335; coprolite, ii, 117; copyhold, ii, 90; farms, ii, 82, 83; labourers' wages, ii, 80; mans., i, 312; ii, 79, 294-6, 374; iii, 238; mills, ii, 293, 297; park, ii, 297; Nonconf., ii, 299; place-names ii, 294; poor-house, ii, 104; Rom. rem., ii, 13, 294; sch., ii, 184, 293
Shillington Bury, man. (Shillington), i, 307; ii, 295
Shingay (Shengay), preceptory of (Cambs), ii, 277; iii, 23, 213, 324, 330, 332, 376, 378, 420, 437
Shipley, Ellis, iii, 146
Shipman, Eliz. (Lucy), ii, 204
Ship-money, ii, 41; iii, 35, 162, 180, 197, 227, 267
Shire Horse Society, ii, 137, 140
Shirley (Sherley), John, ii, 316; Thos., iii, 167
Shitlington, *see* Shillington
Shoe-making ind., iii, 157
Shone, Will., ii, 318
Shortewood (Bolnhurst), iii, 126
Shortgrave, man. (Studham), ii, 31, 145, 376, 430, 449 *n*, 456
Shotbolt, Thos., iii, 432
Shotesbrook (Shottesbroke, Shottisbrook), Edith, Lady, iii, 136; John de, iii, 136; Sir Rob., iii, 107, 136, 137, 317

Shouldham Priory, i, 391
Shrewsbury, earls of, ii, 203, 223, 227, 261; Fran., ii, 340; Gilb., ii, 261; John, ii, 223
Shropshire, wool, price of, ii, 91
Shutlyngdene, *see* Shillington
Shuttleworth, Caroline, iii, 255; Col. Frank, ii, 197; iii, 202, 205, 209, 240, 251, 253-5, 257, 264; Jos., iii, 205, 253, 257
Shyfforth, *see* Shefford
Shyngay, *see* Shingay
Shytlington, *see* Shillington
Sibelthorpe, Edw., iii, 18
Sibley, Anne, iii, 429; Edm., iii, 429; Edw., iii, 429; Eliz., iii, 429; John, iii, 429; R. G., ii, 374; Thos., iii, 346, 429; Will., iii, 346; fam., iii, 194, 348
Sickling, Thos., iii, 425
Sidegate (Suff.), iii, 229
Sidney (Sydney), Algernon, ii, 57; Mary, iii, 177 *n*, 290; Sir Phil., iii, 290; Sir Will., iii, 177 *n*
Sidney Sussex Coll. (Cambridge), ii, 180; iii, 179, 296, 328, 332
Silchester (Toddington), Rom. rem., ii, 2, 13, 15
Sill, Simeon, ii, 212
Silsoe, i, 174, 297, 318; ii, 36, 146, 289 *n*, 325-33, 335, 336, 382; chant., ii, 326, 330, 331, 332; chaps., i, 315 *n*, 318, 325 *n*; gold coin, ii, 326; man., ii, 329, 330; iii, 292; mkt. and fairs, ii, 88, 330; pop., ii, 114; sch., ii, 184
Silsoe, John of, ii, 336
Silver End (Haynes), ii, 338
Silverton Grange, *see* Goldington Grange
Silvester, ii, 78
Simley, —, ii, 44
Simmons, F., iii, 351; Thos., ii, 120
Simon, anchorite, i, 350; the hermit, i, 350
Simons, Hen., ii, 318
Simpson (Bucks), iii, 349
Simpson, F., ii, 198; Rich., iii, 132 *n*
Sinclair, Geo., ii, 135
Sindry, John, iii, 21
Sismey, John, iii, 155
Sitegate (Sharnbrook), iii, 91
Siward, ii, 237
Skeffington, Ant., iii, 162 *n*; Geoff. de, iii, 168; John, iii, 163; Thos., iii, 163; Sir Will., iii, 163; Will., iii, 163; fam., iii, 162
Skegness, Bridg. F. A., ii, 295; Frances, ii, 295
Skinner, Tom, ii, 188
Skippon, —, ii, 46
Skipworth, Eliz., Lady, iii, 435; Greg., iii, 344; Sir Will., iii, 435
Skroges, *see* Scroggs
Slade House, The (Hinwick), iii, 81
Slade Plantation (Podington), iii, 80
Slater (Sclater), Chris., i, 338 *n*; iii, 414; Rob., ii, 118; Will., ii, 312; —, ii, 119; fam., iii, 411
Slayny, Marg., Lady, iii, 250
Sleaford (Lincs), A.S. rem., i, 182, 184
Slingsby, Abija, iii, 398; Hezekiah, iii, 385; Kath., iii, 385; Mark, iii, 399; Rebecca, iii, 385; Rob., iii, 398
Slip End (Caddington), ii, 314
Slipp (Luton), ii, 361
Slow, Rog., ii, 204
Slye, John, iii, 18
Smalman, Jas., iii, 159
Smart, Arth., ii, 375; Gerard, iii, 107
Smartwick (Welden), iii, 223
Smeaton, —, iii, 235
Smith, Abra., iii, 226; Alice, iii, 429; Anne, iii, 177; Rev. A., iii, 429; Barbara, iii, 177; Benett, ii, 336; Charlotte O., iii, 387, 388; Chris., iii, 395; Cyrus, ii, 185 *n*; Rev. C. H., iii, 179; Diana, iii, 60; Dorothy, iii, 205; Edm., iii, 177; Rev. Edw., iii, 60; Rev. Edw. O., iii, 388; Eliz., iii, 429; E., ii, 174; Frances, iii, 256, 261; Geoff., iii, 49; Geo., ii, 221, 408; Hen., ii, 241; iii, 251; Jas., ii, 241; John, iii, 392, 429, 432; Magdalen, ii, 233; Martha, iii, 432; Mary, ii, 162; iii, 432; Matth., iii, 125; Nich., i, 387; Rich., iii, 226; Roach, i, 176; Rob., ii, 241; iii, 156; Sim., ii, 336; Thos., ii, 316; iii, 246, 247; Sir Will., iii, 255; Will., i, 335; ii, 162, 335; iii, 201, 346, 348, 349, 367, 432; Worthington G., i, 269, 270; ii, 3 *n*; Mrs. Chernock, iii, 386, 387, 388, 425; —, ii, 165; *see also* Smyth and Smythe
Smithies, Rev. H. Y., ii, 133
Smyth, Alice, iii, 393; Edw., ii, 256; Geo. E., ii, 256; Jas., ii, 256; John (de), iii, 137, 255; Rev. Laur., iii, 255 *n*; Rich., i, 353; iii, 225; Rob., iii, 293; Susanna, iii, 255; Thos., iii, 456; Will., ii, 150; iii, 293; *see also* Smith and Smythe
Smythe, Geo., ii, 40, 382; iii, 106; Hugh, ii, 382, 383; Jas., ii, 382, 383, 385; Jasper, ii, 263; John, ii, 263, 305, 382; Marg., ii, 385; Rev. Rog., ii, 265; Thos., iii, 106; Will., ii, 162; iii, 106, 394; Mrs., ii, 382; *see also* Smith and Smyth
Snagge, Agnes, iii, 13, 313; Anne (Anna), iii, 13, 298, 312; Beatrice, iii, 13; Chas., iii, 298; Edw., iii, 306, 308, 309; Eliz., iii, 298, 306, 309; Geo., ii, 363; Mary, ii, 363; Ralph, iii, 298; Sir Thos., iii, 13, 240, 298, 309, 321; Thos., ii, 296; iii, 11, 12, 13, 14, 298, 299, 306, 307, 309, 312, 313; —, iii, 217
Snell, Will., i, 402
Snetteshall Priory, iii, 184
Snitch, John, ii, 241
Snowe (Snow), Alice, iii, 301; Dan., ii, 270, 271; Edw., ii, 271, 275, 276, 344; iii, 301; Eliz., ii, 271, 276, 342; iii, 301; Emma, ii, 271; Joan, ii, 363; Lawr., ii, 336, 378; Rebecca, iii, 165, 301; Rich., ii, 270, 271, 275, 276, 342; Sarah, iii, 301; Thos., ii, 336; Will., ii, 334, 378; fam., iii, 297
Soame, Judith, ii, 231, 233; Sir Steph., ii, 231, 233
Social and economic hist., ii, 73-116
Socon, *see* Eaton Socon
Soham (Cambs.) i, 189
Sok, Godf. le, iii, 196; John le, iii, 196; Rog. le, iii, 196; Sim. le, iii, 196; Will. le, iii, 196
Sokes Manor (Laurence Place) (Eaton Socon), iii, 196
Soleby, Hen. de, iii, 162, 164; Joan de, iii, 162; Rob. de, iii, 162; Will. de, iii, 162
Solemn Thrift (Bromham), *see* Salem Thrift
Someries, man. (Luton), ii, 350, 352 *n*, 358, 372
Someries Castle (Luton), i, 305; ii, 348, 364
Somers, Rich., ii, 315
Somerset, Marg., dchss. of, iii, 41, 137, 181; dks. of, ii, 37, 316; iii, 137; Edw., iii, 158; Hen., iii, 173; John, iii, 41
Somerset, Sir Chas., iii, 173; Geo., iii, 173; Hen., iii, 173; Thos., iii, 14
Somersham, Agnes de, ii, 248; Alex. de, ii, 248; John de, ii, 248; Marg. de, ii, 248
Somery, Agnes de, ii, 364; Joan de, ii, 364; John de, ii, 364; Marg. de, ii, 364; Rog. de, ii, 364
Sondeye, *see* Sandy
Sondon (Sonedone), *see* Sundon
Son of Æthelwine, Ailward, ii, 21
Son of Alan, Will., ii, 81
Son of Alchetil, Will., ii, 78
Son of Alex., Jordan, iii, 431; Walt., iii, 173
Son of Ascelin, Rob., ii, 296
Son of Azon, Will., iii, 159
Son of Azor, Hen., iii, 57, 58
Son of Baldwin, John, iii, 216
Son of Benedict, Cok, iii, 2
Son of Bernard, Thos., iii, 248
Son of Brun, Mossy, i, 321; iii, 363
Son of Bryan, Rob., iii, 418 *n*, 419, 421
Son of Drew, Ad., iii, 98
Son of Edwin, Lewin, ii, 314
Son of Erfast, Nigel, ii, 281, 285
Son of Ernest, Arnold, iii, 377
Felicia, w. of Arnold, iii, 377
Son of Ernis, Rob., iii, 144
Son of Eudo, Will., iii, 211
Son of Flemengo, Leo, iii, 363
Son of Frane, Oswulf, iii, 426
Son of Fulcher, Amabel, d. of Will., iii, 285; Osmunda, w. of Will., iii, 285; Will., iii, 285
Son of Gerard, Warren, iii, 343
Son of Gerold, Hen., ii, 267, 268; Warine, ii, 267, 268
Son of Gilbert, Rich., *see* Clare, Rich. de
Son of Godric, Eadnoth, iii, 150
Son of Godwin, Gyrth, ii, 20; Harrold, ii, 20; Leofwine, ii, 20; Swegen, ii, 20; Tostig, ii, 20
Son of Gozelin, Hugh, iii, 408
Son of Gregory, Walt., iii, 424
Son of Henry, Guy, iii, 302
Son of Hordfast, Nigel, ii, 263
Son of Hubert, Eudo, ii, 248, 253 iii, 245, 247; *see also* Dapifer
Son of Hugh, Barth., ii, 326; Geoff., iii, 314; Hen., ii, 244
Son of Ilger, Rannulf, iii, 78
Son of Ivo, Herb., iii, 49, 50, 97
Son of Jocelyn, Hugh, i, 371 *n*
Son of John, Ad., iii, 427; Rob., ii, 310
Son of Jordan, Rich., iii, 155; Rog., iii, 155; Thos., iii, 166
Son of Juliana, Hen., ii, 85
Son of Margaret, Rob., iii, 38
Son of Mary, Ad., iii, 58
Son of Nigel, Rob., iii, 78
Son of Olympeas, Rob., ii, 275
Son of Osmund, Levric, iii, 433
Son of Peter, Hamon, iii, 106
Son of Pictavus, Benedict, iii, 2; Jacob, iii, 2
Son of Rainald, Will., iii, 324
Son of Raineward, Will., iii, 219
Son of Ralph, Rob., ii, 44; iii, 181
Son of Richard, Gilb., iii, 428; Osbern, iii, 159; Paschasia, w. of Gilbert, iii, 428; Ralph, i, 325 *n*; Will., iii, 324, 325
Son of Robert, Sim., ii, 286
Son of Roger, Hen., ii, 351; Ralph, iii, 113

INDEX

Son of Roland, Abel, i, 371 *n*; iii, 29
Son of Rozelin, Rob., iii, 90
Son of Salaman (Salomon), Gilb., ii, 288; iii, 59
Son of Sampson, Rob., ii, 379
Son of Sewale, Thos., iii, 36
Son of Simon, Rich., ii, 360; Rob., ii, 360; Walt., iii, 436
Son of Siward, Alan, ii, 81; Waltheof, iii, 168
Son of Teodric, Rog., iii, 206
Son of Turkill, Rob., ii, 78
Son of Walter, Osbern, ii, 207, 208; Rob., iii, 396; Walt., ii, 315
Son of Warin, Agnes, w. of Walt., ii, 234 *n*; Walt., ii, 234 *n*
Son of William, Gilb., iii, 60; Hen., ii, 244; Rich., ii, 225
Son of Wymark, Ralph, iii, 74
Sonyngdon, *see* Sundon
Sopwell Priory (Herts), i, 351 *n*; ii, 324; iii, 237
Sorthegrave, *see* Shortgrave
Soulbury (Bucks), i, 162; iii, 368, 404, 415; ch., i, 370; rectory, i, 370
Soulbury, Hugh of, i, 370
Souldrop (Soulthorp), i, 327 *n*, 394; ii, 90, 115; iii, 34, 94-5; adv., iii, 95; char., iii, 95; ch., i, 314 *n*, 394; iii, 95; lace ind., iii, 94; man., iii, 95; place-names, iii, 95; schs., ii, 184; iii, 139
Souldrop, Steph. of, i, 314 *n*; Will. of, i, 382 *n*; ii, 244
Souldrop Would, iii, 94
Soulthorp, *see* Souldrop
Southampton, Thos. Wriothesley, earl of, ii, 57 *n*
South Brook (Wilden), iii, 223
Southill, i, 364, 365, 380, 393; ii, 44, 55*n*, 60, 61, 66, 116, 179, 197, 266, 338; iii, 69, 175, 176, 246, 256-261, 281, 283; adv., iii, 261; agric., ii, 134; char., iii, 261; ch., i, 315 *n*, 378 *n*; iii, 260; man., iii, 257; mill, ii, 278; place-names, iii, 257; priest's stipend, i, 341; iii, 261; schs., ii, 184; vicarage, i, 317; warren, iii, 260
Southill Park, ii, 147, 190; iii, 234, 235, 256, 258, 261
Southill with Rowney, iii, 256
South Mills, man. (Blunham), iii, 228, 231
Southoe, man. (Hunts), iii, 172
Southouse, Edw., ii, 361; Hen., iii, 211; Sarah, iii, 211
Southwater Mead, ii, 266
Southwell, Thos., iii, 82, 419
Southyevell, *see* Southill
Sowerby, John, ii, 361; Col., ii, 359; Maj., ii, 196; —, ii, 359, 361
Spark, Sir John, i, 326
Sparrow, Rob., iii, 20
Spech (Spec), hon. of, iii, 219
Spech (Spec, Espec), Albreda, iii, 176, 257; Aubrey, iii, 219; Hadwisa, ii, 230; iii, 252; Walt., i, 361, 362 *n*, 364; ii, 230, 233; iii, 36 *n*, 175, 176, 243, 252, 253, 255, 257, 259; Will., ii, 143, 230, 383 *n*; iii, 36, 38, 85, 120, 134, 219, 220, 221, 248, 252, 257-8, 324, 386, 439; fam. iii, 207
Speedwell Belt (Potsgrove), iii, 421
Spelman, Sir Hen., i, 343 *n*
Spence, John, iii, 194; Rob., iii, 194
Spencer, baron, ii, 243; earls, ii, 180, 220, 222; iii, 104, 310; John, iii, 306; Chas., Ld., ii, 220; Rob., Ld., ii, 222
Spencer, Alice, iii, 102; Arnold, iii, 314; Eliz., iii, 208; Frances L., iii, 301; Hen., *see* Sunderland, earl of; Sir John, ii, 243; iii, 102, 208; John, i, 393; ii, 62, 163, 220, 232, 245; iii, 104, 182, 240, 306, 310; John W., *see* Brownlow, earl; Mary, ii, 232, 243; Nich., iii, 29, 184, 240; Rev. Oliph L., iii, 301; Rob., ii, 43, 220, 222, 243; iii, 182, 240; Thos., ii, 245; iii, 240; Will., ii, 220, 243; iii, 182, 240, 242; fam., iii, 205
Spendlove, John, ii, 360 *n*
Spensley, Howard, iii, 451; Mrs. iii, 453
Spicer, John, iii, 166; Rich., iii, 154; Thos., ii, 40; iii, 332
Spiders (Arachnida), i, 88-90
Spigurnel, Alice, i, 360; Sir Hen., iii, 428; Hen., ii, 276, 286; iii, 129, 130, 429; Joan, iii, 429; Lucy, iii, 429; Phil., iii, 129 *n*; Sarah, iii, 130; Sir Thos., ii, 276, 280; Thos., ii, 286 *n*; iii, 129, 428; Will., ii, 286-7; iii, 429; —, iii, 216
Spiller, Sir Hen., iii, 113
Spinneyhole (Maulden), iii, 316
Spittle Close (Dunstable), iii, 364
Splashyard Wood, *see* Palace Yard
Spokes, Rev. J. H., ii, 308
Sports, ancient and modern, ii, 187-200
Springfield House (Kempston), iii, 297
Springs, chalybeate and medicinal, i, 39; iii, 44, 59, 69, 96, 284; petrifying, ii, 308; iii, 82
Spurling (Spurlyng), Anne, ii, 224, 232; John, ii, 224, 232
Spynk, John, iii, 52
Squire, Gaius, iii, 191, 198; John, ii, 204, 205, 320; Mary, iii, 191; Rob., ii, 204, 205; Rowland (Roland), iii, 191, 196; Miss, iii, 193
Stacheden, *see* Stagsden
Stachesdene, *see* Stagsden
Stacy, Agnes, iii, 247 Edw., iii, 244, 248; John, iii, 247; Thos., iii, 247, 248; Will., iii, 28
Stacy's Wood (Northill), iii, 245
Stafford, man. (Kempston), iii, 302
Stafford, Anne, ctss. of, iii, 171; earls of, Edm., iii, 156, 171; Ralph, iii, 36; Thos., iii, 36; Lady Marg., iii, 36; Will. Howard, visct., iii, 192, 196
Stafford, Anne, iii, 14; Ant., iii, 196; Bridg., iii, 196; Edw., *see* Buckingham, dk. of; Eliz., iii, 195, 196, 283, 298; Sir Humph., iii, 14; Humph., iii, 195, 196; Sir Hen., iii, 298; Jane, iii, 302; John, iii, 196; Kath., iii, 195; Marg., Lady, iii, 298; Mary, iii, 196; Nigel de, i, 353; Thos., iii, 277, 302; Walt., iii, 196; Sir Will., iii, 195, 298; Will., iii, 196, 302; fam., iii, 76
Stagsden (Stagesden, Stachesdene), ii, 115; iii, 32, 34, 96-100; adv., iii, 100; ch., i, 315 *n*, 380; iii, 98; char., iii, 100; farms, iii, 96; lace ind., iii, 96; man., iii, 96; mills, iii, 96; park, ii, 143; sch., ii, 184; vicarage, i, 316 *n*
Stagsden, John of, i, 352; fam., iii, 199
Staines (Stands), Capt. John, iii, 12; *see also* Stane
Staismore fam., *see* Staysmore
Stamford (Lincs), ii, 276 *n*, 290, 299
Stamford, Rich. of, ii, 178
Stampe, John, iii, 277
Stanbridge, ii, 375; iii, 368, 399, 400, 402, 407, 415, 417, 447; chant., iii, 415; chap., i, 324, 341; iii, 414; ch., iii, 412; man., i, 381 *n*; iii, 405; Nonconf., iii, 415; pop., ii, 114; schs., ii, 184; vicarage, iii, 414
Stanbridge, half-hund., iii, 336
Stanbridge, Hugh of (de), iii, 347, 442; Isabel of, iii, 347; Joan of, i, 360; Sim. of (de), iii, 347, 442
Stanbridge Ford (Totternhoe), iii, 400, 447
Stanbrig (Stanbrugge), *see* Stanbridge
Standon (Beds), *see* Stondon, Upper
Standon (Herts), i, 312
Standon, Ralph de, ii, 296; Walt. de, i, 352
Stands, *see* Staines and Stane
Stane (Stanes), Christina de la, ii, 321; Eliz. de la, ii, 321; Margery de la, ii, 321; Pet. de la, ii, 321; Will. de, ii, 350; *see also* Staines
Stanford (Southill), i, 365, 393; iii, 227, 256, 258; fishery, iii, 259; man., iii, 258; mills, iii, 256, 259; Rom. rem., ii, 1, 13
Stanford, Ld., ii, 44
Stanford, Eliz., ii, 289; Geoff. of, i, 365; Joan, ii, 289; John, ii, 289; iii, 97; Mary, ii, 289; Will., ii, 291
Stanfordbury Farm (Southill), iii, 257, 258; Rom. vault, ii, 13
Stanfordbury Manor (Southill), iii, 258, 259
Stanhope, Edw., iii, 236, 418; Mich., iii, 236, 418; Phil., *see* Chesterfield, earl of
Stanley, Ld., iii, 230; Thos. Ld., iii, 140, 172
Stanley, Edw., iii, 102, 119; Eliz., Lady, iii, 405; Ferdinand, iii, 119; Sir Geo., iii, 119; Geo., *see* Strange, Ld.; Hen., *see* Derby, earl of; Sir John, iii, 145; Marg., iii, 283; Thos., *see* Derby, earl of; Sir Will., iii, 405; Will., iii, 102
Stanton, *see* Staunton
Stanwick (Northants), i, 312; ii, 71, 72; iii, 123
Stap, Dorothy, ii, 373; Roland, ii, 373
Stapleford Mill (Luton), ii, 366
Stapleton, Sir Phil., ii, 45 *n*
Staple Wood (Eaton Socon), iii, 189
Staploe (Nether Staploe) (Eaton Socon), i, 297; iii, 190, 192 *n*, 193, 197, 198
Staploe, Upper (Over), (Eaton Socon), iii, 190, 193, 201
Starcher, iii, 402
Stare, Edw., iii, 405; Mary, iii, 405; Will., iii, 405
Staresmore, *see* Staysmore
Starkey, —, ii, 166
Starling (Starlyng), Sir Sam., ii, 359; Will., ii, 360 *n*
Staughton, Little, ii, 71, 86, 115, 133; iii, 123, 136, 146 *n*, 153, 165-8; adv., iii, 167; char., iii, 168; ch., i, 315 *n*, 349, 394*n*; iii, 146 *n*, 166; man., iii, 165; Nonconf., iii, 165; place-names, iii, 165; sch., ii, 183
Staunton (Stanton), Edw., iii, 461; Eliz., iii, 461; Sir Fran., ii, 40; iii, 418, 461, 462; Fran., iii, 418; John de, iii, 376; Rob., ii, 44; iii, 259; Stavely, iii, 461; Will., iii, 418; —, iii, 321

Staysmore, man. (Carlton), *see* Carlton Hall
Staysmore (Staresmore), John, iii, 51, 384; Will., iii, 51, 384
Stead, Geo., iii, 313
Steingrave (Steyngreve), Ida, iii, 45, 235, 295, 330; Isabel, iii, 14; John de, iii, 14, 235, 295, 424; Mabel de, iii, 330
Steph, Will., iii, 50
Stephen, king, i, 372 *n*; ii, 24, 25; iii, 9, 352
Stephen, priest, iii, 286
Stephen, Maj. J. Y., iii, 428; *see also* Steven
Stephens, Agnes, i, 361; Jeremy, i, 338, 343; Thos., ii, 268; *see also* Stevens
Steppingley (Stepigelai, Stepingle), i, 394; ii, 115; iii, 267, 324-5, 458; adv., i, 376; iii, 325; char., iii, 325; ch., i, 315 *n*, 321, 371 *n*, 374 *n*; iii, 325; 'French Horn' Inn, iii, 324; man., i, 364; iii, 23, 324; mills, iii, 325; Nonconf., iii, 324; place-names, iii, 324; sch., ii, 184; warren, ii, 136; iii, 324
Steppingley (Steppingly, Steppingle), Hen. de, iii, 324; John de, iii, 324; Maud de, iii, 324; Nichola de, iii, 324; Rich. of, i, 371 *n*; iii, 324, 325; Walt., iii, 220 *n*; iii, 324, 325
Steppingley Park, iii, 325
Steppingley Park Farm, iii, 324
Steppingley Wood, ii, 145; iii, 324
Stepynge, Matth., iii, 240
Sterne, Susan, ii, 329, 330, 378; Thos., ii, 329, 330, 378
Stethintun, *see* Stevington
Steven, Hen., ii, 379; *see also* Stephen
Stevenage (Herts), ii, 4; iii, 293
Stevens, —, ii, 118; *see also* Stephens
Stevenson, Rob., iii, 282; W. H., i, 310 *n*
Stevington, i, 388 *n*; ii, 77, 91, 115; iii, 34, 44, 100-4; adv., i, 389; iii, 103,; Black Death in, iii, 100; char., iii, 104; ch., i, 315 *n*, 324 *n*, 388, 389; iii, 102; cross, iii, 100; fishery, iii, 102; ind., iii, 100; man., ii, 88; iii, 74, 78, 100; mill, ii, 89; iii, 100; place-names, iii, 103 *n*; rents, ii, 132; sch., ii, 184; vicarage, i, 316 *n*
Stevington, Alwold of, iii, 114
Stevington Hall, iii, 102
Stevington Park, ii, 187; iii, 102
Stewart (Steward), Anne, ii, 281; Eliz., iii, 32; Geo., ii, 281; Lt.-Col. Jas., ii, 67; Will., ii, 210; *see also* Stuart
Stewkley (Bucks), i, 370, 404
Steyngreve, *see* Steingrave
Steynton, *see* Stevington
Stigand, archbp., ii, 210, 219; iii, 260
Stilton (Hunts), i, 386 *n*; ii, 120
Stirling, Thos., ii, 318
Stirman, John, iii, 453
Stivecle (Stivecele, Styvecle), Alice, ii, 334; Aline de, ii, 334; Barnabas, ii, 334; iii, 252; Joan, ii, 334; Joscelin de, ii, 333, 334; Nich. de, iii, 194; Walt. de, ii, 334; iii, 252; *see also* Stukeley
Stiventone (Stivetone), *see* Stevington
Stoakes, *see* Stokes
Stobart, F. W., iii, 44
Stobell, Anne, iii, 300; Will., iii, 300
Stocker (Stokker), Hen., iii, 201; John, iii, 201; Oliver, iii, 197; Rich., iii, 197; Sir Will., iii, 201
Stock Grove (Bucks), iii, 404
Stocking Croft (Ravensden), iii, 210
Stockinge (Shillington), ii, 295 *n*
Stockinge Close (Kempston), iii, 302
Stocking Pelham (Herts), ii, 214, 304
Stockwood Close (Luton), ii, 361
Stockwood Park (Luton), ii, 147, 197, 319, 348, 360, 361; iii, 105, 177
Stocton (Stokton), John de, iii, 165; Rich. of, ii, 149; fam., iii, 166
Stocton Parva, *see* Staughton, Little
Stocwell, Urian, iii, 295
Stodden, hund., ii, 115; iii, 123, 180
Stodham, *see* Studham
Stoke, man., i, 376; mill., iii, 91
Stoke, John de, iii, 67
Stoke d'Abernon (Surrey), iii, 78
Stokehammond, man. (Bucks), i, 376
Stoke Rochford (Lincs), iii, 145
Stokes (Stoakes, Stokys), John, iii, 121; Rob. de, i, 370; iii, 152; Will. de, iii, 286, 288
Stokesby, man. (Norfolk), i, 360
Stokesholt, ii, 291
Stokker, *see* Stocker
Stokton, *see* Stocton
Stokton Parva, *see* Staughton, Little
Stokys, *see* Stokes
Stolfalt, *see* Stotfold
Stolferth, iii, 383
Stonbury, *see* Etonbury
Stondon, Lower (Shillington), ii, 260, 293, 294, 296, 304; char., ii, 287
Stondon, Upper, ii, 113, 260, 275, 288, 304-5; adv., ii, 305; ch., i, 315 *n*, ii, 304; coins, Brit. and Rom., i, 173, 174; ii, 304; man., ii, 304
Stondon, Will. de, iii, 51
Stone (Bucks), Rom. well, ii, 6
Stone, John, iii, 321; Rich., iii, 322; Thos., iii, 321; Will., ii, 40, 130, 131; iii, 322, 340; —, ii, 96, 136
Stoneham, Mary, ii, 243; Rob., ii, 243
Stoneley Priory (Hunts), iii, 173
Stoneworts (Characeae), i, 59
Stoneylove, Thos., ii, 286
Stonley, Rich., iii, 212
Stony Hill (Limbury), Rom. rem., ii, 8
Stoppesley, *see* Stopsley
Stopsley, ii, 306, 308, 348, 349, 350, 357, 361, 374; adv., ii, 374; ch., i, 346; ii, 374; man., ii, 350, 352 *n*, 359, 363, 365; Nonconf., ii, 374
Stopsley (Stoppesley), Alex. (de), ii, 365; iii, 130; Edw., ii, 365; Hugh de, ii, 366 *n*; John of, i, 352; Matilda de, iii, 130
Stortewayle, Will., i, 402
Story, John, ii, 40; Phil., ii, 227
Stotfold (Stotfeld), i, 379, 380; ii, 113, 206, 214, 260, 261, 300-4; adv., ii, 303; agric., ii, 134; char., ii, 184 *n*, 303; ch., i, 315 *n*, 392; ii, 300, 302; Cook's Close, ii, 304; ind., ii, 117, 120; mans., i, 381, 393; ii, 300; iii, 12; mills, ii, 302; Morrells Close, ii, 304; Nonconf., ii, 303; place-names, ii, 300; poor-house, ii, 104; priest's stipend, i, 336; Rom. rem., ii, 14; Rom. rd., ii, 4, 300; schs., ii, 184, 304; vicarage, i, 316 *n*
Stotfold (*cont.*)
Stotfold, Joan, iii, 221; Walt., iii, 221
Stotfold Brayes, man. (Stotfold), ii, 300, 302; iii, 44; mills, ii, 300, 301 *n*
Stotfold Common, ii, 300
Stotfold Green, ii, 300
Stotfold Newnham, man. (Stotfold), ii, 301
Stotford, Geoff. of, ii, 289 *n*
Stotham, *see* Studham
Stotton, ii, 83
Stoughton, Little, *see* Staughton, Little
Stoughton (Stouton), Joc. of, i, 386 *n*; Rich. of, i, 386, 387; Thos., i, 387; Walt. de, iii, 137; Will., i, 387
Stouton, *see* Stoughton
Strabolgi, Dav. de, iii, 3, 281
Strafford, Lady Anne, ii, 277; iii, 441; Ld., ii, 52; Thos., Ld., ii, 277; iii, 441
Straillei, *see* Streatley
Strange, Geo. Stanley, Ld., iii, 172
Strange, Marg., iii, 145; Rog. le, iii, 418; Thos., iii, 384; Walt., iii, 145; Will., iii, 144, 145, 368, 394
Strangeways, Sir John, iii, 391
Strangward, Will., iii, 132
Stratford (Sandy), i, 271; ii, 242
Stratford, Thos. of, ii, 384
Stratford, Langthorne Abbey (Essex), ii, 227, 252, 253
Strathum, Eliz., iii, 129; Thos., iii, 129
Stratlei, *see* Streatley
Stratton (Biggleswade), ii, 45 *n*, 201, 209, 248; iii, 69, 258, 259; chap., ii, 214; man, ii, 210; water-mill, ii, 212
Stratton Park (Biggleswade), ii, 190, 209
Straw-cutting industry, ii, 120
Straw plaiting industry, ii, 107, 108, 109, 118-22, 212, 349, 350; iii, 5, 35, 234, 317 *n*, 345, 351, 363, 369, 390, 426, 435, 439, 447
Streatley, ii, 89, 114, 306, 313, 324, 345, 381, 384; adv., i, 360; ii, 383; char., ii, 384; ch., i, 315 *n*; ii, 383; man., ii, 346, 381; mill, ii, 381 *n*; place-names, ii, 381; sch., ii, 184, 384; vicarage, i, 317
Streatley Field (Streatley), ii, 313
Stredlegh, *see* Streatley
Streeter, John, ii, 315
Street Field (Dunstable), Rom. coins, ii, 6
Strickland, Chris., iii, 179
Strigul (Chepstow), prior of, ii, 265
Stringer, Anne, ii, 291; Hen., ii, 290; John, i, 398; Rich., ii, 289, 291; Thos., ii, 290; iii, 204
Strode, Edw., iii, 332; Litton, ii, 301; Rob., ii, 316; Will., ii, 316
Stuart, Lt.-Col. Dugald, ii, 251, 252; Col. Geo., iii, 106; Hen., ii, 66 *n*; Jas., iii, 106; May, iii, 106; Lt.-Col. Will., ii, 70; Will., ii, 66 *n*, 184 *n*, 252; Col., ii, 69; —, ii, 197; fam., ii, 66; *see also* Stewart
Studde, Eliz., iii, 400
Studham, i, 404; ii, 71, 84, 92 *n*, 114, 314; iii, 336, 337, 368, 426-32, 455; adv., i, 314 *n*, 376; iii, 431; char., iii, 432; ch., i, 311 *n*, 315 *n*, 318, 371 *n*; iii, 428 *n*, 430; Ch. Farm, iii, 427;

Studham (*cont.*)
ind., iii, 426; man., i, 376; iii, 426; Nonconf., iii, 432; place-names, iii, 426; schs., ii, 184; iii, 432; vicarage, i, 316 *n*; woollen hat petition, iii, 429
Studham (Stodham), Alex. of, i, 371 *n*; iii, 427, 428, 431; Alice de, iii, 428; Jordan de, iii, 428; Lavinia de, iii, 428; Paschasia de, iii, 428; Rob. de, iii, 428, 431; Sarah de, iii, 428; Thos. de, iii, 428; Will. de, iii, 428, 431
Studham House (Studham), iii, 428
Studley, Thos., iii, 331
Studleys, man. (Wootton), iii, 329, 331, 332, 333
Stukeley, Nich. de, iii, 22; Mrs., iii, 145, 246; *see also* Stivecle
Sturges, Barnard C., iii, 424
Sturmere (Essex), i, 184
Sturminster, ii, 352
Style, John, iii, 325; Oliver, iii, 449; Thos., iii, 325
Styrop, Rich., iii, 145
Styvecle, *see* Stivecle
Styventon, *see* Stevington
Suckling, Thos., ii, 289
Sudbury (Eaton Socon), iii, 180; man., iii, 193 *n*, 195
Sudbury, Joan de, iii, 195; John de, iii, 195; Kath. de, iii, 195; Margery de, iii, 195; Rog. de, iii, 195; Simon, archbp., ii, 35; Will. de, iii, 195
Sudgible (Sudgivele), *see* Southill
Sudington, John de, ii, 239
Sudtone, *see* Sutton
Sueteman, ii, 271 *n*
Suffolk, assessment, ii, 48 *n*; straw-plait ind., ii, 121; wool, ii, 91
Suffolk, Sarah, ctss. of, iii, 332; dchsses. of, Alice, iii, 401, 403, 415; Eliz., iii, 403; dks. of, Hen., iii, 156; John, iii, 403, 415; Will., iii, 403; Hen., earl of, iii, 332
Sulgrave, Hugh of, ii, 309, 310
Sunderland, Hen., earl of, ii, 243; Rob., earl of, ii, 220
Sunderland, Rev. Thos. S. J., iii, 211; Lt.-Col., iii, 209, 211; Mrs., iii, 211
Sundials, ii, 208, 303, 387; iii, 38, 81, 128, 217, 287, 303, 312, 347
Sundon, ii, 114, 135, 189, 306, 384-7; iii, 192; adv., ii, 387; char., ii, 387; ch., i, 315 *n*; ii, 385; ind., ii, 384; mans., ii, 223, 384; iii, 362; mkt., ii, 88; mill, ii, 385; Nonconf., ii, 387; place-names, ii, 384; sch., ii, 184; vicarage, i, 316 *n*, 341; work-house, ii, 105
Sundon, Will. Clayton, Ld., ii, 385
Suppethorp, Rob. de, iii, 181
Surive, Pet. de, iii, 119, 122
Surrey, Eliz., ctss. of, ii, 340; earls of, John, ii, 340; Thos., ii, 301, 340; iii, 13 *n*, 263; *see also* Norfolk, dk. of
Surtees, Frances, iii, 434
Sussex, ctsses. of, Eliz., iii, 283; Marg., iii, 283; earls of, iii, 281; Edw., iii, 281; Rob., iii, 283
Suthlingdon, *see* Shillington
Sutton (Suttone), i, 335 *n*, 384; ii, 90, 96, 98, 113, 201, 211, 237, 246-51; iii, 109; adv., ii, 250; char., ii, 251; ch., i, 335 *n*; ii, 248; earthworks, i, 300; ii, 246; mans., ii, 238, 246, 250, 256, 257; pack-horse bridge, i, 301; ii, 246; place-names, ii, 246; rector, i, 328; sch., ii, 184; vicarage, ii, 246
Sutton, Drew de, iii, 247; Eustace de, iii, 247; Sir John de, ii, 364; Marg., ii, 364; Olimpas of, ii, 279; Oliver, *see* Lincoln, bps. of; Rich., iii, 259; Rob. of, ii, 279
Sutton Park, ii, 197, 246
Swaffham Prior (Cambs), i, 365
Swanbourne (Bucks), i, 370; vicar, iii, 418
Swann, Rev. E., ii, 174
Swanton, man. (Harrold), ii, 83; iii, 66
Swart (Sweart), Æthelwine (Ailwin), ii, 21; iii, 128, 297
Swathyng, Marg., iii, 220; Thos., iii, 220
Swayne, Thos., ii, 330; *see also* Sweyn
Swaynes Orchard (Wootton), iii, 331 *n*
Sweart, *see* Swart
Swell, the (Colworth), iii, 89
Sweyn, ii, 20
Sweyn, Hen. le, ii, 212; Will., iii, 98; *see also* Swayne
Swift, Will., iii, 442
Swifte, Sir Fran., iii, 314
Swinburn, Ad. de, iii, 78
Swineshead, ii, 71; iii, 123, 136, 168-70; adv., iii, 170; char., iii, 170; ch., iii, 169; man., iii, 134, 168; Nonconf., iii, 168; sch., ii, 184; Three Horse Shoes Inn, iii, 168
Swineshead, Isabella de, iii, 168; Ralf de, iii, 168, 170; Rob. de, iii, 168; Walt. of, i, 397; iii, 168, 169
Swinford (Swynford), Eliz., ii, 248; Sir Thos. de, ii, 87; Thos., ii, 248
Swynerton (Swynnerton), Hugh, ii, 329; John de, iii, 456
Sydney, *see* Sidney
Syer, Rev. Thos., iii, 214
Sykes, —, ii, 374
Sylam, Agnes, ii, 363; Eliz., ii, 363; Joan, ii, 363; John, ii, 362, 363, 366, 373; Mary, ii, 363
Symcotts, —, ii, 277
Symgwyn, ii, 332
Symond, Ad., i, 402
Symonds, Thos., iii, 250
Synnot, Henrietta L., iii, 419
Syon Abbey (Midd.), ii, 151; iii, 394

Taddy, Edw. G., ii, 222, 242, 251; Rev. John, ii, 222, 251
Tadelowe, John, ii, 213 *n*; Maud, ii, 213 *n*
Tadlow, man. (Cambs), i, 392, 393
Tags End (Wootton), iii, 328, 329
Taillebois (Taillebosc, Talgebosc, Tallebosc), Azelina, ii, 215, 216, 232, 271, 275, 304, 305, 322; iii, 199, 253, 344, 383; Cecily, ii, 257; Elias, ii, 257, 258; Ivo, ii, 22; iii, 206, 390; Ralph (Ralf), i, 297 *n*, 312; ii, 153, 215, 232, 248, 271, 275, 281, 305, 306 *n*, 321 *n*, 322, 361; iii, 9, 37, 171, 199, 203, 206, 253, 344, 383, 402
Taisso (Taissel), Rob. de, iii, 186; Rog. de, iii, 186; Wimund de, iii, 181, 186
Talbot, Lady Anne, ii, 340; Lady Beatrice, ii, 224 *n*; Lady Eliz., ii, 332
Talbot, Eliz., ii, 223; Hugh, iii, 343; John, *see* Shrewsbury, earl of; Rich., ii, 223, 227; iii, 159; Rob., iii, 159; Thos., iii, 159; Will., iii, 343
Talgebosc, Tallebosc, *see* Taillebois
Tamiseforda, *see* Tempsford
Tanfield, Clem., ii, 227, 238, 262; Eliz., ii, 227; Fran., ii, 227; Rob., ii, 228 *n*; Will., ii, 227; fam., ii, 262
Tanners, Dr., ii, 170
Tanqueray, Chas., iii, 91
Tansley, Alf. J., ii, 120
Tarleton, Alf. H., iii, 276
Tartlett End (Cranfield), iii, 275
Tasciovan (Tasciovanus), coins of, i, 173
Tattenhoe (Bucks), iii, 302
Taverner, Fran., iii, 328
Tavistock, mqss., of, ii, 64, 69, 70, 187; Fran., iii, 290; Will., ii, 43, 61
Taylor (Taylard), Alice, ii, 244; Anne, ii, 238; iii, 329; Cath. (Kath.), ii, 239; iii, 130, 150, 198; Eliz., iii, 126, 150; F. G., iii, 278; Geoff., iii, 150; Humph., ii, 238; John, ii, 238, 244; iii, 31, 50; Sir Laur., iii, 150; Laur., ii, 238; Mich. A., ii, 204, 265; Nath., ii, 54 *n*; Nich., iii, 54, 329; Rich., ii, 43, 55, 281 *n*; iii, 126, 130, 198; Rob., ii, 241; iii, 43, 80, 116, 293, 325; Rog., ii, 238, 358; Sim., iii, 154, 322; Thos., iii, 126, 130, 131, 132; Ursula, iii, 130, 131, 132; Will., ii, 43, 238; iii, 130, 150; W. J., iii, 116; Mrs., ii, 182 *n*; —, bell founder, ii, 213, 292, 319; iii, 25, 68, 121, 179, 255, 278, 288, 304, 334, 342, 378, 382, 385, 393, 398, 420, 454
Tebault, *see* Theobald
Tebb, Jonathan, iii, 157
Tebworth (Chalgrave), iii, 343, 345, 347, 438; chant., iii, 349; chap., i, 318, 325 *n*; iii, 349
Teken, Will. de, iii, 139 *n*
Temesforda, *see* Tempsford
Templars, i, 315 *n*, 349, 362, 366, 394; ii, 144, 216; iii, 11, 59 *n*, 66, 67, 70, 78, 90, 134, 154, 158, 165, 315, 318, 324, 437; Aimery, master of, iii, 165; Rob. de Sanford, master of, iii, 66
Templars' Lands (Pertenhall), iii, 154
Temple, Sir Will., ii, 275
Temple Hills, man. (Sharnbrook), i, 394; iii, 90
Tempsford, i, 273, 284, 297, 307, 346 *n*, 403; ii, 19, 20, 44, 65, 113, 130, 201, 206, 226, 251-5, 276; iii, 209; adv., ii, 254; chant., i, 329; ii, 151, 233, 245, 254, 255, 258; char., ii, 255; ch., i, 315 *n*; ii, 251; earth-works, i, 280-2; ii, 251; fishery, ii, 253; mans., ii, 251; mills, ii, 253; Nonconf., ii, 255; prehist. rem., i, 145; ii, 251; place-names, ii, 251; rector of, i, 341 *n*, 342; Rom. rd. at, ii, 4; schs., ii, 150, 151, 184, 251
Tempsford Hall, ii, 197, 251
Temysford, *see* Tempsford
Teobbanwynthe, *see* Tebworth
Terle, Thos., iii, 332
Tesserae, ii, 7, 12, 13, 15
Tessington, Rich., iii, 139
Tetbald, *see* Theobald
Tetbaud, iii, 181
Tetebury, Rich., iii, 137; *see also* Tutbury
Tethbald, *see* Theobald
Tetricus, coins of, ii, 7
Tettesworth, John, iii, 456; Nich. iii, 456

Tetworth (Hunts), ii, 71, 226, 228, 230; sch., ii, 182
Tewkesbury, abbot of, i, 320, 362
Teye (Teyes), Isabel, iii, 14; Walt. de, iii, 14, 45
Teynturer, Laur. le, iii, 358 *n*
Thame Sch. (Oxon), ii, 162, 164, 173
Thanet, earl of, iii, 441
Thatchford mill, ii, 355
Thaxted (Essex), ii, 241
Thayne, Jas., ii, 355
The, John de la, ii, 145
Thebrugg, Rog. de, i, 352
Thebworthe, *see* Tebworth
Theed, Eliz., iii, 198; Hen., iii, 199; Will., iii, 198, 199
Theistic church, iii, 31
Themes, Nich. de, iii, 219
Theobald (Tebault, Tethbald, Tetbald), ii, 315; iii, 85
Theobald, Fran., iii, 291; Rich., ii, 204 *n*
Theodore, archbp., i, 346
Thimelby, Eliz., iii, 291
Thirning, Sir Will., iii, 130
Thody, Oliver, ii, 268
Thomas (Cancellarius), i, 400 *n*
Thomas, Rob., iii, 18
Thomlynson, *see* Tomlinson
Thompson, Cath., iii, 396; Dorothy, iii, 397; Edw. H., ii, 282; Eliz., iii, 328; Geo., iii, 195; Jane, iii, 398; Sir John, iii, 395; John, iii, 74, 286, 307, 333, 395-8; Judith, iii, 395; Mary, iii, 332; Maurice, iii, 296; Rob., iii, 395; Sam., iii, 332; St. John, iii, 395, 396, 398; Ursula, iii, 396, 398; Sir Will., iii, 332; Will., iii, 328; —, ii, 135
Thomson, John C., iii, 242; Will., iii, 107
Thorn (Houghton Regis), ii, 8; iii, 390
Thornbury, man. (Houghton Regis), iii, 391
Thorncote (Northill), ii, 92; iii, 242, 248, 250, 251
Thorne, Edw., ii, 160, 161; Giles, i, 337-40, 342, 343; iii, 28; Obed, ii, 320; Will., iii, 28; Mrs., i, 338, 339
Thorney Abbey (Cambs), i, 312, 314, 315 *n*; iii, 124, 125, 127, 143, 179, 188, 396
Thornton, Col. Godf., iii, 231, 246, 247; Godf., ii, 252; iii, 231; Harry, ii, 189; iii, 205; Rob., iii, 231, 247; Steph., iii, 231; Thos. de, i, 370; Col. Will., iii, 231; Will., ii, 228; Miss, iii, 419; Mrs., iii, 228
Thorowgood, Sir John, iii, 380 *n*; *see also* Thurgood
Thorpe (Thorp), Geo. de, ii, 382, 383; John de, i, 398; ii, 382, 383; Matilda, de, ii, 382; Rob., ii, 382, 383; Will. of, i, 381
Thrale, Agnes, ii, 359
Thrayle, Mich., ii, 39
Three Counties (Arlesey), ii, 265
Three Counties Asylum, ii, 300
Threkeston, Rich., iii, 30
Threlkeld, Launcelot, iii, 91; Laur., iii, 118; Marg., iii, 91, 118, 121
Thrift Wood (Silsoe), ii, 326
Thring, Llewellyn C. W., ii, 179
Throckmorton, Bromsall, iii, 247; Sir Geo., iii, 220; Geo., iii, 219; Judith, iii, 183; Rich., iii, 183; Rob., iii, 219
Throckmortons, man. (Roxton), iii, 220
Thrupp, Fred., iii, 30
Thrupp End (Lidlington), iii, 305
Thrupp End Farm (Lidlington), iii, 306
Thuand, fam., iii, 210
Thurald, John, ii, 253
Thurgood, John, iii, 258; Nich., iii, 258, 259; Thos., iii, 258; *see also* Thorowgood
Thurkytel, ii, 19
Thurleigh, i, 384; ii, 44, 115, 342; iii, 15, 31, 34, 51, 60, 69, 82, 104-9, 126, 136, 143, 146, 147, 150, 210, 212, 226, 235, 283, 331; adv., iii, 108; char., iii, 109; ch., i, 287, 315 *n*; iii, 107; College Farm, iii, 104; earthworks, i, 287, 308; iii, 104; Jas. I. at, iii, 107; mans., i, 325 *n*; iii, 104; mills, iii, 105; sch., ii, 184; iii, 109
Thurleigh Hall, iii, 104
Thurley, *see* Thurleigh
Thurston, Thos., iii, 415
Thynne, Lady Sophia, iii, 132; Lds.; Geo., ii, 341; John, ii, 182 *n*, 185 *n*, 339, 341, 343
Thynne (Thynn), A. C., iii, 326, 328; Fran., iii, 363, 402; Fran. J., ii, 147, 341, 344; iii, 293, 296; Hen. F., *see* Carteret, Ld.; John, *see* Carteret, Ld.
Tickford Moulsoe, iii, 271
Tickmarsh (Tichemersh), Hen. de, iii, 57; Isabel de, iii, 57; Maud de, i, 390
Til, riv., i, 289, 291; iii, 132, 171, 176
Tilbrook (Hunts), ii, 71, 81, 115; iii, 59 *n*, 115 *n*, 123, 168, 171-5; adv., iii, 175; char., iii, 175; ch., iii, 156, 173; Hardwick Farm, iii, 171; Manor Farm, iii, 171; mans., iii, 156, 171; mills, iii, 171; Nonconf., iii, 171; rector of, i, 338, 342 *n*
Tilbrook, Rohese de, iii, 172
Tilbrook Grange, iii, 171
Tilbrook Hall, iii, 171
Tilebroc, *see* Tilbrook
Tile industry, ii, 117; iii, 157
Tiles, 15th cent., iii, 450; Rom., ii, 7, 11, 15
Tileword, *see* Tilsworth
Tillebrok, *see* Tilbrook
Tillisword, Tillsworth, *see* Tilsworth
Tilly (Tilley), Hen., iii, 224; Matilda, iii, 224; Rob., iii, 3
Tilsworth, ii, 41, 114, 375; iii, 336, 400, 432-5; adv., iii, 435; char., iii, 435; ch., i, 315 *n*, 324 *n*; iii, 434; earthwork, i, 291; man., iii, 433; manor-house, iii, 432; vicarage, i, 316 *n*
Tilwick (Ravensden), iii, 212, 213
Tilwick Farm (Ravensden), iii, 210, 212
Tinden (Finedon, Northants), ch., i, 378
Tingey, Hen., ii, 253; Will., ii, 253
Tingeys House (Tempsford), ii, 253
Tingre, Tingrei, Tingriff, *see* Tingrith
Tingrith, i, 335 *n*; ii, 114, 324; iii, 286, 336, 382, 435-8; adv., iii, 438; Castle Farm, iii, 435; char., iii, 438; ch., i, 324 *n*, 357; iii, 437; ind., iii, 435; manor-house, iii, 435; mans., iii, 435; sch., ii, 184
Tingrith (Tingry), Cecilia de, iii, 442; Gilb. of, i, 321; Nich. de, iii, 395; Pet. de, iii, 436 *n*, 437; Thos. de, iii, 436 *n*; Will. de, iii, 442
Tingrith Mead (Westoning), iii, 455
Tingry, *see* Tingrith
Tipper, Will., iii, 117 *n*, 173, 385
Tipper and Dawe, iii, 173
Tipping (Tippinge), Anne, Lady, iii, 376; Sir Thos., iii, 376; Capt., iii, 242
Tiptot, Eliz., ii, 385; John (de), ii, 384, 385; Marg., ii, 385; Millicent, ii, 385; Rob. (de), ii, 384, 385
Tirell (Tirrell), *see* Tyrrell
Tissington (Derb.), chap., i, 372 *n*
Tithe Farm (Stevington), iii, 104
Tithe Mills (Clifton), iii, 258
Tivill (Tyville), Elena de, ii, 334; Hugh de, ii, 333, 334; Ralph, ii, 294, 297, 333
Tocke, *see* Tooke
Tocotes, Eliz., Lady, ii, 296; iii, 230; Sir Rog., ii, 296; iii, 187, 230, 326
Tod, Gilb., ii, 26 *n*
Toddenham (Tudenham), John de, iii, 15; Kath. de, iii, 15, 330; Marg. de, iii, 15; Rob. de, iii, 15, 330; Thos. de, iii, 15; fam., iii, 329
Toddington, i, 176, 286, 325 *n*, 338 *n*, 344, 367 *n*, 400, 402; ii, 2, 45, 56, 58, 84, 114, 277, 363 *n*; iii, 336, 346, 368, 438-47, 451; adv., iii, 446; A.S. rem., i, 181; iii, 439; chant., i, 325 *n*; iii, 446; chaps., iii, 446; char., ii, 185 *n*; iii, 446; ch., i, 185, 315 *n*; iii, 439, 444; farms, iii, 438; hosp. of St. John Baptist, i, 330, 331 *n*, 368, 402-3; ind., iii, 439; Jas. I. at, iii, 440; mans., i, 287 *n*; iii, 380, 383, 439; mkt. and fairs, ii, 88; iii, 441; mills, ii, 278; Monmouth at, iii, 441; place-names, iii, 439; plague in, iii, 440; Portionaries, the, iii, 444; prehist. rem., i, 169, 174; iii, 439; Rom. rem. at, ii, 14-15; Rom. rd. at, ii, 4; schs., ii, 184, 185
Toddington Park, iii, 439
Toddington Place, iii, 440
Todeni, *see* Tony
Tofte, The (Tofts), man. (Sharnbrook), iii, 88-92, 95
Tofte, Will., iii, 90
Tole, Rob., iii, 80
Toller, Ralph le, iii, 22
Tolleshunt Major (Essex), ch., i, 382, 384
Tolls, iii, 356, 362, 408
Tolthorp, Rob. de, iii, 139
Tomlinson (Thomlynson), Alice, ii, 160; Thos., ii, 160
Tompion, Thos., iii, 250
Tompson, *see* Thompson
Tongue, W., ii, 189
Toni (Tony, Todeni), Agnes de, iii, 426; Rob. de, iii, 112, 149, 426; Rog. de, ii, 315; Will. de, iii, 112; fam., iii, 57
Tooke (Tocke, Took), John H., ii, 64; iii, 20; Will., iii, 187
Top End (Renhold), iii, 214
Toplers Hill (Edworth), ii, 209; Rom. rem., ii, 7
Torfeye, *see* Turvey
Torksey, Walt. of, i, 399
Tornai, *see* Turvey
Torrington, Marg., Lady, iii, 145; Geo., visct., ii, 61, 69, 238, 291, 346; iii, 145, 246, 253, 255, 258, 260, 261
Torveie, *see* Turvey
Tostig (Tosti), earl, ii, 21 *n*, 153, 203, 216, 226, 321; iii, 248

INDEX

Totternhoe, i, 336; ii, 84, 114, 356; iii, 69, 294 *n*, 336, 368, 430, 447-51; adv., i, 376; iii, 450; char., iii, 451; ch., i, 315 *n*, 371 *n*; iii, 450; Cross Keys Inn, iii, 447; ind., iii, 447; man., iii, 371, 448; mill, iii, 447; place-names, iii, 448; prehist. rem., i, 172, 174; iii, 448; quarries, iii, 373, 448; Rom. rem., i, 172; ii, 15; iii, 448; sch., ii, 185; vicarage, i, 316 *n*
Totternhoe Castle, i, 293, 294; iii, 448
Totternhoe Downs, ii, 15
Totternhoe Hill, iii, 350; prehist. rem., i, 170
Tottman, Mary, ii, 241
Tovi, housecarl, iii, 61; priest, iii, 126
Towcester (Northants), ii, 2, 3, 46, 49
Tower, Chris., ii, 282 *n*
Tower Hill (Sandy), Rom. rem., ii, 9, 10
Towersey, Rev. —, ii, 172, 173
Toweslonde, John de, ii, 257
Town Close (Cardington), iii, 238
Towne, Rev. Leonard, iii, 187
Town Farm (Eversholt), iii, 378
Town Field (Maulden), iii, 316
Townley, —, iii, 142
Town Row (Maulden), iii, 316
Towns End House, *see* Sharnbrook House
Townshend (Townsend), Eleanor, ii, 382; Rog., ii, 382; Thos., ii, 382; Will., iii, 37
Towse, Will., iii, 133
Tracy, Hugh, i, 402
Trailly, bar. of, iii, 36, 54, 110, 175, 219
Trailly, hon. of, iii, 36, 257
Trailly, Albreda de, iii, 243, 257; Eleanor, iii, 36, 56, 176; Geoff. de, iii, 54, 175, 176, 179, 243, 257; Joan, i, 357; Sir John, i, 329, 357 *n*, 403; iii, 244, 250; John, iii, 51, 54, 55, 110, 176, 177, 179, 211, 243, 244, 330; Mary, iii, 176, 243; Maud de, iii, 176, 243; Nich. de, i, 361 *n*; 362 *n*; ii, 233, 243; Norman de, iii, 55; Sir Reg., iii, 244, 250; Reg., iii, 51, 211, 243, 330; Reynold, i, 329, 403; Walt. de, iii, 36 *n*, 55, 56, 74, 175, 176, 179, 211, 244; fam., iii, 85, 249
Traillys Close (Ravensden), iii, 211
Trailly's Manor (Ravensden), iii, 211
Tranecroft (Sharnbrook), iii, 90
Trawles Close (Wootton), iii, 333
Trayles Fields Farm (Ravensden), iii, 210, 211
Tregoz, John, ii, 80; iii, 452; Mabel, iii, 452
Tresham, Sir Thos., iii, 354
Treswell, Rob., iii, 113
Tretheny, Hen., ii, 381
Trevanion, John B., ii, 357
Trevor, Lady Ann, iii, 48; Lds., iii, 54; John, iii, 45; Rob., iii, 37; Thos., iii, 45, 47, 48, 55, 96
Trevor, Cath., iii, 437; Eliz., iii, 437; Sir John, ii, 46 *n*, 60; Lt.-Col. John, ii, 70; John, iii, 45; Capt. Lewis, iii, 48; Mary, iii, 436; Rob., iii, 436; Sir Thos., *see* Trevor, Ld. Thos.; fam., iii, 37
Trevor-Battye, Capt. C. E., iii, 435, 437
Tribal or Military earthworks, i, 269
Trice, —, ii, 277
Triket (Tricket), Bald., iii, 90, 94; Sim., iii, 90; Will., iii, 90; W., i, 315 *n*
Trikynham, Walt. de, iii, 60
Trimer, Will., ii, 304
Trinity College (Camb.), ii, 179, 180, 299, 302, 303, 304, 335; iii, 59, 61, 63, 80, 100, 139, 185, 221, 222, 237, 374, 375, 458
Trinity College (Oxford), ii, 171, 374
Trinity Hall (Camb.), ii, 380; iii, 349
Tristran, Lawr., ii, 304
Trowley Bottom (Flamstead), ii, 375
Troy Hall (Cranfield), iii, 275
Trubleville Hen. de, iii, 101
Trumpington, man., *see* Perots
Trumpington, Blanche, Lady de, iii, 230; Eleanor, iii, 230; Giles de, iii, 230, 248; Marg., iii, 230, 248; Maud de, iii, 230; Sir Rog. de, iii, 230; Rog. de, iii, 230; Sir Walt., iii, 230
Trusse, John, iii, 18
Trussell, Isabel, iii, 71; Marg., iii, 299; Sir Will., iii, 71; Will., iii, 299
Tryon, Eliz., iii, 102; Sir Sam., iii, 102
Tryvet, Eliz., ii, 360; Thos., ii, 360
Tubb, Will., ii, 165
Tucker, Jos., ii, 184 *n*; iii, 60, 80; J., iii, 145
Tuckey, Will., iii, 432
Tudenham, *see* Toddenham
Tudingetone, *see* Toddington
Tudor, Jasper, ii, 39
Tuke, Geo., iii, 78, 102
Tumuli, *see* Burials
Turbert, iii, 54
Turchil, iii, 120, 424
Turford, Thos., ii, 309
Turgis, iii, 90, 146, 286, 375, 396, 435
Turk, Beatrice (Beatrix), ii, 256 *n*, 354; Joan, ii, 354; Rob., ii, 256 *n*
Turneley, John, iii, 349
Turner, *see* Turnor
Turney, Thos., iii, 278
Turneyes Ground (Leighton Buzzard), iii, 404
Turnhall Mill, i, 352
Turnor (Turner), Anne, iii, 131; A. J., ii, 199, 200; Sir Chris., iii, 144; Chris., iii, 144, 148; C. H., iii, 148; Sir Edm., iii, 145, 149; Edm., iii, 144; Sir Edw., iii, 144, 149; Jacob, iii, 125; John, iii, 145; Sam., iii, 427; Sir Thos., iii, 131
Turnor Almshouses (Milton Ernest), iii, 149
Turold, priest, iii, 384
Turri, Elias de, iii, 428; Lavinia de, iii, 428
Tursa, iii, 169
Turstin (Turstan), ii, 267, 322; iii, 76, 83, 85, 248
Turvey (Turveia), i, 335, 380 *n*; ii, 40, 60 *n*, 71, 115, 147, 187, 324, 326; iii, 34, 49-51, 70, 104, 109-17, 175, 183; adv., i, 315 *n*; iii, 116; almshouses, iii, 117; char., iii, 117; ch., i, 315 *n*; ii, 72; iii, 115; farms, iii, 111; mans., iii, 110; mills, iii, 112, 114; place-names, iii, 110; rents in, ii, 132; sch., ii, 185; Three Fishes Inn, iii, 109
Turvey Abbey, ii, 188; iii, 109, 111, 114 *n*, 115
Turvey Hall Farm, iii, 109, 111
Turvey House, ii, 147; iii, 51, 109 111, 116
Turvey Lees, iii, 114
Turvey Lodge Farm, iii, 111
Turvey Old Hall, iii, 109
Turvyll, Will. de, ii, 34 *n*
Tutbury, Kath. of, i, 389, 390; *see also* Tetebury
Tutty, —, ii, 344
Tuward, Will., iii, 138
Twamley, J. H., iii, 132
Twinberrow, Miss, iii, 211
Twylesworth, *see* Tilsworth
Tyley, Rev. Jas., ii, 384
Tyndale, Mary, ii, 382; Will., ii, 382
Tyngree, Tyngreve, *see* Tingrith
Tyringham, Ant., iii, 77; Eleanor, iii, 77; Geoff., iii, 212; John (de), iii, 77, 83, 150, 212; Rob., iii, 64, 67, 77; Rog., iii, 212; Sim. de, iii, 150; Sir Thos., iii, 57, 58, 83, 139; Thos., iii, 77
Tyrington, Joan, iii, 339; Sir Will. de, iii, 340; Will., iii, 339
Tyrell's End (Eversholt), iii, 375
Tyrrell (Tirell), Alice, iii, 224; Anne, ii, 78; Dorothy, iii, 78; Edw., ii, 385; iii, 106; Geo., iii, 91; Joan, iii, 91; John, iii, 78; Pet., iii, 224; Ralph, iii, 224, 225; Rich., ii, 385; iii, 78, 106; Thos., iii, 73, 224, 225; Will., iii, 78; fam., iii, 126
Tyrwhitt, Rob., iii, 90, 106, 160 *n*
Tyville, *see* Tivill

Ufford, Eliz., iii, 13; Rob. (de), i, 382; iii, 13
Ulf, iii, 426
Ulf, Thos., i, 399
Ulfech, iii, 195
Ulfkytel, ii, 20
Ulmar (Almar, Wolfmar), i, 300; ii, 215; iii, 92; (priest), iii, 38
Ulsi, ii, 263; *see also* Alsi
Ulster, Matilda, ctss. of, iii, 403
Ulverton, Rich., i, 402
Ulveva, iii, 162
Ulvric, *see* Alvric
Umfreville (fam.), iii, 43
Underhill, Thos., iii, 248
Underwood, Thos., ii, 59, 166; Will., iii, 462
Unitarians, iii, 9, 421
University Coll. (Oxford), iii, 275
Upbury man. (Pulloxhill), ii, 378
Upbury moat, ii, 376, 378
Up End (Kempston), iii, 297
Up End (Stagsden), iii, 96
Up End Wood (Stagsden), iii, 96
Upper Fields (Radwell), iii, 305
Upper Ossory, ctss. of, ii, 63 *n*; earls of, ii, 61, 64, 69, 70, 146; iii, 268, 272, 288, 291, 306, 307, 318, 319; John, iii, 286, 291, 310, 311, 317; Ld., iii, 270
Upton, Chas., ii, 44; Rich. de, iii, 419 *n*; Will. de, iii, 419
Upwood, Mary, iii, 261; Thos., ii, 280; Thurgood, iii, 261
Urlin, Geo., ii, 385; Sir Sim., iii, 268
Urns, cinerary, *see* Burials and Burial Urns
Urry, —, ii, 45 *n*, 46
Ursel, Will., iii, 148 *n*
Utcoate (Hudicote) Grange (Woburn), iii, 458, 461
Utteford, Rob. de, iii, 91

Vale Farm (Lidlington), iii, 305
Valence, bps. of, i, 400

Valence (Valencia), Agnes de, iii, 229; Aymer de, ii, 223, 275; Joan de, ii, 223; Will. de, ii, 223
Valence End Farm (Dunstable), i, 170
Valery, Guy de, iii, 339
Vardon, Alf., ii, 199
Varney, *see* Verney
Vaseys, man. (Gt. Barford), *see* Veseys, man.
Vaudey, monastery, i, 367 *n*
Vaughan, Eliz., G., ii, 304; Geo., iii, 246; Mrs. W., ii, 304
Vaux, Lds., iii, 51, 101, 130, 150, 151; Edw., iii, 191; Hen., iii, 51; Nich., iii, 45, 51, 77, 130; Thos., iii, 45, 51, 77, 191; Will., iii, 131
Vaux, Eleanor de, ii, 351; Eliz., iii, 77; Ernest, *see* Harrowden, Ld.; Geo., iii, 78; John, ii, 44; Maud, ii, 354; iii, 422; Sir Nich., *see* Vaux, Ld.; Nich., iii, 126; Rob., iii, 456; Sir Thos., *see* Harrowden, Ld.; Thos., ii, 69; iii, 432, 456; Sir Will. de, ii, 351, 354; iii, 51; Will., iii, 201, 405, 422; fam., iii, 77, 235 *n*, 361
Vauxes, man., *see* Ocle-cum-Clapham
Vavasour, John, iii, 299
Veale, Rich., ii, 380; *see also* Viel
Vendôme, count of, ii, 36
Ventris (Ventriss), Sir Chas., ii, 44, 266, 268, 343; Sir Fran., ii, 268, 278, 343; Fran., ii, 268, 343; iii, 49; Henrietta, ii, 268; Hen., ii, 342, 343; iii, 61; Joan, ii, 268; John, ii, 59, 268, 342, 343, 343 *n*; Mary, ii, 268, 343 *n*; iii, 61; Will., ii, 342
Ver, riv., i, 29, 146, 151; ii, 314
Vere, Aubrey de, i, 378 *n*; ii, 23; Eliz., iii, 115; John de, *see* Oxford, earl of; fam., iii, 459 *n*
Verey, J. G., ii, 195
Verney (Varney), Cath., iii, 432; Sir Ralph, iii, 148; Will., ii, 164-5; iii, 432
Vernon, Lady Harriet, iii, 441
Vernon, Chris., iii, 113; Henrietta, ii, 277; Hen., ii, 278; iii, 441 *n*; Rich., ii, 63; iii, 20; —, ii, 64, 192
Verulam (town), *see* St. Albans
Verulam, Alice, vsctss., ii, 233
Vesey, Hen. Bromflete, Ld., *see* Vessy
Veseys (Vaseys), man. (Gt. Barford), iii, 181
Vessy (Vesey), Hen. Bromflete, Ld., iii, 91, 118
Viel, Rev. John de, iii, 128; *see also* Veale
Villiers, Philippa, iii, 97; Will., iii, 97, 404
Vine Farm (Langford), ii, 203
Vinegar Hill (Northill), iii, 251
Vipont, Ida, ii, 230; Isabel, ii, 230; Rob. de, ii, 230
Vitella de Ferentino, Pet. de, i, 321
Vivian, Chris., iii, 58; Humph., iii, 58
Vivian's Croft (Studham), iii, 432
Vivonia, *see* Vyvon
Vollans, Will., iii, 95
Volunteers, ii, 70
Vyall, John, i, 395
Vynter, John, iii, 231; Sir John, ii, 205
Vyvon, Cicely de, ii, 351; Heloise de, iii, 71; Hugh de, iii, 71; Joan de, ii, 351, 352 *n*; Mabel de, ii, 351; Maud de, ii, 351; Sybil de, ii, 351; Will. de, ii, 351
Wade, Hester, iii, 198; Rev. Hugh, iii, 198
Wade-Gery, Rev. Rob., iii, 189; Will., iii, 105, 190; W. H., i, 385 *n*; iii, 105, 198; fam., ii, 23; *see also* Gery
Wadehelle (Wadelle), par., *see* Odell
Wadelowe, *see* Wadlowe
Wadhull, fam., *see* Wahull
Wadlowe (Wadelowe), Hugh de, iii, 442; John de, iii, 442
Wadlowes, man. (Toddington), i, 376; iii, 380, 442, 454
Wadsworth, John, iii, 156
Waferer, Anne, iii, 131; Arden, iii, 129, 130; Eliz., iii, 130; Jas., iii, 130
Wagstaffe (Wigstaffe), Eliz., iii, 214; Geo., iii, 224; Hen., ii, 363; iii, 224 *n*; Jane, iii, 84; John, iii, 214, 282; Rich., ii, 55; iii, 84; Will., iii, 224
Wahull, bar., *see* Odell, bar.
Wahull, par., *see* Odell
Wahull (Wodhull, Woodhull), Agnes, ii, 234, 234 *n*; iii, 70-2; Albreda, ii, 283 *n*; Alice, iii, 70 *n*; Ann, iii, 72; Ant., ii, 234; iii, 72; Cecily de, iii, 70 *n*; Eleanor, ii, 204 *n*, 234; iii, 71; Eliz. de, ii, 204 *n*, 234; iii, 71, 72, 384; Fulk de, iii, 72; Heloise de, iii, 71; Isabel, iii, 71; John de, ii, 204 *n*, 234 *n*, 283, 326; iii, 70-4, 76, 82, 118, 285; Mary de, iii, 70 *n*; Mich. de, iii, 70 *n*; Nich. de, ii, 234; iii, 71-2; Rose de, iii, 70; Saer (Saher) de, ii, 234; iii, 69, 71-4, 76; Sibyl, i, 394 *n*; Sim. de, i, 371 *n*, 394 *n*, ii, 235; iii, 71, 321, 323; Thos. de, iii, 70, 71, 104, 105, 384; Walt., i, 371 *n*; ii, 26, 234, 234 *n*, 283 *n*; iii, 70-1, 74, 104, 448, 450; Will. de, iii, 211; fam., ii, 204; iii, 69, 321; *see also* Odell
Wainright, Abigail, iii, 444; Geo., iii, 444; John, iii, 443
Wake, man (Cardington), ii, 235
Wake, Lady Alina, iii, 252; John, Ld., iii, 101
Wake, Alice, iii, 45; Aline, ii, 334; Alinor, iii, 221; Bald., ii, 30, 31; iii, 12, 14, 45, 74, 78, 101-2, 136 *n*, 215, 375; Blanche, iii, 101; Ela, ii, 30 *n*; iii, 12, 215, 375; Eliz., iii, 14, 46, 375; Hadwisa, iii, 101; Hugh, iii, 162, 252; Ida, iii, 14, 215; Isabel, ii, 30 *n*; Jas., ii, 334; iii, 252; Joan, iii, 14, 15, 46, 215; John, iii, 101; Marg., iii, 101; Maud., iii, 45, 252; Sir Thos., iii, 45, 235; Thos., iii, 101; Sir Will., ii, 64; iii, 20; fam., iii, 206, 237
Wakefield, John, iii, 216
Wakes, man. (Bromham), iii, 45
Wakes, man. (Eversholt), iii, 377
Wakes End Farm (Eversholt), iii, 375
Walcot, Eyre, iii, 159; John, iii, 272 *n*
Waldegrave (Walgrave), iii, 391
Waldegrave (Waldgrave, Walgrave, Walgrove), Eliz., iii, 298; John, ii, 233; Rose, i, 357; Warin, iii, 298; Will., ii, 65; fam., iii, 43
Walden Abbey, i, 390, 391 *n*
Waldeouf, count, *see* Huntingdon, Waltheof, earl of
Waldeshef, John de, iii, 165
Waldgrave, *see* Waldegrave
Waleis, *see* Waleys and Whalley
Waleran, Matilda, iii, 301; Rob., iii, 301
Wales, man. (Eaton Socon), iii, 198-9
Waleys (Waleis, Walley, Wally), Beatrice, ii, 354; Eleanor le, iii, 299; Joan, ii, 334, 354, 362, 363; iii, 77, 198 *n*; John, ii, 354, 362; iii, 393; Joyce, ii, 362; Rich. le, ii, 180; iii, 299; Sir Will., iii, 393; Will. le, ii, 334; iii, 393
Walgrave, Walgrove, *see* Waldegrave
Walker, John, ii, 194, 221; iii, 392; Jos., iii, 287, 325; Rich., iii, 416; Dr. Walt., i, 337
Wallace, J. W., ii, 141
Wall Close (Eversholt), iii, 375
Waller, Edm., ii, 42; iii, 140; John, ii, 119, 342 *n*; Rob., iii, 140; Thos., ii, 349; —, ii, 47; fam., iii, 194
Walley, *see* Waleys
Wallinger, John, i, 337
Wallingford, hon. of, iii, 129, 130, 150, 154
Wallingford, prior of, ii, 252
Wallington, Nehemiah, ii, 42
Wallop, Eliz., Lady, iii, 405; Sir Hen., iii, 405; Rich., ii, 179; Rob., iii, 405
Wall paintings, iii, 43, 108, 115, 121, 127, 163, 164, 178, 295, 303
Wallud's Bank (Luton), *see* Waulud's Bank
Wally, *see* Waleys
Walsall, Fran., i, 343; ii, 245
Walsham How, Rev. W., i, 332 *n*
Walshe, Walt., ii, 250
Walsingham, Sir Fran., iii, 294
Walter, i, 313; ii, 271 *n*, 326, 383 *n*; iii, 85, 120, 173, 206, 248, 253, 321
Walter (Wylter), Rich., ii, 157
Waltham Abbey, i, 312, 323, 348*n*; ii, 154, 155, 220, 261, 262, 263, 265
Waltheof, earl, *see* Huntingdon, earl of
Walton, Cecyle, iii, 241; Christina de, iii, 456; Hen. de, iii, 456; Sir Thos., iii, 241; Thos., iii, 194
Walweyn, Joan, iii, 437; Phil., iii, 437
Walweyns man. (Tingrith), iii, 437
Wanwyle, *see* Wavyle
Warburton, Rich., ii, 301
Ward, Hen., ii, 241; John, i, 403; ii, 237; iii, 226, 250; —, ii, 353
Ward, B. & Co., ii, 127
Warden, Old, i, 270, 305, 361, 364, 365, 393; ii, 96, 116, 197, 336; iii, 219 *n*, 227, 245, 251-6, 259, 261, 264; adv., i, 361 *n*; iii, 255; Celtic rem., i, 170, 174; iii, 252; char., iii, 255; ch., i, 361, 362, 364; iii, 254; crown property, iii, 271; forest offences, ii, 144; inclosures, ii, 96; mans., iii, 248, 252, 317; mkts. and fairs, ii, 88; iii, 254; Park Farm, iii, 254; parson, i, 323; place-names, iii, 252; Rom. rem., ii, 15; iii, 252; sch., ii, 184
Warden, bar., iii, 57, 70, 85, 120, 243, 252, 257, 258
Warden, hon., iii, 175, 176, 248
Warden, John, i, 403; iii, 57, 250
Warden Abbey, i, 349, 351, 356, 361-6; ii, 28, 43, 53, 60, 144, 275, 277, 278, 281, 283, 288, 290; iii, 7, 24, 97, 98, 107, 147, 190 *n*, 204, 206, 207, 210, 212, 225, 233, 237, 246, 247, 251,

INDEX

Warden Abbey (*cont.*)
253, 254, 255, 257, 258, 259, 285, 315, 317, 318, 324; abbots, i, 365, 367; ii, 84, 204, 230, 233, 275, 281 *n*; iii, 12, 38, 97, 98, 147, 204, 206, 212, 225, 245, 248, 255, 259, 273; mill, ii, 283; seal, i, 365; iii, 252
Warden Hill, prehist. rem., i, 171, 172, 280; ii, 280
Warden Park, iii, 251, 253
Warden Tunnel, iii, 251
Warden Warren, iii, 251
Warden Woods, iii, 251
Wardle, Col., iii, 4
Wardone, *see* Warden, Old
Ware (Herts), i, 297 *n*; ii, 141; iii, 203, 206
Ware, —, ii, 273
Waren fam., *see* Warenne and Warren
Warenne, earl, ii, 301 *n*
Warenne, Will. de, iii, 133, 134, 168, 169, 171; *see also* Warren
Wareton, Thos., iii, 162
Warham, John, i, 353
Warin (Warine), *see* Warenne and Warren
Warison, John, ii, 248
Warner, iii, 114
Warner, Edw., ii, 326, 333; John, iii, 94, 326, 345, 383; —, ii, 265; iii, 446, 450
Warre, Anne, iii, 410; John la, iii, 162; Rog., iii, 410; *see also* De la Warr
Warren (Waren, Warin(e)), Anne, ii, 373; Elinor, i, 389, 390; Eliz., ii, 328, 331, 332; Humph., ii, 329, 332; John, iii, 133, 142; Thos., ii, 328, 331, 332; Will., iii, 92; fam., iii, 132; *see also* Warenne
Warren Farm (Millbrook), iii, 316
Warren Farm (Ridgmont), ii, 141
Warren Hill (Suff.), i, 182 *n*
Warren-Vernon, Eliz. G., iii, 439, 441, 443
Warwekhyll, John, iii, 450
Warwick, earls of, i, 373; ii, 37, 327; Rich., iii, 403; Thos., i, 373; Will., iii, 129
Warwick, Gilb. de, iii, 277; Phil., ii, 52
Washers Wood (Tingrith), iii, 435
Washinglenes Gate (Wootton), iii, 329
Washingley, man. (Cranfield), iii, 276
Washington, —, ii, 257
Wassingle, John de, iii, 277; Will. de, iii, 276, 277
Wast, Nigel (Neil) de, i, 351 *n*; ii, 324; iii, 60, 260, 271, 316, 317, 318
Wastell, John, i, 377
Water, Alice atte, iii, 92; Hen. atte, iii, 92; *see also* Waters
Waterbeach convent, i, 326; iii, 40
Water Eaton (Bucks), ii, 30 *n*
Water End (Eversholt), iii, 375
Waterend (Wrestlingworth), ii, 255
Watergate Farm (Battersden), iii, 343
Waters, Edm. T., ii, 318; *see also* Water
Wateson, Rev. Geo., iii, 275; *see also* Watson
Watford (Herts), i, 358, 360
Watford, Giles de, iii, 449; Ralph, iii, 449; Will. de, iii, 449
Watkins, man. (Steppingley), iii, 324
Watkins (Watkin), Eliz., iii, 91; Hen iii, 325; Jas., iii, 91
Watling St., i, 371; ii, 1, 3, 17, 23; iii, 350, 351, 354, 390
Watson, Frances, ii, 289; Rob., iii, 157 *n*; Thos., iii, 226; Will. C., iii, 92; —, ii, 44; *see also* Wateson
Watton Priory (Yorks), ii, 274
Watts, Hugh, ii, 269, 299; iii, 29, 54, 63, 68, 76, 135, 160, 164, 179, 185, 208, 214, 226, 233, 283, 304, 313; Will., ii, 279; iii, 382; —, iii, 57
Wauberge (Waybridge, Hunts), forest, iii, 22
Waudari, Rob. de, i, 315 *n*; ii, 350, 356
Waukelyn, Hen., iii, 137; Marg., iii, 137; Steph., iii, 137
Waulud's Bank (Luton), i, 160, 162, 163, 164, 166, 174, 175, 268, 269; ii, 8, 348
Wauton, Anne, Lady, iii, 193; Cicely, iii, 193; Eliz., iii, 105; Ellen, iii, 193; Emma (de), iii, 192, 193 *n*; Joan de, i, 357, John, iii, 193; Rob., iii, 192, 193; Sir Thos., ii, 36; iii, 193; Thos. de, iii, 193; Will. of, i, 381
Wautons (Eaton), iii, 193
Wavendon (Bucks), iii, 271, 336, 461
Wavendon Heath (Bucks), ii, 15 *n*, 329
Wavyle (Wanwyle, Weavile), Alan de, iii, 173; Hen. de, iii, 391; John de, iii, 173; Rog. de, iii, 173; Rich. de, iii, 391; *see also* Wyvell
Wayte, Agnes, iii, 218; Edm., iii, 218; Hen., ii, 329; Joan, ii, 329; John, ii, 329
Weald, Will., iii, 50; *see also* Weld
Weapons, bronze, i, 169; Iron Age, i, 170; neolithic, i, 160, 166
Weavile, *see* Wavyle and Wyvell
Webbe (Webb), John, ii, 329; iii, 233; Thos., iii, 212; Will., iii, 233
Webster, John, iii, 184, 221; Will., iii, 184, 201, 221
Weddel, Thos. P., ii, 327
Wederhore, Will. de, i, 377
Wedewessen, Alice, ii, 302; John, ii, 302; Sim., ii, 302
Wedon, *see* Weedon
Weedon (Bucks), ii, 68
Weedon (Wedon), Isabel, iii, 110; Ralph de, iii, 129, 133
Weedon Beck (Northants), i, 376 *n*, 377
Weedon Pinkney, man., iii, 424
Wehsnade, *see* Whipsnade
Welbey, Rich., ii, 278
Welbourne, Rob., iii, 32
Welch, Will., iii, 449
Weld (Welde), Frances, Lady, iii, 441; Mary, Lady, ii, 301
Welfitt, S. J., ii, 195
Welitone, *see* Willington
Well, Geoff. atte, ii, 89; John atte, ii, 89; Rog. atte, ii, 89; Steph. atte, ii, 89; Thos. atte, ii, 89; *see also* Wells
Wellefed, *see* Wellesford
Welles, *see* Wells
Wellesford (Wellefed), Alice, ii, 353 *n*; iii, 292
Well Estate, the (Steppingley), iii, 325
Wellesworth, Rog. de, iii, 299
Wellhead Plantation (Maulden), iii, 313
Wells, i, 13, 26; ii, 2, 5, 7; iii, 44, 74, 83, 94, 100, 114, 153, 157, 228, 320, 349, 390, 402, 457
Wells (Welles), Arth. C., ii, 318; Edw., iii, 32; Ellen, iii, 456;
Wells (*cont.*)
Fran., iii, 411; Hugh de, *see* Lincoln, bps. of; John, iii, 30, 411, 432; Marg., iii, 411; Rich., ii, 185 *n*; iii, 328; Thos., iii, 53, 456; —, ii, 190
Welstead, Leonard, iii, 436
Welton, Alelmus de, iii, 448, 449; Joan de, iii, 118; John de, iii, 118; Rog. de, iii, 118, 448; Will. de, iii, 118, 448
Weltone, par., *see* Willington
Wendover (Bucks), iii, 54, 372
Wendover, Rog. of, ii, 28
Weneslai, half-hund., ii, 201
Weneslai (Wennesli), Hen. de, ii, 263
Wenlock, Lds., i, 400; ii, 36, 37, 355, 368; iii, 292; John, ii, 351 *n*, 352, 358, 364; iii, 299
Wenlock, Sir John, ii, 36, 305; Marg., ii, 305; iii, 292; Sir Thos., ii, 372; Will., i, 400; ii, 305, 351 *n*, 352, 372; iii, 292; fam., ii, 307
Wennesli, *see* Weneslai
Wensi, the chamberlain, iii, 402
Wensleydale, iii, 270
Wentworth, Henrietta M., baroness, ii, 56, 58; iii, 441, 445, 453; Martha, baroness, iii, 441; Philadelphia, Lady, iii, 441; Lds., ii, 42, 43; iii, 381; Hen., iii, 440; Thos., iii, 346, 440-1, 445
Wentworth, Anne, iii, 266; Sir Giles, iii, 283; Jane, iii, 346, 445; John, iii, 266; Marg., iii, 283; Maria, iii, 445; Sir Thos., iii, 445; *see also* Strafford, Ld.; Will., iii, 441; fam., ii, 56; iii, 283
Wernher, Sir Julius, ii, 349, 353, 355
Weseham, Hamon de, iii, 284 *n*; Rog. de, iii, 284 *n*
Wesley, John, i, 344-6
Wesleyans, ii, 214, 237, 241-2, 246, 255, 265, 270, 299, 303, 312, 320, 333, 335, 344, 374, 387; iii, 31, 59, 63, 76, 117, 128, 136, 139, 144, 157, 168, 171, 175, 181, 190, 234, 268, 275, 284, 296, 297, 305, 307, 308, 313, 314, 316, 320, 326, 328, 338, 345, 367, 383, 389, 414, 415, 418, 424, 432, 458
Wessex, kingdom of, i, 309; ii, 20
Wessex, Godwin, earl of, ii, 20
West, Edm., iii, 286; Fran., iii, 348, 349, 386; Ida, iii, 380; Marmaduke, iii, 18; Nich., iii, 286, 442; Rich., ii, 289; Thos., iii, 380; Walt., ii, 334 *n*; Will., iii, 286
Westbury (Bucks), ch., i, 357
Westbury, Agnes of, i, 357; Will., iii, 150 *n*
Westcotes (West Cotton), man. (Wilshampstead), ii, 324; iii, 326
West End (Cranfield), iii, 275
West End (Little Staughton), iii, 165
West End (Silsoe), ii, 326, 338
West End (Stagsden), iii, 96
Westende, man. (Gt. Barford), *see* Creakers, man.
Westerdale, Nich., iii, 247
West Field (Westoning), iii, 455
Westhey, Thos. de, ii, 346 *n*
Westhey and Faldo, man. (Higham Gobion), ii, 346
Westminster Abbey, i, 312; ii, 153, 211, 235, 286, 341; iii, 12, 260, 401; John, abbot of, ii, 212 *n*
Westminster Pond (Thurleigh), i, 289
Westmoor Field (Radwell), iii, 305

Westmorland, price of wool in, ii, 91
Westmorland, Ralph, earl of, iii, 13; Ld., iii, 94
Westnynge, *see* Westoning
Weston, Jeremy, iii, 277; John, ii, 330; Rich. iii, 116, 272, 277, 396; Sir Will., iii, 142; Will. de, ii, 227; iii, 157
Westoning, i, 315 *n*; ii, 44, 72, 81, 86 *n*, 88, 92, 114, 185; iii, 179, 336, 451-5; adv., iii, 454; chant., ii, 285, 299; iii, 453; char., iii, 455; ch., i, 314 *n*, 325 *n*, 357; iii, 453; dean of, i, 347; ind., iii, 451; inns, iii, 451; mans., i, 303, 370; ii, 80, 226; iii, 443, 451-3; mkts. and fairs, ii, 88; iii, 452-3; mills, iii, 453; Nonconf., iii, 451; place-names, iii, 451; prehist. rem., iii, 451; sch., ii, 185; vicarage, i, 316 *n*
Westoning Wood End, iii, 451
Weston Tregoz, *see* Westoning
West Wood (Knotting), iii, 139
Westwood (Lidlington), iii, 305
Wetaway, Will., iii, 291
Wettele, *see* Wortele
Weylondon, Agnes de, iii, 452; John de, iii, 452; Juliana de, iii, 452
Whalley, Edw., iii, 173 *n*; Rich., iii, 173 *n*; Col., ii, 50, 52; iii, 458
Wharley End (Cranfield), iii, 276
Wharton, Lady Anne, ii, 340; Lady Dorothy, iii, 236; Phil., Ld., iii, 236
Wharton, Geo., ii, 378
Whatwell Mill (Shillington), ii, 297
Wheathampstead (Herts), prehist. rem., i, 150
Wheathampstead, John of, i, 351, 352; ii, 342, 368, 369; iii, 148 *n*, 448
Wheatley, Eliz., iii, 184
Wheeler, Will., ii, 329, 382; iii, 333
Whetham, Thos., iii, 192, 197
Whethamstede, *see* Wheathampstead
Whikey, man. (Little Staughton), iii, 166
Whiperley, man. (Luton), ii, 350, 358, 360
Whipsnade, i, 315 *n*, 318; ii, 113 *n*, 114, 185; iii, 336, 337, 407 *n*, 426, 430, 449, 455-7; adv., iii, 457; chap., i, 318; char., iii, 457; ch., i, 315 *n*; iii, 456; Hill Farm, iii, 455; mans., iii, 371, 455; Nonconf., iii, 455; place-names, iii, 455; sch., ii, 185
Whipsnade, Ad. de, iii, 455, 457; Alice de, iii, 456; Christina de, iii, 456; Gilb. de, iii, 456; Joan de, iii, 456; Margery de, iii, 456; Matilda de, iii, 456; Nich. de, iii, 456; Phil. de, iii, 456; Rich. de, iii, 455; Will. de, iii, 455
Whipsnade Heath, iii, 448, 455
Whipsnade Wood, iii, 369, 455
Whitaker (Whitacre, Whiteacre, Whytacre), Bennet (Benedicta) of, i, 360; Hen., ii, 162; John, ii, 41; P. A. O., ii, 189; Rich., iii, 129
Whitbread, Emma, iii, 41; John, iii, 259; Sam., ii, 64, 65, 66, 176, 238, 299; iii, 9, 15, 20, 21, 32, 41, 140, 206, 226, 234, 235, 236, 237, 238, 253, 254, 255, 256, 257, 258, 259, 261, 281, 283, 327; Lt.-Col. Sam., ii, 70; Sam. C., iii, 236; Sam. H., ii, 66; iii, 234; Steph., iii, 238; S. C., ii, 189; Will., ii, 334; iii, 259; Will. H., ii, 65, 194; iii, 15, 235, 253; Miss, iii, 234; —, ii, 132, 197; iii, 139; fam., ii, 108, 130, 338; iii, 258
Whitby, fam., *see* Whytbie
Whitchurch (Bucks), i, 370; man., iii, 310
Whitchurch, Bald. of, iii, 427; John A., iii, 181; —, ii, 190
White (Whyte), Agnes, iii, 225; Bertram le, iii, 46; Fran., *see* Norwich, bp. of; John, ii, 359; iii, 236, 366; Sir Thos., ii, 158, 159; Thos., iii, 225; Will., iii, 225
Whiteacre, *see* Whitaker
Whitehead, Eliz., ii, 289; Hen., ii, 337; Thos., ii, 151, 182 *n*; iii, 394; W., ii, 195, 337; Mrs., iii, 160, 162
Whiteman, Eliz., iii, 238
Whitemore, *see* Whitmore
White Way (Rom. rd.), ii, 4
Whitfield, Ralph, iii, 201
Whiting and lime manufacture, ii, 117; iii, 350, 363
Whiting (Whyting), Will., ii, 89
Whitlocke (Whitlock, Whitloke), Bulstrode, ii, 54 *n*; iii, 8; John, iii, 414; J., iii, 194; Kath., iii, 411; Rich., iii, 411
Whitmore (Whitemore, Whittmore), Geo., iii, 175 *n*; Tom, ii, 189; Will., iii, 331, 374
Whitnoe (Whitnow) Grange (Woburn), iii, 459 *n*, 461
Whittington, Jacob J., ii, 256, 257
Whittlebury (Northants), iii, 462
Whittmore, *see* Whitmore
Whitwick, man. (Thurleigh), iii, 106
Whitwick Green Farm (Thurleigh), iii, 104
Whitworth, John, iii, 285; Kath., iii, 285; Miles, iii, 277; Will., iii, 92
Whytacre, *see* Whitaker
Whytbie, Oliver, i, 337; Thos., i, 336
Whyte, *see* White
Whyting, *see* Whiting
Wiboldestune, *see* Wyboston
Wichalse, Arth., iii, 274, 316, 319, 323
Wiche, Matth. atte, iii, 98
Wick End (Stagsden), iii, 96
Wickend Spinney (Stagsden), iii, 96
Wicker-work ind., ii, 124-5; iii, 35, 76
Wickey Farm (Little Staughton), iii, 166
Widville, *see* Woodville
Wiffen, Benj. B., iii, 338, 458; Jer., iii, 458
Wigain (Wigan), Hen., iii, 206; Hugh, iii, 206; Ralph, iii, 206; Rog., iii, 206; Walt., iii, 240; Will., iii, 206
Wigg, fam., iii, 407
Wiggons, man. (Cople), iii, 240
Wightman, Will., ii, 257
Wigmore, hon. of, ii, 328
Wigram, F. S., ii, 189
Wigstaffe, *see* Wagstaffe
Wilbarston (Northants), ch., i, 357
Wilbon, Will., iii, 293
Wilbraham (Cambs), ch., ii, 217
Wilbraham, Little (Cambs), A. S. rem., i, 179 *n*
Wilde, *see* Wylde
Wildeboef, *see* Oyldeboef
Wilden, ii, 113, 145, 147; iii, 126, 168, 180, 182 *n*, 214, 223-6; adv., iii, 226; char., iii, 226; ch., iii, 225; mans., iii, 211, 223; place-names, iii, 223; schs., ii, 185; iii, 226
Wildman, Jas., ii, 316
Wilford, Christiana, iii, 443 *n*; Thos., iii, 443 *n*
Wilkes, Charlotte, iii, 416; Edw., iii, 411, 415; Joan, iii, 411; John, iii, 415, 451; Luke, iii, 411; Matth., iii, 415; fam., iii, 411
Willaume, *see* William
Willes (Willis), Edw., ii, 181 *n*, 310, 313; Sir Fran., ii, 210; Will., ii, 101, 166, 167
Willesdon, Barth., ii, 310
Willett, H., ii, 200; Willmer M., iii, 189
Willey, hund. of, ii, 115; iii, 34-58
Willey (Willy, Wilye), Bern., iii, 310, 313; Brown, ii, 170; Hugh de, iii, 34, 113; Rog. de, iii, 34, 113, 147
William, iii, 57, 302; the chamberlain, i, 311, 314, 315 *n*, 344; the clerk, i, 319 *n*; iii, 404; the steward, iii, 302
William (Willaume), Chas. D., iii, 91, 436, 444; Dav., iii, 436, 438, 444; Dionisia, iii, 105; Edw., iii, 436; John, iii, 436
Williams, Dav., ii, 173; Edw. G., iii, 383; Rev. Hamilton J., iii, 304; John, archbp., *see* York, archbps. of; John, i, 368; ii, 256; iii, 461; Rich., ii, 239; Will., iii, 285; — (Ld. Keeper), iii, 458
Williamson, Anne, iii, 119; Chas., iii, 119; Rev. Edm., iii, 398; Edm., iii, 396, 398; Rev. Edm. R., iii, 298; John, ii, 207, 301; Ralph, iii, 122; Sara, ii, 207, 301; Talbot, iii, 396; Mrs., iii, 298, 299
Willington, i, 284, 324, 392; ii, 60, 96, 101, 116, 138, 339; iii, 227, 262-6; adv., iii, 266; ch., i, 134, 315 *n*, 380; iii, 262; earthworks, i, 280, 282; Manor Farm, iii, 262; mans., iii, 12, 184, 203, 204, 262; mill, i, 392; Rom. rem., ii, 15; iii, 262; sch. ii, 185; vicarage, i, 316 *n*
Willington, man. (Cople), iii, 240
Willington, Eleanor, iii, 298; Hen. de, iii, 298; Will. of, i, 399
Willis, *see* Willes
Willoughby, Eliz., ii, 211; Mary, iii, 335, 435; Rob. de, ii, 211
Willoughby de Broke, Ld., ii, 203 *n*
Willoughby de Eresby, Ld., iii, 13, 14
Willow Close (Ampthill), iii, 274
Willowes, Mrs., i, 335 *n*
Willy, *see* Willey
Wilshamstead (Wilsamstead), i, 352-4, 356; ii, 115, 293, 341, 342; iii, 267, 279, 281, 284, 325-8; adv., iii, 328; chant., i, 326; char., iii, 328; ch., i, 315 *n*, 326, 357; iii, 326; farms, iii, 274, 326; mans., i, 313; iii, 326; Nonconf., iii, 326, 328; sch., ii, 185; iii, 328
Wilshamstead Wood, iii, 325
Wilshire (Wilshere), John, ii, 252; J., ii, 181 *n*, 313; Thos., ii, 313
Wilson, Eliz., ii, 268; Felix, ii, 278, 310, 323; Jas., ii, 285; Tim., ii, 268
Wilstead (Cardington), iii, 238
Wiltone, *see* Willington

Wiltshire, Edm. earl of, iii, 125; John earl of, iii, 106
Wilye, *see* Willey
Wimberville, Rog. de, iii, 405 n
Wimington (Wimmentone), *see* Wymington
Wimund, iii, 114
Wimund (Wymund), Pet., iii, 30
Winch (Wynche), Eliz., ii, 340, 375; Sir Humph., ii, 60 n, 227, 229, 241, 340 n; iii, 8; Humph. ii, 55, 227, 235; John, ii, 235; Sir Onslow, ii, 201, 202, 227, 228, 340, 341 n; iii, 35, 227; Rich. atte, i, 400; fam., ii, 60
Winchelsea, archbp., i, 375
Winchendon, Lower (Bucks), iii, 317
Winchester, archd. of, i, 327; Pet. des Roches, bp. of, ii, 29; iii, 439; Rich. Fox, bp. of, iii, 138
Winchester, earls of, ii, 28; Rog., iii, 101, 230; Saher, iii, 230
Windmill Field (Potton), ii, 241
Windmill Hill (Eaton Socon), iii, 189
Windmill Hill (Leighton Buzzard), iii, 404
Windmill Hill (Silsoe), ii, 326
Windmill manufacture, ii, 127
Windsor, St. George's coll. ch., i, 376 n, 404; ii, 218; iii, 366, 401, 416, 429
Windsor, Maurice de, iii, 229
Winessamestede, *see* Wilshamstead
Winfeud, Winfield, *see* Wingfield
Wingate (Wyngate), Anne, iii, 410; Arth., ii, 362; iii, 381; Button, iii, 331, 335; Edm., ii, 54 n; iii, 331, 335, 381; Edw., ii, 354, 355, 362, 374; iii, 393; Eliz., ii, 363; iii, 335; Sir Fran., ii, 362, 363 n; iii, 367, 381, 382; Geo., ii, 362, 363; iii, 367, 410; John, ii, 43, 362, 363; iii, 367, 381; Kath., i, 356; Mary, ii, 354, 363; Ralph, ii, 286; iii, 366; Rob., iii, 410; —, Lady, iii, 381; fam., iii, 379
Wingfield, iii, 345, 347; man., iii, 346, 348
Wingfield (Wyngfield), Ant., iii, 270; Chas., iii, 172; Edw., iii, 37; Sir Jas., iii, 168, 172; Sir Rich., iii, 172, 396; Rich., iii, 82, 172, 272; Thos., iii, 172; Trevor, iii, 40, 45, 55; Misses, iii, 268
Winkbourn (Notts), i, 394
Winslow, Will. of, i, 353
Wintremelc, Alric, iii, 206
Wintroe Corner (Ridgmont), iii, 321
Wiscard, Hen., ii, 329; Rich., ii, 378, 379; iii, 260; Will., ii, 329
Wisdom, Geoff., ii, 215 n; Mabel, ii, 215 n
Wiseman, Anne, ii, 338
Witchcraft, ii, 100; iii, 402
Witham, riv., i, 187
Witintona, Hen. of, ii, 293 n
Wits End (Eversholt), iii, 375
Wittenham, Long (Berks), A. S. rem., i, 178, 183, 188
Witton, Rev. —, iii, 435
Wixamtree, hund., ii, 18, 113 n, 116, 242; iii, 227, 267
Wlui, bp., iii, 314
Wlward, *see* Wulfweard
Woad, ii, 130; iii, 44
Woburn, i, 362, 363 n, 370, 374; ii, 17, 47, 52, 67, 102, 114, 132, 135, 171, 197, 377; iii, 4, 336, 343, 353, 382, 383, 400, 457-62; adv., iii, 462; agric., ii, 133, 134, 138, 140, 141; iii, 394; chap., i, 318, 331, 368, 369, 370; iii, 422; char., iii, 462; Chas. I. at, ii, 50, 51; iii, 458; chs., iii, 461; crown property, iii, 271; farms, iii, 458; fires in, iii, 458; hosp., iii, 457; ind., iii, 458; inns, ii, 99; iii, 458; mans., i, 366, 367, 370; iii, 459; mkts. and fairs, ii, 88; Nonconf., iii, 458; place-names, iii, 459; racing, ii, 191; Rom. rem., ii, 15; schs., ii, 185; iii, 462; sheep-shearing, iii, 459
Woburn, Walt. de, iii, 449, 450, 456
Woburn Abbey (anct.), i, 318, 330, 331, 349, 350, 351, 366-70, 371, 372 n, 402; ii, 40, 346, 376; iii, 24, 324, 347, 362, 370, 375, 376, 377, 379, 380, 385, 387, 397, 418, 419, 422, 442, 443, 448, 453, 458, 459, 461, 462; abbots, i, 318, 370, 374, 402; mill, i, 366
Woburn Abbey and Park, ii, 47, 69, 107, 133, 146; iii, 320, 338, 375, 394, 417, 421, 458, 459; royal visits, iii, 458, 459, 460
Woburn Hills, ii, 71, 129
Woburn Sands (Aspley Guise), ii, 117, 129; iii, 275, 336, 338; ch., iii, 338; fuller's earth, ii, 117
Wode, *see* Wood
Wodehouse, Rob., ii, 287
Wodemancote, Emma de, ii, 379; Rob. de, ii, 379
Wodhull, *see* Odell and Wahull
Wolaston, *see* Wollaston
Wolf, John le, iii, 51, 60
Wolfmar, *see* Ulmar
Wollascott (Woolascote), Joan, ii, 227-52; Will., ii, 227, 228, 252
Wollaston (Northants), ii, 190; iii, 209
Wollaston (Wolaston), Sir John de, iii, 90; Marg., iii, 90; Sim. de, iii, 49, 49 n
Wolley, Rich., ii, 364; Rob., ii, 364
Wolstenholme, Sir John, iii, 73 n; Lady Temperance, iii, 68, 76; Lady, iii, 66, 74
Wolston, *see* Wollaston
Wolverton man. (Bucks), i, 391, 393
Woobourn, *see* Woburn
Wood (Wode), Marg., iii, 456; Nigel atte, iii, 52; Oliver, iii, 456; Rich., ii, 266; Thos., iii, 110; Will. (atte), iii, 245, 450
Woodburn, Mrs. Pen, ii, 289
Woodcock, Edw., iii, 23
Woodcroft (Luton), ii, 354, 374; man., ii, 350, 354, 356-8, 362, 364, 366; iii, 405, 422; mill, ii, 354 n
Wood Croft (Ravensden), iii, 210
Woodcroft (Stevington), iii, 100
Wood End (Bolnhurst), iii, 124
Woodend, man. (Cople), iii, 238, 239
Wood End (Cranfield), iii, 276
Woodend (Harlington), iii, 380, 442
Wood End (Marston Moretaine), iii, 308
Wood End (Ravensden), iii, 209, 211
Woodend Plant (Sharnbrook), iii, 89
Woodfield (Luton), ii, 361
Woodford, Hen. of, ii, 381; Will. of, ii, 381
Woodhall, man. (Meppershall), ii, 290
Woodhall Farm (Meppershall), ii, 288
Woodhill, *see* Odell and Wahull
Woodhull, *see* Odell and Wahull
Wooding, Rob., iii, 58
Woodleys (Melchbourne), iii, 142
Woodmanley man., iii, 456
Woodmer End (Shillington), ii, 294
Woodside (Caddington), ii, 314 n, 319
Woodstock, Mary of, iii, 403
Woodville (Widville, Wydville, Wydvile), John, iii, 36, 386; Kath., iii, 36, 386; Sir Rich., iii, 118, 386; Thos., iii, 36, 48, 424
Woodward, Edm., iii, 295; Ellen, iii, 346; Mary, iii, 425; Rob., iii, 425; Tristram, iii, 346, 440; Walt., i, 356 n; Dr., iii, 425; —, ii, 166
Woodweston, John of, i, 399; Will. of, i, 399
Woodyard Close (Luton), ii, 361
Wooldridge, Thos., iii, 25
Wool ind., ii, 91, 101, 363
Woolsey Wood (Turvey), iii, 114
Woolward, Rev. S. A., i, 172
Wootton, i, 174, 338; ii, 44, 115, 187, 213, 245, 292, 303, 312, 324, 335; iii, 39, 132, 147, 156, 233, 267, 278, 297, 315, 328-35, 348, 378, 398, 414, 435, 454; adv., iii, 334; chants., iii, 335; char., iii, 335; ch., i, 315 n, 325 n, 333, 334 n, 379, 380; iii, 333; ind., iii, 329; man., iii, 13, 89, 329, 330, 332; sch., ii, 185; vicarage, i, 317
Wootton (Wotton), Alex. de, iii, 132; Constance de, iii, 309; Isabella de, iii, 358 n; John de, iii, 358 n; Rich. de, iii, 132; Rob. de, iii, 309, 313; Walt. of, i, 324; iii, 313
Wootonbourne (Wootton), iii, 331
Wootton Green (Wootton), iii, 329
Wootton Hoo, man. (Wootton), iii, 329, 330
Wootton House (Wootton), iii, 328
Wootton Pilling (Wootton), iii, 332
Wootton Shelton, man. (Wootton), iii, 333
Worcester, Walt. Cantilupe, bp. of, ii, 32
Worcester, Eliz., ctss. of, ii, 354; earls of, iii, 173; John, ii, 354; iii, 329
Workhouse End (Renhold), iii, 214
Workhouses, ii, 104
Wormleghton, Wormleighton, par., *see* Wrestlingworth
Wormleighton, Rob. Spencer, Ld., ii, 220
Worship, Joan, iii, 403; John, iii, 403
Wortele (Wettele), Nich. de, iii, 145
Wortham, Hale, iii, 428
Worthing, Thos., ii, 326
Worthington, Will., ii, 310
Wotton, *see* Wootton
Woughton, *see* Wauton
Wrastlingewurde, *see* Wrestlingworth
Wray, Sir Chris., iii, 381
Wresle, John de, iii, 247
Wrest, man. (Silsoe), ii, 184 n, 283, 290, 305, 326, 331, 334, 336, 345; iii, 65, 82; ch., ii, 333; mill, ii, 331; vicarage, ii, 333
Wrestlingworth (Wrestlingforth), i, 345; ii, 72, 113, 201, 230, 233, 243, 255-9; adv., ii, 257, 258; char., ii, 258, 259; ch., i, 315 n; ii, 257; mans., ii, 255; mills, ii, 257; Nonconf., ii, 258; place-names, ii, 255; sch., ii, 185
Westmead (Flitton), ii, 330
Wrest Park, ii, 36, 44, 61, 146, 197, 308, 325, 331, 333; iii, 451

Wright, Geo., iii, 409; Sir Hen., iii, 140; John, ii, 214; iii, 129; Dr. Jos., ii, 18 *n*; Lawr., iii, 95; Sir Nathan, iii, 105; R. S., ii, 174, 175; Will., iii, 409; —, ii, 40
Wriothesley, Ld., ii, 299; Thos., Ld., ii, 57 *n*; iii, 203
Wroxhill (Marston Moretaine), *see* Roxhill
Wroxill, Will., i, 398
Wulfhere, king of Mercia, i, 309
Wulfig (Wulfwig), *see* Dorchester, bp. of
Wulfmar, iii, 190
Wulfweard (Wlward), 'Levet,' iii, 439
Wutton, *see* Wootton
Wyatt (Wyat), Geo., iii, 129; Sir Hen., ii, 359; iii, 396; Hen., iii, 272; Jas., i, 176; ii, 273; Rev. Paul, iii, 21 *n*; Sam., iii, 125, 146; Thos., ii, 161; iii, 164; —, ii, 326
Wyboston, i, 308, 312; ii, 324; iii, 189-90, 191, 193, 196, 198, 199; chant., i, 329 *n*; iii, 201; chap., i, 326 *n*, 329 *n*; man.-house, i, 305-6; mans., iii, 191, 196, 197, 199
Wycombe, West (Bucks), ii, 45 *n*
Wye, Thos., ii, 380
Wygod, Hugh, iii, 225
Wygood (Wilden), iii, 225
Wylde (Wilde, Wild), Dorothy, Lady, iii, 216, 293; Edm., ii, 180, 182 *n*; iii, 296; Sir Edm., iii, 216, 293; Eliz., iii, 48; Sir John, iii, 300; Thos., iii, 48, 179; Will., iii, 7; Mrs., iii, 179
Wylibesende, *see* Whipsnade
Wyllyngton, Wyliton, *see* Willington
Wylter, *see* Walter
Wymington, ii, 71, 115, 185; iii, 34, 70, 80, 87, 117-22, 178; adv., iii, 122; bronze impl., i, 169, 174; char., iii, 122; ch., iii, 120; ind., iii, 117; man., iii, 117; man.-house, iii, 117; mill, iii,

Wymington (*cont.*)
119; Nonconf., iii, 117; sch., ii, 185
Wymington, John, i, 383; Rog. of, i, 382, 384; Will. de, iii, 196
Wymondley, Little (Herts), i, 294
Wymund, *see* Wimund
Wynche, *see* Winch
Wyndham, Thos., ii, 271, 275
Wyngate, *see* Wingate
Wyngfield, *see* Wingfield
Wynn (Wynne), Hen., iii, 259; John, ii, 246; iii, 259
Wynum, Walt., iii, 322
Wyrell, Joan, i, 361
Wyscard, *see* Wiscard
Wytham, Hercules, iii, 432
Wythes, Fran., iii, 210 Fran. A. W., iii, 210
Wythes Close (Stotfold), ii, 304
Wyttelbury, Rob., iii, 126
Wyvell, Agnes, ii, 352 *n*; Nich., ii, 352 *n*; Will., ii, 352; *see also* Wavyle

Yarborough, Chas. A. Pelham, Ld., ii, 231
Yarborough, Geo. C., ii, 245
Yardley, John, ii, 95
Yarlswood (Thurleigh), i, 308
Yarrow's charity (Sandy), ii, 246
Yarway, Rob., iii, 298, 331, 335; Thos., iii, 331, 335; —, ii, 44
Yeaveley preceptory (Derb.), ii, 276 *n*
Yelden, i, 290; ii, 71, 115; iii, 36 *n*, 123, 134, 136, 160, 168, 175-9, 330; adv., iii, 179; char., ii, 185 *n*; iii, 179; ch., iii, 177; man., iii, 54, 175, 179; Nonconf., iii, 175; sch., ii, 185
Yelden Castle, iii, 175; earthworks, i, 289, 291; Rom. rem., ii, 1, 15; iii, 175
Yelnoe Wood (Odell), iii, 69
Yelverton, Sir Chris., iii, 82, 119; Sir Hen., iii, 201; Hen., iii, 82, 119; Sybil, ii, 82, 119

Yielden, *see* Yelden
Ympie, *see* Impey
Yon, *see* Gravenhurst, Lower
York, archbps. of, Murdak, i, 390 *n*; Oskytel, i, 311; Rotherham, ii, 157, 219, 295, 352; iii, 292, 299; Thurstan, i, 361; Williams, i, 339 *n*; iii, 264
York, Anne, ctss. of, ii, 301, 340; dks. of, ii, 57, 67, 192, 301, 340; iii, 4, 404; Rich., ii, 301, 340; iii, 13
York, Nich. of, iii, 277
Yorke, Amabella, ii, 327; Phil., ii, 61, 380
Yorkshire Farm (Ravensden), iii, 210
Young, Arth., ii, 96, 97, 119, 130, 131, 133, 134, 140; Barth., i, 326 *n*; Freeman, iii, 432; Gabriel, iii, 125; Mark, iii, 264
Younges, man. (Westoning), iii, 453
Yprês, John of, i, 382
Ythingaford, iii, 401

Zoology, i, 69-143
Zouche, Lds., iii, 394; John, ii, 316; Will., iii, 371
Zouche, Alan la, ii, 328; Alice, la, iii, 440 *n*; Ellen la, ii, 328; Eudo de la, i, 373; ii, 225, 282, 315; iii, 118, 370, 371, 392, 449; Geo. la, iii, 452; Ivo de la, ii, 336; Joan, i, 360, 361; ii, 336; iii, 449, 452; John de la, ii, 225 *n*, 282; iii, 144, 371, 452; Mary la, ii, 243; Maud la, ii, 328; iii, 176, 243; Milicent, ii, 225, 282, 373; iii, 370; Rich. de la, ii, 282; Rog. la, ii, 328; Thos., ii, 243; Sir Will. la, iii, 360; Will. de la, ii, 282, 316; iii, 176, 243, 370, 371, 372, 391, 394, 440 *n*, 449, 452; fam., ii, 282, 315; iii, 118
Zouches, man. (Caddington), ii, 315, 316
Zouches Farm (Caddington), ii, 316

318

CORRIGENDA AND ADDENDA

Vol. I, page 41, line 9, *for* ' Charad ' *read* ' Chara '
,, ,, 41, line 16, *for* ' Flora of Bedfordiensis ' *read* ' Flora Bedfordiensis '
,, ,, 173, line 27, *for* ' Tascovian ' *read* ' Tasciovan '
,, ,, 272, line 3 from end, *for* ' west ' *read* ' east '
,, ,, 272, line 4 from end, *for* ' eastern ' *read* ' western '
,, ,, 355*b*, line 3 from end, *for* ' fourteenth century ' *read* ' fifteenth century '
,, ,, 365*b*. The following names of additional abbots of Warden have been supplied by Mr. Hight Blundell, M.D. :

Geoffrey, occurs 1244, 1254, and 1259 (*Cal. Chart.* 1226–57, p. 279 ; Assize R. no. 23, m. 72 ; Feet of F. Beds. file 25, no. 67)
Robert of Harrold, occurs 1272–5 (Assize R. no. 1247)
John de Dallinger, occurs 1287 and 1290 (Assize R. no. 1276, m. 20 ; *Cal. Pat.* 1281–92, p. 371)
Thomas, occurs 1318 (*Cal. Pat.* 1317–21, p. 275)
William, occurs 1406 (*Cal. Pat.* 1405–8, p. 236)

,, ,, 393*a*. The following names of additional priors of Chicksand have been supplied by Mr. Hight Blundell, M.D. :

Hugh de Ledenham, occurs 1242–6 (Feet of F. Beds. file 20, no. 7)
Alan, occurs 1272 and 1284 (Assize R. no. 1223, m. 6 ; ibid. Northants, no. 620, 622)
Walter, occurs 1292 (Assize R. no. 1298, m. 80 d.)
Simon, occurs 1330 (Assize R. Northants, no. 633)
Roger, occurs as predecessor of John Lechworth (Assize R. Beds. no. 32)
John Lechworth, occurs 1355 (Assize R. Beds. no. 32)
William, occurs 1426–8 (Assize R. no. 1539)
Richard Spencer, occurs 1503–4 (De Banco R. Hil. 18 & 19 Hen. VII)

,, ,, 403. The following names of masters of Northill College have been supplied by Mr. Hight Blundell, M.D. :

Richard Hethe, occurs 1422–40 (Ct. R. [Gen. Ser.], portf. 153, no. 34)
Thomas Greneley, occurs 1459–61 (ibid.)
Thomas Taylard, occurs 1477 and 1478 (ibid.)
William Porter, occurs 1494 (ibid. no. 35)
Thomas Randolfe, occurs 1494 and 1498 (ibid.)
Andrew Benstode, occurs 1499 and 1505 (ibid.)
John Underhill, occurs 15— (Dugdale, *Mon.* vi, 1399)

,, ,, 404*a*, line 6, *for* ' Almesbury ' *read* ' Amesbury '
Vol. II, page xvii, line 5, *for* ' Austen ' *read* ' Austin '
,, ,, 57, note 406, line 2, *for* ' south ' *read* ' north '
,, ,, 145, line 40, *for* ' Beckening ' *read* ' Beckering '
,, ,, 149, line 15, *for* ' £30,000 ' *read* ' £13,000 '
,, ,, 176, line 34, *for* ' and the buildings completed ' *read* ' and completed '
,, ,, 235*a*, line 43, *for* ' Knights Hospitallers ' *read* ' Knights Templars ' (cf. Assize R. no. 4, m. 19)
,, ,, 243*a*, line 13, *for* ' Henry III ' *read* ' Henry II '
,, ,, 251*a*, line 21 from end, *for* ' Stewart ' *read* ' Stuart '
,, ,, 305*a*, line 14, *for* ' one knight's fee ' *read* ' half a knight's fee '
,, ,, 326*b*, lines 29, 41, *for* ' Lee in Podington ' *read* ' Lee in Thurleigh '
,, ,, 384*b*, line 7, *for* ' Rodenham ' *read* ' Bodenham '
,, ,, 384*b*, line 33, *for* ' passed to Isabel's son by her first marriage, Richard de Clare, Earl of Gloucester,' *read* ' passed to Gilbert de Clare, grandson of Isabel, her son Richard having died in 1262 '
Vol. III, page 20*b*, line 5, *for* ' Sanbridge ' *read* ' Sawbridge '
,, ,, 37*a*, line 30, *for* ' Butler ' *read* ' Boteler '
,, ,, 46*b*, line 9 from end, *for* ' Osiel ' *read* ' Osiet '
,, ,, 110*a*, line 3, *for* ' Easton Mandit ' *read* ' Easton Maudit '
,, ,, 181*b*, line 35, *for* ' Tetband ' *read* ' Tetbaud '
,, ,, 219*b*, line 5 from end, *for* ' Grymband ' *read* ' Grymbaud '
,, ,, 220*b*, line 2, *for* ' Grymband ' *read* ' Grymbaud '
,, ,, 258*b*, line 15, *for* ' Ordin ' *read* ' Ordui '
,, ,, 295, note 163, *delete* ' She later married Walter de Teyes '
,, ,, 298*b*, line 16, *for* ' May ' *read* ' Mary '
,, ,, 335*a*, line 4, *for* ' Britton ' *read* ' Button '
,, ,, 338*a*, line 1, *for* ' Aspslea ' *read* ' Aepslea '
,, ,, 338*a*, ,, *for* ' Aspleia ' *read* ' Aspeleia '
,, ,, 338*a*, line 6 from end, *for* ' 1690 ' *read* ' 1711 '
,, ,, 339*a*, line 2, *for* ' Valery ' *read* ' St. Valery '
,, ,, 342*a*, line 2, *for* ' Wishaw ' *read* ' Wysham '
,, ,, 342*b*, line 14, *for* ' Booth ' *read* ' Ansell '
,, ,, 343*b*, line 3, *delete* ' in labour in connexion therewith '
,, ,, 345*b*, line 24 from end, *for* ' Guthruin ' *read* ' Guthrum '
,, ,, 385*a*, line 17, *for* ' Hamstead ' *read* ' Flamstead '
,, ,, 390, note 8, *for* ' Buckwood Stables ' *read* ' Buckwood Stubbs '

SUBSCRIBERS TO THE VICTORIA COUNTY HISTORY OF BEDFORD

HIS MAJESTY THE KING

C. Alington, Esq.
W. H. Allen, Esq., J.P.
A. R. Alston, Esq.
Capt. F. Alston
The Rt. Hon. The Lord Ampthill, G.C.I.E., G.C.S.I.
The Rt. Hon. The Lord Annaly, K.C.V.O.
His Grace The Duke of Argyll, K.G., K.T.
William Austin, Esq.
C. B. Balfour, Esq., J.P., D.L.
Mrs. Barclay
His Grace The Duke of Bedford, K.G., F.R.S.
The Rt. Hon. The Lord St. John of Bletsoe, D.L.
Hight Blundell, Esq., M.D.
J. Hight Blundell, Esq.
Rev. C. Bromley, M.A.
Miss Brooks
A. C. Buckmaster, Esq., LL.B.
Mrs. Eleanor Carroll
The Rt. Hon. The Earl of Carysfort, K.P.
Major E. F. Clayton
E. C. Coleman, Esq.
Francis Crawley, Esq., J.P.
Miss Crewdson
William Deane, Esq., J.P.
J. Griffith Deardon, Esq.
The Rt. Hon. The Earl of Derby, G.C.V.O.
Col. C. Villiers S. Downes
Sir Robert Edgecumbe, LL.D., D.L.
Charles Emmerton, Esq.
William Farrer, Esq., D.Litt.
Miss Harriet Fitzpatrick
The Rt. Hon. The Lord Foley, D.L.
Edward Snow Fordham, Esq., M.A., LL.M.
G. Herbert Fowler, Esq., B.A., Ph.D.
C. J. Fox, Esq., M.R.C.S.
Maurice G. C. Glyn, Esq., J.P.
O. E. D'Avigdor Goldsmid, Esq., D.L.
Sir Laurence Gomme, F.S.A.
H. E. Gregory, Esq.
The Right Hon. The Viscount Hambleden
John Hamson, Esq.
Henry Edward H. Harris, Esq.
W. H. Harrison, Esq.
A. Conning Hartley, Esq., M.D.
F. J. Haverfield, Esq., M.A., LL.D., F.S.A., Camden Professor of Ancient History
Charles C. Hawkins, Esq.
Lawrence Higgins, Esq., J.P.
F. R. Hockliffe, Esq.
Mrs. Mary A. Hollingsworth
W. Horey, Esq.
Rev. Campbell B. Hulton, M.A.
The Rt. Hon. The Viscount Iveagh, K.P., G.C.V.O., LL.D., F.R.S.
Lt.-Col. Frederick John Josselyn
C. W. Kaye, Esq., M.A.
The Rt. Hon. The Lord Kenyon, K.C.V.O.
John C. Kershaw, Esq.
Graham Charles Lawson, Esq.
E. T. Leeds-Smith, Esq., J.P.
F. Seymour Lloyd, Esq., M.D.
Henry Longuet Longuet-Higgins, Esq.
Walter Thomas Lye, Esq.
John Charles Mason, Esq.
Mrs. Cyril Maude
Joseph Miller, Esq.
The Hon. Algernon H. Mills
W. Gifford Nash, Esq., F.R.C.S.
Clement Buckley Newbold, Esq.
T. Newton, Esq.
The Rt. Hon. The Lord Northcliffe
J. Crewe Orlebar, Esq.
Richard Orlebar, Esq., D.L., J.P.
Sir A. Kerr Butler Osborn, Bart.
Charles G. Pace, Esq., F.R.M.S.
Rev. John Parr, M.A.
C. R. S. Payne, Esq., J.P.
The Rt. Hon. The Viscount Peel
The Hon. William Peel, M.P.
Mrs. Penton
George Phillips, Esq.
Sir Lionel Phillips, Bart., D.L.
Cecil Polhill, Esq.
His Grace The Duke of Portland, K.G., G.C.V.O.
Mrs. Edward Pratt
W. W. G. Prosser, Esq.
Rowland Edmund Prothero, Esq., M.V.O., M.A., F.R.Hist.Soc., &c.
Capt. Charles Guy Pym, D.L., J.P., F.G.S.
The Rt. Hon. The Earl of Radnor, V.D.
His Excellency The Hon. Whitelaw Reid
Robert Richmond, Esq., J.P.
Lady Roscoe
Charles Julius Ryland, Esq.
Mrs. Rylands
James Saunders, Esq.
Frederick Sharman, Esq.
W. R. Sheldon, Esq., M.A.

LIST OF SUBSCRIBERS

The Rt. Hon. The Lord Sherborne
Clement K. Shorter, Esq.
B. Shuttleworth, Esq.
Col. Frank Shuttleworth, J.P.
C. Charnock Smith, Esq., M.R.C.S., L.R.C.P.
F. Gouldthorpe Smith, Esq.
H. H. Smith-Carington, Esq., J.P.
His Honour Sir Thomas Snagge, K.C.M.G., M.A., LL.D., D.L.
John Tricks Spalding, Esq., J.P.
Miss Stanton
J. Steele-Elliott, Esq.
The Hon. Frederick Strutt
F. W. Styan, Esq.
Lady Sutton
John Taylor, Esq.
Alfred Trapnell, Esq.
Percival Fox Tuckett, Esq.
Charles Robert Wade-Gery, Esq., M.A., J.P.
J. H. Wall, Esq.
William Clarence Watson, Esq., D.L., J.P.
Charles Wells, Esq.
Lady Wernher
Samuel Whitbread, Esq., D.L., J.P.
J. Arnold Whitchurch, Esq.
J. W. Willis-Bund, Esq., M.A., LL.B., F.S.A.
Anthony Henry Wingfield, Esq., J.P.
Alexander Wood, Esq.
H. Wood, Esq., M.A., J.P.
Rev. H. B. Workman, LL.D.
Rev. Paul Williams Wyatt, M.A.
Henry Young, Esq.

PUBLIC AND PRIVATE LIBRARIES

London

The Athenæum
The Bath Club
Battersea Central Public Library
Bermondsey Public Library
Bishopsgate Institute
The Board of Agriculture
The British Museum
The Carlton Club
Chelsea Public Library
The Conservative Club
The Guildhall Library
Hammersmith Public Library
Hampstead Public Library
The House of Commons Library
The Incorporated Law Society
The Junior Carlton Club
The Junior Naval and Military Club
Kensington Public Library
Lincoln's Inn Library
The London Library
The National Liberal Club
The New University Club
The Reform Club
The Royal Societies' Club
Sion College
The Society of Antiquaries of London
The Surveyors' Institution, Westminster
Tottenham Central Library
The Travellers' Club
The United University Club
The Victoria and Albert Museum
Westminster Public Library
Westminster and Southland Training College
Dr. Williams' Library
Wimbledon Public Library

The Provinces

Bedford Arts Club
Bedford County Library
Bedford Grammar School
Bedford Modern School
Birmingham Corporation Reference Library
Bolton Central Reference Library
Bradford Free Public Library
Brighton Public Library
Bristol Public Library
Cambridge Free Library
Cambridge University Library
Cardiff Free Public Library
Cheltenham College
Croydon Public Library
Gloucester Public Library
Hitchin Public Library
Hull Public Library
Kingston-on-Thames Public Library
Leeds Library
Leeds Public Library
Leicester Free Public Library
Leigh (Lancs.) Public Library
Liverpool Public Library
Luton Free Library
Chetham's Library, Manchester
Manchester Free Library
John Rylands Library, Manchester
Victoria University Library, Manchester
Newcastle-on-Tyne Literary and Philosophical Society
Newcastle-on-Tyne Public Library
Northampton Public Library
Nottingham Free Library
Bodley's Library, Oxford
Christchurch, Oxford
New College, Oxford
Oxford Union Society
Preston (Lancs.) Free Library
Reading Free Public Library
Reading University (presented by The Lady Wantage)
Royal Library, Windsor Castle

Scotland

Aberdeen University Library
The Advocates' Library, Edinburgh

LIST OF SUBSCRIBERS

Edinburgh Public Library
Edinburgh University Library
The Signet Library, Edinburgh
Glasgow University Library
Mitchell Library (Moir Collection), Glasgow
St. Andrews University Library

Ireland

King's Inn Library, Dublin
The National Library of Ireland
Trinity College, Dublin

The Colonies

Adelaide Public Library, South Australia
New South Wales Public Library, Sydney
Victoria Public Library, Melbourne, Australia
Toronto Public Library, Canada
Toronto University Library, Canada
Victoria Public Library, British Columbia
The General Assembly Library, Wellington, New Zealand

America

Albany State Library
Boston (Mass.) Athenæum
Boston (Mass.) Public Library
Brookline (Mass.) Public Library
Cambridge (Mass.) Public Library
Chicago Public Library
Cincinnati Public Library
Columbia University, New York
Connecticut Historical Society
Cornell University Library, Ithaca
Forbes Library, Northampton, Mass.
Harvard University Library
Illinois University Library
Indiana State Library
Iowa State Library
Maine State Library
Massachusetts State Library
Michigan State Library
Newberry Library, Chicago
New Hampshire State Library
Grosvenor Public Library, New York
New York Historical Society
New York Public Library
New York State Library
Ohio State Library
Peabody Institute, Baltimore
Pennsylvania State Library
Philadelphia Free Library
Providence Free Library
The Library of Congress, Washington
Wisconsin State Historical Society
Worcester (Mass.) Free Public Library
Yale University Library

The Continent

Royal Library, Berlin
Royal Library, Copenhagen
Royal Public Library, Dresden
Royal University Library, Göttingen
Lille University Library
Royal Library, Münich
National Library, Paris
Imperial Public Library, St. Petersburg
Royal Library, Stockholm
Upsala University Library